Masculinity Studies &
FEMINIST THEORY

Masculinity Studies &
FEMINIST THEORY

NEW DIRECTIONS

EDITED BY
Judith Kegan Gardiner

COLUMBIA UNIVERSITY PRESS / NEW YORK

COLUMBIA UNIVERSITY PRESS
Publishers Since 1893
New York   Chichester, West Sussex
Copyright © 2002 Columbia University Press
All rights reserved

"Masculinity and the (M)Other" copyright © 2002 Isaac Balbus, adapted from *Emotional Rescue* by Isaac Balbus. Reproduced by permission of Taylor and Francis, Inc./Routledge, Inc., http://www.routledge-ny.com
"Studying Masculinities As Superordinate Studies" copyright © 2002 Harry Brod
"The Enemy Outside: Thoughts on the Psychodynamics of Extreme Violence with Special Attention to Men and Masculinity" copyright © 1998 Nancy J. Chodorow; originally published in *JPCS: Journal for the Psychoanalysis of Culture and Society* 3 (1998)
"Long and Winding Road: An Outsider's View of U.S. Masculinity and Feminism" copyright © 1997 R. W. Connell; first published in Barbara Laslett and Barrie Thorne, eds., *Feminist Sociology: Life Histories of a Movement* (Rutgers University Press, 1997)
"Foreword" copyright © 2002 Michael Kimmel
"Masculinity Studies" copyright © 2002 Judith Newton
"Unmaking: Men and Masculinity in Feminist Theory," by Robyn Wiegman, adapted from "Object Lessons: Men, Masculinity, and the Sign Women," published in *Signs* 26.2 (Winter 2001), copyright © 2000 University of Chicago; all rights reserved

Library of Congress Cataloging-in-Publication Data
Masculinity studies and feminist theory : new directions / edited by Judith Kegan Gardiner.
　　　p.　　cm.
Includes bibliographical references and index.
ISBN 0-231-12278-0 (cloth : alk. paper) — ISBN 0-231-12279-9 (pbk. : alk. paper)
1. Men's studies.　2. Masculinity.　3. Feminist theory.　I. Gardiner, Judith Kegan.
HQ1088 .M375 2001
305.31'07—dc21

2001047017

∞

Casebound editions of Columbia University Press books are printed on permanent and durable acid-free paper.

Printed in the United States of America
Designed by Lisa Hamm

c 10 9 8 7 6 5 4 3 2 1
p 10 9 8 7 6 5 4 3 2 1

for Annika

CONTENTS

FOREWORD

With this volume, "masculinity studies" comes of age as an intellectual field, both in dialogue with and in alliance with feminist theory. Judith Kegan Gardiner has assembled some of the most distinguished practitioners of both masculinity studies and feminist theory working in universities today, and they have collectively thought through the different ways in which feminist theory and masculinity studies are related. In many ways, *Masculinity Studies and Feminist Theory* explores the insights of three decades of feminist theory on the construction of masculinities.

This project is politically important because it demonstrates that, although it is not self-evident, masculinity studies is a significant outgrowth of feminist studies and an ally to its older sister in a complex and constantly shifting relationship. Masculinity studies is not necessarily the reactionary defensive rage of the men's rights groups, the mythic cross-cultural nostalgia of mythopoetry, nor even the theologically informed nostalgic yearning for separate spheres of Promise Keepers. Rather, masculinity studies can be informed by a feminist project to interrogate different masculinities, whether real (as in corporeal) or imagined (as in representations and texts). These essays are about men, but also about gender—as a system, individually embodied and institutionally embedded, and as a set of practices, independent of the actors' struggles to accomplish it.

Generally there are two big divisions in the essays. First, there are those essays that explore the theoretical, pedagogical, political, and intellectual links between feminist theory and masculinity studies. These essays "do" feminist theory by exploring masculinity as an important dimension of gender relations, hierarchy, inequality, and power. Then there are those that "use" feminist theory to explore some aspect of masculinity; that is, they "do" masculinity studies by using feminist theory. The cumulative effect of such essays is to show the myriad ways in which theorists and researchers are attempting to bridge the two domains—those that do feminist theory "on" men and those who do masculinity studies "through" feminism.

To engage masculinities through the prism of feminist theory or to write feminist theory using masculinities as an analytic dimension requires two temperamental postures. One must engage masculinity critically as ideology, as institutionally embedded within a field of power, as a set of practices engaged in by groups of men. And yet given the contradictory locations experienced by most men, men not privileged by class, race, ethnicity, sexuality, age, physical abilities, one must also consider a certain forgiveness for actual embodied men as they attempt to construct lives of some coherence and integrity in a world of clashing and contradictory filaments of power and privilege.

Though it is fashionable these days to say that feminists "hate" men, indulge in "male bashing," and otherwise reinscribe men as the center of their lives, even in anger, the essays in this book confirm that feminism is not "antimale," but rather that feminists are capable of using feminism to empathize with men when they challenge and critique masculinity as ideology and institution. (Actually, the right-wing antifeminists are the real "male bashers" who assert that males are biologically programmed to be violent beasts, incapable of change, that will rape and pillage if women do not fulfill their biological mandate of sexual and social constraint.)

Thus the second division in the volume, essays by women and essays by men, proves instructive along this dimension. While they do not divide neatly along the first axis described above, the essays by women tend to be the more theoretical, but mostly they tend to be far more for-giving of men's fumbling, inarticulate, and often contradictory ways that we have begun to think through issues of gender through a feminist lens. And this they accomplish without losing one drop of theoretical acuity. By contrast, many of the essays by men are more sharply critical of masculinity, more pointedly unforgiving—perhaps of self, certainly of others.

Some of these essays take enormous intellectual risks, attempting to use elements from a variety of theoretical and political discourses such as queer theory and critical race theory. This is especially important be-cause these discourses too are vital components of masculinity studies; indeed, I would estimate that fully half the empirical research in mas-culinity studies today comes not through the door of feminist theory but through queer theory. More important than the weight of numbers are the ways in which queer theory and multiculturalism transform and complicate feminism. In particular, queer theory enables one to theorize masculinity as a system of power relations *among men* as well as as a system of power relations *between women and men.*

This fuller integration, it seems to me, is one of the core intellectual projects of the coming decade—to construct the bridges between the different axes of power and to illuminate how those systems both rein-force each other and also may contradict each other. For it is in the seams of power that those structural weaknesses are exposed, where re-sistance is born and coalitions are built.

Michael Kimmel

Masculinity Studies &
FEMINIST THEORY

INTRODUCTION

Judith Kegan Gardiner

What has masculinity to do with feminism?[1] Why is there so much talk of a "crisis" of masculinity? How do feminist theories shape masculinity studies, and how, in turn, have feminist theories been altered by the insights of masculinity studies? Why is masculinity's supposed complement, femininity, so rarely mentioned? The essays in this volume address central questions about the analysis and construction of masculinity in contemporary society. They discuss how male power and privilege are constituted and represented. They explore the effects of men's masculinity on women and on diverse men, and they seek to foster more egalitarian forms of manhood. They demonstrate that masculinity studies can help feminist theories break free from theoretical impasses and that feminist attention to the institutionalizations of power can ensure masculinity studies against superficial celebrations of the mobility of gender. In addition, they examine who has a stake in retaining masculinity as a coherent category, of restricting it to men, and of valorizing it as a goal of individuals and a necessary component of society. They show how nuanced feminist analyses of masculinities are necessary to adequately theorized gender studies. Thus this book advances new dialogues between masculinity studies and feminist theories.

The relationships between masculinity, masculinity studies, feminism, and feminist theories are asymmetrical, interactive, and changing: I sketch a few such changes here. The women's liberation movement of the 1960s and 1970s assumed an antagonism between feminism and masculinity that was reciprocated in much popular discourse, while masculinity studies within the academy in the 1970s and 1980s developed a conflicted dependency on feminist theories and often housed its courses within women's and gender studies programs (Brod, *Making;* Franklin, *Changing*). The 1990s masculinist men's movements, which sought to restore male dominance over women and reverse feminist advances, rose and fell, while in the academy queer theories altered gender studies and feminists associated with cultural studies turned toward masculinity as a pressing theoretical concern (Clatterbaugh "Literature"; Wiegman,"Unmaking," this volume). The present situation appears more complicated and perhaps more promising, despite a rhetoric of crisis applied to masculinity in society, to feminism as a social movement, and to academic gender studies. Academic masculinity studies have matured as an independent field that is influenced by queer theory, "race" studies, and various poststructuralisms as well as by the full range of feminisms (Kimmel and Messner, *Men's Lives*). Current masculinity studies have reached consensus on a number of issues, which the essays in this book both build upon and dispute. In particular, they help deconstruct static binaries in gender studies between victims and oppressors, difference and dominance, and hegemonic (or socially validated) and alternative masculinities (Robinson, "Pedagogy," this volume; Connell, *Masculinities*). They examine parallelisms, interdependencies, and asymmetries between men and women, masculinity and femininity, masculinity studies and feminist theories, gender and other distributions of social power. Concerned with gender relationships now and the theories that describe them, these essays map sites of change as they build toward ethical and political engagement.

MASCULINITY AND FEMINISM: ANTAGONISMS AND DEPENDENCIES

Second-wave feminism of the 1960s and 1970s in the United States is frequently represented by the rhetoric of the most vocal, if not the most populous, of its perspectives, that of a radical feminism that sometimes did charge men as a group with being the enemies and oppressors of women and saw men's masculinity as both an instrument and a sign of their power. These radical feminists presented themselves as spokeswomen and popularly represented feminism in the media and the historical record (MacKinnon, *Feminism*). To take one widely anthologized statement, for example, the "Redstocking Manifesto" claimed that "all men have oppressed women": "we do not need to change ourselves, but to change men," who should "give up their male privileges and support women's liberation in the interest of our humanity and their own" ("Redstocking," 534–35). This rhetoric upstaged the arguments of liberal feminists, who wanted women to have parity with men's power, prestige, and position, and the perspectives of materialist feminists and feminists of color who included race and social class as well as gender in their analyses and who held social structures, not men as individuals, responsible for women's disadvantaged position.[2] For instance, the Combahee River Collective rejected biological determinism and categorical denunciations of men: "actively committed to struggling against racial, sexual, heterosexual, and class oppression," they sought an "integrated analysis and practice based upon the fact that the major systems of oppression are interlocking" ("Black Feminist," 63).

Thus the assumption that feminist thinking and masculinity were mutually antagonistic was not entirely unfounded, but not entirely accurate either. Many feminists did have problems with masculinity in at least two different senses. First, much feminist thought associates masculinity with the institutional practices, attitudes, and personality traits of men—like aggression and competitiveness—that uphold male dominance and oppress women. It casts such masculinity as itself a social problem antithetical to feminist goals. Second, the concept of masculinity poses problems for feminist theory because it is a slippery entity without consistent content. Some feminists think it can be restructured so that it does not depend on male dominance over women. Others wish to abolish it, believing that a "feminist degendering movement" is necessary "to undo gender" as an organizing principle of institutions, attitudes, and values (Lorber, "Using," 88). Yet gender appears to be so deeply structured into society, individual psychology, identity, and sexuality that eradicating it will be extremely difficult. The political stakes of this controversy are considerable, and efforts to make gender matter less may well collaborate with efforts toward its reformulation.

Second-wave antagonisms between feminism and masculinity were often mutual. Whereas early feminists attacked men, according to Kenneth Clatterbaugh, most men's initial "reactions to the contemporary women's movement of the 1960s were negative and derisive" ("Literature," 883). They ridiculed feminist analyses of women's disadvantage, claimed men as victims, and attributed men's traditional traits and privileges to hormones, evolution, or logic, all views still prevalent today (Goldberg, *Inevitability;* Farrell, *Myth*). The "masculinist" men's movement argued in favor of male dominance and blamed widespread psychological and social problems on feminist attacks and men's loss of status. In the early 1990s, it notoriously bewailed male victimization and gathered men into supportive enclaves (Bly, *Iron John;* Kimmel, *Politics*). Although profeminist men happily note the waning of such male supremacist men's movements, Clatterbaugh warns that this decline may in fact result from successful mainstreaming, so that misogyny and antifeminism have at the same time lost their distinctive organizational forms and their marginality within U.S. society (Clatterbaugh, "Literature").

If masculinist men's movements saw feminism as a powerful enemy, a smaller group of profeminist men agreed with feminists that the two traditional genders distorted both sexes (Pleck, *Myth*). These profeminists sought gender equality by changing men, reeducating the abusive, and seeking to dismantle the male privileges enjoyed by dominant men. These profeminist men constituted themselves as male supporters of the women's liberation movement, and they sought to disestablish sexism from within men's territory, sometimes by attacking masculinity. For example, John Stoltenberg argued for the necessity of "refusing to be a man" in favor of being an ungendered human with a penis.

Clatterbaugh judges that all men's movements are now in "serious decline" and that the profeminist men's movement "has almost no life outside the university" ("Literature," 890, 887). There, however, it is institutionalized, and its influence in sociology, history, and cultural studies, as well as in gender studies more generally, may be increasing. As Judith Newton reports, even progressive academic men did not do much scholarly academic work on gender until the 1980s, when masculinity studies provided them a validating professional context ("White," 574–75). Meanwhile, feminists influenced by psychoanalysis debated whether the Lacanian phallus was necessarily the signifier of social power and questioned Freud's idea that gender and heterosexuality must develop simultaneously through the Oedipus complex in order for society to cohere (Sprengnether, *Spectral;* Segal, *Slow*). Attempts to understand the cinematic "male gaze" and misogynous culture led feminist scholars to pay more attention to male subjectivities and male bonding, inaugurating feminist masculinity studies as an academic field (Sedgwick, *Between;* Jeffords, *Remasculinization;* Silverman, *Male;* Wiegman, "Unmaking," this volume). Queer theory of the 1990s, galvanized by Judith Butler, focused on the man in drag as paradigmatic of the performative attributes of all gender, inspiring fruitful skepticism about naturalized biological assumptions (Halberstam, *Female;* Fausto-Sterling, *Myths*).

Academic men's studies became established in college courses and programs, associations, and journals, though remaining marginal in comparison with women's studies and gender studies focused on sexuality. According to Lynne Segal, men's studies literature still depends on women's studies for its methodology and "uncannily mirrors" feminist texts: "it focuses upon men's own experiences, generates evidence of men's gender-specific suffering and has given birth to a new field of enquiry," all based on a victimization model, despite the fact that men overall still have greater power, cultural prestige, political authority, and wealth than women (*Why,* 160). Thus, if one relationship between the terms *masculinity* and *feminism* in American culture at large is an antagonism, a dependency developed in academic studies that gave priority to feminist analysis of gender as constructed through power and hierarchy (Newton, "White," 579–82).

Profeminist men argued that men should support feminism because most are harmed by idealizing the characteristics of socially powerful men and by defining the masculine in opposition to women and subordinate men, especially homosexuals and men of color (Connell, *Masculinities;* Kimmel, *Manhood*). All men were harmed by this "hegemonic masculinity," they claimed, because it narrowed their options, forced them into confining roles, dampened their emotions, inhibited their relationships with other men, precluded intimacy with women and children, imposed sexual and gender conformity, distorted their self-perceptions, limited their social consciousness, and doomed them to continual and humiliating fear of failure to live up to the masculinity mark. According to Michael Kimmel, "Men are just beginning to realize that the 'traditional' definition of masculinity leaves them unfulfilled and dissatisfied" (*Gendered,* 268). As they argued about whether men or women were more advantaged or more suffering, both antagonistic and sympathetic male responses to feminism helped articulate men, as well as women, as "marked" by gender (Robinson, *Marked*).

CURRENT "CRISES"

If both feminist and men's movements seem less active now than in past decades, it is not because society considers either masculinity or feminism unproblematic. On the contrary, popular discussion of these issues is often phrased in the heightened rhetoric of an impending crisis (Horrocks, *Masculinity*). In her pioneering book of 1963, *The Feminine Mystique,* Betty Friedan located a contradiction in the lives of white, suburban, middle-class women who were educated equally with men but then tracked into a stultifying domesticity, and she helped channel their dissatisfaction into second-wave feminism and activism. A generation later, the majority of married American women are in the paid labor force, and other contradictions now appear more salient, for example, the one between white men's expectations of masculine privilege and a polarizing economy where many men perceive themselves falling in status as women's economic and social power rises—even if it remains below full parity with men's (Coontz, *Really;* Sidel, *Keeping*).

Talk of a masculinity crisis frequently implicates feminism, and this language of crisis extends, as well, to feminist and gender theories. These arousals of anxiety depend reciprocally on each other. Feminists are anxious that after generations of struggle not enough has changed: sexism, male dominance, and traditional masculinity still hold sway. Conversely, the media frets that American culture has changed too much, so that men's masculinity is undermined and social stability therefore imperiled. These contradictory assessments rest on the common assumption that masculinity and feminism are both antagonistic and interdependent, the rise of one determined by the fall of the other, with anxiety on both sides. This talk of crisis, with its deliberate exaggerations and fomenting of anxieties, echoes the rhetoric of advertising and extends into academic feminism and masculinity studies. Segal notes that many people see the presumed " 'crisis of masculinity' in the Western world" as "a, if not *the*, burning issue of our time" (*Why*, 160). Alluding to Friedan's hallmark "problem that has no name" of postwar women, Gail Sheehy warns of a new midlife "male malaise" that has "no name" (*Understanding*, 22). If it seems implausible that men, everywhere visibly in power, are in crisis, the rhetoric of crisis is deployed even more urgently where men are most vulnerable and where men are made, that is, as boys. "Boys today are in crisis," says William Pollack in *Real Boys: Rescuing Our Sons from the Myths of Boyhood*, a title that trumpets an emergency to save "our sons," here not from the erosion but from the development of traditional masculinity.

One widely publicized writer on the "masculinity crisis" is Susan Faludi, the feminist journalist who a decade ago analyzed the media "backlash" against women. Her book about men, *Stiffed: The Betrayal of the American Man*, demonstrates American culture's transformation by feminism, the ideological containment of that transformation, and the limitations of a simplistic gender rhetoric based on victimization. She reports a serious "masculinity crisis" in the increase of such "male distress signals" as anxiety, suicide, and criminality, but she is unclear about where to assign responsibility for these problems, vaguely blaming men's "betrayal" on manipulative media and disappointing fathers who are themselves disappointed by their country. She thinks men now should act as feminism inspired women to act thirty years ago, and for the same reason, a perception of victimization by the culture. Yet the men she interviewed did not view feminism as their model; instead, they blamed "women's advancement as a driving force behind their own distress" (594). Faludi struggles against the notion that women can rise only if men fall, but she escapes the gender binary only through vague liberal humanism expressed in generically male terms: "Because as men struggle to free themselves from their crisis, their task is not, in the end, to figure out how to be masculine—rather, their masculinity lies in figuring out how to be human," so they can "learn to wage a battle against no enemy, to own a frontier of human liberty, to act in the service of a brotherhood that includes us all" (607). Faludi tries vainly to transmute this masculine "battle" into a common cause that could ally feminists and men in crisis, then gives up: "Maybe women's role is just getting out of the way" (quoted in Jacobs, "Male," 68). She therefore agrees with the masculinists that masculinity is in "crisis," instead of seeing dominant masculinity, which subordinates women and distributes power unevenly among men, as itself a cause of men's problems. Yet, vague and contradictory though it is, such popularized feminism does illustrate insights from both feminism and masculinity studies, most clearly, the idea that men as well as women are shaped by gender. Faludi's evidence that individual men feel powerless against economic forces and social institutions does not mean that these forces are inexorable laws of nature or that they are not largely man-made. Rather, one strategy of established power is its erasure of human agency, its masquerade of naturalness, which perplexes popular discussions of gender but contemporary feminist masculinity studies can unveil.

At the same time that a "crisis" of masculinity is invoked, there is also a crisis perceived in contemporary feminism. Assessments of twentieth-century feminisms vary from assertions that it has harmed men, society, and even women to the triumphalism of some of its scholars and participants (Minnich, "Feminist"). For instance, Rosalyn Baxandall and Linda Gordon claim that "the women's liberation movement, as it was called in the sixties and seventies, was the largest social movement in the history of the United States—and probably in the world. Its impact has been felt in every home, school, and workplace, in every form of art, entertainment and sport, in all aspects of personal and public life in the United States" ("Second-Wave," 28). Yet the popular press often describes feminism as ailing, defunct, passé, and a failure at the same time that, contradictorily, individual accomplishments and social problems are attributed to its success.

One popular view is that feminism has helped American women become more assertive and fulfilled, while men have remained relatively unchanged, watching the women's revolution march past them. Yet feminists note that men retain social power, progressive change has been capped, glass ceilings and frozen attitudes inhibit women's gains, and male violence still threatens households and nations. They question why it currently seems so difficult to mobilize women, to sustain a movement, and to intervene effectively in politics and culture, and they decry the rise of antifeminist ideologies like "Darwinian fundamentalism" and "genetic determinism" (Segal, *Why*, 6). They note that much of the gain in the ratio of women's to men's wages over the last thirty years resulted from the decline in working men's hourly wages. While some feminists empathize with men's losses, others believe the instability of men's position offers unprecedented opportunities for feminism (Faludi, *Stiffed*; Bordo, *Male*). Segal argues that women need feminism now, when "the resilience of images of masculinity as power are shaken [*sic*] by the actualities of shifting gender dynamics" but feminist values are not yet in place: "What we have yet to see is movement towards fairer and more caring societies" (Segal, *Why*, 8, 7). This is also an argument that feminists need to engage masculinity studies now, because feminism can produce only partial explanations of society if it does not understand how men are shaped by masculinity. Reducing men's resistance to feminism, moreover, is a necessary goal of a masculinity studies that responds to feminism's crisis of frustrated progress toward equality.

Besides seeing crises in masculinity and in feminism, some scholars also perceive crises in feminist and gender theories as these fields try to accommodate the increasingly sophisticated insights of postmodernist and queer theories and those that demonstrate how racialized formations and sexuality construct and are constructed through gender. Some scholars question whether it is even possible to use the traditionally gendered categories of men and women, masculine and feminine, in the face of poststructuralist warnings about the exclusions performed by all such categories and the limits of purely binary systems. They ask whether political mobilizations in the name of gender are still possible or desirable (Riley, "*Am I*"; but see Pfeil, *White*). Thus among the problems facing feminist and masculinity theorists today are how to conceptualize their categories and how to articulate the interdependencies and conflicts between them, their divisions, the effects of masculinities and men on women and of women and femininities on men.

One cause for the anxiety so often expressed in masculinity studies, then, may be its ambivalent dependency on and antagonism toward feminism, hegemonic masculinity, and gay, lesbian, and queer studies. When masculinity is the object of feminist study, the customary specular relationship of subject and object between a male gaze and a female body is reversed (Mulvey, "Visual"; Bordo, *Male*). Feminist-inspired masculinity studies also alter the traditional division between a masculine public and a feminine private sphere, since feminism denotes a public politics of women's rights and masculinity studies analyze men's most private attributes: by considering embodiment, sexuality, and emotion, they show men not as generically human but as gendered male persons (Thomas, *Male*). Male sexuality is of particular interest to queer studies, as well, that have developed analyses of homophobia and heterosexuality. While men's and masculinity studies are growing as academic specialities, the boundaries of the field continue to be contested: should masculinity studies be autonomous or conjoined with women's studies, or gay, lesbian, bisexual, transgender and queer studies, lodge under the variously capacious tents of gender or cultural studies, or disperse among other programs identified by ethnicity, geographical area, or traditional academic discipline (Auslander, "Do Women's"; Wiegman, "Object")? Bryce Traister suggests that *masculinity studies* is now a coded term for "heterosexual masculinity studies," a field shaped by a "two-pronged 'crisis theory,' " which finds crisis so ubiquitous in the psychology of the masculine subject and in the history of American masculinities that it becomes normative and exculpatory ("Academic," 275–76). "The history of American men as men now not only proceeds as a historiography of masculine crisis but collectively writes itself as an actual history of American masculinity *as* crisis," Traister says, pondering, "Why at this particular historical moment is there not merely a perceived crisis of masculinity, but an academic and intellectual preoccupation with this crisis and its history?" (287, 298).

One answer to Traister's question may be adduced from the anatomy of "crises" sketched here and from the asymmetrical interdependencies of masculinity and feminism as cultural formations and academic subjects. Masculinity and feminism are fantasies, but they invoke differently situated desires. As contemporary social phenomena, the two exist in complex presents with which individuals and groups identify differently, yet both simultaneously appear as ideals that are not realized here and now. Masculinity is a nostalgic formation, always missing, lost, or about to be lost, its ideal form located in a past that advances with each generation in order to recede just beyond its grasp. Its myth is that effacing new forms can restore a natural, original male grounding. Feminism, in contrast, is a utopian discourse of an ideal future, never yet attained, whose myths celebrate alliances that manage conflicts within comprehensive metanarratives and narratives of comprehension. Both fantasies risk simplifying the political—into the invisible hand of the natural or the dichotomous ally or enemy of the ethical—and both mystify collective action as too futile or too effective. Both are myths of power: masculinity of the natural congruence of male self with social privilege and feminism of a perfectly self-regulating collectivity. In both cases, adherents often believe they can picture their ideals brightly outlined against the gray confusions of the present, yet without a clear path to reach them. This unmapped gap, then, this zone of frustration and anxiety, is the "crisis," the loss of the past or the deferral of the future ideal. In contrast, the project of this book is to map the intersecting territories of masculinity and feminism, masculinity studies and feminist theories.

CURRENT CONSENSUS AND NEW DIRECTIONS

Current masculinity studies, including the essays collected here, are invigorated by a range of feminist, humanist, and poststructuralist theories, and current feminist theories are in turn being changed by the insights of masculinity studies. At present, feminist-inflected masculinity studies have reached consensus about some previously troubling issues. Chief among these is the initial insight that masculinity, too, is a gender and therefore that men as well as women have undergone historical and cultural processes of gender formation that distribute power and privilege unevenly.

Second is the consensus that masculinity is not monolithic, not one static thing, but the confluence of multiple processes and relationships with variable results for differing individuals, groups, institutions, and societies. Although dominant or hegemonic forms of masculinity work constantly to maintain an appearance of permanence, stability, and naturalness, the numerous masculinities in every society are contingent, fluid, socially and historically constructed, changeable and constantly changing, variously institutionalized, and recreated through media representations and individual and collective performances. According to Robyn Wiegman, early second-wave feminists paid far too little attention to "the masculine" or to differences between men for strategic reasons: "the assumption of masculinity as an undifferentiated position aided feminism's articulation of its own political subjectivity," while "the representation of men as the common enemy" disrupted women's previously unquestioned heterosexual alliances with men and so permitted the fleeting if "utopic myth" of sisterhood (*American*, 167). Yet, as the present volume demonstrates, feminists now join masculinity theorists in unpacking this "myth of masculine sameness" (*American*, 180).

A third area of consensus within feminist and masculinity theories is that both genders can and should cooperate both intellectually and politically, a previously contested point that now seems moot (Jardine and Smith, *Men;* Modleski, *Feminism*). Women contribute to masculinity studies, men to feminist theory as well as to masculinity studies, heterosexuals to queer theory, and gay-identified scholars to the study of heterosexuality, even though the standpoints of differently situated scholars will not be identical (Digby, *Men;* Thomas, *Straight*).

A fourth area of consensus is more broadly methodological. The authors represented here are skeptical about essentialist conceptions of gender and sexuality as fixed by God, nature, or immutable psychological or sociological laws, even though they may acknowledge biology's role in the unfolding of gender. They join poststructuralist suspicion of universal truths with queer and antiracist caution about the dangers of categorical exclusions and cultural imperialisms. They agree that the critique of essentialist categories is politically imperative, since belief in traditional polarized genders as static, inevitable, universals precludes social change by insisting that change is impossible, deeply undesirable, or both.

Whereas masculinity scholars and feminist theorists generally have achieved consensus around these broad premises, the contributors to this volume question, critique, and clarify the prevailing paradigms of academic masculinity studies and so create new approaches to understanding gender. They question older binaries that now seem simplistic and potentially distorting and exclusionary—for example, the binaries that divide men and women, masculine and feminine, heterosexual and homosexual, white and black, individual and society, structure and agency. In particular, they critique the limited binaries within feminist theories and masculinity studies of oppressors and victims, of difference and dominance, and of hegemonic versus alternative masculinities (Robinson, "Pedagogy," this volume).

As we have seen, second-wave radical feminism galvanized women's support with the simplification that "all men have oppressed women," and some men's movements, too, have found an identity as victims useful for themselves. Both these tendencies have come under repeated recent attack. For example, Aída Hurtado assails masculinist white men's masculinity studies for adopting a fallacious posture of victimization. She charges that "Western male intellectual tradition cannot theorize from a position of privilege but, rather, one of victimhood, because paternalism is the only viable political solution that leaves the status quo untouched" (*Color*, 126). Contemporary discourses continually refer to but distrust this language of victimization; they are anxious, as well, about naming oppressors. For example, in an issue of *Ms* magazine that asks, "What's Up with Men?" editor Marcia Ann Gillespie replies, "There are no villains here, only menfolk struggling" in "male country at a time when the old rules about manhood no longer seem to apply, men are floundering, and the terrain is fragile" (1). Bordo agrees that "within a Foucaldian/feminist framework . . . it is indeed senseless to view men as the enemy" because "most men, equally with women, find themselves embedded and implicated in institutions and practices that they as individuals did not create and do not control—and that they frequently feel tyrannized by" (*Unbearable*, 28). This rejection of a simplistic binary between victims and oppressors facilitates analyzing the subtle complicities of both women and men in upholding inegalitarian institutions; it does not invalidate investigations into dominance (Clatterbaugh, "Are Men"). Rather, differences between genders, within genders, and outside of the standard gender binary need always to be articulated with reference to social hierarchies.

Using feminist theories about gender inequality, the authors in this volume advance the investigation of men and masculinities in more nuanced ways. Using the perspectives of masculinity studies about differences between men as well as between men and women, they question earlier feminist formulations in order to develop more comprehensive theories of gender. With differing conclusions, they explore the now dominant paradigm of masculinity studies: that the power maintained by a hegemonic masculinity attributed chiefly to privileged white heterosexual men can be effectively unsettled by the representation of alternative masculinities, especially those of queer men and men of color. In addition, they show how the scholarship and pedagogies of masculinity studies replicate the contradictions within contemporary gender relations.

As we have seen, the language of a "masculinity crisis" falsifies history by implying there was once a golden time of unproblematic, stable gender, when men were men, women were women, and everyone was happy with their social roles—"the way we never were" (Coontz, *Never*). In an individualistic culture, crisis rhetoric frequently mandates introspection to change the self, but it also forebodes that historical conditions have gradually built up to a unique moment of dramatic, even violent, social change to which individual responses will be inadequate. Popular talk of "crisis" demands attention and action while remaining vague about the alleged problem, who is troubled by it, and who stands to benefit either from its incitement or its resolution. The essays in this book reveal some answers about the contemporary "crisis of masculinity," finding it, among other things, both a rationalization for the drive to maintain patriarchal entitlement and a sign of many men's legitimate search for new forms of vulnerability, responsibility, intimacy, and maturity.

Current masculinity studies focus less on men's power over women and more on relationships between men, as these are regulated by regimes of masculinity. They look at the positive potentials of male bonding as well as at divisive effects of racial, class, sexual, and other differences between men. They significantly expand the insight that gender is relational by analyzing gender as it varies according to a number of axes that cannot be reduced to the rubric of "alternative" masculinities. To the familiar categories of race, class, and sexuality, the essays gathered here add age, nationality, and institutional location. They argue that genders form through power relationships that are mobile and both temporally and site specific, asymmetrical relationships that may appear different to those who are differently situated. They thus illustrate that masculinity and femininity are not necessarily parts of a zero-sum game. Rather, these abstractions are defined in relation to one another, but not only in relation to one another—and not necessarily in relationships of simple opposition or negation. The dynamics of both intraracial and cross-racial, same-sexual relationships, for example, include far more than the binary of homoeroticism and homophobia, as Marlon Ross proves in this volume ("Race, Rape, Castration").

The contributors to this book expose asymmetries in the relationships among gender terms, showing, for instance, that masculinity and femininity hold neither parallel nor complementary roles in feminist theory, that the relationships between men and masculinity differ from those between women and femininity, and that all these relationships are textured by historically variable axes of power and difference, social location and individual experience. The conflation of emasculation, castration, femininization, and femininity is a political maneuver, not a psychological law, and masculinity and femininity have differing meanings and uses in male and female bodies and in differing cultural contexts.

In this volume, the authors clarify the operations of gender through specific examples and case studies, many drawn from film and literature. In contemporary culture, which creates and maintains gender differences largely through reinforcing its representations, through replicating and consuming images, the cultural critics' tasks of making masculinities visible and locating social agency and responsibility are always in dialogue with the erasures and naturalizations of the ubiquitous market culture. In recent years, cultural critics have questioned if and how power surges, market forces, and public works. They have declared that race matters, class acts, identity fragments, age benefits, sex practices, and, persistently, gender troubles (West, *Race;* Butler, *Gender*). These phrases refer simultaneously to entities and actions, and they thus highlight both the mobility of social categories and our agency as scholars in creating them. The essays gathered here point the way to movements for practical action and for closer institutional, academic, and intellectual affiliations with other branches of feminist and gender studies. Redefining masculinity as a submerged political and ethical arena, they unlock opportunities to resist individual isolation and so foster meaningful collective action in the struggle for gender justice. In this book, too, "masculinity studies" are studied, feminists theorize and have their theories altered, and both feminist theories and masculinity studies advance in new directions through these mutual investigations.

THE ESSAYS

The essays in this volume are arranged to converse with one another in seven pairs that address common questions, often from highly divergent perspectives. The book begins with two theoretical essays that argue its central premise—the necessity of the project to connect feminist theories and masculinity studies. These essays propose questions that reverberate throughout the volume as a whole. The first essay, Robyn Wiegman's "Unmaking: Men and Masculinity in Feminist Theory," explains feminism's turn toward the study of masculinity by surveying the challenges originally leveled at the category of women as deployed by U.S. white feminists at the end of the twentieth century. As unified gender categories were attacked by feminists of color, by post-structuralist theorists, and by queer political activists, the falsely unified and normative category of men also came under scrutiny. The "unmaking" of the category of men, Wiegman argues, is necessary both to remake masculinity as pertinent to female subjectivity and to complicate feminism's understandings of the interconnections between sex, sexuality, and gender.

Whereas Wiegman shows how changes in feminist theory alter available interpretations of masculinity, Calvin Thomas asks that the political test of masculinity studies be their results for women. "For this male feminist," Thomas writes in his essay, "Reenfleshing the Bright Boys; or, How Male Bodies Matter to Feminist Theory," "what is ultimately at issue in masculinity studies is, or should be, the effect of masculinity construction on women. . . . Situated within this horizon, masculinity studies can be, not the betrayal or appropriation of feminism, but rather one of its valuable and necessary consequences." In particular, he wishes to reinstate the vulnerable male body in masculinity studies in order to deter the displacement of that vulnerability onto the feminine and the queer, a formulation that provides insights into relationships between men as well as the significance of masculinity for women.

While essays throughout the book highlight interdependencies between the traditionally cited categories of race, class, and gender, the next two essays further expand the theoretical grid through which feminist theories can study masculinities. My own essay, "Theorizing Age and Gender: Bly's Boys, Feminism, and Maturity Masculinity," complicates the usual categories of analysis by adding age to the mix. I suggest the advantages to feminist theory of thinking gender through analogies with the multiple categories of age rather than in exclusively binary terms. A developmental, age-inflected theory of gender, I argue, could oppose the challenge of "being a man," not to being a woman or a male homosexual but to being a boy. Such a theory could allow feminists to affirm rather than reject some forms of masculinity in men and to build on the insights and emotional needs evoked in men by the masculinist men's movement without subscribing to its sexism. At the same time, this approach historicizes masculinity, responding to changes over the individual life course as well as to the changes in society that have eroded breadwinner models of masculinity in the contemporary United States.

In "Getting Up There with Tom: The Politics of American 'Nice,' " Fred Pfeil examines masculinity as a national as well as historical phenomenon, one he too associates with a contrast between childishness and maturity. Pfeil explicates one of dominant masculinity's current ruses by describing a transformation in culturally validated representations of masculinity from the familiar ideal of the tough rampager to a new kind of oedipal hero who progresses from childish man to man authorized by his inner child. Taking the roles played by film actor Tom Hanks as symptomatic, Pfeil shows how the "perpetually innocent niceness" of this boyish, heterosexual white masculinity functions as ideology: it provides an alibi for the continuation of ruling-class American male privilege and forecloses social commitments to maturity and community. In this instance, power is preserved not by knowledge but by willful ignorance, and a supposedly progressive alternative masculinity turns out to be a prop rather than a challenge to the dominant social order. While this volume as a whole elaborates the insights that men as well as women are gendered and that both masculinity and femininity have complex histories, Pfeil specifically illustrates how the normative characteristics of masculinity—and of whiteness, middle-classness, and Americanness—require constant cultural work in order to appear the effortless attributes of a privilege they simultaneously justify and disguise.

The third set of essays discusses the connections between feminism and masculinity through the temporary community of the masculinity studies classroom. A woman teacher facing men in her classes, Sally Robinson finds herself repeatedly confronted not only with her students' hesitation about connecting masculinity with feminism but also with the implication that feminists are out to destroy or emasculate men.

These two concerns highlight the interrelationship in the classroom setting of academic inquiry, which seeks to theorize both masculinity and feminism, and of the popular perceptions that make these issues so emotionally charged for both students and teacher. In "Pedagogy of the Opaque: Teaching Masculinity Studies," Robinson learns from her students the dangers of the static, ahistorical, individualistic, and binary conceptions of masculinity that mirror larger problems in the academy, and she also grapples with the ambivalent feelings the masculinity studies classroom can generate.

In contrast, philosopher Harry Brod reflects in his essay, "Studying Masculinities As Superordinate Studies," on his experiences as a male teacher of masculinity studies in classrooms where women outnumber men. Brod is relatively sanguine about transforming his students through a "superordinate studies" approach that makes masculinity analogous to other such forms of social privilege as whiteness, middle-classness, and heterosexuality, without disparaging women as victims or disparaging men as oppressors. By assigning social, not individual, blame for sexism, he claims he can facilitate productive conversations between male and female students as well as recognition of their personal responsibility for the continuation of sexism. Both Robinson and Brod grapple with the oscillations among theoretical, moral, and political investments common in feminist masculinity studies classrooms and find some practical suggestions for responding to their students' concerns. Even though both these teachers challenge hegemonic masculinity in their courses, their differing experiences suggest the symbolic power of gendered bodies. Men are not the only experts on masculinity, but the visibly male masculinity studies teacher may produce an automatic effect of reassurance in his students in contrast to the female feminist teacher who is perceived even before she speaks as a potential attacker of men's masculinity. Like the other authors in this book who write on parallel topics, this pairing is comprised of a man and a woman, not to privilege a heterosexual model but to demonstrate, as Brod argues, the broad range of cross-gendered relationships that are intellectual, affiliative, and political rather than sexual.[3]

The essays by Judith Newton and R. W. Connell are also concerned with masculinity studies in the academy, but with the distinctive trajectories of differing national formations and with the institutionalization of fields rather than pedagogical practices. Newton looks at masculinity studies in the contexts of men's responses to successive waves of feminism over the past thirty years. Are "masculinity studies" the longed for "profeminist movement for academic men?" she asks. Noting some of the "global developments that have helped produce the very 'crisis' over masculinity" to which men's movements both contribute and respond," she finds men both in popular men's movements and in academic masculinity studies inventing new, empathetic, and socially responsible male subjectivities congruent with feminist goals. Yet she also worries that men's studies communities may exclude women. She argues, instead, that masculinity studies should continue to develop as a collective political project that crosses "gendered territorializations."

Australian sociologist Connell shares this emphasis on collaboration between the sexes in his autobiographical account, "Long and Winding Road: An Outsider's View of U.S. Masculinity and Feminism." However, he doesn't think the collaboration is easy, and he gives some examples of the trouble to be expected. Because he is concerned about the interplay between American academic feminism and American universities' place in global capitalism, he does not assume that feminist-inspired masculinity studies are automatically and in all respects progressive. He criticizes defensive accounts of masculinity that obscure the power imbalances between men and women, ones that focus on male difference without acknowledging male dominance. Among other problems, these accounts do not allow for the complexities and contradictions in men's gender practices. Yet there are starting points for progressive theory and practice. Connell argues, as does Newton, for the difficult alliances of male friends of feminism with female feminists and for an unconditional commitment to human equality.

The next pair of essays turns from masculinity studies as an academic field to the place of masculinity within the framework of psychoanalysis in order to examine psychodynamic theories of masculinity formation from loving fatherhood to warrior brutality. These essays revise the gender schema of Freud, Lacan, and more recent psychoanalytic theorists and, like other essays in this book, connect personal and psychological with larger social issues. Political philosopher Isaac D. Balbus argues that individual psychological mechanisms, especially a son's identification with a nurturant parent, may produce positive variations on traditional masculine self formation. His essay, "Masculinity and the (M)Other" moves toward a synthesis of feminist mothering theory with psychoanalytic theories of narcissism that emphasizes the influence of different maternal practices on masculine identity formation. He critiques the well-known feminist mothering theories of Nancy J. Chodorow and others as too preoccupied with a polarized model of gender domination to account for individual differences and suggests a more balanced model of masculine development that integrates the effects of actual parenting practices with the structures of child rearing.

Nancy J. Chodorow has herself modified her earlier, extremely influential "mothering theory," which attributed the differences between masculine and feminine personality formation to mother-dominated child-rearing. In "The Enemy Outside: Thoughts on the Psychodynamics of Extreme Violence with Special Attention to Men and Masculinity," Chodorow scrutinizes the moral and political consequences of binary gender, especially in the culturally validated links between masculinity, nationalism, and violence that she attributes to transformations of intrapsychic representations of being a humiliated and subordinated boy in relation to an adult man. Thus Chodorow's argument resonates with other theorizing in this volume on the complex interdependencies between gender, sexuality, ethnicity, national identity, and age, and it also revisits and particularizes feminist theories of male dominance and aggression. In so doing, it points toward other areas not developed in this book, for example, the ecofeminist argument that the "global devastation caused by militaries is directly a product of the militarized 'cult of masculinity' " in which man conquers nature (Seager, "Patriarchal," 168).

The subsequent essays by King-Kok Cheung and Michael Awkward continue to articulate specific connections between masculinities and national or racialized identities. In "Art, Spirituality, and the Ethic of Care: Alternative Masculinities in Chinese American Literature," Cheung joins other authors of this volume in urging feminists to attend to the differences between men and so participate in the process of rethinking masculinity. She stresses how manhood is inflected by various determinants, such as age, race, sexuality, class, and geographic location, determinants that are often interactive rather than additive. But she is optimistic about the power of representations to undermine traditional patriarchies through the depiction of alternative masculinities, both gay and straight, in Chinese American literature of the 1990s.

In "Black Male Trouble: The Challenges of Rethinking Masculine Differences," Awkward, too, analyzes the effects of representations of alternative masculinities, but he is more cautious than Cheung about celebrating the progressive potential of nonmonolithic masculinities. He questions the simplistic theories of both black cultural nationalists and some white feminists concerning race and gender, especially those that associate black masculinity with violence and predatory sexual power. Recent films directed by African American women, he claims, dispute myths of black matriarchy and of black male impotence that assume black men's categorical estrangement from hegemonic phallic power. Within heterosexuality as well as outside it reside multiple alternative masculinities that need not be either idealized or demonized. Thus Awkward cooperates with the project of such feminist theorists as Beverly Guy-Sheftall, who has charged that "we race black men, but we don't gender them" and has proposed that looking at black masculinity should "be a focus of black Women's Studies" ("Whither," 43).

Taken together, the essays in this book question both the model of a static hegemonic masculinity and the political efficacy of celebrating various alternative masculinities. They critique conflations of blame and responsibility that sort "good" from "bad" masculinities too simply, and they expose the dangers of universalizing and dehistoricizing masculinity. The two powerful essays that conclude this volume complicate these matters further by valorizing categories that are completely effaced in most current discourses about both masculinity and feminism—the male-male erotics of racialized sexual violence and the abjected monstrosity of female masculinity. Like other essays collected here, they demonstrate that the insights of queer theory are essential to feminist thinking about the interactions between race, ethnicity, and gender. In his essay, "Race, Rape, Castration: Feminist Theories of Sexual Violence and Masculine Strategies of Black Protest," Marlon B. Ross analyzes the odd conflation of the castration of African American men with the rape of African American women in the rhetoric of race outrage against African American men's historical deprivation of manliness. Rather than assuming an equal or analogous relation between these acts, he considers the forces that obscure the agency of women as both perpetrators and victims of race violence, the sexual violence committed against black men and that which they perpetrate, and, most deeply, the cross-racial, same-sexual undercurrents implicit in such violence.

Finally, Judith Halberstam closes *Masculinity Studies and Feminist Theories: New Directions* with the deliberately controversial essay, "The Good, the Bad, and the Ugly: Men, Women, and Masculinity." Dramatically challenging naturalizations of gender, she discovers contemporary anxieties about heterosexuality and dominant masculinity that are prevalent in recent films and adumbrated in nineteenth-century fiction. While men's maleness remains protected in these narratives, feminism is feminized and rendered ineffectual; initially independent women are repeatedly represented as unhappy until they achieve heterosexual families and domestic security. For Halberstam, such popular images of the relationships between masculinity and feminism reverberate with those found in academic feminist theory and masculinity studies. From this perspective, a major problem with both academic masculinity studies and many feminist theories is their commitment to a binary gender system, which supports male dominance and heteronormativity instead of imagining the new arrangements of gender, race, class, and sexuality that could make female masculinities intelligible.

Halberstam's speculations about the missing discourse of female masculinity implicitly invite inquiry into other gaps in contemporary gender discourses. For example, in comparison to men's—or even women's—masculinity, women's femininity has been of little theoretical interest lately. Discussions of women's work, sexuality, maternity, or other matters rarely refer to the concept, one so discredited that literary critic Sharon Holland chastises an author who uses "the word 'feminine' rather than 'female' to describe both subjectivity . . . and identity," explaining that in work that otherwise "engages feminist concerns so adeptly, it is distressing to find the use of the word 'feminine' with little attention to its lack of currency within feminist circles" ("On Waiting," 110).[4] This lack of theoretical interest in women's femininity may tell us something as well about the rhetoric of crisis so obsessively applied to masculinity. If masculinity and femininity were indeed formed in complementary relationship to one another, so that men's masculinity and women's femininity were really necessary for individual mental health and for successful social functioning, as conservatives argue, the collapse of one should imply the collapse of the other, presumably with dire results. But, across a wide political spectrum, pundits seem to agree that the women's movements of the twentieth century have brought women both expanded opportunities and increased pressures, but neither these conflicts nor these advances are seen as endangering women's "femininity," which is rarely mentioned as an area of concern and is certainly not connected with lost sexuality or a body part in the way characteristic of the rhetoric of masculinity and emasculation. In contrast, anxiety about men's imperiled masculinity indicates how tied masculinity is to the assumption of privilege and how uneasy has become the justification for that privilege. In this context, the attention to men's so-called feminine side may act to shore up their privilege through the alibis of androgyny, completeness, and personal transformation rather than undermine that privilege, as men, no longer able to escape the mark of gender, seek to appropriate its full range for themselves (Robinson, *Marked Men*).

Moreover, separating masculinity from an automatic association with men, as Halberstam implies, may facilitate other theoretical breakthroughs, for example, disentangling masculinity's normative associations with sexual and cultural power and so dethroning those symbols, like the Lacanian phallus, that naturalize men's privilege as necessary to the maintenance of social order (Brenkman, *Straight;* Cornell, *At the Heart*). The essays collected here suggest that there is much to be gained by trying to discriminate those gendered aspects of power and privilege, like comfort with one's own body, that all people might be thought to deserve, even though at present few enjoy them, from those coercions that diminish the potential of others.

Thus, even as they seek to forward the movement toward gender justice inaugurated by twentieth-century feminism, the authors in this book dispute the old, tidy binaries of difference and dominance, men and women, masculine and feminine. Instead, they exemplify the possibilities that open when feminist theories and masculinity studies ally in the project to reformulate gender. They find feminist, queer, and other gender theories necessary but not sufficient in themselves to understand the obstacles that impede gender justice, and they demonstrate that such theories are neither interchangeable nor universally applicable. They cast neither men nor women as invariably oppressors or victims. Charting the mobile manifestations of power in all its registers, they recognize that men and women, in their multiplicity of circumstances and locations, have changed as their circumstances have changed from the mid twentieth to the twenty-first centuries. They know, too, that seeking to change others requires tact, ethical concern, political savvy, and a willingness to interrogate and change one's self, as well as theoretical analysis. Cumulatively, then, these essays help make masculinities visible in their many representations and effects, but they also question easy divisions of good from bad, hegemonic from alternative masculinities. Persistently pointing to practical goals, they reveal how tenacious are claims to male entitlement, even as many men's access to economic and cultural power diminishes. At the same time, they demonstrate how much contemporary feminisms stand to learn, and to gain, from dialogue with the insights of masculinity studies.

As a feminist theorist interested in masculinity studies, I initiated this book by calling for scholars working at the intersections of both these fields to speak on two panels at Modern Language Association conventions, one in 1998 and one in 2000. Seven of the fourteen authors gave brief versions of the essays published here at these panels.[5] The other authors responded to my invitation to contribute to this volume. Eleven of the book's fourteen essays were written specifically for this volume: the other three were previously published in specialized contexts.[6] Although wide-ranging, the essays in this book are not comprehensive. They emphasize the contemporary United States and the cultural work of theory, literature, the academy, and the media.[7]

NOTES

I thank all the authors in this volume for their energy, enthusiasm, insights, and care in writing and revising their ideas. I am also grateful for the support of my home institution, the University of Illinois at Chicago, especially its English department, Gender and Women's Studies Program, and Institute for the Humanities, and for a fellowship from the Rockefeller Foundation to attend its individual residency program at Bellagio, Italy. Thanks also to Noel Barker, Harry Brod,

John Huntington, Sally Robinson, Calvin Thomas, Robyn Wiegman, and the Colum-
bia University Press readers for comments and suggestions about this introduction.

1. See Robinson, "Pedagogy of the Opaque," this volume. Citations of outside sources in this introduction are brief, focusing on a few recent studies: see the bibliographies of individual essays for more extensive coverage of feminist and masculinity studies literature.

2. Such classifications of feminisms are used, for example, in the feminist theories textbooks by Tong, *Feminist Thought,* and by Jagger and Rothenberg, *Feminist Frameworks,* but explicitly rejected by other current texts like Nicholson, *Second Wave.*

3. Having paired the essays by subject and discovered that they were all male-female pairs, I tried to rearrange them but lost useful thematic connections and returned to this order.

4. Though scholarly interest in women's femininity may be about to return. For example, see Ussher, *Fantasies.*

5. The 1998 panelists were Michael Awkward, Judith Kegan Gardiner, Judith Halberstam, and Judith Newton. The 2000 panel, which convened after this volume went to press, included Harry Brod, Calvin Thomas, and Sally Robinson, plus Susan Fraiman, who declined participating in the book project.

6. These were written by Ike Balbus, Nancy J. Chodorow, and Bob Connell. As this book was in press, a longer version of Robyn Wiegman's essay appeared.

7. Omitted from this volume because of its cultural focus were excellent essays by anthropologists Steven Caton and Norma Fuller, by Ingeborg Breines, director of the Women and a Culture of Peace Programme for the United Nations Educational, Scientific and Cultural Organisation, and by former men's studies student Ben Herold. These essays expanded the scope of material covered here, and I am grateful to their authors for initially contributing to this project.

WORKS CITED

Auslander, Leora. "Do Women's + Feminist + Men's + Lesbian and Gay + Queer Studies = Gender Studies?" *differences: A Journal of Feminist Cultural Studies* 9.3 (1997): 1–30.

Baxandall, Rosalyn, and Linda Gordon. "Second-Wave Soundings." *Nation* 271.1 (July 3, 2000): 28–32.

Bederman, Gail. *Manliness and Civilization: A Cultural History of Gender and Race in the United States, 1880–1917.* Chicago: University of Chicago Press, 1995.

Bly, Robert. *Iron John: A Book About Men.* Reading, Mass.: Addison-Wesley, 1990.

Bordo, Susan. *The Male Body: A New Look at Men in Public and Private.* New York: Farrar, Straus and Giroux, 1999.

———. *Unbearable Weight: Feminism, Western Culture, and the Body.* Berkeley: University of California Press, 1993.

Brenkman, John. *Straight Male Modern: A Cultural Critique of Psychoanalysis.* New York and London: Routledge, 1993.

Brod, Harry, ed. *The Making of Masculinities: The New Men's Studies.* Boston: Allen and Unwin, 1987.

Butler, Judith. *Gender Trouble: Feminism and the Subversion of Identity.* New York: Routledge, 1990.

Chodorow, Nancy J. *The Reproduction of Mothering: Psychoanalysis and the Sociology of Gender.* Berkeley: University of California Press, 1978.

Clatterbaugh, Kenneth. "Are Men Oppressed?" In Larry May, Robert Strikwerda, and Patrick D. Hopkins, eds., *Rethinking Masculinity: Philosophical Explorations in Light of Feminism,* pp. 289–305. 2d ed. London: Rowman and Littlefield, 1996.

———. "Literature of the U.S. Men's Movements." *Signs* 25.3 (Spring 2000): 883–94.

Combahee River Collective. "A Black Feminist Statement." In Linda Nicholson, ed., *The Second Wave: A Reader in Feminist Theory,* pp. 63–70. New York: Routledge, 1997.

Connell, R. W. *Masculinities.* Berkeley: University of California Press, 1995.

Coontz, Stephanie. *The Way We Never Were: American Families and the Nostalgia Trap.* New York: Basic, 1992.

———. *The Way We Really Are: Coming to Terms with America's Changing Families.* New York: Basic, 1997.

Cornell, Drucilla. *At the Heart of Freedom: Feminism, Sex, and Equality.* Princeton: Princeton University Press, 1998.

Digby, Tom, ed. *Men Doing Feminism.* New York and London: Routledge, 1998.

Faludi, Susan. *Backlash: The Undeclared War Against American Women.* New York: Doubleday, 1991.

————. *Stiffed: The Betrayal of the American Man.* New York: William Morrow, 1999.

Farrell, Warren. *The Myth of Male Power.* New York: Berkley, 1996.

Fausto-Sterling, Anne. *Myths of Gender.* 2d ed. New York: Basic, 1992.

Franklin, Clyde. *The Changing Definition of Masculinity.* New York and London: Plenum, 1984.

Friedan, Betty. *The Feminine Mystique.* New York: Dell, 1963.

Fuller, Norma. "The Social Constitution of Gender Identity Among Peruvian Urban Men." *Men and Masculinities* forthcoming.

Gillespie, Marcia Ann. Editor's page. *Ms.,* April/May 2000, p. 1.

Golderg, Steven. *The Inevitability of Patriarchy: Why the Biological Difference Between Men and Women Always Produces Male Domination.* New York: William Morrow, 1974.

Guy-Sheftall, Beverly, with Evelynn M. Hammonds. "Whither Black Women's Studies: Interview." *differences: A Journal of Feminist Cultural Studies* 9.3 (1997): 31–45.

Halberstam, Judith. *Female Masculinity.* Durham: Duke University Press, 1998.

Harper, Phillip Brian. *Are We Not Men? Masculine Anxiety and the Problem of African-American Identity.* New York and Oxford: Oxford University Press, 1996.

Holland, Sharon. "On Waiting to Exhale: Or What to Do When You're Feeling Black and Blue, a Review of Recent Black Feminist Criticism. *Feminist Studies* 26.1 (Spring 2000): 101–12.

Horrocks, Roger. *Masculinity in Crisis: Myths, Fantasies, and Realities.* New York: St. Martin's, 1994.

Hurtado, Aída. *The Color of Privilege: Three Blasphemies on Race and Feminism.* Ann Arbor: University of Michigan Press, 1999.

Jacobs, Gloria. "The Male Book." *Ms.,* April/May 2000, pp. 63–69.

Jaggar, Alison M., and Paula S. Rothenberg, eds. *Feminist Frameworks: Alternative Theoretical Accounts of the Relations Between Women and Men.* 3d ed. New York: McGraw Hill, 1993.

Jardine, Alice, and Paul Smith, eds. *Men in Feminism.* New York: Methuen, 1987.

Jeffords, Susan. *The Remasculinization of America: Gender and the Vietnam War.* Bloomington: Indiana University Press, 1989.

Kimmel, Michael S. *Manhood in America: A Cultural History.* New York: Free, 1996.

————. *The Gendered Society*. New York: Oxford University Press, 2000.

Kimmel, Michael S., ed. *The Politics of Manhood: Profeminist Men Respond to the Mythopoetic Men's Movement (and the Mythopoetic Leaders Answer)*. Philadelphia: Temple University Press, 1995.

Kimmel, Michael S., and Michael A. Messner, eds. *Men's Lives*. 5th ed. Boston: Allyn and Bacon, 2000.

Lorber, Judith. "Using Gender to Undo Gender: A Feminist Degendering Movement." *Feminist Theory* 1.1 (April 2000): 79–95.

MacKinnon, Catharine A. *Feminism Unmodified: Discourses on Life and Law.* Cambridge: Harvard University Press, 1987.

Minnich, Elizabeth Kamarck. "Feminist Attacks on Feminisms: Patriarchy's Prodigal Daughters." *Feminist Studies* 24.1 (Spring 1998): 159–75.

Modleski, Tania. *Feminism Without Women: Culture and Criticism in a "Post-feminist" Age*. Routledge: New York and London, 1991.

Mulvey, Laura. "Visual Pleasure and Narrative Cinema." *Screen* 16.3 (Autumn 1975): 6–18.

Newton, Judith. "White Guys." *Feminist Studies* 24.3 (Fall 1998): 572–98.

Nicholson, Linda, ed. *The Second Wave: A Reader in Feminist Theory*. New York: Routledge, 1997.

Pfeil, Fred. *White Guys: Studies in Postmodern Domination and Difference*. London and New York: Verso, 1995.

Pleck, Joseph H. *The Myth of Masculinity*. Cambridge: MIT Press, 1981.

Pollack, William. *Real Boys: Rescuing Our Sons from the Myths of Boyhood*. New York: Random House, 1998.

"Redstocking Manifesto." In Robin Morgan, ed., *Sisterhood Is Powerful: An Anthology of Writings from the Women's Liberation Movement*, pp. 533–36. New York: Vintage, 1970.

Riley, Denise. *"Am I That Name?" Feminism and the Category of "Women" in History*. Minneapolis: University of Minnesota Press, 1988.

Robinson, Sally. *Marked Men: White Masculinity in Crisis*. New York: Columbia University Press, 2000.

Ross, Marlon B. "In Search of Black Men's Masculinities." *Feminist Studies* 24.3 (Fall 1998): 599–26.

Seager, Joni. "Patriarchal Vandalism: Militaries and the Environment." In Jael Silliman and Ynestra King, eds., *Dangerous Intersections: Feminist Perspectives on Population, Environment, and Development*, pp. 163–88. Cambridge: South End, 1999.

Sedgwick, Eve Kosofsky. *Between Men: English Literature and Male Homosocial Desire.* New York: Columbia University Press, 1985.

Segal, Lynne. *Slow Motion: Changing Masculinities, Changing Men.* New Brunswick, N.J.: Rutgers University Press, 1990.

———. *Why Feminism?* New York: Columbia University Press, 2000.

Sheehy, Gail. *Understanding Men's Passages: Discovering the New Map of Men's Lives.* New York: Random House, 1998.

Sidel, Ruth. *Keeping Women and Children Last: America's War on the Poor.* New York: Penguin, 1996.

Silverman, Kaja. *Male Subjectivity at the Margins.* New York and London: Routledge, 1992.

Sprengnether, Madelon. *The Spectral Mother: Freud, Feminism, and Psychoanalysis.* Ithaca: Cornell University Press, 1990.

Stoltenberg, John. *Refusing to Be a Man: Essays on Sex and Justice.* Portland: Breitenbush, 1989.

Thomas, Calvin. *Male Matters: Masculinity, Anxiety, and the Male Body on the Line.* Urbana: University of Illinois Press, 1996.

Thomas, Calvin, ed., with Joseph A. Aimone and Catherine A. F. MacGillivray. *Straight with a Twist: Queer Theory and the Subject of Heterosexuality.* Urbana: University of Illinois Press, 1999.

Tong, Rosemarie Putnam. *Feminist Thought.* 2d ed. Boulder: Westview, 1998.

Traister, Bryce. "Academic Viagra: The Rise of American Masculinity Studies," *American Quarterly* 52.2 (June 2000): 274–304.

Ussher, Jane M. *Fantasies of Femininity: Reframing the Boundaries of Sex.* New Brunswick, N.J.: Rutgers University Press, 1997.

West, Cornel. *Race Matters.* Boston: Beacon, 1993.

Wiegman, Robyn. *American Anatomies: Theorizing Race and Gender.* Durham: Duke University Press, 1995.

———. "Object Lessons: Men, Masculinity, and the Sign of 'Women.' " *Signs* 26.2 (Winter 2001): 355–88.

UNMAKING: MEN AND MASCULINITY IN FEMINIST THEORY

Robyn Wiegman

Imagine Bill Clinton's surprise in 1999 to discover that the privileges attending the U.S. presidency had so radically changed in thirty years that something as banal as an Oval Office blow job could raise the question of his qualifications for the nation's number one post! Poor Bill. How could he not have known that promiscuous Camelot masculinity was no longer one of the perks of the White House's homosocial culture of male heterosexuality? Time had betrayed him and he, sadly for all of us, was the last to know. Dear Bill: what did you take these to mean: the smart bomb, the patriot missile, gays in the military, even a professional women's basketball league? Technology as a prophylactic for male bodies, homosexuality at the center of the nationalist imaginary, powerfully embodied women threatening to dunk? The authoritative norms of conventional masculinity were everywhere in flux. Not that Monica-gate had nothing to do with women's bodies as the territory of masculine truth and its displaced consequences, but even Chelsea knew that Bill's body could not be abstracted from the muck. The 1990s were, after all, the decade in which masculinity's marking had become a primary feature of U.S. popular culture, not to mention a burgeoning academic subfield, even—indeed especially—among feminists.

I raise the presence of the popular and academic at the outset of this consideration of masculinity studies less to explore their overlapping and quite often contradictory political investments than to foreground the status of the contemporary that has become the overdetermined tense of masculinity's crisis. In cultural commentary, Hollywood film, and the academic marketplace, masculinity has become "new"—newly marked and newly in crisis—through a retrospective rearticulation of the meaning of the counterculture of the 1960s.[1] Its crisis is thus one born of sexual and racial social movement on one hand and the failure of militarization to sustain a cold war consensus on nationalist manhood on the other. While a number of academic studies have made cogent arguments for understanding masculinity as by definition in perpetual crisis (in part through analyses of earlier historical periods),[2] the very emergence of masculinity as an entity to be interrogated and understood finds its raison d'être in the popular acknowledgment and open representational display of masculinity as a domain seemingly beside itself: that is, internally contested, historically discontinuous, and popularly a mess.

This essay attempts to construct a critical history of feminism's turn toward the study of men and masculinity by discussing three trajectories of analysis. The first identifies how questions of differences among women, especially racial, compelled a rearticulation of feminism's hegemonic understanding of gender, making legible how difficult are such overarching concepts as "women's oppression" and "patriarchy" as precise terms for social worlds that operate along multiple axes of power and difference. By focusing on the transition from *identity* as the favored ground for feminist critical vocabularies to *difference*, I demonstrate how critical interest in inequalities among men has advanced feminist theoretical understanding of the structure and ideological function of "male bonding" on one hand and the production of alternative masculinities on the other. The second trajectory takes up the poststructuralist challenge to the category of women in order to define how the broad critique of identity as a coherent referent for feminism has worked to reconfigure normative assumptions about the relation between sex and gender. This reconfiguration has profoundly challenged ideals of corporeality as gender's natural domain of truth, making possible considerations of gender's performativity apart from the normative mapping of bodies, identities, and desire. In the third trajectory, the poststructuralist critique is taken to its critical extreme as masculinity and men are severed altogether in order to generate attention to female masculinity, transsexuality, and the politically activist theorizing on intersexuality. These critical domains raise issues about the structure and performance of gender identifications irreducible to the body as determinant sex.

In tracking the theoretical elaboration of men and masculinity as objects of study, I hope to contribute to this volume by demonstrating, along with Judith Halberstam, how feminism's critical interrogations of gender have productively disassembled the normative cultural discourse that weds masculinity to men and thinks about women only in the register of the feminine. Such "unmaking," if you will, of the category of men importantly remakes masculinity as pertinent to if not constitutive of female subjectivity, thereby rendering complex feminism's ability to negotiate the distinctions and interconnections between sex, sexuality, and gender. At the same time, I hope to map, as does Marlon Ross, the historic significance of issues of race and racialization for the study of masculinity within feminism, providing productive linkages to questions of power and difference among men. And finally, this essay sketches the intellectual history, contradictions, and terms of debate that Sally Robinson confronts in her essay on the pedagogical dimensions of masculinity studies. In particular, I trace the way that feminist theories of gender and power have functioned in tension with critical analyses of sexuality, making masculinity a site for the complex negotiation of feminism's own understanding of identities, bodies, and both political and erotic desire.

FEMINISMS'S MAL(E)CONTENTS

Before feminism's constitution of men and masculinity as discrete objects of study, these entities became known as the effect of the way knowledge was produced. The English literary canon, traditional history: these arenas taught us a great deal about the relation of men to masculinity, but only as evidence of the male body's abstraction into the normative domain of the universal where, shielded by humanism, both specificity and diversity were lost in the generic function of "man." To

remove the generic fallacy, to unveil masculinity as a particularized on-
tology linked to a normative rendering of the male body: this was the
task that feminism in the mid-1980s began to pursue as a necessary political intervention. The pursuit was not, however, without anxiety, for
the turn toward examining men and masculinity brought pressure to
bear on a variety of earlier feminist assumptions. In the first heady
decade of the contemporary women's movement, for instance, men and
masculinity tended not only to be melded together in a normative reit-
eration of the sex-gender equation but were also articulated as the foundational identity form for understanding such concepts as patriarchy
and women's oppression. By collapsing men and masculinity into a generalized category of man and wedding that generalization to the organizational practices and privileges of patriarchy, much feminist critical
analysis relied on what seemed to many scholars and activists an un-
problematical linkage between maleness, masculinity, and the social order of masculine supremacy. While this linkage is legible today as the
site of a certain kind of critical incomprehension concerning the complexity of power, it enabled feminist discourse to posit a political subjectivity for women that seemingly disrupted the sexual arena of women's
primary social bonding: the heterosexual. By bringing into question
women's allegiances to men as products of heterosexuality's compulsory production, feminism made imperative political solidarity among
women. Thus, sisterhood became powerful, and the personal, in its multiple aspects of the everyday, took on a decidedly political signification.

As we all know, however, this utopic narrative of identitarian collectivity is itself a site of contestation as both concrete political struggle
and the recognition of women's differences in power and privilege have
combined throughout the second wave of the feminist movement to undermine the saliency of *women* as a coherent identity project. For this
reason, our narrative of second-wave origins might more accurately say
that while identity served at times productively to isolate woman's difference from man and to generate a collective identification in the face
of that difference, the imperative toward differences among women—
the race, class, national, and sexual dynamics of women's engendering—
has from the outset unsettled any easy collapse of *women* into a monolithic or unified construction.[3] For some feminist thinkers, the concept of men as the common enemy was never an adequate explanatory

framework, as it obviated the way that women's political solidarities quite often transgressed the identitarian logics of gender. As feminists of color have routinely discussed, a monolithic understanding of man avoids the violent and discriminatory implications of white racial supremacy, displacing both white women's complicity with men of their own racial group and antiracist bonding across gender among the disenfranchised.[4] Because all men do not share equal masculine rights and privileges—because some men are, in fact, oppressed by women of the prevailing race and class—assumptions about power as uniformly based on sexual difference (men as oppressor, women as oppressed) have long been under pressure to give way.

One of the most important expressions in the 1970s of how an examination of the social position of women of color rearticulates the status of men within a feminist theoretical framework was the Combahee River Collective's "A Black Feminist Statement." Founded in 1974, the collective wrote its statement in 1977 in order to establish "as our particular task the development of integrated analysis and practice based upon the fact that the major systems of oppression are interlocking" (13). Dedicated then to what we would later call intersectional analysis, the collective explained the political relationship between black women and men:

> Although we are feminists and lesbians, we feel solidarity with progressive Black men and do not advocate the fractionalization that white women who are separatists demand. Our situation as Black people necessitates that we have solidarity around the fact of race. We struggle together with Black men against racism, while we also struggle with Black men about sexism. (16)

What remains striking today about this passage is the "although" that opens it, which demonstrates how overwritten were the categories of feminist and lesbian by the force of a foundational and oppositional sexual difference, one that seemed to preempt the work of affiliation and collectivity across lines other than those of gender.[5] By drawing out the implications of an analysis of women's differences from one another in the context of socialist feminism's attention to race and class, the collective identified the ways in which the category of men could not be monolithically rendered. As other black feminists—bell hooks, Michele

Wallace, Audre Lorde, and Angela Davis—added their critical analysis of the complexity of social power arrangements to the feminist theoretical archive, the study of men and masculinity was disarticulated from its status as patriarchal business as usual.

My training in graduate school in the 1980s was drawn quite heavily toward the theoretical and political project of understanding differences among women, which led me (to my own surprise) to write a dissertation about men. As a feminist project, the dissertation was not fully legible to everyone on my committee, and indeed I felt a great deal of anxiety about the political consequences of its focus. What was a feminist project that didn't take women as its object of study? How could feminist theory find some kind of critical future in the study of men? These questions were made all the more urgent by the end of the decade when conference presentations and articles began appearing that quite forcefully critiqued feminist interest in studying masculinity because of the way it seemed to reproduce the centrality of "man" against which women's studies as a broad, interdisciplinary field had long defined itself. While various scholars were concerned both before and after 1991 about the implications of masculinity studies (and many remain so today), it was Tania Modleski's *Feminism Without Women: Culture and Criticism in a "Postfeminist" Age* that brought such anxieties center stage. For Modleski, the turn toward masculinity studies in general and the inclusion of men as critics of and speakers for feminism in particular evinced a triumph "of a male feminist perspective that excludes women" (14), thus returning critical practice to a "pre-feminist world" (3) where women could be politically recontained within the masculine universalism that constituted every tradition of knowledge production in the humanities. As her title charged, any feminism that articulated itself without women as both subject and object—as knower and the category to be known—had acquiesced to the conservative political project of the 1980s, which succeeded, thanks to the nationalist masculinity of both Ronald Reagan and George Bush, in rendering *feminism* a very dirty word. The "postfeminism" that Modleski hoped both to diagnose and combat needed, in politically strategic and ideologically pointed terms, *women.*

While *Feminism Without Women* took its urgency from the transformations in the popular public sphere that had indeed changed, radically, the conditions under which feminism (like other leftist discourses that proliferated in the 1960s) operated, Modleski identified the academic re-cuperation of feminism via masculinity studies as a consequence of theoretical shifts as well, namely, poststructuralism's antihumanist ap-proaches to identity, experience, and subjectivity. The postfeminist for-mation that she critiqued in the study of masculinity was not, then, a consequence of the genealogy of analysis put into play by black femi-nism but was instead the effect of feminist "intercourse" with French intellectual culture. From Judith Butler to Donna Haraway to Denise Riley, she cited the critique of the subject and its attendant interroga-tion of the category of woman as a massive rejection by feminists of feminism's political imperative. Lamenting that "every use of the term "woman," however "provisionally" it is adopted, is [now] disal-lowed" (14), Modleski argued for a nonessentialist though identity-grounded epistemology, a category of "women's experience" that could serve as locus for both political organization and "a sense of solidarity, commonality, and community" (17). Without this epistemological assur-ance, Modleski wrote, "it is easy to see how a "man" can be a 'woman' " (15), which is to say it was easy to see how an antiessentialist deconstruc-tive move could banish the material implications of living in a body de-fined as *woman,* and hence how women within feminism could entirely disappear. Thus indicting both male and female scholars for abandoning feminism's political project of doing justice to and for women, Modleski cast the study of men and masculinity as a theoretically driven appro-priation, if not displacement, of feminist political struggle.

If the occasion of this volume implicitly unsettles Modleski's argu-ment by defining masculinity studies within and not against feminism as an intellectual and political project, it should not be assumed that Modleski's anxieties have disappeared from the critical scene or, further, that we have nothing to learn from her book. From the vantage point of nearly a decade later, we might interpret Modleski's work as an attempt to slow down the commodification of feminist knowledge that acceler-ated at the end of the 1980s and defined whole field imaginaries as criti-cal arenas of the past tense. She wanted, it seems to me, to stay put for awhile longer with the problematic of differences among women, in part because the various critical moves that had transformed feminism's theoretical imperative from *identity* to *difference* had assumed that identity and difference were so antithetical that no subjective affiliation or critical transportation could occur between them. It is this, finally, that a great deal of critique about masculinity studies a decade ago seems symptomatically to speak: a desire to forge identification and political solidarity not to the exclusion of women's differences but from within them—and hence from within those very contradictions that had animated *women* as the referent, no matter how troubled, for feminism. Modleski was not alone in assuming that a critical intimacy between women and feminism provided the immunity necessary to resist patriarchal appropriations and recuperations. For her as for others, *women* as an object of critical analysis and as a category of political subjects was what differentiated feminism from its foe and thereby guaranteed feminism's political effectivity.

THINKING HOMOSOCIALITY

While Modleski sounded a powerful warning about the dangers she saw in the burgeoning rise of masculinity studies and of a male feminism that "banishes women," she tried in her introduction "to make it clear that I do not consider [the dangers] to comprise the whole picture" (*Feminism,* 12, 11). She thus turned, as have many feminist critics, to the work of Eve Kosofsky Sedgwick, whose 1985 *Between Men: English Literature and Male Homosocial Desire* not only extended feminist analysis by partaking in an important deconstructive move that gave both legibility and critical complexity to the dominant term of gender's powerful binary, but did so in the context of linking feminism to antihomophobic critique. Modleski praised *Between Men* for "making feminists sensitive to issues of homophobia and making gay men aware of how constructions of homosexuality intersect with misogynist constructions of femininity," even as she felt obliged to cite Sedgwick's inattention to the lesbian as a lurking postfeminist danger (12).[6] In her acknowledgment of Sedgwick, Modleski recognized gay studies (and what would later be called, via Sedgwick, queer theory) as one of the most important analytic trajectories of masculinity studies to be developed in the 1980s.

Between Men worked in tandem with Gayle Rubin's controversial 1984 essay "Thinking Sex: Notes for a Radical Theory of the Politics of Sexuality" to forge a series of important deliberations on terms that had rather loose interchangeability in feminist studies: gender, sex, and sexuality. Interestingly, it was Rubin who had written in 1975 the foundational essay, "The Traffic in Women: Notes on the 'Political Economy' of Sex," that had cogently articulated the relation between sex and gender as a systemic one. As Sedgwick would later describe it, Rubin defined "the system by which chromosomal sex is turned into, and processed as, cultural gender," a strategy that yielded "analytic and critical leverage on the female-disadvantaging social arrangements that prevail[ed] at a given time in a given society, by throwing into question their legitimative ideological grounding in biologically based narratives of the 'natural' " (Sedgwick, "Gender," 274). Rubin's critical intervention was a deessentializing one, giving anthropological weight to the analysis of cultural practices and providing feminist theory with a distinct and powerful way to ward off simple biological determinism.[7] Rubin's social analysis superseded the "nature/nurture" framework of analysis that held biology and culture in a dynamic tension by yielding primary analytic power to the "nurture" side of the equation. By wrenching the authority of sexual difference from the supposed natural domain of the body to the realm of the sociocultural, Rubin's sex-gender distinction has profoundly affected nearly two decades of critical analysis by providing a theoretical perspective for a host of interconnections between the power arrangements of sexuality and gender.

In *Between Men*, which Naomi Schor has called the inaugural text in the "rise of gender studies" (276), Sedgwick used Rubin to thoroughly interrogate, to brilliant effect, the power dynamics of the erotic triangle of two men and one women found throughout British literature (from Shakespeare to the English readers of Walt Whitman). As Sedgwick described it, Rubin's early essay revealed how "patriarchal heterosexuality can best be discussed in terms of one or another form of the traffic in women: it is the use of women as exchangeable, perhaps symbolic, property for the primary purpose of cementing the bonds of men with men" (*Between*, 26). By linking the traffic in women to the homophobic injunction against male to male sex, Sedgwick's text transformed the kinds of questions feminist theory thought to ask not only about patriarchy as a historical organization of masculine supremacy but about male sexuality in both its hetero and homosexual dimensions. In particular, *Be-*

tween Men returned issues of genital sexuality among men to the critical understanding of patriarchy as a structure of masculine bonds, challenging the important, but, in Sedgwick's words, "expensive leap of register" that accompanied Luce Irigaray's formulation (*Between*, 26): "The exchanges upon which patriarchal societies are based take place exclusively among men. . . . This means that the *very possibility of a sociocultural order requires homosexuality* as its organizing principle. Heterosexuality is nothing but the assignment of economic roles" ("Commodities," 192). For Sedgwick, "the quicksilver of sex itself" was critical to thinking historically about the male "homosocial continuum" that structured patriarchal organization (*Between*, 26). While, for the ancients, this continuum functioned without injunction to articulate sex between men as a part of the pedagogical instruction of class-based gender privilege— activities that consolidated male bonds and normative masculinity—the violent homophobia of contemporary Western culture was quite clearly another story. And it was that story, as one deeply entangled with feminist aspirations to understand interconnected discriminatory structures, that interested Sedgwick. "The importance of women . . . in the etiology and the continuing experience of male homosexuality seems to be historically volatile (across time, across class). . . . Its changes are inextricable from the changing shapes of the institutions by which gender and class inequality are structured" (*Between*, 26–27).

Sedgwick's historicist approach to the issue of male bonds revealed some of the ways in which both patriarchy and masculinity had been discussed and analyzed throughout humanistic-based feminist inquiry in a metaphoric register that collapsed both cultural and temporal distinctions. Where Irigaray and others read the realm of the masculine as an "economy of the same" and posited women as outside the symbolic orbit of male relations, Sedgwick simultaneously facilitated and came to represent a turn toward the ruptures, contradictions, and inconsistencies that had to be repressed, negotiated, or violently eradicated in the continual process of constituting and extending patriarchal power. More dissertations than mine were written under the auspices of this attention to differences among men, and it is striking that while *Between Men* took class and sexuality as the main determinants for understanding the historical function and structure of gender, the author recognized in her introduction how powerful her analysis would be for interrogations into race and masculinity in U.S. culture. By turning briefly to Margaret Mitchell's *Gone with the Wind,* Sedgwick compared the two "rape" scenes in the novel—one by the black man seeking money he was told was hidden in Scarlet's bosom, the other the blissful marital moment of Scarlet and Brett's union—in order to argue against the *categorical* deployment of rape in U.S. feminism as a crime against women and tool of patriarchal domination.[8] "To assume that sex signifies power in a flat, unvarying relation of metaphor or synecdoche will always entail a blindness," she wrote, "not to the rhetorical and pyrotechnic, but to such historical categories as class and race" (*Between,* 10–11). Calling then for "more different, more complicated, more diachronically apt, more off-centered . . . applications of our present understanding of what it may mean for one thing to signify another," Sedgwick challenged the dominant imaginary of feminism not simply to think its own historicity but to rethink most seriously a great deal of what it assumed it already knew (*Between,* 11).

Susan Jeffords extended Sedgwick's intervention into feminist understanding of patriarchal social formation in general and male bonds in particular in 1989 by considering the prolific figure of the Vietnam veteran that had dominated U.S. popular culture throughout the 1980s. Taking film, television, cultural history, and contemporary fiction as its objects of analysis, *The Remasculinization of America: Gender and the Vietnam War* studied the way that these texts stressed, in a compulsive fashion, the significance of masculine bonds as the ideological counter to the feminizing influences of both a corrupt, betraying government (the United States) and an enemy (the Vietcong) who refused to fight, in Western parlance, "like a man." For Jeffords, these representational formulations established differences between men and women as the necessary precondition for defining and celebrating a commonality of gender among men. "The masculine bond," she wrote, "insists on a denial of difference—whether black or white, wealthy or poor, high school or college-educated, from north or south, men are the 'same'—at the same time that the bond itself depends for its existence on an affirmation of difference—men are not women" (59–60). Jeffords understood the postwar reassertion of a mythic masculine bond not only as a strategy for reinvigorating the national imaginary in the aftermath of the loss of the war but as a response to the feminist, civil rights, and gay rights strug-

gles that forcefully criticized the exclusionary practices on which traditional structures of power had long depended. Her interest in the male
bond was thus in its function as a scene for the negotiation, indeed celebration, of masculine sameness in the face of a variety of potentially dis-
rupting differences (race, sexuality, class, as well as gender).

In linking her project to *Between Men,* Jeffords reiterated, in the context of a different century and in texts widely disparate from the canonical British tradition, the theoretical paradigm Sedgwick had witnessed
in *The Country Wife:* "Men's heterosexual relationships . . . have as their
raison d'etre an ultimate bonding between men . . . [which] if successfully achieved, is not detrimental to 'masculinity' but definitive of it"
(*Between,* 50). Because the so-called theater of war functions in modern
technological cultures as the primary scene of masculinity's hegemonic
performance, Jeffords's investigation simultaneously situated the homosocial prominently within the national imaginary and detailed the ways
in which popular culture by the end of the twentieth century functioned
as the symptomatic domain for the production of masculinity as spectacle. In the proliferation of this spectacle, which is to say in its incessant
visuality, Jeffords culled a vocabulary for thinking not only about crucial
distinctions between patriarchy and masculinity but about the historically specific structural relationships between gendered discourses and
social differences among men. For Jeffords, then, as for Sedgwick, a feminist "analysis of the patriarchal system [limited solely] to relations between men and women . . . overlook[ed] much of its force" (xii).

In hoping to pry apart masculinity and patriarchy as conceptual terms
in the context of Vietnam War narration, Jeffords encountered a certain
resistance in her objects of analysis, which seemed to propel the analytic
gaze away from those differences repressed by the homosocial bond and
toward the mechanisms of their recuperation and hegemonic recontain-
ment, as her study's signal term, *remasculinization,* would suggest. Other
scholarship in the late 1980s and early 1990s would move, analytically
speaking, in the opposite direction, finding in the figure of a multiple
object of study—masculinities—a way to productively fracture the consolidation of male bonds that underwrote patriarchal investments in
sexual difference. Important studies in *masculinities* thus focused on the
sexuality, race, and class differences that unsettled the ideological desti-

nation of homosocial bonding, hailing men not into a monolithic vision of essential sexual difference but toward contrary intellectual and political claims.[9] In *Slow Motion: Changing Masculinities, Changing Men* (1990), for instance, Lynne Segal sought to plumb the disparity between being male and being normatively masculine by focusing on what she called "competing masculinities." As she explained, "by looking not at 'masculinity' as such, but at certain specific '*masculinities*', it is . . . *differences* between men which [become] central to the struggle for change" (x).

Taken together, the critical projects by Sedgwick, Jeffords, and Segal are important indexes of the ways in which the study of men and masculinity has developed from Rubin's early intervention into the normative naturalization of sex as gender. As the forgoing discussion should suggest, the focus on the male bond has deepened feminist critical understanding of the way that patriarchal investments are reproduced not only in the management of erotic and intimate life but in the spheres of popular culture and national politics. In reading the dynamics of power in these realms, scholars draw our attention to the constructedness of masculinity and its complex dependence on discourses of sexual difference (sometimes with, sometimes without the figure of woman), thereby making visible and theoretically credible the analysis of the constitutional performativity of a variety of masculinities, from dominant heterosexual formations to more subversive gay, black, or antisexist articulations. The seeming naturalness of adult masculinity—heterosexuality, fatherhood, family governance, soldiery, and citizenry—can thus be viewed as a set of prescriptive norms that contain potential contradictions within and between men. These norms repress the male subject's constitution along multiple lines of the social: race, class, and sexuality in addition to gender. In unleashing masculinity from its assumed normativity and reading its function and structure as the product of a contested and contradictory field of power, a great deal of feminist work in masculinity studies has been motivated by the desire to intervene in the practices of patriarchal domination while locating the possibilities for men to challenge their constitution as men. That much of this challenge begins, analytically, in a rethinking of the patriarchal structure of homosocial relations—what by shorthand we now call the male bond—is hardly a surprise, given the profound impact of feminist theoretical concern with the patriarchal "traffic in women" *and* its own utopic imagining of women's political bonding with one another.

MASCULINITY WITHOUT MEN

Careful readers will note that my discussion of the fracturing of the monolithic understanding of the category of men and of the male bond in the previous section mentioned without adequate commentary Gayle Rubin's important 1984 essay "Thinking Sex." While we might think of it as a piece historically akin to Sedgwick's *Between Men*, published a year later, its significance in this discussion of masculinity inaugurates what I consider a different line of critical investigation, one that disarticulates the feminist imperative to link gender and sexuality that had been a consistent call in lesbian feminist discourses since the early sixties. For Rubin, the dominant discourse in feminism by the end of the 1970s concerning sexuality, by which she meant sex acts and activities, was so heavily prohibitive as to make feminism resemble a sexual temperance movement. In its antipornography and antilesbian SM discourses, feminism was courting the state, quite literally, in order to resolve forms of discrimination and violence that sexuality as a realm not of pleasure but of coercion had come to represent. Rubin's essay, still one of the most controversial statements against sexual prohibition in the feminist archive, challenged the movement's conceptions not of sexual difference per se but of sex itself, forcing a reconsideration of feminism's understanding of the political struggles of various sexual minorities: homosexuals, prostitutes, sadomasochists, transvestites, pederasts, and onanists. Revising her theoretical stance in "The Traffic in Women," Rubin now argued "that it is essential to separate gender and sexuality analytically," to see them "as two distinct arenas of social practice" ("Thinking," 33). Most crucially, she asserted that "feminist thought simply lacks angles of vision which can fully encompass the social organization of sexuality" (34).

Rubin's position, as she would later explain it to Judith Butler in a 1994 interview, "Sexual Traffic," was not a rejection of feminism per se, nor was it a claim that gender and sexuality should have no analytic traffic. Rather it was a studied response to the increasing moralism and desexualization of critical analysis within the dominant imaginary of feminism in the 1970s, where even sexual relationships between women had been cast outside a sexual register, as "woman identification," and every act of non-normative sexual behavior was interpreted as part of the system maintaining women's subordination. "I looked at sex 'deviants,' " she explained, "and frankly they didn't strike me as the apotheosis of patriarchy" (78).[10] Rubin's desire to make *sex*, analytically speaking, a domain of practices and to think about how specific practices have been historically cast in juridical terms as deviant identities (as in the cases of homosexuality, prostitution, transsexualism, fetishism, and sadomasochism) opened a productive wedge between acts and identities that would enable greater critical commentary about not only feminism's own "abjected" categories but the definitional relationship between what bodies *do* and what bodies *are*. By interrupting the normative emplotment of the relationship between bodies, acts, and identities, a whole range of scholarly investigation has emerged to rethink desires, identifications, and psychic formations that, while not articulated directly under the banner of masculinity studies, has nonetheless made possible the trajectory of inquiry described by this section's title: masculinity without men. This domain is epitomized by queer theory's poststructuralist critique of identity's coherence, intersex activism and criticism, transsexual theory and political criticism, and deliberations on butch-femme, drag kings, and "female masculinity," to use Judith Halberstam's term in her 1998 book of the same title.

Each of these arenas is critically inaugurated by a certain refusal to accede to the domain of the biological as the prior condition for gender's construction, as the "natural" material on which gender dimorphically depends. No text is more famous for making this point than Butler's *Gender Trouble: Feminism and the Subversion of Identity* (1990), which argued that while the idea of a male or female body functions as gender's seemingly neutral sexed referent, it can only do so as a consequence of the ideological structure of sexual difference. Hence, gender— as the name we give to the social apparatus that produces and maintains various kinds of sexual divisions—provides the conceptual framework for rendering the body biologically determinant. "Sex itself is a gendered category," Butler wrote, thereby defining "sex" not as gender's necessary precondition but as one of gender's most powerful effects (7). In this, she reconfigured Rubin's argument in "The Traffic in Women" while challenging feminist scholarship that used a corporeal logic to define woman's difference from man.

While so much critical memory of *Gender Trouble* has involved Butler's use of gay male drag as an example of what she defined as the constitutive performativity of gender, she actually devoted more pages to a figure far more important to her argument: the hermaphrodite in Michel Foucault's *Herculine Barbin, Being the Recently Discovered Memoirs of a Nineteenth-Century Hermaphrodite.* Butler's discussion of Barbin, which focused on the seeming referential realness of what Sandy Stone has called "genetic" gender, was crucial to *Gender Trouble*'s analysis of the heterosexual regulatory strategies that normatively align sex, gender, and sexuality.[11] The intersexuality of Barbin's genitals and her/his passage in the course of a truncated lifetime through the categorical designations of both male and female challenged any definitive account of the trajectory of sexual desire—was s/he homosexual or heterosexual, seemingly "normal" or sexually "deviant"? The failure of gender identity to be mapped back onto the body, and for the body to function as gender's founding alibi, gave Butler one way, among many explored in *Gender Trouble*, to conclude that

> gender ought not to be construed as a stable identity or locus of agency from which various acts follow; rather, gender is an identity tenuously constituted in time, instituted in an exterior space through a *stylized repetition of acts.* . . . This formulation moves the conception of gender off the ground of a substantial model of identity to one that requires a conception of gender as a constituted social temporality. (140–41)

In turning to Barbin, Butler was staging an argument with Michel Foucault, whose editorial introduction to Barbin's autobiography strove to figure the hermaphrodite as outside the law precisely because of the body's failure to conform to the law's regulatory schema of dimorphic sex. More recent work on intersexuality returns, sometimes only implicitly, to Foucault's earlier work on the establishment of the clinic and prison where he traced the production and productivity of medical-juridical discourses as disciplinary regimes that normalized and made bodies docile. In "Hermaphrodites with Attitude: Mapping the Emergence of Intersex Political Activism," Cheryl Chase documents the development in the twentieth century of intensive medical intervention into intersex births, detailing how a culture of experts has emerged to manage what is deemed a "medical crisis." This crisis necessitates swift action, often days after birth, in order to prevent the intersexed individual from knowing about his/her bodily history. Chase, who has been assigned at different times to both categories of dimorphic sex, questions not only the cultural invisibility of intersexed people but the profound structure of medically sanctioned silence and secrecy that functions to eradicate the very possibility of intersex subjectivity. "We as a culture have relinquished to medicine the authority to police the boundaries of male and female, leaving intersexuals to recover as best they can, alone and silent, from violent normalization" (193). As a counter to this disciplinary tactic, Chase's essay also provides an important theoretical account of the recent emergence of "intersex people [who] have begun to politicize intersex identities, thus transforming intensely personal experiences of violation into collective opposition to the medical regulation of bodies that queer the foundations of heteronormative identifications and desires" (189). Intersex theory and activism thus draws its critical edge from a refusal to assent to the invasive maneuvers of medical science where the consolidation of the ideology of gender functions to inscribe dimorphic sex onto bodies and subjectivities in the violently ironic hope of returning such bodies to "nature."

This refusal, which seeks not only to instantiate ambiguity in the relationship between sex and gender but to establish as a political project the intersexed subject's own authority in the decision to be "remade" (or not) in the image of categorical completeness, has important parallels with Sandy Stone's foundational work in transsexual theory, "The *Empire* Strikes Back: A Posttranssexual Manifesto" (1992). As Stone's title begins to demonstrate, the "posting" of the transsexual reveals a political imperative to refuse the trans-position of one unambiguous sex for another. By arguing against the social injunction for transsexuals to "pass," to render their interruption into the naturalized regulations of bodies and identities invisible, Stone calls for "a political action begun by reappropriating difference and reclaiming the power of the refigured and reinscribed body" (298–99). Here, as Stone puts it, "on the gender borders at the close of the twentieth century, with the faltering of phallocratic hegemony and the bumptious appearance of heteroglossic origin accounts," the possibility of speaking "beyond the constructed opposi-tional nodes which have been predefined as the only positions from which discourse is possible" begins (294, 295).[12] In the theoretical archive of intersexuality and transsexuality, with their differing political and his-torical genealogies on one hand and their complex relation to medical practices and knowledges on the other, we encounter a powerful reartic-ulation of the meaning of the sexed body and those regulatory dis-courses, including feminism, that have utilized genetic normativity to stabilize not only identity-based social struggle but theoretical under-standings of sex and gender.

It would be inaccurate, however, to suggest that this work has been critically accepted into the dominant formation of feminist theory or that its implications for thinking about the political project of feminist struggle have been realized, for this certainly is not the case. In everyday feminist and lesbian spaces, debates continue to rage, as they do each year at the Michigan's Womyn's Music Festival, concerning the partici-patory status of male-to-female transsexuals (MTFs) and their relation-ship to the categorical designation that was created to exclude them, "women born women." That female-to-male transsexuals (FTMs) have rarely been a significant aspect of this conversation demonstrates the in-coherence that organizes and constrains feminist deployment of origi-nary sex designation, a situation that is all the more striking given the rejuvenation in the 1990s of the butch lesbian—and with it, notions of *transgender* identity and identifications—in critical and community for-mations alike.[13] While there are significant points of difference and dis-continuity between FTMs and butches, according to Gayle Rubin, the boundaries have been more permeable than either lesbians or feminists (or lesbian feminists) seem to want—and with that permeability comes a variety of anxieties, disavowals, and negations. "Many of the passing women and diesel butches so venerated as lesbian ancestors are also claimed in the historical lineages of female-to-male transsexuals," ex-plained Rubin in her 1992 essay, "Of Catamites and Kings." But lesbian cultural recognition of this overlap has been rare; instead, as Rubin writes, "many lesbians are antagonistic toward transsexuals, treating . . . female-to-male transsexuals as treasonous deserters. . . . A woman who has been respected, admired, and loved as a butch may suddenly be despised, rejected, and hounded when she starts a sex change" ("Catamites," 474, 475). In pointing to the way that lesbian culture has a history of celebrating a variety of transgender identifications and of investing the "mannish woman" with the status of icon in the war against gender normativity, Rubin revealed how profoundly disruptive was the abandonment of a female sexed domain, which is to say how deeply invested has lesbian feminism been in arranging its own gender productions within a dominant feminist imaginary anxiously attached to biological women.

While Rubin's essay was notable precisely for its desire to refuse genetic sex as the precondition for licensing either gender's performative display or feminism's political project, her text was constrained by the linguistic divide that governs the lesbian butch on one hand and the FTM on the other: the transformation in self and social identification that "she" and "he," as the structural language of personhood in English, profoundly signify. By defining butch as a category of persons in its own right, Rubin put pressure on the linguistic domain of sexed subjectivity, trying to construct a continuum that could conceptualize masculinity across a range of bodies, identities, and practices. And yet her definition began in sexual difference: "Within the group of women labeled butch, there are many individuals who are gender dysphoric to varying degrees. Many butches have partially male gender identities. Others border on being, and some are, female-to-male transsexuals" ("Catamites," 468). The move from the beginning of this definition to the end is an illogical one, for certainly if butch is a group of women, it is not possible for that term to frame, as a conceptual category, the FTM who has precisely and decisively left the sexed category of woman. The continuum that Rubin thus constructed was haunted from the outset by the status of sex as a form of linguistic identification—this even as her analysis repeatedly refused sex as a political identification by exploring butch as a domain of complex and diverse identificatory practices that confounded the normative routes of dimorphic sex, gender, and desire.

If it seems that this discussion has strayed quite far from a consideration of men and masculinity, that is of course precisely the point. For Rubin, the diversity of lesbian gender in general and butch gender in particular posed theoretical questions for thinking about masculinity as a structure of identification in ways that could be wholly disconnected from genetic male bodies (if not fully from female ones). The analytic focus on "masculinity without men," as Judith Halberstam theorized it in her 1998 study *Female Masculinity,* not only functioned to valorize those butch gender styles that mainstream feminism had often been embarrassed, if not scared, of but, more to the point, it allowed for a deeper consideration of the relationship between gender variance and homosexuality.[14] While, for much of the twentieth century, gender variance was located in both medical and political discourse as internal to homosexuality, indeed one of its most legible signs, "in the last part of this century," Halberstam wrote, "the invention of transsexuality as a medical category has partly drained gender variance out of the category of homosexuality" (142–43). Halberstam was interested in pursuing the theoretical implications of this shift, especially as it made possible interrogation of a range of female masculinities (of women who do not identify according to the logics and bodily tropes of femininity), without assuming that same sex-object choice defined either the horizon or parameter of such masculinities. By offering a kind of taxonomy of female masculinities from the androgyne, tribade, and invert to the stone butch and drag king—and differentiating from within and not simply across each "type"—Halberstam studied the cultural repression of gender variance in women. While she was clearly committed to the project as a revalorization and diversification of the lesbian butch, it would be incorrect to limit her analysis of female masculinity to the province of lesbians. Indeed, at its broadest and most crucial critical intervention, *Female Masculinity* turned the tables on normative gender imaginaries by refusing to concede that most sacred terrain, masculinity, to men, seeking instead to figure *women* as a category of profound gender difference itself.

The theoretical distinctions between sex, gender, and sexuality that Halberstam both inherited and refined have had an enormous impact on masculinity studies, producing the three different and overlapping trajectories of critical investigation I have now defined. The first identified how differences among women mobilized an inquiry into the ways in which patriarchal power was consolidated by examining both the structure of the male bond and the various forms of masculinity and social hierarchy that the bond functions to deny. Through a social construction rubric that disarticulates the normative wedding of sex and gender, alternative masculinities could be both politically imagined and critically analyzed. Using poststructuralism, the second trajectory builds radically on the sex-gender distinction to rethink the very idea of genetic sex, turning to considerations of gender's performativity apart from the normative mapping of bodies, identities, and desire. The third trajectory relocates the question of masculinity from genetic corporeality to the realm of identification, thereby defining a new species, so to speak, of masculinities that cannot be assimilated into the framework of patriarchal constructions of men. In these various conversations, the political stakes for feminism are high, so high in fact that we must now pause over one of the central questions that gave rise to the study of masculinity—what do men have to do with feminism? By deemphasizing the normative relationship between men and masculinity and seeking not simply alternative masculinities for men but a broad rearticulation of masculinity as a production of gender, distinct from, if not in contradiction with, so-called male bodies, feminist work in the 1990s has radically transformed the content, scope, and political project of masculinity as a domain of critical inquiry.[15] If the decade began with critical concern that feminism was abandoning women, it ended with the counterintuitive suggestion that even masculinity was no longer the proper domain of men. In other words, the knowledge objects once unquestioned as the definitive property of feminism—and those accepted as fully outside feminism's critical scope—had lost the logic of their critical place. Gender trouble indeed.

From the dire predictions of *Feminism Without Women* to the seemingly outrageous postulation of masculinity without men, then, feminist critical analysis covered a great deal of theoretical ground in the 1990s in its attempt to understand the complex relationships between and among bodies, identities, sexualities, and genders. Where Modleski feared the loss of women, Halberstam celebrated woman's normative undoing, making sex and gender mobile across bodies and identities *and* feminism mobile across sexed bodies and gender identities. For some critical observers, these critical differences are evidence that feminist theory is, at the beginning of the twenty-first century, decidedly torn between a modernist and postmodernist political interpretation—which is to say between a desire for a materialist articulation of bodies versus their liberation in indeterminate and/or multiple resignifications. This rendering of the contradictions and contestations within feminist theory perpetuates the clichéd taxonomy that has occluded our present understanding of the paradox—the unresolvable constitutive constant—that feminism is not the scene of a seamless identification between so-called women and *women* but is crisscrossed and overwritten by a whole range of disidentifications, incongruities, and remappings of the material (bodies and identities) that it has taken as its primary knowledge objects. To say that the study of men and masculinity has been another route for confirming this insight is not to return women to the center of feminist analysis. Rather it is to demonstrate what the theoretical archive seems to implicitly assert: that feminism as an intellectual and political project is not finally bound to any prescribed domain of gender's complex universe.

NOTES

My thanks to Judith Gardiner for comments on earlier drafts of this essay.

1. See Robinson, *Marked,* for the most comprehensive and astute reading of the contemporary cultural archive of white masculinity's crisis.
2. In 1991, Tania Modleski posited that "however much male subjectivity may currently be 'in crisis' . . . we need to consider the extent to which male power is actually consolidated through cycles of crisis and resolution, whereby men ultimately deal with the threat of female power by incorporating it" (*Feminism,* 7). Dana Nelson's more recent *National Manhood* offers an important investigation into the way that ideologies of "national manhood" in the early republic worked to abstract white men from localized affiliations and domains of embodiment in order to project them into a national imaginary. Racial, gendered, and ethnic difference was thus rendered incompatible, through a series of repressions and omissions, with the emergent understanding and material practices of democratic governmentality.
3. My narrative of the identity-difference axis of twentieth-century feminist thought is devoted to countering the now normative assumption that early second-wave feminism was indifferent to race, class, sexuality, or nationality—an assumption that disturbingly casts both women of color and lesbians as belated arrivals to feminist critical practice and movement. Actual examination of

documents from the 1960s and 1970s demonstrates that issues of race and sexuality, especially, were given more than incidental discussion, and many of us trained as the first undergraduate generation of women's studies students were schooled in the lengthy discussions by Barbara Smith, Audre Lorde, and others about the content and politics of black women's studies. This is not a defense against the charges that feminism or women's studies were racist in their second-wave articulation; rather it is an argument against writing out of the history of contemporary feminist thought the early and vibrant discussion of race and sexuality.

4. See Davis, *Women;* hooks, "Men"; and Lorde, "Man Child."

5. In "Lesbian Feminism and the Gay Rights Movement," Marilyn Frye read gay male culture as "congruent with and a logical extension of straight male-supremacist culture," a position that privileged the differential of gender over that of sexuality in the competing regimes of patriarchy and compulsory heterosexuality (144). While her essay was intended as a call to gay men to abandon the "unconscious" of male privilege, it nonetheless performs the fundamental move of a great deal of lesbian feminist theorizing and organizing that the Combahee River Collective critiques.

6. In citing the absence of the lesbian from the analysis, Modleski reiterated a persistent criticism of *Between Men*. And yet, in her introduction, Sedgwick establishes her analysis within the context of feminist theory and identifies the ways in which the asymmetries of gender arrangements and of sexual practices within homosocial networks will not yield comprehensive analytic purchase. For a discussion of the way that Modleski mobilizes the figure of the lesbian, see Jagose," 'Feminism,' " 124–35.

7. Critics have since noted that Rubin does not challenge the biological notion of sexual difference so much as rearticulate the power of gender hierarchies to the realm of the cultural. See, for instance, Nicholson, "Interpreting."

8. In her use of the example of rape, Sedgwick was drawing from a lengthy conversation in African American scholarship on the way that white supremacy had used rape throughout the nineteenth and twentieth century as a provocation for racial violence. Rape was thus not simply a crime against all women but a vehicle for criminalizing black men, for whom, as Richard Wright put it in Native Son, "rape was the death before death came." In the figure of the black male rapist, which proliferated as a popular icon after the Civil War, the contestation between patriarchal and white supremacist social formations is simultaneously made legible and managed. See Davis, *Women*, 172–201; Hall, " 'Mind' "; Harris,

Exorcising; Smith, "Split"; Wallace, *Black;* Wells, *Crusade;* and Wiegman, *American,* chapter 3.

9. For the historical archive on black masculinity, see Hine and Jenkins, *Question.* Lowe, *Immigrant* (especially 11–12), examines the way that immigration law dovetailed with discourses of feminization to produce images of the Asian American male as emasculated.

10. In calling for an end to feminism's internal compulsion to police the proper domain of sexed, gendered, and sexual expression, Rubin would later specify an arena of discussion—transsexuality—that had been an important impulse for writing "Thinking Sex," though one that did not appear as central in the essay's final form. As she explained in her interview with Butler,

> "Thinking Sex" wasn't conceived in a direct line or as a direct departure from the concerns of "Traffic." I was trying to get at something different. . . . I started to get more and more dissatisfied with what were then the stock feminist explanations for certain kinds of sexual behaviors. . . . A number of different debates . . . forced me to starting questioning the wisdom, if not the relevance, of feminism as the privileged political movement or political theory for certain issues of sexuality and sexual difference. One was the debate on transsexuality. Even before that debate hit print toward the late 1970s, the discussion really flipped me about because it was so biologically deterministic. When it finally erupted into print over the hiring of Sandy Stone, a male to female transsexual, by Olivia Records, there were a number of articles in the lesbian press about how women were born and not made which I found rather distressing. ("Sexual," 67, 72)

11. "Genetic gender" does not seek to describe a biological truth about sexed embodiment; rather it is a term that refers to the coherence between medically assigned sex and gender identification and performance. See Stone, *Empire,* 294.

12. In *Second Skins,* Jay Prosser challenges the *post*transsexuality of Stone's political imperative. He writes,

> Fundamental to posttranssexuality is the belief that political subjectivity for transsexuals requires not simply a revision but a refusal of sexual difference—of what has been transsexuality's very purpose: passing, belonging, attaining realness in one' gender identity. In Stone's posttranssexuality there is no space for transsexuality as a progressive narrative—for continuing

to value belonging, for an ongoing desire for a sexed realness and coherent embodiment: precisely the desire for a sexed place that galvanized transsexuality's narrative in the first place. . . . In pushing past a transsexual narrative ("post"), in ceding our claims to sexed location, we relinquish what we do not yet have: the recognition of our sexed realness; acceptance as men and women; fundamentally, the right to gender homes. (203, 204)

The political project of *Second Skins* is thus a reconfiguration of the desire and demand for gender belonging, a belonging couched in the language of embodied coherence. Prosser is eloquent in his readings of the autobiographical narratives of transsexuals where this desire is most profoundly expressed—and in the claim that transsexuality itself must be thought of as and through narrative. But in thinking about Stone's work (or Butler's, for that matter), Prosser relies on a crucial contextual erasure: that of feminism. Instead, he locates queer theory as the generative discourse for transsexuality as a theoretical issue, without linking queer theory to feminism and its grappling with sex and gender.

This is not to say that any text dealing with transsexuality needs to have feminism as its object of study or its political commitment, especially given the historical difficulty that feminism has had in relinquishing its own disciplinary hold on a normative idea of woman. But the decontextualization of Stone's "Manifesto" from its place within feminist political analysis and organization is a costly critical omission. In the late 1970s, after all, it was literally around Stone's body that a major political eruption occurred when Olivia Records, a woman run and owned company, hired her. For a time, Stone, as an MTF, was the single individual around whom lesbian feminism's passionate commitment to "women born women" was expressed. "Manifesto" takes its political intervention in feminism as its primary domain, not queer studies, and it is precisely its lament that feminism has reproduced a discourse of regulation, shame, and critical abjection that motivates the imperative toward what Stone describes in the essay's closing words, "the next transformation" (299), which is a transformation not of the individual but of the social: "Although *individual* change is the foundation of all things, it is not the end of all things" (299), she wrote.

For an account of the critical archive within feminist and lesbian theory concerning transsexuality, see Chapman and Du Plessis, " 'Don't.' " 13. Prosser has noted this inconsistency in which the notion of "transgender" does the vanguard work of delinking gender from sex by constituting identifications, desires, and pleasures in ways unmapped by normative regulatory schemas, but without displacing the status of originary sex embodiment. According to Prosser, *transgender* was derived from "transgenderist," a term "coined in the late 1980s to describe a male subject with a commitment to living as a woman more substantial than that denoted by 'transvestite' or 'cross-dresser' " (*Second*, 176). While *transgender* tends now to function as an umbrella term for transsexuals, transvestites, intersexuals, butches, drag queens and kings, cross-dressers and the gender dysphoric of all kinds, it was forged precisely to differentiate between acts, identifications, and performances that do or do not remake the body (or hope to) at the level of sex. For an articulation of the political utility of transgender as an umbrella term, see Stryker.

14. "Masculinity without men" is the subtitle of Halberstam's introduction (see *Female*). The phrase appeared a year earlier in the title of an essay that sought to think about straight femininity and its relation to masculine identifications. See Cox et al., "Masculinity."

15. It is important to stress, as Halberstam does, that the emphasis on alternative masculinities is not, in and of itself, enough to guarantee its political effectivity. She writes,

> Not all models of masculinity are equal, and as butches and transsexuals begin to lay claims to the kinds of masculinities they have produced in the past and are generating in the present, it is crucial that we also pay careful attention to the function of homophobia and sexism in particular within the new masculinities. . . . Gender variance, like sexual variance, cannot be relied on to produce a radical and oppositional politics simply by virtue of representing difference. . . . I suggest we think carefully, butches and FTMs alike, about the kinds of men or masculine beings that we become and lay claim to: alternative masculinities, ultimately, will fail to change existing gender hierarchies to the extent to which they fail to be feminist, antiracist, and queer. (173)

WORKS CITED

Butler, Judith. *Gender Trouble: Feminism and the Subversion of Identity.* New York: Routledge, 1990.

Chapman, Kathleen, and Michael Du Plessis. " 'Don't Call Me *Girl*': Lesbian

Theory, Feminist Theory, and Transsexual Identities." In Dana Heller, ed., *Cross-Purposes: Lesbians, Feminists, and the Limits of Alliance*, pp. 169–85. Bloomington: Indiana University Press, 1997.

Chase, Cheryl. "Hermaphrodites with Attitude: Mapping the Emergence of Intersex Political Activism." Transgender issue, ed. Susan Stryker. *GLQ* 4.2 (1998): 189–211.

Combahee River Collective. "A Black Feminist Statement." In Gloria T. Hull, Patricia Scott Bell, and Barbara Smith, eds., *All the Women Are White, All the Blacks Are Men, But Some of Us Are Brave*, pp. 13–22. Old Westbury, New York: Feminist Press, 1982.

Cox, Ana Marie, Freya Johnson, Annalee Newitz, and Jillian Sandell. "Masculinity Without Men: Women Reconciling Feminism and Male-Identification." In Leslie Haywood and Jennifer Drake, eds., *Third Wave Agenda: Being Feminist, Doing Feminism*, pp. 178–99. Minneapolis: University of Minnesota Press, 1997.

Davis, Angela. *Women, Race, and Class*. New York: Vintage, 1983.

Foucault, Michel, ed. *Herculine Barbin, Being the Recently Discovered Memoirs of a Nineteenth-Century Hermaphrodite*. Trans. Richard McDongall. New York: Colophon, 1980.

Frye, Marilyn. "Lesbian Feminism and the Gay Rights Movement: Another View of Male Supremacy, Another Separation." *The Politics of Reality: Essays in Feminist Theory*, pp. 128–51. Trumansburg, N.Y. Crossing, 1978.

Halberstam, Judith. *Female Masculinity*. Durham: Duke University Press, 1998.

Hall, Jacquelyn Dowd. " 'The Mind That Burns in Each Body': Women, Rape, and Racial Violence." In Ann Snitow, Christine Stansell, and Sharon Thompson, eds., *Powers of Desire: The Politics of Sexuality*, pp. 329–49. New York: Monthly Review Press, 1983.

Harris, Trudier. *Exorcising Blackness: Historical and Literary Lynching and Burning Rituals*. Bloomington: Indiana University Press, 1984.

Hine, Darlene Clark, and Earnestine Jenkins, eds. *A Question of Manhood: A Reader in Black Masculinity in the United States*. Bloomington: Indiana University Press, 1999.

hooks, bell. "Men: Comrades in Struggle." *Feminist Theory: From Margin to Center*. Boston: South End, 1984.

Irigaray, Luce. "Commodities Among Themselves." *This Sex Which Is Not One*, pp. 192–97. Trans. Catherine Porter. Ithaca: Cornell University Press, 1985.

Jagose, Annamarie. " 'Feminism Without Women': A Lesbian Reassurance." In Dana Heller, ed., *Cross-Purposes: Lesbians, Feminists, and the Limits of Alliance*, pp. 124–35. Bloomington: Indiana University Press, 1997.

Jeffords, Susan. *The Remasculinization of America: Gender and the Vietnam War.* Bloomington: Indiana University Press, 1989.

Lorde, Audre. "Man Child: A Black Lesbian Feminist's Response." In *Sister Outsider*, pp. 72–80. Trumansburg, N.Y.: Crossing, 1987.

Lowe, Lisa. *Immigrant Acts: On Asian American Cultural Politics.* Durham: Duke University Press, 1996.

Modleski, Tania. *Feminism Without Women: Culture and Criticism in a "Postfeminist" Age.* New York and London: Routledge, 1991.

Nelson, Dana. *National Manhood: Capitalist Citizenship and the Imagined Fraternity of White Men.* Durham: Duke University Press, 1998.

Nicholson, Linda. "Interpreting Gender." *Signs* 20.1 (Autumn 1994): 79–105.

Prosser, Jay. *Second Skins: the Body Narratives of Transsexuality.* New York: Columbia University Press, 1998.

Robinson, Sally. *Marked Men: White Masculinity in Crisis.* New York: Columbia University Press, 2000.

Rubin, Gayle. "Of Catamites and Kings: Reflections on Butch, Gender, and Boundaries." In Joan Nestle, ed., *The Persistent Desire: A Femme-Butch Reader*, pp. 466–82. Boston: Alyson, 1992.

———. "Sexual Traffic." Interview by Judith Butler. *differences: A Journal of Feminist Cultural Studies* 6.2–3 (1994): 62–99.

———. "Thinking Sex: Notes for a Radical Theory of the Politics of Sexuality." In Henry Abelove, Michèle Aina Barale, and David M. Halperin, eds., *The Lesbian and Gay Studies Reader*, pp. 3–44. New York: Routledge, 1993.

———. "The Traffic in Women: Notes on the 'Political Economy' of Sex." In Rayna R. Reiter, ed., *Toward an Anthropology of Women*, pp. 157–210. New York: Monthly Review, 1975.

Schor, Naomi. "Feminist and Gender Studies." In Joseph Gibaldi, ed., *Introduction to Scholarship in Modern Languages and Literatures*, pp. 262–87. 2d ed. New York: Modern Language Association of America, 1992.

Sedgwick, Eve Kosofsky. *Between Men: English Literature and Male Homosocial Desire.* New York: Columbia University Press, 1985.

———. "Gender Studies." In Stephen Greenblatt and Giles Gunn, eds., *Redrawing the Boundaries: The Transformation of English and American Literary Studies*, pp. 271–302. New York: Modern Language Association of America, 1992.

Segal, Lynne. *Slow Motion: Changing Masculinities, Changing Men.* New Brunswick, N.J.: Rutgers University Press, 1990.

Smith, Valerie. "Split Affinities: The Case of Interracial Rape." In Marianne Hirsch and Evelyn Fox Keller, eds., *Conflicts in Feminism,* pp. 271–87. New York and London: Routledge, 1990.

Stone, Sandy. "The *Empire* Strikes Back: A Posttranssexual Manifesto." In Julia Epstein and Kristina Straub, eds., *Body Guards: The Cultural Politics of Gender Ambiguity,* pp. 280–304. New York: Routledge, 1991.

Stryker, Susan. "The Transgender Issue: An Introduction," *GLQ* 4.2 (1998): 145–58.

Wallace, Michele. *Black Macho and the Myth of Super Woman.* 1979. London and New York: Verso, 1990.

Wells, Ida B. *Crusade for Justice: The Autobiography of Ida B. Wells.* Chicago: University of Chicago Press, 1970.

Wiegman, Robyn. *American Anatomies: Theorizing Race and Gender.* Durham: Duke University Press, 1995.

2

REENFLESHING THE BRIGHT BOYS; OR, HOW MALE BODIES MATTER TO FEMINIST THEORY

Calvin Thomas

For hours each day the child Genet
roosted in the silken peace of the outhouse,
a confessional where we bare our intimate parts,
feeding his imagination on the odor and darkness.
For myself, it was many years before I could
get near the poetry section in a bookstore
or PS3521 in library stacks
without a sudden urge to shit,
I don't know why, unless envy, or emulation,
a need, like a coyote's or hyena's,
to set down my identity in scat.
—Galway Kinnell, "Holy Shit"

It is much harder for man to let the other come through him.
Writing is the passageway, the entrance, the exit, the
dwelling place of the other in me—the other that I am and
am not, that I don't know how to be, but that I feel passing,
that makes me live—that tears me apart, disturbs me,
changes me, who?—a feminine one, a masculine one, some?
—Hélène Cixous, "Sorties"

I am one thing, my writing is another matter.
—Friedrich Nietzsche, *Ecce Homo*

The proliferation of masculinity studies has been viewed with understandable suspicion by some feminist theorists. Such studies are seen as integral to, if not responsible for, a critical and institutional shift away from a specifically feminist project and toward what is considered a politically neutralized "gender studies." On this view, the argument that men are *no less* gendered than women, that masculinity is *no less* a social construction or performative masquerade than is femininity, is complicitous with the assumption that men and women are equally installed into symmetrically gendered positions. This assumption of equal or symmetrical gendering, supposedly inscribed in the phrase "no less" above, would obviously evacuate the feminist argument that the social and symbolic process of gendering sexed bodies maintains unequal and asymmetrical relations of power. Masculinity studies and the "turn to gender" are thus charged with perpetuating rather than interrogating the reproduction of male dominance.[1]

In some cases, charges such as these are justified. Some versions of "men's studies," particularly those influenced by the mythopoetic school of Robert Bly, are spectacularly uninformed by and hostile to feminism, while even more well-intentioned interventions, based on the argument that the confines of normative masculinity are damaging to men, can seem perilously close to a whiney men-have-it-bad-too line of defensive reaction against feminism. They seem motivated by the desire to ameliorate the condition of men, while ignoring or minimizing the oppression of women.[2] These sorts of masculinity studies can seem quite suspect, and their specific modes of reaction, appropriation, and celebration can seem to compromise the very possibility of profeminist masculinity studies by men.

On the other hand, to leave masculinity *un*studied, to proceed as if it were somehow not a form of gender, is to leave it naturalized, and thus to render it less permeable to change. For feminist theorists who recognize the importance of this fact, a "gender studies" that focuses on masculinity need not necessarily entail the depoliticization or betrayal of feminism. Quite to the contrary, it can also designate the critical process by which (some) men learn *from* feminism in order to make subversive interventions into reproductions of normative masculinity itself. There are a number of reasons and motivations for such intervention, and certainly the strategic point that normative masculinity harms men, that it can be in men's best interests—their most fully humanizing interests—to want to escape or demolish masculine norms, can be salutary. But from a specifically feminist perspective, interventions into masculinity—

by feminist women and men—are not only desirable but necessary for one overarching reason: as Kaja Silverman puts it, "Masculinity impinges with such force upon femininity [that] to effect a large-scale reconfiguration of male identification and desire would, at the very least, permit female subjectivity to be lived differently than it is at present" (*Male*, 2–3). In terms of a masculinity study whose point is change, the criticism most "supportive of the feminist project," writes Tania Modleski, is "the kind that analyzes male power, male hegemony, with a concern for the effect of this power *on the female subject* and with an awareness of how frequently male subjectivity works to appropriate 'femininity' while oppressing women" (*Feminism*, 6–7).

For this male feminist, Silverman's and Modleski's points are crucial: what is ultimately at issue in masculinity studies is, or should be, the *effect* of masculinity construction *on women*. In other words, for a truly *critical* masculinity studies the feminist project must remain what Fredric Jameson, in quite another context, calls "the absolute horizon of all thought and all interpretation" (*Political*, 17). Situated within this horizon, masculinity studies can be not the betrayal or appropriation of feminism but rather one of its valuable and necessary consequences.

But how best to study, so as to transform, the reproduction of the masculine in men? Perhaps the question, with its emphasis on competitively locating and inhabiting the superior mode of critical operation, is itself a bit too masculinist. My argument—which isn't necessarily "the best" but simply the one I find most compelling—has been, and will continue here to be, that *one* possibly productive way to analyze male power and hegemony, and to reconfigure male identification and desire, involves a specific sort of attention to the "matter" of the male body and to the materialization of that body *in writing*—in writing as what Cixous calls "the passageway, the entrance, the exit, the dwelling place of the other in me" ("Sorties," 583).

Referring to my title, then, I would say that male bodies do matter to feminist theory, and in two ways. First, in a simple sort of "warm bodies" appeal, I would argue for sheer numbers: the more profeminist men, straight and queer, the better for feminism. In this sense, male bodies matter to feminism because men can and sometimes do *materialize* feminism in their writing, their teaching, and their public and private lives.[3] Second, and more to more my concerns here, I suggest the significance of the question of how the repression of the abject vulnerability of the male body—a repression necessary for the construction of heteronormative masculinity—demands a displacement of that vulnerability, and all that it materially entails, onto the feminine. Here is where the matter of writing emerges as a "scene of visibility" in which male subjectivity can be led to confront its effaced embodiment, its constitutive otherness, the femininity that has always functioned as "the bearer" of its "meaning."[4] Again, what is ultimately (but not always evidently) at issue in this confrontation is the effect *on women* of a specific sort of masculinity construction, a specific form of straight male anxiety assuagement. The question is not one of the way male authors represent themselves or women in their writing, but rather of writing itself as a "bodily function" carrying the potential to alienate, to abject, to "feminize," to "de-mean"—and even to "queer"— a heteromasculine subjectivity "caught in the act" of writing (to) itself.

Readers of this essay who are familiar with my *Male Matters* will recognize these allusions to that book's central argument, about which I will have more to say here. Before doing so, however, I want to return to the institutional and methodological questions of feminism, gender studies, and masculinity with which I opened this essay. My context is a set of discussions by Judith Butler: her introductory essay "Against Proper Objects" and her interviews with Rosi Braidotti and Gayle Rubin in the 1994 "More Gender Trouble: Feminism Meets Queer Theory" issue of the feminist journal *differences*. As the issue's title suggests, its central topic is not masculinity but the tensions between feminism, gender studies, and queer theory. However, the relevance to masculinity studies, particularly to the question of the formation of masculine subjectivity through a "defiling" linguistic difference, will become evident as we proceed.

Butler's immediate aim in "Against Proper Objects" is to counter the methodological and political boundary between feminism and gay/lesbian studies that she sees being erected by the editors of the Routledge *Lesbian and Gay Studies Reader,* both in their introduction and in their placement of Gayle Rubin's "Thinking Sex"—which challenges feminism as "the ultimate and complete account" (34) of the oppression of sexual minorities—as the volume's lead essay. In the course of this discussion, Butler begins to examine "the significant differences between feminists who make use of the category of gender and those who work within the framework of sexual difference" ("Against," 17). Roughly, the difference in framework involves the split between social constructionist approaches to the question of sexual identity and those influenced by Lacanian psychoanalysis. At issue is the question of the formation of the subject. Butler writes:

> Those who work within the framework of sexual difference argue against "gender" on the grounds that it presupposes a notion of cultural construction in which the subject is taken as a given, and gender then acquires a supplementary meaning or role. Some would argue that such a view can recognize neither the way in which the workings of sexual difference in language establish the subject nor the masculinity of that subject—and the exclusion of the feminine subject from subject formation that that subject requires. . . . Gender theory misunderstands the ways in which that asymmetrical relation between the sexes is installed through the primary workings of language, which presuppose the production of the unconscious. The turn to gender, for those who emerge from a Lacanian or post-Lacanian tradition, signals a papering over of this more fundamental structuring of language, intelligibility, and the production of the subject along the axis of a split which also produces the unconscious. ("Against," 16)

Butler situates Rosi Braidotti as representative of this particular argument against gender. She writes that "according to Braidotti, some versions of the gender studies model consider the cultural construction of femininity and masculinity as homologous kinds of constructions, which suggests that the study of gender directly contradicts the political impetus of feminist analysis—to mark the constitutive asymmetry of sexed positions by which language and the unconscious emerge" ("Against," 17). For Braidotti, Butler writes, "the turn to gender is understood as an antifeminist move and a deradicalization of the feminist political agenda" ("Against," 17). Gender is thus "a sign of a politically defused feminism, a framework which assumes the symmetrical positioning of men and women along the homologous means of their construction" ("Against," 17). Such defusion, Butler writes, has even prompted the call "Death to gender!"—offered not by Braidotti but by "a feminist friend objecting to the replacement of a feminist perspective on sexual difference by a theory of the cultural or social construction of gender" ("Against," 17).

In the subsequent interview with Braidotti, "Feminism by Any Other Name," Butler draws Braidotti out on these points. Braidotti is indeed opposed not only to gender studies, basing her opposition on "the realization of its politically disastrous institutional consequences" (43), but to masculinity studies and gay male studies as well. Among the disasters Braidotti lists are "the take-over of the feminist agenda by studies on masculinity," incidents of academic positions "advertised as 'gender studies' being given away to the 'bright boys,' " and the "special significance" of "the role of the mainstream publisher Routledge" in "promoting gender as a way of de-radicalizing the feminist agenda, re-marketing masculinity and gay male identity instead" ("Feminism," 43–44). In the course of comments such as these, Braidotti offers the following analysis:

> The focus on gender rather than sexual difference presumes that men and women are constituted in symmetrical ways. But this misses the feminist point about masculine dominance. In such a system, the masculine and the feminine are in a structurally dissymmetrical position: men, as the empirical referent of the masculine, cannot be said to have a gender; rather, they are expected to carry the Phallus—which is something different. They are expected to exemplify abstract virility, which is hardly an easy task. Simone de Beauvoir observed fifty years ago that the price men pay for representing the universal is a loss of embodiment; the price women pay, on the other hand, is at once a loss of subjectivity and a confinement to the body. Men become disembodied and, through this process, gain entitlement to transcendence and subjectivity; women become over-embodied and thereby consigned to immanence. This results in two dissymmetrical positions and to opposing kind of problems. ("Feminism," 38)

Several questions emerge from Braidotti's formulation. First of all, although it's a small concern, one might expect Braidotti to cite some particular examples of gender theorists who have missed the point about systemic male dominance. There are no specific citations other than the mention of Routledge, though I doubt that Braidotti would want to implicate everyone who has published in that "mainstream" as pointmissers, since the list would have to include Braidotti herself (see her *Patterns*). More important, however, one might ask how we are to understand all of the expectations, entitlements, confinements, and consignments that Braidotti mentions here as *not* being gender. If we understand gendering not as a set of characteristics "added on" to a given preexisting subjectivity but as constitutive of the very social formation of any subject, as "a social category imposed upon a sexed body" (Scott, *Gender*, 32), as "the process of assuming, taking on, identifying with the positionalities and meaning effects specified by a particular society's gender system" (De Lauretis, "Habit," 302), then it is difficult to understand the tropes Braidotti deploys as corresponding to or arising from anything other than a specifically *sociohistorical* sex/gender system.[5] Particularly in regard to the expectation of Phallus-carrying and abstract-virility-exemplification that Braidotti suggests exempts men from having a gender, it is difficult to understand where such expectations *come from,* if not society and culture. And if one responds, in supposedly good Lacanian fashion, that Phallic expectations originate from "the primary workings of language, which presuppose the production of the unconscious" (Butler, "Against," 16), then, since language and the unconscious don't just fall out of the sky, one still has to account, as Butler stresses, for the relationship between social production and linguistic production, between social structures and psychic structures, as well as for how their relationship might be reconfigured. Moreover, from a feminist perspective, one might want to account for the possibility of conditions under which men might productively *fail* to "live up" to Phallic expectations or even consciously *choose* to betray them—a choice that would be something other than what Braidotti calls "a self-regulating masculine agency" ("Feminism," 39). In other words, if, with Braidotti, we recognize the feminist value of an Irigarayan "double syntax" that inscribes the "difference not only of Woman from man, but also of real-life women from the reified image of Woman-as-Other" ("Feminism," 39), can we not also ask about the feminist value of another syntactic doubling that opens up the difference between real-life men and the reified image (or nonimage) of Man-as-Same, of Man as bearer of the Phallus?

To begin to answer this question, I want briefly to consider the Lacanian take on linguistic difference as sexual difference, a take that supposedly supports the "sexual difference" framework to which Braidotti opposes the "turn to gender." As Butler explains in her interview with Gayle Rubin, Lacan's theory concerns "the structure of language" and "the emergence of the speaking subject through sexual differentiation." There is, Butler writes, a Lacanian tendency "to understand sexual difference as coextensive with language itself," so that "there is no possibility of speaking, of taking a position in language outside of differentiating moves," the *primary* differentiating move being that "differentiation from the maternal which is said to install a speaker in language for the first time" ("Sexual," 69).

To unpack these comments, let's say that in Lacan's theory what precedes the primary differentiation that installs us into positions of speaking subjects is the Real. The Real in Lacan is that prelinguistic, undifferentiated realm of sensation and perception, without discernable subjective or corporeal locus, that characterizes our immediately postuterine, infantile existence and that will always resist or exceed symbolization. Roughly, the Real can be related to the "oceanic feeling" (11) that Freud describes at the beginning of *Civilization and Its Discontents* and by Lacan is directly related to the maternal body as what Jacqueline Rose calls "undifferentiated space" (*Feminine*, 54). For Freud, the development of the ego marks a separation from the oceanic feeling: the ego is what Freud strikingly calls a "shrunken residue" (*Civilization*, 15) of that earlier, much larger field of sensation and perception. In Lacan's theory of ego development, we are "shrink-wrapped," so to speak, into our subjectivities in two successive stages. The first instance of shrinkage is the mirror stage, the second our accession to the Symbolic Order of language. In the mirror stage, the infant's first (mis)recognition of its own image in the mirror is a moment of both jubilation ("that's *me*") and alienation ("*that's* me").[6] This mixture of jubilant and alienating identification/*méconnaissance* forecasts what Lacan calls "the self's radical ex-centricity to itself" (*Écrits*, 171) and foregrounds the fact that the price of a fledgling subjective coherence will have been the irrecuperable expulsion from/loss of the Real: in other words, one begins to sense in the mirror stage that, by virtue of being one, being imagistically delineated *as* one, one isn't everything, isn't "all."

This loss of the "all" of the Real is further ratified upon accession to the Symbolic Order of language, since language demands that one must differentiate from the Real in order to signify the objects that now inadequately stand in for it. Or rather, one must have *been* separated from the objects of the Real—say, by paternal prohibition, the father's name and no (*nom du pére* and *non du pére*)—to be in the position of *having* to signify or symbolize them at all. Moreover, and importantly, since one must signify or symbolize oneself, one's own position as a subject of desire in the form of the first-person pronoun, that very positionality is objectified in the body of the sign, and a significatory self-alienation becomes the inevitable condition of being-in-language/being-in-the-world.

Lacan, following Saussure, defines the sign (and hence the world) as "a presence made of absence" (*Écrits*, 65). In other words—or in *all* words—the presence of the signifier presupposes the absence, or the possibility of the absence, not only of the referent but of all the other signifiers that lend any particular signifier its value (language being, in Saussure's sense, a differential system without positive terms). For Lacan, the defining and defiling characteristic of the symbol is its capacity to "murder" the symbolized "thing"—to make present its absence—by the same significatory stroke that grants "the world of things" its very intelligibility. Thus, upon our accession to the Symbolic Order, "there is born the world of meaning of a particular language in which the world of things will come to be arranged. . . . It is the world of words that creates the world of things. . . . Man speaks, then, but it is because the symbol has made him man" (*Écrits*, 65).

Of course, the emphasis here on *man* and *his* symbol—or perhaps *the* symbol and *its* man—is not coincidental. Since the primary object of the Real is for Lacan the maternal body, the primary differentiation from the Real that language effects corresponds to the sexual difference between the *male* subject and the mother. This Lacanian imposition of sexual difference onto the primary differentiation of language has a number of consequences. Linguistic difference is metaphorized as sexual difference, which is itself figured as the difference between (masculine) being and (feminine) nothingness: "The subject is presented with the question of his existence . . . as an articulated question: 'What am I there?,' concerning his sex and his contingency in being, namely, that on the one hand, he is a man or a woman, and, on the other, that he might not be, the two conjugating their mystery, and binding it in the symbols of procreation and death" (*Écrits,* 194). The "loss of the Real" that every subject suffers upon entry into language is metaphorized by Lacan in terms of the mother's "lack" of the Phallus: thus are we all "castrated" in and by the Symbolic Order. The mother's specific "castration," and hence her putative desire for the Phallus, is figured as the very essence of our general "lack of being" and of our desire to mean, our desire to be viable and intelligible. The Phallus, as "signifier of lack," comes to symbolize the compensatory essence of symbolization itself, inscribing and necessitating our differentiation from the Real, compensating us, always inadequately, for the very thing of which it deprives us. The Phallus thus becomes the privileged term of "union" by virtue of which our very desire to speak links up "successfully" with whatever meaning we manage to make.

In other words, the Lacanian conflation of linguistic difference with sexual difference installs what Butler calls a "heterosexual pathos" not merely into "the mystery" of physical procreation and/or the death drive but into the very process and possibility of "successfully" making sense ("Against," 19).⁷ I repeat and scare-quote the word "successfully" here not only to foreground the way heteronormativity (and hence male dominance) subtends virtually all culturally legitimated forms of "success" or subjective viability but also, conversely, to suggest the political productivity, for certain kinds of men, of certain forms of embodied discursive *failure* or *desubjectivation.* It is the productive possibility of antiphallocentric, corporeodiscursive failure that I want to keep in mind as we return to Butler and Braidotti's exchange regarding the sedimentations of heteronormativity in Lacan.

In the course of their discussion, Butler repeatedly suggests to Braidotti that "when sexual difference is understood as a linguistic and conceptual presupposition or, for that matter, an inevitable condition of writing, it falsely universalizes a social asymmetry, thereby reifying social relations of gender asymmetry in a linguistic or symbolic realm, maintained problematically at a distance from socio-historical practice" ("Feminism," 38). Sexual difference, Butler argues, reifies "a social asymmetry as an eternal necessity" ("Feminism," 39). Braidotti's response—that one "must not confuse the diagnostic function of sexual difference with its strategic or programmatic aims" ("Feminism," 39)—is not particularly satisfying, since it is difficult at first to understand what strategies for change can be possible given the "irreducible and irreversible" nature of the diagnosis itself ("Feminism," 39). As Gayle Rubin puts it, the Lacanian symbolic seems to stick us with, and in, "a primary category of gender differences which might as well be inscribed in granite" ("Sexual," 70).

Such inscription would indeed seem to be the effect of the Lacanian symbolic. On the other hand, lest I seem to be unduly picking on Braidotti here—playing one feminist off another at the other's expense, which probably isn't the most feminist way for a man to do feminism— let me say that I do find myself attracted to some of the strategies she enumerates. In fact, though I obviously agree with Butler against Braidotti in terms of the question of gender versus sexual difference, I find some of Braidotti's formulations somewhat more compelling than Butler's because of Braidotti's specific recourse to the materiality of the body (one of my reservations about Butler being that there aren't *enough* bodily matters in her *Bodies That Matters*). In "Against Proper Objects," Butler writes that "the heteropathos that pervades the legacy of Lacanian psychoanalysis and some of its feminist reformulations can be countered only by rendering the symbolic increasingly dynamic, that is, by considering the conditions and limits of representation and representability as open to significant rearticulations and transformations under the pressure of social practices of various kinds" ("Against," 20). In "Feminism by Any Other Name," however, Braidotti brings the matter of embodiment, of corporeal materialism, into this dynamization—or dynamiting—of the symbolic. She writes that "the best strategy for moving out of this contradiction [of asymmetrical sexual difference] is radical embodiment and strategic mimesis . . . a strategy of deconstruction that also allows for temporary redefinitions, combining the fluidity and dangers of a process of change with a minimum of stability or anchoring" ("Feminism," 43). In the context of "a psychic and social guerrilla warfare against the kingdom of identity per se," Braidotti joins Irigaray in calling "for the melt-down of the male symbolic in order to provide for the radical re-enfleshing of both men and women" ("Feminism," 50, 54). Finally—indeed, these are the closing words of the interview—Braidotti advocates "a merrier brand of idiosyncratic and hybrid thinking, something that is neither conceptually pure nor politically correct: a joyful kind of feminist 'dirty-minded' thinking" ("Feminism," 58).

Now, because Braidotti's main concern is "the political will to assert the specificity of the lived, female bodily experience," it is understandable that she has nothing to say about what a radical reenfleshing of men would look like or how it might proceed ("Feminism," 40). However, if we recall Kaja Silverman's point about the way masculinity impinges upon femininity, if we consider the history of male disembodiment's specific effects on lived female bodily experience, then the project of male reenfleshment takes on a certain feminist urgency. This urgency, again, is what justifies critical masculinity studies, provided that the studies are truly critical, and even, perhaps, the institutional "give-away" of gender studies positions to "bright boys," provided that the boys are not merely "bright" but radically reenfleshed.[8]

So how might a profeminist reenfleshment of male subjectivity proceed? And how might that proceeding be related to the possibility of a *male* feminist "dirty-mindedness"? I find the latter question particularly intriguing in that expressions of male feminism are sometimes marked by just the sort of politically correct conceptual purity that Braidotti wants merrily to sully.[9] In my view, one way of dirtying the mind of male subjectivity, and thus rendering the symbolic increasingly dynamic, is through a recognition of the way that mind is already sullied—not "castrated," but abjected[10]—in and by the materiality of language itself, by abjection as the "inevitable condition" of all writing, by the written trace as the hybrid soil(ing) that pulls the kingdom of identity down into the realm of the body, by writing as what Lee Edelman calls "a category-subverting alterity within the conceptual framework of 'the masculine' itself" ("Tearooms," 564), by writing as that which always already "set[s] down my identity in scat" (Kinnell, *Imperfect,* 65).

To unpack this set of assertions, let's say that the phrase "inevitable condition" compels us to scat momentarily back to Lacan. Let's say that although there is nothing inevitable, and everything quite arbitrary, about Lacan's conflation of linguistic difference with sexual difference, language can be said to involve certain inevitable and irreducible differentiations—such as the split between the subject of the enunciation and the subject of the enounced, between the I that speaks and the

"I" that is spoken of—differentiations that, with significant revisions, might still be productively *sexualized*, or corporealized. There may, in other words, be something inevitable, and inevitably sexual, about the I/"I" split, about the "the self's radical ex-centricity to itself" (*Écrits*, 171) in language, but there is nothing inevitable about what we *make* of that ex-centricity, about *how* we rearticulate it, *how* we sexualize it. I very much agree with Gayle Rubin when she writes "there is something intrinsically problematic about any notion that somehow language itself or the capacity for acquiring it requires a sexual differentiation as a primary differentiation. If humans were hermaphroditic or reproduced asexually, I can imagine we would still be capable of speech" ("Sexual," 69). On the other hand, I want strategically to hold on to the connection between linguistic difference and *sexualized differences,* not the "primary" genital difference between male and female (much less "Phallic" and "castrated") but a mobile constellation of differences involving various corporeal sites and openings—with, importantly, the recognition that such openings are themselves open "to significant rearticulations and transformations under the pressure of social practices of various kinds" (Butler, "Against," 20).

Obviously, the opening that I want strategically to foreground here is the male anus, and it was Lacan (along with Joyce, Bataille, and Kristeva) who, with formulations such as the following, first compelled my considerations in *Male Matters* of the anal dynamics of the self-alienations of language: "For this subject, who thinks he can accede to himself by designating himself in the statement, is no more than such an object. Ask the writer about the anxiety he experiences when faced by the blank sheet of paper, and he will tell you who *is* the turd of his phantasy" (*Écrits*, 315). But Lacan, in good heteronormative psychoanalytic fashion, always seems to manage recuperatively to turn the turd back into the Phallus and thus return it to its "inevitable" destination, to which, for him, the "letter" always arrives.[11] It has, rather, been up to certain feminist and gay male critics to open the male anus and anality up to nonphallogocentric rearticulations. Indeed, the anus has been getting a fair bit of theoretical attention lately, mostly following from Leo Bersani's important essay, "Is the Rectum a Grave?" Because I have extensively articulated my own relation to Bersani's work elsewhere,[12] I will turn here to two other theorists who have employed

Bersani's insights to propose reconfigurations of the straight male body.

For our purposes, let's say that Bersani's main insight involves proposing the rectum as a site of radical desubjectivation: receptive male anal eroticism, serving as a metaphor for "de-meaning" sexuality per se, also metaphorizes the radical humiliation or exuberant discard of a hyperbolic ego that, for a number of reasons, is most closely associated with the swellings of conventional phallic masculinity.[13] In her essay "Destruction: Boundary Erotics and Refigurations of the Heterosexual Male Body," Catherine Waldby tropes Bersanian desubjectivation as "erotic destruction," as "the temporary ecstatic confusions wrought upon the everyday sense of self by sexual pleasure" ("Destruction," 266). With reference to Jeanette Winterson's novel *Oranges Are Not the Only Fruit*, Waldby writes that while lesbian relationships seem to "offer the possibility of a reciprocity of destruction" ("Destruction," 266), most heterosexual men

> are so concerned with the maintenance of their sovereign selfhood that they cannot tolerate its infringement by another. They seek instead to be always the destroyer, to refigure women in their own interests but to resist such refiguration themselves. In this case the transformational possibilities offered by the limited destructions of erotic intimacy are perverted into the very real destruction of one partner, the woman, whose sense of self is not merely refigured but systematically dissipated. (267)

Waldby contends that "while the rituals of heterosexual sex can and often do enact the non-reciprocity of destruction that [Winterson] condemns, they can also play out disturbances and secret reciprocities in this erotic economy" (267). Because conventional heterosexual non-reciprocity depends upon a "hegemonic bodily imago of masculinity" (268) that conforms with the man's status as sovereign ego and with an understanding of the male body as "phallic and impenetrable" (268), the male anus can become a site of significant disturbances in, and destructions of, the rituals of straight sex. As Waldby writes:

> Anal eroticism carries disturbingly feminizing connotations. Part of the significance of intercourse understood in its ideological aspect is its assertion

not just of the woman's penetrability but of the man's *im*penetrability, the exclusive designation of his body by its seamless, phallic mastery. Intercourse can count as demonstration of the idea that women's bodies lack the means to penetrate another body, and that male bodies are impenetrable. When a man puts his penis in a woman's vagina he is saying, 'look, it is she who is the permeable one, the one whose body accommodates, takes in and lets out, *not I.*' But the possibilities of anal erotics for the masculine body amount to an abandonment of this phallic claim. The ass is soft and sensitive, and associated with pollution and shame, like the vagina. It is non-specific with regard to genital difference in that everybody has one. It allows access into the body, when after all only women are supposed to have a vulnerable interior space. All this makes anal eroticism a suasive point for the displacement or erasure of purely phallic boundaries. In a sense then, anal eroticism is the sexual pleasure which conformation to a phallic imago most profoundly opposes. If the point of the phallic imago is to guard against confusion between the imaginary anatomies of masculine and feminine, and to shore up masculine power, then anal eroticism threatens to explode this ideological body. (272)

Given this threat of anal explosion, Waldby suggests, the self-supporting masculine response is a projective violence against others who represent the dissolution, pollution, and shame of permeability. Not only does the maintenance of the sovereign male ego depend upon "projecting the permeable possibilities of the male body on to women," but homophobia and homophobic violence "might also be ways of adjudicating the anxiety aroused in heterosexual men by their own penetrability" (272). The denial of receptive anal eroticism "can be acted out as a violence against, or contempt for, those who are interpreted as wishing to . . . experience such pleasure themselves. . . . In this sense the repression or elision of anal eroticism in heterosexual men can be seen to work not only along the lines of the masculine/feminine division, but also along the homosexual/heterosexual divide" (272–73). Thus, as a strategy for combating both misogynist and homophobic violence, Waldby calls for "celebratory alliances between feminism and other groups with political/erotic interests in dephallicizing the straight male body" (274–75). In line with Braidotti's joyously feminist dirty-minded thinking, Waldby suggests that "feminism needs to develop something like a pornographic imagination in relation to masculine bodies, and bodies in general" (275). Maybe, Waldby writes, "what theoretical feminism needs now is a strap-on" (275).

If a strap-on is what theoretical feminism needs, Brian Pronger is happy to assist with the straps. In "On Your Knees: Carnal Knowledge, Masculine Dissolution, Doing Feminism," Pronger suggests that the issue is less men "doing" feminism than feminism doing men, or rather, that the masculine aversion to being done, being penetrated, by the feminist strap-on or by other men, is what specifically prevents men "from embodying feminist insights" (69). Defining "masculine desire" not as heterosexual attraction but as refused homosexuality, Pronger writes that "masculine desire is essentially homophobic" and that homophobia "is an obstacle to the embodiment of feminism" (74). The "point of masculinity," he suggests, is

> to become larger, to take up more space, and yield less of it. It is the opposite of feminine anorexic desire. The transformation of the limp penis into the large, hard phallus is the flowering of masculine desire. The expanding phallus is protected by the other side of this desire: the closed anus. Just as the phallus realizes its masculinity by taking space, so the tight anus protects masculine space by repelling invasion. Masculine desire protects its own phallic production by closing orifices, both anus and mouth, to the phallic expansion of others. Rendered impenetrable, the masculine body differentiates itself as distinct and unconnected. It is conquering and inviolable. . . . The discourse of gender territorializes men's bodies by constructing this form of desire, simultaneously channeling it and damming it up . . . through metaphorically generalized or sexually specific phallic expansions and anal contractions. (72–73)

Although I find Waldby's and Pronger's formulations tremendously attractive and productive, I do have some reservations about what might be taken as their *apparent* literalism. At the risk of sounding like just another anxious straight boy who wants to keep his own literal ass covered, I would submit that Waldby's and Pronger's essays *might* leave the impression that only, literally, ass-fucked men can reconfigure heterosexuality and embody feminism.[14] I stress "apparent" and "might" because Pronger in particular alludes to the possibilities of extraliteral forms of bodily deterritorialization, even if he tends to leave those possibilities undeveloped. For example, after elaborating homophobia as "the reluctance to give up masculine space" and "the fear men have of the inversion of the expanding phallus and closed anus into a deferential phallus and an open anus," Pronger points out that "this fear is evident beyond the physical space of the body in the reluctance some men have to give way in sport, commerce, academic debate, or interpersonal relationships" (76). To counter this reluctance, Pronger writes, "we need to extend the joy of the eroticization of opening spaces and deterritorializing masculine desire in the anus and mouth to the joy of erotically opening up such spaces in conversation, in interpersonal relations, in games, in academic discourse, in economics, etc." (77). Although Pronger does not elaborate on how we might open up such spaces in, say, academic discourse and debate, the important point to be retained is that if the phallic expansions and anal contractions that define masculinity can be both "sexually specific" and "metaphorically general," then so too must be the phallic deference and anal opening that dissolve it. Straight masculinity needs, in other words, to confront its figural as well as its literal penetration.

Again, at the risk of seeming to let this recourse to the figural allow an anxious, ass-covering evasion of the very thinkability of the literal, one still might ask what metaphorical forms this deferential opening, this masculine dissolution through penetration, might take—particularly, say, in academic discourse. And, leaving aside for a moment the literal strap-on, is there a feminist point to be taken in terms of this opening? I submit, again, that we (men) have always been *in* this opening—in it, near it, metonymically contiguous with it—to the extent that our subjectivities have always been set down *in writing*, to the extent that written symbols have always *made* us "men": *in writing* as sexually specific and metaphorically general, as the physical, spatial, visible representation of the self's inevitable ex-centricity to itself in language, as the fault line—the very crack, if you will—of the masculine/feminine and the heterosexual/homosexual divides. We have always been in that opening, not simply to the extent that we are writers, facing the blank white page with anxiety (since not all of us are), but to the extent that we are written. And we are all written. But not in granite. I submit that if we (straight men) can recognize how our being writers/written abjects us, how our phantasmatic fears about self-abjection in writing relate to the lived bodily experiences of those who are literally abjected in the social realm, how our fears fuel and provoke their abjection, how both misogyny and homophobia can inhabit our anxiety about our ex-centricity to ourselves in the written trace, then we might begin to rewrite and reenflesh ourselves by writing those forms of fear and hatred *out*. We might begin to reconfigure ourselves—and deabjectify "our" others—by producing ourselves as writing that does something other than simply take up space. This deferentially expansive and dirty-minded writing would not necessarily depend literally upon, but would always figuratively refer us to, the possibility of our permeability and penetrability. It would entail the radical recognition—radical in the sense of "going to the roots"— that to the extent that we write and are written, to that extent are we also abjected, feminized, queered—which is to say, deeply and constitutively *fucked*. But it would also entail the recognition that, as Drucilla Cornell puts it, " 'to be fucked' is not the end of the world" (*Beyond*, 154). Indeed, it might actually be the beginning of a new one.

That, in so many words, is my argument in *Male Matters,* where, for mainly feminist purposes, I attempt to foreground the most sexual and most abject features of the defiling signifier, the devalued graphic mark, the de-meaning written trace.[15] I will close—but not, I hope, contract— my remarks here by considering three things I wish I had known while writing that book.

First, and rather incidentally, there is the transcultural information that, in traditional Indian society, there are four occurrences after which one is expected to wash one's hands: having sex, urinating or defecating, touching dead bodies, and writing.[16] Other than remark that it ties writing to abjection fairly neatly, I will let that information speak for itself.

Second, and much more important, there is Lee Edelman's concept of "homographesis," a concept that I particularly regret not knowing while writing *Male Matters* and whose omission from that book rather damages its queer aspirations.[17] As employed by Edelman, the term homographesis "refers to the disciplinary and projective fantasy that homosexuality is visibly, morphologically, or semiotically, written upon the flesh, so that homosexuality comes to occupy the stigmatized position of writing itself within the Western metaphysics of presence" ("Tearooms," 571). It refers "to the process by which homosexuality is put into writing through a rhetorical or tropological articulation that raises the question of writing as difference by constituting the homosexual as text" (571).

> Thus while homographesis signifies the act of putting homosexuality into writing under the aegis of writing itself, it also suggests the putting into writing—and therefore the putting into the realm of difference—of the sameness, the similitude, or the metaphors of identity that the graphesis of homosexuality deconstructs. For the insistent tropology of the inscribed gay body testifies to a deep-seated heterosexual concern that a widely available conceptualization of homosexual personhood might subvert the cognitive security that the categories of sameness and difference serve to anchor; it indicates, by its defensive assertion of a visible marker of sexual otherness, a fear that the categorical institutionalization of homosexual difference may challenge the integrity and reliability of sameness as the guarantor of identity, that this hypostatized difference between socially constructed and biologically determined understandings of maleness can vitiate the certainty by which one's own self-identity can be known. (572)

If homographesis signifies the act of putting homosexuality into writing, it also signifies the vitiations of certainty, and of heterosexual self-identity, that are inscribed in writing itself, in the very act of putting identity down in script. If "I—mark(s) the division," as Derrida remarks in *Glas* (165), then any mark "I" make(s) divides me from myself and potentially challenges the integrity and reliability of the very identity I am trying to guarantee. And in a culture in which division is lived (pervasively but not exclusively) along the lines of masculine/feminine and hetero/homo, the self-division of the straight male subject in writing is inevitably feminizing and queering. To meet this graphic challenge to straight self-identity, the heteromasculine subject must write out—cast out or abject—the internal markings of femininity and homosexuality. Edelman is clear enough about the terms of this project, which

> bespeaks a narcissistic anxiety about the definition of (sexual) identity that can only be stabilized and protected by a process of elimination or casting out. It betokens, that is, a cultural imperative to anal sadistic behavior that generates the homophobic definition of masculinity itself—that generates, we

might say, masculinity as such for our culture through the anal sadistic projection or casting away that inheres in homophobia . . . [and through] the aggressive anality of a culture compelled to repudiate the homosexuality it projectively identifies, definitionally, with anality. That abjectifying—and therefore effeminizing—anality is a condition that homophobic masculinity repudiates by construing it as the distinguishing hallmark of a recognizable category of homosexual person. (568–69)

That homophobic masculinity construes anality as the hallmark of the recognizably queer suggests that there may always potentially be something anally queer—abjectifying and therefore effeminizing—about *any* recognizable mark. If, again, "I mark(s) the division" between, say, my self-presence and my self-alienation, between private self and public meaning, then I also furtively recognize, in the mark of otherness that "I" always *is*, the potential dissolution of whatever determinate entities are erected on either side of that division into an unstable, differential relation. One of Edelman's contexts in "Tearooms and Sympathy" is the public restroom, "the threat to stability—that is, to the fixity of (heterosexual) identity and to (heterosexual) mastery of the signifiers of difference—portended . . . by the men's room itself" (563). Edelman writes that this threat

can be intuited more readily when the restroom is considered, not, as by Lacan, in terms of "urinary segregation" [*Écrits*, 151]—a context that establishes the phallus from the outset as the token of anatomical difference—but instead as the site of a loosening or relaxation of sphincter control, with the subsequent evocation of an eroticism undifferentiated by gender, in Freudian etiology, because anterior to the genital tyranny that raises the phallus to its privileged position. Precisely because the phallus marks the putative stability of the divide between "Ladies" and "Gentlemen," because it articulates the concept of sexual difference in terms of "visible perception," the "urinary" function in the institutional men's room customarily takes place within view of others—as if to indicate its status as an act of definitional display; but the private enclosure of the toilet stall signals the potential anxiety at issue in the West when the men's room becomes the locus not of urinary but intestinal relief. For the satisfaction that such relief affords abuts dangerously onto homophobically abjectified desires. (563)

Citing several instances in 1960s journalistic and literary discourse of an anxious troping of the men's room as a stinking, "cloacal" cavern, Edelman writes that "these displaced but insistent spatial tropes suggest the anxiety of an internal space of difference, an overdetermined opening or invagination within the male, of which the activity of defecation may constitute an unnerving reminder" (563). Following Edelman, I would reiterate that it is not only these particular spatial tropes but writing itself—which is always, insistently, tropaically spatial and displaced—that suggests or provokes anxiety, that serves as the unnerving reminder not only of defecation but, by nervous extension, of that overdetermined opening or invagination within the male. Thus, to the extent that writing is an inevitable condition of identity formation within a dynamic symbolic order, writing always potentially undoes any identity that sequesters or "stalls" itself in terms of its very resistance to being done, to being fucked, to homophobically abjected "feminine" desires that are both sexually specific and metaphorically general.

Edelman's writing on the stalling and destalling of masculine subjectivity in terms of homographesis allows an interesting point of entry into the third thing I wish I had known while writing *Male Matters*, Galway Kinnell's poem "Holy Shit." Opening with a set of epigraphs spanning the history of idealism from Plato to Jung, all concerning the turd and its abject confederates (my favorite among the epigraphs being Valentinus's "Jesus ate and drank but did not defecate" [61]), Kinnell's poem laments the human hostility to shit and shitting, argues against the idealist desire to "sever the chain of linked turds / tying us to some hole in the ground" (*Imperfect*, 64). Most valuable, from my perspective, the poem concerns the political consequences of this hostile desire. In a sort of etymological/editorial aside, Kinnell blasts the absurdity of the fact that the American newspapers "that were so enamored / of the smart weapons of the Gulf War" would never print that "indecent word" shit, "despite a lineage going back / to the Indo-European, from *skheid*, / to shed, to drop" (*Imperfect*, 65). Kinnell also brilliantly depicts the violently imperialist projection of abject vulnerability onto the other, what Edelman calls "a cultural imperative to anal sadistic behavior" ("Tearooms," 568), when he writes of Americans "imagining we are a people who don't die, / who come out of the sky like gods and drop / not shit but bombs on people who shit" (*Imperfect*, 66–67).

Kinnell, however, drops a little bomb of his own here. In the section of the poem that I have included as an epigraph to this essay, we find "the child Genet" stalled "in the silken peace of the outhouse . . . feeding his imagination on the odor and darkness" (*Imperfect,* 64). Kinnell then writes:

> For myself, it was many years before I could
> get near the poetry section in a bookstore
> or PS3521 in library stacks
> without a sudden urge to shit,
> I don't know why, unless envy, or emulation,
> a need, like a coyote's or hyena's,
> to set down my identity in scat. (Imperfect, 64–65)

Now, what interests me about this passage is the way Kinnell brings his most intimately confessional conflation of writing with defecation (none of the rest of the poem so explicitly concerns the act of writing or Kinnell's own "urge") into such close proximity with the homosexual writer Genet (none of the rest of the writers mentioned—Dante, Swift, etc.—are queer). One is tempted to call this proximity "homographic" in that it seems to signify a recognition of the way Kinnell's mixed urge to write/shit abuts with the adult Genet's abjectified homosexual desire. But one might also discern here Kinnell's own sense of the danger of that abutment, so that the line beginning "For myself" may signal not an identification with but rather a nervous distantiation from the roosting Genet. Indeed, Kinnell's baring of his urges leads him, mysteriously ("I don't know why"), not back into Genet's outhouse but rather to the land of coyotes and hyenas, to "the white-tailed deer" and "the canary" (*Imperfect,* 65), to the "wilder" but perhaps less dangerous realm of the animal kingdom, in which there is plenty of scat, but, conspicuously, neither identity nor writing.

This totemized animalization, this positively naturalized unhumanization of Kinnell's desire can be read as an abjectifying and dehumanizing flight from Genet's. In *Bodies That Matter,* Butler writes that

> the notion of abjection designates a degraded or cast out status within the
> terms of sociality. Indeed, what is foreclosed or repudiated . . . is precisely

what may not reenter the field of the social without threatening . . . the dissolution of the subject itself. I want to propose that certain abject zones within sociality also deliver this threat, constituting zones of uninhabitability which a subject fantasizes as threatening its own integrity with the prospect of a psychotic dissolution ('I would rather die than do or be that!'). (*Bodies*, 243)

On the one hand, I do not see enough evidence in Kinnell's poem to justify the claim that he finds Genet's outhouse a zone of uninhabitability the entry to which would threaten him with psychotic dissolution. On the other, I do see unfortunate evidence, in a poem I otherwise admire, that, when it comes to facing up to what writing sets down, Kinnell would rather emulate a coyote or a canary than a queer, would rather be a hyena than a homo. Granted, this preference is not as extreme as Butler's "I would rather die than do or be that," since the animals in question are supposedly alive, but it still seems an abjectifying move that has the effect of consecrating "Holy Shit" by separating it from the wholly shit. This subtle but urgent move on Kinnell's part leads me to be somewhat suspicious of the sanctimoniousness of the poem's closing lines—"Let us sit bent forward slightly, and be opened a moment, / as earth's holy matter passes through us" (*Imperfect*, 67)— lines that urge me to hope (but not pray) for openings of a slightly less reverential bent.

In this essay, I have moved from a consideration of discussions between feminist women (Butler, Braidotti, Rubin) to an examination of matters that might seem strictly "between men" (Edelman, Genet, Kinnell). If the essay's movement thus seems to be away from feminism and toward queer theory, its primary urge, to the contrary, has been in solidarity with Butler's desire "not only to link feminism and queer theory . . . but to establish their constitutive relationship" (*Bodies*, 240). Now, if that relationship were *obviously* established, there would perhaps be no such thing as misogyny among gay men or homophobia among feminist women, which of course there continues to be. But my concern here has not been with these aspects of gay male or feminist female subjectivities, for which, respectively, misogyny and homophobia have complex valences and which, in any case, are not exactly identical with the reproduction of straight male hegemony (though they're not exactly removed from such reproduction either). My concern *has* been with straight male subjectivity and with the possibility of its productive dissolution, its dirty-minded, corporeodiscursive failure to uphold the Phallus. It is the constitutive relationship between misogyny and homophobia in the formation of properly phallic, straight male subjects that makes the link between feminism and queer theory crucial for those interested in de-forming and transforming masculinity. My particular take involves the ways misogyny and homophobia are inscribed in writing as well as the possibilities of deformation and transformation that a radically reenfleshed writing might open up. There are, of course, many ways of opening masculinity to change, but by recognizing what is actually on the line when straight male identity is put down in writing, is set down in script (if not in scat), we may also see new ways, metaphorical and specific, of beginning to bring down—or at least fundamentally disturb—that identity's disembodied kingdom.

NOTES

1. The situation is complicated by the emergence of queer theory, whose tension with gay and lesbian studies resonates with that between gay/lesbian studies and feminism, which itself corresponds to certain debates and divisions within feminist activism and theory (essentialist versus antiessentialist, antiporn versus pro-sex).

2. An exception is Michael Kimmel, who advocates using the masculinity-hurts-men line *strategically* to get men interested in changing gender relations, while making it clear that his primary investment is profeminist. See "Who's Afraid?"

3. See Smith and Jardine, *Men;* and Digby, *Men Doing.* For my commentary on men teaching feminism, and straight men teaching queer theory, see my essay "Straight."

4. My reference here is to Laura Mulvey: "Woman then stands in patriarchal culture as signifier for the male other, bound by a symbolic order in which man can live out his phantasies and obsessions through linguistic command by imposing them on the silent image of woman still tied to her place as bearer of meaning, not maker of meaning" ("Visual," 586).

5. The phrase "sex/gender system" hails from Gayle Rubin's essay "The Traffic in

Women: Notes on the 'Political Economy' of Sex." Perhaps the following from that essay—particularly the phrase "oppresses everyone"—could be cited as evidence for Braidotti's claim that gender theorists miss the point about the asymmetries of sexual difference:

> Gender is a socially imposed division of the sexes. It is the product of the social relations of sexuality. . . . Far from being the expression of natural differences, exclusive gender identity is the suppression of natural similarities. It requires repression: in men, of whatever is the local version of "feminine" traits; in women, of the local definition of "masculine" traits. The division of the sexes has the effect of repressing some of the personality characteristics of virtually everyone, men and women. The same social system which oppresses women in its relations of exchange, oppresses everyone in its insistence upon a rigid division of personality. (546)

Also potentially problematic from a feminist perspective would be Rubin's later essay, "Thinking Sex: Notes for a Radical Theory of the Politics of Sexuality." There Rubin writes that "feminist thought simply lacks angles of vision which can fully encompass the social organization of sexuality. The criteria of relevance in feminist thought do not allow it to see or assess critical power relations in the area of sexuality. . . . Feminism is no more capable than Marxism of being the ultimate and complete account of all social inequality" (34). For discussion of both essays, see Rubin, with Butler, "Sexual."

6. These interjections are of course literally preposterous ("pre" what is "post") since in the mirror stage the infant, being without language, is not yet in a position to articulate anything about its image in the mirror, one way or the other.

7. In addition to Butler's critique of "the hetero-pathos that pervades the legacy of Lacanian psychoanalysis" ("Against," 20), see Michael Warner, "Homo-Narcissism."

8. In the fall of 1999, in the interest of finding out, among other things, to what extent men have been hired in positions advertised as "gender studies" in English language and literature departments in the United States, I conducted a survey in which I mailed a questionnaire to the heads of the 144 departments whose doctoral programs were listed in the "Rankings of Research-Doctorate Programs" in the September 1995 issue of the *Chronicle of Higher Education* (a list that ranged from Yale to Middle Tennessee State University). I cannot do full justice to the responses to this survey here. Suffice it to say that my research in-

dicates that appointments such as Braidotti describes have indeed been made. One respondent reported a case in which a long-fought-for "women's studies" position was changed to "gender studies" specifically so that a man might be hired. My thanks to all respondents, and to Elizabeth Wurz of the English Department at Georgia State University for her assistance in the survey.

9. Since I fault Braidotti for not giving examples, I should say here that I am thinking of the work of John Stoltenberg.

10. I assume the reader's familiarity with the concept of abjection, but provide the following for the unimmersed: As Butler informs us in *Bodies That Matter,* the word "abjection (in Latin, *ab-jicere*) literally means to cast off, away, or out and, hence presupposes and produces a domain of agency from which it is differentiated. . . . The notion of *abjection* designates a degraded or cast out status within the terms of sociality. Indeed, what is foreclosed or repudiated . . . may not reenter the field of the social without threatening . . . the dissolution of the subject itself" (243). In *Powers of Horror,* Julia Kristeva writes of the abject as that which "disturbs identity, system, order. What does not respect border, positions, rules" (4). She associates the abject with "what is jettisoned from the '*symbolic system*' . . . what escapes that social rationality, that logical order on which a social aggregate is based" (65). To the extent that what is jettisoned from any "symbolic system" relates symbolically to what is expelled from the individual body and its orifices, the abject is for Kristeva always related to fluids and products that traverse the body's boundaries, "polluting objects" that "always relate to corporeal orifices as to so many landmarks parceling-constituting the body's territory" (71): blood, saliva, milk, urine, mucus, semen, feces, tears. Thus abjection is the general realm of bodily fluidity, of filth, pollution, and defilement.

11. What allows Lacan to turn the turd back into the Phallus is, among other things, that triumvirate unity of feces, baby, and penis that Freud discusses in "On Transformations of Instinct as Exemplified in Anal Erotism" and elsewhere. See Freud, *On Sexuality,* 296. Typically, Freud and Lacan attempt to stabilize this unity through the always ultimately phallic appeal to castration anxiety. In my chapter on Freud in *Male Matters,* I attempt to destabilize the same unity by submitting, as it were, the penis to abject fecality. The bit about the letter arriving at its destination is a reference to Lacan's "Seminar on 'The Purloined Letter.'"

12. In *Male Matters,* in "Straight," and in an essay called "Cultural Droppings: Bersani's Beckett," forthcoming in *Twentieth Century Literature.*

13. In "Is the Rectum a Grave?" Bersani posits sexuality as self-shattering, and the

"self-shattering into the sexual as a kind of nonanecdotal self-debasement . . . in which, so to speak, the self is exuberantly discarded" (217–18). Bersani writes that

> the self which the sexual shatters provides the basis on which sexuality is associated with power. It is possible to think of the sexual as, precisely, moving between a hyperbolic sense of self and a loss of all consciousness of self. But sex as self-hyperbole is perhaps a repression of sex as self-abolition. It inaccurately replicates self-shattering as self-swelling, as psychic tumescence. If, as these words suggest, men are especially apt to "choose" this version of sexual pleasure, because their sexual equipment appears to invite by analogy, or at least to facilitate the phallicizing of the ego, neither sex has exclusive rights to the practice of sex as self-hyperbole. (218)

On Bersani's analysis, the hyperbolic self or phallicized ego cannot experience sexuality as anything but power, cannot give itself over to the "strong appeal of powerlessness, of the loss of control" (217). It cannot exuberantly discard and shatter itself *into* sexuality and so can have contact *with* sexuality only as the shattering discard of the devalued other. Phallocentrism, therefore, is according to Bersani "not primarily the denial of power to women (although it has obviously also led to that, everywhere and at all times), but above all the denial of the *value* of powerlessness in both men and women. I don't mean the value of gentleness, or nonaggressiveness, or even of passivity, but rather of a more radical disintegration and humiliation of the self" (217). But this subversion of phallocentrism through radical self-disintegration is, for Bersani, not only sexual but ethical, for it is, he says, "the sacrosanct value of selfhood [that] accounts for human beings' extraordinary willingness to kill in order to protect the seriousness of their statements. The self is a practical convenience; promoted to the status of an ethical ideal, it is a sanction for violence" (222).

14. Pronger explicitly refutes the suggestion "that men need to take on homosexual identities in order to be feminist. Indeed homosexual identity is no guarantor of feminist insight" ("On Your Knees," 77). Nor, it should be pointed out, are celebrations of male anal effusiveness per se any guarantor of feminism. In this regard, see Gardiner's essay, " 'South Park.' " For more on straight-male ass covering, see my essay in *Straight with a Twist* as well as "Afterword(s)," the conversation between Catherine MacGillivray and myself that concludes that volume.

15. We of course owe the notion that writing is devalued in the Western philosophical tradition to Jacques Derrida. See *Of Grammatology*.

16. The source of this information was a lecture by Professor Jan Nattier, of the Department of Religion at Indiana University, delivered at the Bodhi Manda Zen Center, Jemez Springs, New Mexico, June 1997. The information is, as I say, transcultural, but not universal for, as Nattier pointed out, in traditional Chinese culture, writing is highly valued and carries no such abject associations or proscriptions.

17. Though here I am working from Edelman's condensed definitions in the essay "Tearooms and Sympathy," see also *Homographesis*.

WORKS CITED

Abelove, Henry, Michèle Aina Barale, and David M. Halperin. "Introduction." In Henry Abelove, Michèle Aina Barale, and David M. Halperin, eds., *The Lesbian and Gay Studies Reader*, pp. xv–xvii. New York: Routledge, 1993.

Bersani, Leo. "Is the Rectum a Grave?" *October* 43 (Winter 1987): 197–222.

Butler, Judith. "Against Proper Objects." *differences: A Journal of Feminist Cultural Studies* 6.2/3 (1994): 1–26.

——. *Bodies That Matter: On the Discursive Limits of "Sex"*. New York: Routledge, 1993.

Braidotti, Rosi. *Patterns of Dissonance*. New York: Routledge, 1991.

Braidotti, Rosi, with Judith Butler. "Feminism by Any Other Name." *differences: A Journal of Feminist Cultural Studies* 6.2/3 (1994): 27–61.

Cixous, Hélène. "Sorties." In Julie Rivkin and Michael Ryan, eds., *Literary Theory: An Anthology*, pp. 578–84. New York: Blackwell, 1998.

Cornell, Drucilla. *Beyond Accommodation: Ethical Feminism, Deconstruction, and the Law*. New York: Routledge, 1991.

De Lauretis, Teresa. "Habit Changes." *differences: A Journal of Feminist Cultural Studies* 6.2/3 (1994): 296–313.

Derrida, Jacques. *Glas*. Trans. John P. Leavey and Richard Rand. Lincoln: University of Nebraska Press, 1986.

——. *Of Grammatology*. Trans. Gayatri Spivak. Baltimore: Johns Hopkins University Press, 1974.

Digby, Tom, ed. *Men Doing Feminism*. New York: Routledge, 1998.

Edelman, Lee. *Homographesis: Essays in Gay Literary and Cultural Theory.* New York: Routledge, 1993.

———. "Tearooms and Sympathy, or, the Epistemology of the Water Closet." In Henry Abelove, Michèle Aina Barale, and David M. Halperin, eds., *The Lesbian and Gay Studies Reader,* pp. 553–74. New York: Routledge, 1993.

Freud, Sigmund. *Civilization and Its Discontents.* Trans. James Strachey. New York: Norton, 1961.

———. *On Sexuality.* Trans. James Strachey. Vol. 7. Pelican Freud Library. Harmondsworth, Middlesex: Penguin, 1983.

Gardiner, Judith K. "*South Park,* Blue Men, Anality, and Market Masculinity." *Men and Masculinities* 2.3 (January 2000): 251–71.

Jameson, Fredric. *The Political Unconscious: Narrative as a Socially Symbolic Act.* Ithaca: Cornell University Press, 1982.

Kimmel, Michael. "Who's Afraid of Men Doing Feminism?" In Tom Digby, ed., *Men Doing Feminism,* pp. 57–68. New York: Routledge, 1998.

Kinnell, Galway. *Imperfect Thirst.* Boston: Houghton Mifflin, 1994.

Kristeva, Julia. *Powers of Horror: An Essay on Abjection.* Trans. Leon S. Roudiez. New York: Columbia University Press, 1982.

Lacan, Jacques. *Écrits: A Selection.* Trans. Alan Sheridan. New York: Norton, 1977.

———. "Seminar on 'The Purloined Letter.' " In John P. Muller and William J. Richardson, ed., *The Purloined Poe: Lacan, Derrida, and Psychoanalytic Reading,* pp. 28–54. Baltimore: Johns Hopkins University Press.

MacGillivray, Catherine A. F., with Calvin Thomas. "Afterword(s)." In Calvin Thomas, Joseph O. Aimone, and Catherine A. F. MacGillivray, eds., *Straight with a Twist: Queer Theory and the Subject of Heterosexuality,* pp. 253–80. Urbana: University of Illinois Press, 2000.

Modleski, Tania. *Feminism Without Women: Culture and Criticism in a "Postfeminist" Age.* New York: Routledge, 1991.

Mulvey, Laura. "Visual Pleasure and Narrative Cinema." In Julie Rivkin and Michael Ryan, eds., *Literary Theory: An Anthology,* pp. 585–95. New York: Blackwell, 1998.

Pronger, Brian. "On Your Knees: Carnal Knowledge, Masculine Dissolution, Doing Feminism." In Tom Digby, ed., *Men Doing Feminism,* pp. 69–80. New York: Routledge, 1998.

Rose, Jacqueline. "Introduction II." In Juliet Mitchell and Jacqueline Rose, eds., *Feminine Sexuality: Jacques Lacan and the école freudienne,* pp. 27–57. New York: Norton, 1982.

Rubin, Gayle S., with Judith Butler. "Sexual Traffic." *differences: A Journal of Feminist Cultural Studies* 6.2/3 (1994): 62–99.

———. "Thinking Sex: Notes for a Radical Theory of the Politics of Sexuality." In Henry Abelove, Michèle Aina Barale, and David M. Halperin, eds., *The Lesbian and Gay Studies Reader*, pp. 3–44. New York: Routledge, 1993.

———. "The Traffic in Women: Notes on the 'Political Economy' of Sex." In Julie Rivkin and Michael Ryan, eds., *Literary Theory: An Anthology*, pp. 533–60. New York: Blackwell, 1998.

Scott, Joan Wallach. *Gender and the Politics of History*. New York: Columbia University Press, 1988.

Silverman, Kaja. *Male Subjectivity at the Margins*. New York: Routledge, 1992.

Smith, Paul, and Alice Jardine, eds. *Men in Feminism*. New York: Methuen, 1986.

Thomas, Calvin. "Cultural Droppings: Bersani's Beckett." *Twentieth Century Literature* forthcoming.

———. *Male Matters: Masculinity, Anxiety, and the Male Body on the Line*. Urbana: University of Illinois Press, 1996.

———. "Straight with a Twist: Queer Theory and the Subject of Heterosexuality." In Calvin Thomas, Joseph A. Aimone, and Catherine A. F. MacGillivray, eds., *Straight with a Twist: Queer Theory and the Subject of Heterosexuality*, pp. 11–44. Urbana: University of Illinois Press, 2000.

Waldby, Catherine. "Destruction: Boundary Erotics and the Refigurations of the Heterosexual Male Body." In Elizabeth Grosz and Elspeth Probyn, eds., *Sexy Bodies: The Strange Carnalities of Feminism*, pp. 266–77. New York: Routledge, 1995.

Warner, Michael. "Homo-Narcissism: or, Heterosexuality." In Joseph A. Boone and Michael Cadden, eds., *Engendering Men: The Question of Male Feminist Criticism*, pp. 190–206. New York: Routledge, 1990.

3

THEORIZING AGE WITH GENDER: BLY'S BOYS, FEMINISM, AND MATURITY MASCULINITY

Judith Kegan Gardiner

> To advance this agenda we would need to rethink our notions of manhood and womanhood. Rather than continuing to see them as opposites, with different "inherent" characteristics, we would need to recognize biological differences without seeing them as markers of specific character traits. This would mean no longer thinking that it is "natural" for boys to be strong and girls to be weak, for boys to be active and girls passive. Our task in parenting and in education would be to encourage in both females and males the capacity to be wholistic, to be capable of being both strong and weak, active and passive, etc., in response to specific contexts. Rather than defining manhood in relation to sexuality, we would acknowledge it in relation to biology: boys become men, girls women, with the understanding that both categories are synonymous with selfhood.
> —bell hooks, *Killing Rage*

Like bell hooks in the passage above, many feminist theorists seek an end to oppositional conceptions of gender and instead call for a move toward androgyny, genderlessness, or "gender independence" (see Lorber, *Paradoxes*, 302; Bem, *Lenses*, 124–25; Burke, *Gender*, 231ff). They may see both masculinity and femininity as results of male dominance, which diminishes the range of personal characteristics culturally available to each sex and awards men power and prestige over women (MacKinnon, *Feminism*, 3). Hegemonic masculinity gives men a sense of superiority and of entitlement to advantages over women, and it valorizes in men characteristics such as aggression that harm women as well as other men

(Connell, *Masculinities*). In the quoted passage, hooks implies that gender should be minimized and redefined simply as a matter of biological maturational development. She argues that it would be healthier for us to understand that "boys become men" with regard to "biology," not "sexuality," in order to avoid reinforcing the kind of masculinity that limits men and demeans women. As I shall discuss, this is not an obvious distinction, since it is not self-evident that *sexuality*, as we usually understand the term, reinforces limiting forms of masculinity in men.

Although contemporary American culture emphasizes masculinity as gender oppositional, current conceptions of masculinity involve its developmental aspects as well. That is, they define being a man not only in opposition to being a woman or a male homosexual but also in opposition to being a boy. In this essay, I suggest that age categories provide useful analogies for nonpolarized ways of conceptualizing gender. In addition, I argue that age categories should play a more prominent role in feminist theorizing about gender, so that gender is always understood developmentally in terms of change over the life course and in history rather than in terms of a static and binary opposition between masculine and feminine. I differentiate feminist from masculinist versions of such theories, with special attention to the books of influential men's movement guru Robert Bly. Bly made a dramatic shift from a gender-based critique of society in his popular book *Iron John*, to a more recent diatribe against American youth culture and its attitudes to aging in *The Sibling Society*. His sexist views indicate potential pitfalls in attempts to theorize gender developmentally, and they also expose fault lines in contemporary patriarchy. Bly's writings help diagnose the popularly decried "crisis of masculinity" in contemporary U.S. culture as in fact a crisis of patriarchal entitlement, yet his developmental focus on both age and gender nonetheless holds open some possibilities for progressive feminist transformation.

Boys become men in more complicated ways than the quotation from hooks implies. Such dissonances indicate problems theorizing gender in terms of developmental categories that a more comprehensive theory would need to solve. Her main goal is to reduce the salience of gender, detaching "manhood" and "womanhood" from inhibiting characteristics of personality and attaching them instead to socially neutral "biological differences" between the sexes. Like proponents of androgyny, she wants positive personal traits like strength and activity distributed among men and women without regard to their anatomical sex, while she would have all people aspire to "selfhood," apparently for her a category of developmental wholeness, completion, perhaps even psychological and spiritual fulfillment. Indeed, she would have all people be "wholistic," containing all positive potentials and characteristics, with specific manifestations of their personalities determined contextually in varying situations rather than consistently stunted by the gender divide. Such a transformation in people's characters would require dramatic changes in the social environment, so that the contexts in which each person could exhibit strength, activity, and other traits would not be polarized, as they are now, by cultural expectations about gender—or, presumably, by other culturally induced inhibitions, like those formed in response to being placed in racialized or ethnic categories. Hooks's most puzzling pronouncement in the passage above is that manhood should not be defined by "sexuality" but rather by "biology," a statement that diverges from her earlier careful gender parallelisms to separate manhood as a highlighted problem in a way that womanhood is not and to substitute *sexuality* for the expected term, *gender,* or for such specifically negative traits as dominance or habitual aggression. The term sexuality, however, is deeply suggestive, especially in light of contemporary queer theories, which remind us that heteronormativity is one of the chief means through which oppositional and dominating masculinity in men is created and sustained (see Ross, "Race, Rape, Castration," this volume).

In saying that "boys become men, girls women," hooks urges developmental rather than oppositional definitions of manhood and womanhood: she posits "men" and "women" as adult states into which children grow. Since she urges both adult sexes to acquire "selfhood," she seems to be requiring more than mere physical maturity to achieve these desired states, but also emotional, psychological, and spiritual growth. In her model, these adult states would seem to be more complete and comprehensive than the conditions of childhood, so that boys and girls would not become narrower as they grow and are socialized, not more constrained but rather freer to express a fuller range of potentials. Thus hooks apparently partitions gender, or whatever it means to be a man or a woman in a given society, into a polarized biology that should bear no social weight and a generalized human potential for individuality. This individuality is understood not as the distinctiveness accrued from a collection of unique and disparate traits but as an internally perceived spiritual and psychological wholeness and fulfillment that require an appropriate social context in which to materialize. In contrast to this complex thinking about gender, however, she effaces the social construction of maturity, taking it as a natural category not requiring careful theorization. Yet her own formulation is not simple. She describes maturity as an individual achievement rather than the automatic consequence of time. Furthermore, she doesn't even acknowledge the possibility, dear to many contemporary pundits, that biology is itself the source of natural and essential gender polarization, so that men's biological development would be shaped by testosterone or other specifically male genetic or hormonal endowments that would produce the "specific character traits" she denies are "inherent." I agree with hooks that developmental conceptions of gender can decrease sexist polarization, but I question her assumption here that the progressions of age are natural, inevitable, universal, and simple.

In its original context, the hooks passage quoted above appears in an essay that appeals to African Americans to repudiate the "patriarchal paradigm" in order to further an autonomous "black liberation struggle" (68). Her effort to depolarize gender thus fosters a larger goal of unifying the African American community against a specific history that infantilized as well as emasculated African American men. This context highlights the fact that age, like gender, is a social, not merely biological, category, and whom a society considers boys or men is very much a feminist issue. Whereas current feminist theory has worked hard to incorporate nuanced understandings of racialized differences and those of sexual orientation, however, it has not seen age as so important a category, a failing that I suggest requires remedy.

CONCEPTUALIZING AGE WITH GENDER

Although not completely ignored in contemporary discourses, age tends to be an undertheorized category in comparison to gender. I think that it has promising attributes for feminist theory and strategy now, especially as both age and gender are taking new shapes in the United States today. I see age as important to feminist theorizing in two separate ways. The first is that age categories can provide useful analogies for thinking about gender more flexibly and thus point to rigidities in current models that inadvertently reinforce the very polarizations that most feminist theories seek to avoid. Thus a new model could facilitate a wider range of ways of thinking about gender. Second, I argue that age categories should form a more integral part in feminist theories of gender so that all gender would be conceptualized developmentally. Moreover, developmental models should also be rethought, not consigned to an automatic progression from girl to woman and boy to man but understood as deeply social and mutable.

With respect to analogies, age has important parallels with gender. All societies recognize and make use of differing age categories, just as they do differing gender categories. Age categories, like gender ones, correlate with differences in social power, status, and access to resources. Like gender, age categories form part of systems of power relations that shape and are shaped by all other social hierarchies (see, for example, Doyle and Paludi, *Sex*). Similarly, like gender, age appears to have an obvious biological basis in a way that many other social categories, like social class, do not, although biological sex manifests itself as more dimorphic than either such markers of gender as aggression or activity or the gradations of biological aging.

These analogies with age can help facilitate more flexible thinking about gender. The most obvious advantage of age categories over gendered ones is that although they are sometimes seen in binary terms, more frequently they are understood as continuous as well as oppositional. Although laws separate age categories into two, those of dependent minors and responsible adults, for many purposes society sees age as a continuum that divides into several broadly differentiated but overlapping, sometimes conflicting, categories. Whereas gender is usually seen as permanent, dichotomous, and stable, age is seen as changing, continuous, and unidirectional. The categories of boy and man are sometimes treated as oppositional, although more frequently as developmental, with one leading to the other rather than conflicting with it. In contrast, both popular opinion and some feminist theories regard gender as oppositional, not merely relational, with masculinity defined in opposition to femininity and frequently as dominant over it (e.g. MacKinnon, *Feminism*). Similarly, whereas masculinity and femininity are felt as internal characteristics that define men and women not only to others but also to themselves, becoming deep and fixed aspects of individual identity, this is less true of age categories, which are sequential through the lifespan. Most people expect to live through the full range of age categories and are expected to behave in rough concordance with the conventions for each stage. Although people are defined in part by their age, however, age is not usually seen as an intrinsic attribute of personality in the way gender is. On the contrary, older persons often say they do not recognize themselves as old but maintain a sense of themselves as forever younger than their chronological age (Woodward, *Aging,* 149). Thus dissonance between biological age and self-perception is considered normal, though often comic, in comparison with dissonance between biological sex and self-defined gender, which is often considered tragic. (Currently, the affluent can resort to surgical remedy for both kinds of dissonance.) Socially, gender has been treated as dichotomous and dimorphic not only as a conceptual category but also in terms of people's experiences. That is, men have rarely experienced life as women, and vice versa, although the fascination with passing narratives and the current possibilities of sexual reassignment surgery have made the gender divide seem more permeable, more like the divisions of age.

Analogies with age may also help clarify the falsity of dichotomizing views about gender between biological essentialism and social constructionism. Age begins as a biological category that is intrinsically tied to those genuinely essential definers of human existence: temporality, embodiment, and mortality. Many markers of age are bodily changes to which people respond strongly, both positively and negatively. At the same time, it is clear that considerable social pressure, not just the passage of time, goes into creating age divisions. Such categories are not innocent, not obvious, and often seem arbitrary. The age of majority is an obvious example, since the legal age varies from place to place and may vary by gender. Even in a single locale, the age of majority may vary for functions that are presumed to be concommitants of maturity, such as the rights to drive, work for wages, buy alcohol or cigarettes, serve in the military, marry, or vote. With respect to gender theory, there has perhaps been too easy an assumption that conservatives take a biological view of gender in believing that genes and innate physical characteristics determine personality, likely behavior, and appropriate social ideals, whereas progressives are assumed to be social constructionists. This political division between biological and social explanations is over-simplifed and confusing. As feminist and queer theorist Eve Sedgwick points out, the belief that a trait is genetic, hormonal, or otherwise bio-logically determined does not mean that the characteristic is socially ac-cepted or free from attempts to control it (*Tendencies*, 163–64).[1] This ea-gerness to alter the "natural" is especially clear in the case of aging. With regard to age, a biological basis for bodily change is acknowledged, even as the changes themselves are persistently contested through social means.

Another advantage of age as a clarifying analogy for thinking about gender is that we understand age as not only biologically and socially constructed but also as performative, with the performance strongly af-fected by evaluative norms that vary by culture. What does it mean to act your age—or to act your gender? Performative theories of gender that are popular among academic theorists remain highly contested in the culture at large (see Butler, *Gender*). In contrast, the idea is wide-spread that people may or may not act in congruity with their chrono-logical age. Transgressions of both age and gender are socially policed, though with varying sanctions. Thus young performers are frequently praised for exhibiting adult poise and accomplishment, while the el-derly, especially old women, are frequently ridiculed for trying to look too young. These standards for behavior according to age vary in emo-tional charge according to gender, indicating the need for a conceptual model that integrates age with gender categories.

The fact that whole societies are always composed of people at differ-ing stages of the life cycle tends to be conceptualized in terms of dis-parate generations and social conflicts. A favorite newspaper drollery is the centuries-old quotation of elders complaining about the wild habits of youth, though older people are also presumed to retain some empa-thy for the younger people they once resembled. More recently, a popu-lar theme has been the reluctance of the young to assume responsibility for the growing cohort of the dependent old. Issues of dependence, in-dependence, and interdependence are intrinsic to American understand-ings of age. Naturalized as part of each person's life cycle, problems in navigating such issues are acknowledged as both normal and difficult, complicating each individual's relationships with authority in the family, other institutions, and the state. Age, unlike gender, is thus a category in which asymmetries of power and experience are overt rather than masked and are openly debated as matters of social policy and communal welfare. Furthermore, it is perhaps more obvious with regard to age than to gender that differences in power between members of different categories are fundamentally affected by social custom and policy. Although some people claim that gender differences can be complementary distinctions denoting equal worth and detachable from differences in power, the model of age categories at least problematizes that belief, especially in the conflation of the categories of women and children as persons needing protection from the valorized category of men. So, too, it is perhaps clearer in the case of age than of gender that the common categories used to describe them continually slip back and forth between descriptions of typical behavior and prescriptions for how people should be and behave, with a wide range of material consequences meted out to those who deviate from the behaviors considered proper for each group.

Temporality is integral to conceptualizing an integrated age-gender system. This appears to be a tautology: age seems to have time built into its very meaning, since each individual experiences physical and emotional changes both inwardly and in interaction with others during the course of the lifespan. However, thinking about age does not in fact always acknowledge temporality as involving historical change. The life cycle may pose as a static model, like a stationary bicycle, which spins in place without going anywhere. In such a model, each person's changing stages over time may become assimilated into an apparently timeless and unchanging society whose components are people ceaselessly turned upon the wheel of time or climbing, then descending, a fixed series of steps from dependence to independence and back again. In contrast, truly historical approaches socially contextualize both gender and age. For example, Phillipe Ariès proposed that childhood, understood as a distinct life stage, is a relatively modern Western invention (*Centuries*, 33–49). Those theorists who historicize age may or may not take gender into account. Psychologist Erik Erikson, for instance, articulated the adolescent "identity crisis" of the mid twentieth century with men in mind; he thought that this stage was activated by a specific cultural context in which middle-class young men sought their vocations and other allegiances after a long period of unspecialized education. Such dilemmas of identification did not explain the lives of young women in the same way, because, he thought, they found their identities, as women had done for centuries, through intimacy and marriage rather than through vocation and aspiration (*Identity*, 265–66). Betty Friedan agreed with Erikson's analysis of men but argued that women, too, were coming to face their own "identity crisis," one manifested in the inchoate unhappiness of the "problem that has no name" among married, well-educated, middle-class mothers (*Feminine*, 11). "For the first time in their history, women are becoming aware of an identity crisis in their own lives," she said (72). Her solution was for these women to join men of their class in seeking vocations other than marriage and motherhood. She thus saw the need for "a new life plan" for women as a historical problem, but she articulated it less as a developmental issue than as an existential crux: "Who knows what women can be when they are finally free to become themselves?" (364).

One reason that today's feminists may not have been thinking of age as a promising category through which to conceptualize gender, I surmise, is that male and female aging are culturally marked in highly asymmetrical ways: the devaluation of older women is a significant part of the the sexist assessment of all women according to their appearance and sexual desirability (Gullette, *Declining*, 56–58). Moreover, age categories are often assumed to demean and separate women so that women are tempted to avoid or obfuscate them. Although for both sexes society imagines a typical developmental ascent from infancy to maturity, followed by decline into old age, men are usually credited with a longer plateau at their prime, whereas women climb the slope of social desirability more swiftly and are more rapidly thrown from its peak (Woodward, *Aging*, 16). Moreover, women's sexual desirability in our society is measured by standards of youthful female beauty that affect the way women of all ages are treated, even women in authority. Older men with power, wealth, or a modicum of physical fitness remain accepted as sexual subjects who are also sexually desirable in a way that older women are not, and older men are still freer than women from even being considered as physical presences or sexual objects, although this seems to be changing (Bordo, *Male*, 168–200). Popular culture emphasizes biological markers more for female than male aging. Menarche, childbearing, and menopause, all related to reproduction, are treated as significant milestones in the female life cycle. In contrast, there are no such socially recognized markers for men. Men retain the advantage of having the male life cycle privileged as normative and conceived of as unimpeded by the abrupt biological changes attributed to women. Those men who claim to envy female life-stage markers, even as they enjoy their freedom from them, may invent ritual substitutes and so imply that men's aging is more spiritual and less physical than women's aging and hence superior to it. The occasional feminist reversal of such sexist terms has seemed shocking when it subjects the aging male body to treatment like that habitually meted out to women. For example, in a climactic scene in *Their Eyes Were Watching God,* Zora Neale Hurston's heroine, Janey, deflates her self-important second husband by publicly claiming that under his pants he, too, looked like the "change of life." He dies of humiliation (123).[2]

Recently, feminists have been increasing their attention to stages in the female life course, especially with regard to education, policy, and law; for example, the fall in contemporary American girls' self-esteem at puberty has garnered considerable attention and calls for school reform (see American Association of University Women, *Growing;* Pipher, *Reviving*). Much of this feminist concern is targeted at specific age groups, for instance, at nonsexist mathematics and science education for girls or pension and health benefits for elderly women, rather than considering the whole life cycle. Such issues as educational success and access to retirement pensions are highly raced and classed as well as divided by age, so that many problems of old women and of very young mothers, for example, are also disproportionately problems of the poor and of people of color, a fact that divides these issues among single-issue activists and obscures them from some feminist theories (see Coontz, *Way;* Hewlett and West, *War;* Males, *Scapegoat;* Sidel, *Keeping*). For both men and women, adulthood usually remains a largely unmarked category, the assumed norm and standard of comparison, as whiteness and masculinity previously were, against which the problems of childhood and old age are discussed.[3] Thus there are many barriers to conceptualizing an integrated theory of the relationships between age and gender categories, but the very effort may also serve to clarify the operations of age and

gender hierarchies as well as those of racialized and other more frequently theorized divisions in our society.

BLY'S BOYS AND STUNTED SIBLINGS

Robert Bly is one influential theorist of masculinity who
has moved from a focus on oppositional gender to one on developmental age categories. Indeed, when I suggested at a meeting of the Men's
Studies Association that feminists might foster developmental models of
masculinity, I was repeatedly referred to Bly as the authority on the subject. His popular book of 1990, *Iron John,* argued that masculinity was in
crisis and that the solution was to reinforce the "deep masculine" in
men. His more recent book, *The Sibling Society* (1996), marked a significant turn from a focus on gender relations to a focus on age categories
in modern society, although his original gender theory was conceived in
age-based terms and his newer age theories remain sexist.[4] Despite significant flaws, I think his effort to focus social awareness on age-based,
as well as gender-based, categories merits further feminist attention.
Furthermore, the very contradictions in Bly's thinking illuminate possibilities and problems for articulating a nonsexist, age-inflected, developmental model of masculinity.

Bly and other members of the Jungian-influenced "mythopoetic"
men's movement have widely disseminated the main tenets of *Iron John.*
Bly's original premise is that men have a deep, biological, essential maleness that is part of their "genetic inheritance" (x). If that "genetic inheritance" in itself were adequate to confirm men's masculinity, Bly would
be in agreement with hooks's feminist viewpoint. However, Bly does
not, like hooks, see this biological maleness simply as a relatively unim-
portant physical fact. Instead, he believes that masculinity determines
what ought to be men's social roles, identity, sexuality, personalities, and
behavior. Despite the fundamental importance and naturalness he sees
in masculinity, however, its contents are hazy. He claims that most men
today experience their own masculinity as fragile and vulnerable. Modern culture vitiates this deep masculinity and feminism, especially, rav-
ages men's self-esteem as men. According to Bly, many men now feel
wounded and ashamed of their maleness, that is, "demasculinized," because, when they were boys, their fathers were absent from their lives or

because they absorbed their frustrated mothers' rages, private rages that feminism now generalizes as public causes (171).

Thus Bly pictures modern masculinity in *Iron John* in mutually contradictory ways that illustrate its confused representations in our culture. Masculinity is at the same time an intrinsic timeless inheritance, or original birthright, of each male human, a modern social problem, and a difficult, elusive developmental goal that requires outside male intervention for its achievement. As his own contribution to the massive task of helping modern men regain their imperiled masculinity, Bly tells stories that he alleges are socially beneficial because they acknowledge men's inner wounds and begin to heal them. He leads his readers through an initiatory fairy-tale journey that shows the necessity of a man's "clean break" from his father and, more crucially, his mother, describes a masculine inner wildness that needs to be honored and preserved, and validates older men's guidance of younger men "into the ancient, mythologized, instinctive male world" of "distinctively male values" (14–15). According to Bly, only fathers and other men, not mothers, can properly develop masculinity in their sons, since masculinity by this definition is a matter of making men more manly. If, as too often happens, a woman brings up a boy alone, her son will suffer a sad loss of identity; overly influenced by a woman, he will have "no male face" (17). Moreover, only under hierarchical forms of male authority can boys develop into proper men: "democratic or nonlinear approaches" will fail to achieve freedom for men or stability for the community (12). Thus Bly's views in *Iron John* rest on a biologically essential, sexist, highly polarized conception of gender that is often vague about the specific content of masculinity but utilizes a language of developmental stages through which a boy may gradually become a man.

In *Iron John* Bly frequently phrases his goals for men and masculinity in age-related terms. Despite his myths about boys becoming men, he addresses middle-aged men, not boys, as his primary audience, that is, as those who are yet undeveloped and need his help to achieve full mature manhood. For example, he claims that "by the time a man is thirty-five he knows that the images of the right man, the tough man, the true man which he received in high school do not work in life. Such a man is open" to the "new visions of what a man is or could be" that he is ready to provide (ix). Whereas the "defective mythologies" of our culture "work to keep men boys," Bly claims that better mythologies and older male mentors can help confused, immature, middle-aged men become simultaneously more masculine and more mature (x). For Bly, therefore, boyhood is a beginning stage that may be prolonged or permanent, rather than automatically ending at puberty, unless the undeveloped man follows the eight stages he describes of the mythopoetic "initiatory path" to manhood, with proper effort and guidance from older men like himself (xi).

Bly's views have been widely criticized as ahistorical, inaccurate, ethnocentric, racist, and sexist. Lambasting Bly as "massively wrong," for example, sociologist Bob Connell attacks his lack of reliable evidence, his incoherent arguments, and his stereotyped thinking, calling *Iron John* "appallingly bad: over-generalised, under-researched, incoherent (and at times self-contradictory)" (Connell, "Men," 81).[5] Some of Bly's profeminist critics specifically attack his handling of age divisions among men, charging that he infantilizes men. For instance, Michael Kimmel sees Bly's quest for "deep" masculinity as "developmentally atavistic" (Kimmel, *Politics*, 320). Kimmel and Michael Kaufman compare Bly to Peter Pan and say that the mythopoetic movement encourages adult men to think of themselves as unfathered sons rather than responsible fathers: "The search for the deep masculine is actually a search for lost boyhood, that homosocial innocence of preadolescence" before work, family, and responsibility to women (36).[6] Yet, unlike critiques of Bly's avowed essentialism, attacks against him for keeping men as boys seem to run counter to his expressed views, where he repeatedly argues that he helps puerile men become more mature. Some of this criticism may spring from the mythopoetic movement's popular representations, in which white men gather around campfires in the woods drumming on tom-toms. Hattie gossett, for example, criticizes the childishness as well as the ethnocentrism of this men's movement by describing it as just "a bunch of boys playing games with the cultures of people they don't know how to live next door to" (gossett, "min's," 21; cf. Steinem, "Forward"; Hagan, *Women*).

Bly's rebuttals of his profeminist critics demonstrate how central age categories are to his thinking and how intertwined with masculinism. He continues to posit men's need for an essential, deep masculinity. "If there is no such thing as masculinity, then a man has no center in himself from which he can speak," Bly says. Yet he distinguishes his position from a defense of patriarchy on explicitly age-related grounds. "None of us wants to reestablish patriarchy," he claims, because its "destructive essence" is that which "moves to kill the young masculine" (in Kimmel, *Politics,* 272). This is an idiosyncratic definition of patriarchy as lethal enmity by fathers against sons. It minimizes patriarchy's baleful effects on women but decries it for pitting men against one another, as some profeminist masculinity theorists also do, yet, in contrast with them, he seeks the reinforcement rather than the restructuring of traditional masculinity: "Patriarchy has damaged masculinity," Bly says. His critics, too, damage masculinity, he claims, because they undermine men's self-confidence in their maleness. Today, "many young men," he says, "rather than being ashamed of being patriarchal, are ashamed of being men. To be ashamed of your gender is not healthful for anyone" ("Thoughts," 274). Bly's mythologizing thus disguises the unequal competitions between men through which some, more socially advantaged, dominate others. Instead, it focuses on men's feelings of shame and disempowerment. In contrast to these negative conditions, he posits an imaginary harmonious and static hierarchy that depends on age gradations for masculine fulfillment: in such a society, all men could presumably mature to the status of proper fathers or wise elders and so fulfill their deep need for a socially validated masculinity. Such a vision is deeply reactionary, fighting change as negative and subsuming age categories into timelessness.

Bly's more recent book, *The Sibling Society,* switches from gender to age categories to propound a bold new thesis: the major problem with the contemporary United States is not that it fails to honor "the masculine" but that it inhibits anyone from becoming an adult and produces, instead, an anarchic "lateral" society of self-indulgent, irresponsible, sometimes violent "half-adults" passively in thrall to the media, the internet, and deconstructionist academics (vii). This thesis builds upon the longing for a society that values mature masculinity expressed in *Iron John* and also responds to Bly's earlier critics. Instead of focusing on boys' individual psychology, this book looks at a historically changing culture in which one can intervene and on multiple causes of social problems, including changes in family structure and child rearing, economic changes, and the increasing power of ideologies transmitted through the media, not on myths or supposedly essential truths of eternal nature. Attacked for sexism, Bly here includes women both among the adolescent "siblings" he decries and the "adults" he values. Moreover, he quotes extensively from feminist scholars and defers to his wife's and daughter's editorial advice (35, 297). Accused of being a Peter Pan, or "Pied Piper," who led men into the woods like little lost boys, in this book Bly attacks the culture at large precisely for its immaturity, an immaturity that has nothing to do with the demographics of an aging American population but rather with the social values he deplores (Connell, "Men," 81).

In contrast to his dualistic conception of gender, Bly's categories concerning age exhibit a number of the positive characteristics I ascribed to age categories more generally—chiefly, a less polarized view of gender, but also a more complex acknowledgment of temporality, history, social forces, and relations of power, authority, and dependence. Rather than the two divisions to which modern gender is usually limited, Bly customarily refers to at least four large divisions of age: childhood, adolescence, adulthood, and old age. These age stages do not progress along the expected developmental curve; rather, he views contemporary adolescence as morally regressing from childhood innocence, and he privileges the wisdom of old age over younger adulthood. Bly expresses particular sympathy for the plight of children. He believes they are too often victims of busy and successful as well as of poor and resourceless adults: "Perhaps this is the first time in human history that children, en masse, have picked up the idea that they are not wanted, not needed," he says (232). In the sibling society he describes, adolescents and their clones rule, while the old and the young are "thrown away" (132). Because this society abandons its children, they express "the deepening rage of the unparented" at adults (132). Bly claims that "capitalism has siphoned off male energy so as to allow deeper exploitation of children. If we knew what children are suffering inside, we would beg every man we meet on the street to give up his career and become a father" (130). This odd statement does not prescribe economic or social solutions for the ills of capitalism but rather displaces the duties of fatherhood from the speaker and his audience to men "on the street," apparently career men who only need exhortation, not better job conditions, to spend more time at home with their children.[7]

Focusing on age categories allows Bly to express more flexible conceptions of gender in *The Sibling Society* than he did in *Iron John,* rendering it as more complex and historically changeable. In particular, he describes masculinity as a variable quantity that properly increases and decreases over each man's lifespan, so that striving for maximum masculinity is not the goal. Bly stresses the adaptability of human infants here, not a biological determinism about gender. Unlike many feminists, however, he sees childhood's original "neutral genderlessness" as a problem that requires men to initiate boys into "genuine masculinity" instead of an opening for alternative possibilities that are stifled in a sexist society (116). Thus he describes masculinity as a singular, though still vague, developmental goal. Boys must slowly travel toward "this unknown, barely imagined place called masculinity," while youth flaunts it and properly mature men stand securely upon it. Bly believes that older people again become more androgynous: "for grown men, serious change today usually means moving into expressiveness," entailing both "reconnection with the feminine" and "reconnection with the deeper side of masculinity" (84). Surprisingly, given his repeated denunciations of the evils of gender approximation, Bly claims that in the mature "vertical thought" he champions, "there is no distinction between men and women" (211). Those people who learn to "think vertically" may advance toward becoming wise elders, and these "highly respected" teachers and "older men and women in each community" will draw "young people over the line" into adulthood "by their very example" (211, 237).

However, Bly's later book often relapses into his old errors of unsupported generalizations, contradictions, racism, sexism, ethnocentrism, and methodological sloppiness. The "sibling society" is a capacious concept that allows him to deride many aspects of contemporary culture, and often his commentary on American age relations gets lost in colorful jeremiads. For example, he claims that American youth has changed "from the optimistic, companionable, food-passing youngsters" of the hippie era "to the self-doubting, dark-hearted, turned-in, death-praising, indifferent, wised-up, deconstructionist audience" of grunge music, a tirade that confuses one French philosophy with American adolescent nihilism (7). Even more fiercely, he attacks "the rise of child prostitution, Satanic sacrifice of infants, Congressional assault on support for children, the abandonment of children to television, a cruelty almost Aztec in its thoroughness," a marvellous mishmash of the mundane and monstrous that equates leaving children in front of television sets with ripping their hearts out and that blithely omits either documenting the alleged atrocities or suggesting realistic solutions to them, like restoring government support programs for poor children (243).

Some of the glaring problems of *The Sibling Society* apparently work against my claim that age categories provide helpful analogies for the feminist theorizing of gender. I take them, however, as useful precisely because they highlight potential pitfalls of sexist age categories as models for rethinking gender. Bly's masculinist use of the age paradigm for social criticism shows his commitment to the project of restoring patriarchy that he disavows elsewhere. He does not claim men's simple superiority over women, as earlier masculinists did, but he still reveals a longing for a kind of male power that shows the alleged modern "crisis of masculinity" as a frustrated sense of entitlement to patriarchy, construed as the sanctioned authority of some older men over the rest of society. The politics of *The Sibling Society* remain committed to allegedly ancient hierarchies and suspicious of any movements toward democracy or equality. Bly lauds a purportedly past "vertical" society in which older generations, embodied in and led by valued mentors, transmitted their timeless wisdom to younger generations in a way that precludes social change. He says this vaguely situated good old order, the "paternal society, now discredited," was based on restraint, control, and the superego (vii). In contrast, today's sibling society is selfish, immature, iddriven, violent, leaderless, and adrift. Bly's imaginary anthropology here is again sexist, as well as racist and elitist: the "paternal" society he describes is structured by the values that some feminists have characterized as the typically male, white Western, and middle-class concomitants of civilization and control, while his other-directed, superficial "siblings" sound like stereotyped versions of the working class, ethnic and racialized groups, women, and children. For example, he decries the "aggression of fatherless gangs among the disadvantaged," one of those implicitly racialized generalizations that make the youthful and nonwhite members of the purported underclass the fall guys for larger social problems (37).

Bly's *Sibling Society* thus reveals a strategy that is also at work in *Iron John* and other masculinist men's studies. It implies that its speaker and audience are real men, opposed to the half-men siblings, and, as such, are all entitled to, and in Bly's ideal system indeed could have, the advantages that a highly hierarchical system in fact restricts to a few wealthy and powerful men and denies to women and most other men. Bly accomplishes this obfuscation by shifts among family metaphors, psychological myths, and political assertions, jumbling attacks on capitalism or Congress with vague appeals to paternal responsibility. Every man is indeed a son and has the potential to be a mature father or mentor, a progressive and egalitarian aspect of Bly's thinking, yet patriarchal practice requires a few men to hold advantages over the many. As Bly illustrates, patriarchy promises all men the advantages of male privilege, inciting feelings of resentment and frustrated entitlement to those who feel deprived of it. At the same time, it categorizes most men as inferior and so unworthy of these privileges, inciting competition to be at the top and meting out humiliation and shame to those who do not succeed (cf. Chodorow, "The Enemy Outside," this volume). One of the evils of the sibling society, Bly says, is that it dangerously teaches that "no one is superior to anyone else" (131). It is the culture of the mass, which is the mob, which is the fatherless who hate older men's authority and therefore want social transformation: "the idea that each of us has the right to change everything is a deep insult" to wise adults who want to preserve past traditions (238). Although in *The Sibling Society* he shifts attention from gender to age, Bly's masculinist notions about gender continue to shape his age categories, which otherwise might substitute age privileges available to everyone who lives long enough for masculinist privileges available only to some men. Acknowledging that women can be wise elders, he nevertheless assumes that elder women should lead only girls, whereas boys need men and all-male institutions, and his solutions for curing the sibling society therefore return to the same nostrums he gave for curing the lost, soft men of *Iron John*.

As sloppy a thinker as Bly is, his shift from gender to age categories is both promising and illuminating—promising, in that it indicates how attention to age categories can complicate, depolarize, and contextualize discussions of gender, and illuminating about the limits of age-related categories when sexist assumptions prevail and undermine their progressive potential. Bly jumbles categories of age, parenthood, familial location, change over the individual life cycle, changing generational and

gendered expectations over historical periods, and metaphorical relations of authority in relation to other discourses of power, nurture, and
concern. Part of Bly's appeal to white, middle-class American men may
be that his writings acknowledge not only the desire to be the big daddy
oneself but also the recurrent pleasures of male bonding and dependency, containing them within a life cycle paradigm that promises an ultimate, but perhaps not continuous, maturity. Kenneth Clatterbaugh objects that Bly minimizes male violence and aggression by calling them
immature rather than evil ("Mythopoetic," 53–55).[8] Without excusing
criminal behavior, however, I think that Bly's approach may sometimes
be more persuasive in modeling preferred behaviors and in allowing
men repeated appeals and dependencies to mentors and fathers.

Thus Bly's thinking illustrates both some positive possibilities and
some limits of a masculinist, age-based model of society. He records
some real changes in the construction of American patriarchy today in
comparison with the past, and his popularity in the 1990s indicates that
he touched a chord resonating to some men's frustrations and expectations of entitlement. I have suggested that by awarding honor to maturity he provides a model for a more egalitarian social ideal than his exal-
tation of essential masculinity. In formulating his social analysis in *The
Sibling Society*, he is sometimes able to use the more empathic, flexible,
nondualistic, and historically variable categories of age, rather than the
more polarized categories of gender, to analyze contemporary society. As
a result, in *The Sibling Society*, Bly is at once a recorder of changing constructions of age in American culture, a compassionate spokesman for
children and the aged, a sexist ideologue, and a figure symptomatic of
the contradictory ideas about age and gender found within masculinist
thinking and patriarchal culture. Moreover, his writings demonstrate
that an analysis of the category of age is necessary to unveil the justifications of patriarchy, even though its rhetoric masks and naturalizes,
rather than explains, inequalities between men and between men and
women.

FEMINIST AGE AND GENDER STUDIES

Perhaps surprisingly, many of Bly's complaints about our
society's attitudes to age reverberate with those made recently by femi-

nist writers who also see a "teening of America," in its commodification
of images of youth and its disrespect for age, although they disagree
with his assessments of the causes of the problems and the preferable alternatives.[9] Barbara Ehrenreich describes the decline of patriarchy as a
change that does not eliminate sexism or misogyny but rather, as Bly
and others complain, the domestic rule of the father and his obligations
to family. Like Bly, she too decries men's decreasing interest in children
and their incorporation into "the post-countercultural world of unisex
consumption," although she blames economic and historical changes for
these conditions more coherently than Bly does (Ehrenreich, *Hearts*, 15;
cf. Faludi, *Stiffed*). The decline of the family wage has decreased men's
authority in the family, she believes, and made them less willing to share
their income with women and children. Like Bly, Ehrenreich thinks
that there were advantages for women in the postwar "breadwinner
ethic" that validated the man who married and supported his wife and
children as a "grown-up," a real man (11). Unlike Bly, however, Ehrenreich sees the loss of older men's authority as a gain for women: "If the
male revolt (against breadwinning) has roots in a narcissistic consumer
culture," it nevertheless moves toward an "androgynous goal"; the "possibility of honest communication between the sexes has been increased,"
she believes, and the "male revolt" may also imply a gain for individual
men's autonomy against corporate conformity and government control (70). Ehrenreich argues that "the decline of patriarchy" can lead to a
better, more egalitarian society, without a hierachy of older over
younger people, exactly the model that Bly finds so appalling: in a world
without fathers or paternalism, "we will have to learn to be brothers and
sisters," she says (182); "potentially, we can be brothers and sisters, comrades and lovers" ("Decline," 290). While she wants a more egalitarian
social order, however, she also seeks to "rebuild the notion of *personal*
commitment, and . . . give new strength and shared meaning to the
words we have lost—responsibility, maturity, and even, perhaps, manliness" (*Hearts*, 182). Ehrenreich's list of personal goals appeals to older
ideals of both age and gender. On the other hand, these "words we have
lost" elegiacally slide past the analogy that makes patriarchal imagery so
slippery and dangerous, that between family and society. What does it
mean to be "brothers and sisters" in civil society or a modern economy?
Can such a conception include necessary but nonoppressive relation-

ships of authority and dependency, a question that is the obverse of analyzing how the metaphorical term *patriarchy* obscures differences
among old men, fathers, and men with economic and social authority in
relation to women and other men.

Other profeminist writers join Ehrenreich in chronicling shifts in
America's ideologies of age and gender and in attempting to prescribe
less patriarchal solutions than those of Bly and other masculinists. So
Margaret Morganroth Gullette claims that the contemporary American
economy seeks self-indulgent consumers and cheap workers unpro-
tected by seniority rules, thus flattering youth and demeaning age. Instead, she recommends reinstating seniority rules and respect for elders
in a democratic, gender-egalitarian manner in order to develop "cohort
solidarity between women and men" as well as within the genders (*Declining,* 241). Similarly, Harry Brod speaks of the transition in our society from private to public patriarchy, a form he calls "fratriarchy, the
rule of the brothers, whose sibling rivalry is a form of competitive
bonding that keeps things in the family of men" ("Politics," 92). He
urges men to realize that this system is not in their best interests and to
join "a political movement to overthrow the capitalist patriarchal state,
which is taking your power from you only to use it against you" (92).

Ehrenreich particularizes patriarchy as the loss of familial power by
fathers without the diminution of male or ruling class supremacy. Many
profeminist writers use *patriarchy* as a catchall term equivalent to any
form of male privilege or domination in society (e.g., Brod, "Studying
Masculinities as Superordinate Studies," this volume). Bly mystifies the
word *patriarchy* by defining it as the fathers' destruction of the "young
masculine," while in *The Sibling Society* he yearns to establish the authority of male spiritual elders detached from a political system he de-
rides as adolescent and immature, even in such relatively geriatric male
institutions as the United States Congress (132). Yet, somewhat perversely, Bly is also helpful in illustrating some complexities to the concept of patriarchy. He is so antidemocratic and antiegalitarian in his
pronouncements that his critics are tempted to compare his ideology
with the "racist, myth-mongering, warrior cults of masculinity" of Germany in the 1920s (Connell, "Men," 85). He justifies male authority and
privilege in society through myths about fathers at a time when many
men seem to feel they are not adequately respected by their children and

simultaneously that their own fathers were too brutish or absent fully to deserve their own respect.[10] Thus, Bly demonstrates the tendency of sexist ideologues to naturalize the power and privilege not only of men over women but of some men over others, with familial metaphors and myths whose psychological resonances have powerful social effects. These myths and metaphors justify the privileges of authority by claiming men's burdens and "natural" obligations. In a polarizing consumer and information-oriented economy, Brod and Ehrenreich point to the declining economic role of individual fathers in many families, while the richest and most powerful men in society may be relatively young (Brod, "Politics"). That is, the patriarchal dominance of some men over the rest of society is changing shape, becoming harder to define within households or a specific age cohort. Feminists and other progressives respond with resolutely egalitarian models of social authority, often using same-generational family metaphors. I've quoted several writers who praise exactly the "sibling" relationship Bly decries. Feminists may well hope that sisterhood is still powerful and brotherhood still sings of justice and equality rather than exclusion and the privilege of men over women and some men over the rest. A genuinely "sibling society" of sisterhood and brotherhood remains an attractive goal, but Bly also raises some questions often elided by such theories, questions about inevitable dependencies within the life cycle, about the scope and limits of legitimate authority, and about the interactions between social categories and that elusive "respect" Americans consider their entitlement. Plausible feminist theories of age and gender, I suggest, should integrate rather than ignore such relationships of authority and dependency into their ideal models and their visions for how to achieve progressive social change in the direction of those ideals.

The idea that gender includes developmental elements, and thus that an adequate feminist theory of gender will also incorporate age categories, is also supported by some contemporary feminist psychologists, who build on the developmental but sexist theories of Freud. Nancy Chodorow is best known for her complementary theories of gender published two decades ago, theories that claim the masculine sense of a separated self is based on opposition to mothers' femininity, whereas the feminine sense of self forms through mother-daughter interdependence and empathy (*Reproduction*). Such theories analyzed the reproduction of social hierarchies through the psychological identifications that infants formed in the family, and they developed a cultural feminist rhetoric that proposed a move from the Law of the Father to "maternal thinking" so as to bring about a more peaceful, caring society based on traditional female values and the motherly role (see Ruddick, *Maternal;* Noddings, *Caring*). More recently, Chodorow argues that gender takes form in individuals in complex and highly variable ways that cannot be reduced to simply opposing and polarized psychological desires and identifications for the two genders (Chodorow, *Femininities,* "Gender"). For example, she describes a woman who constructed her feminine gender identity primarily through fantasies that contrasted girlish smallness with maternal amplitude, not that contrasted femininity with masculinity ("Gender," 530, 538). Her essay in this volume ponders the "psychodynamics of extreme violence with special attention to men and masculinity." It traces extreme violence to the humiliation and shame men produce in one another by aggressive attacks. "For some men, and in some cultures," she says, "masculinity is cast as an adult-child dichotomy: being an adult man versus being a little boy; being humiliated by other men."

I have been arguing that feminists might benefit from the depolarizations of gender consequent on seeing gender "cast as an adult-child" relationship, if not a "dichotomy," and also that the complexities of such relationships need further exploration. Humiliation is only one factor—albeit a baleful one—among many in men's relations with one another that build a gender system in which hierarchies of authority as well as age are inscribed. Humiliation appears as a powerful motive in those psychologically oriented men's studies that look at men's feelings of victimization, rather than their entitlements, and so either justify or deny the existence of male privilege (e.g. Farrell, *Myth*).[11] Freudian theories of psychology naturalize male hostility, competition, generational conflict, and dominance over women into the Oedipus complex as intrinsic to the development of masculine gender identity, and they also generalize from individual psychology to social institutions. Freudian psychoanalysis thus offers one integrated masculinist model of age and gender, in which male social authority is naturalized through generational myths and familial metaphors. "Mythopoetic" masculinist theories of age and gender like Bly's perform similar rationalizations, but their less sophisticated and more familiar authoritarian premises are perhaps easier to discern.[12] Reacting to the changing culture of the United States over the last few decades, Bly provides one example of both the advantages of integrating age categories into gender schema and of the need for less patriarchal, more egalitarian models of developmental gender, ones, for example, that recognize mature women as models of legitimate authority along with mature men of all ethnic groups and social classes and that move from naturalizing familial metaphors to understanding social processes.

According to Gregory Smith, "a very powerful image in our culture is that men do not learn to be men, or men do not develop their manhood, but that men just are. . . . One has it or one doesn't" ("Dichotomies," 38). He thinks U.S. culture lacks the more healthful idea that "degrees of manliness" or masculine identity develop. Instead, society frightens men with continual threats of inadequacy, making most men feel anxious and defensive. Smith suggests that men should understand masculinity in terms of a "sense of development or learning, and becoming more of something," in terms, that is, of "masculine growth" (38, 39). I suggest that feminists may find the concept of developmental gender congenial as well, though we will still need to disentangle analytical descriptions from utopian longings and perhaps disagree about the stages and the content of "masculine growth." Such a model for a developmental masculinity might include in its stages and attributes, for example, fathered childhood and responsible fatherhood, gender egalitarian childhood, a safe risk adolescence, sexual commitment and the ability to please one's partners, a transitional young adult culture marked by both same-sex and opposite-sex friendships, control over one's own potential for violence, moral as well as physical courage, balanced work and family maturity, and democratic citizenship and political and economic activism.[13]

Thus using aging as one model for rethinking gender, while incorporating age into gender categories in historically and culturally specific contexts, allows for the possibility of more adequate models of gender that can validate both women's social authority and men's nonsexist development from boyhood to manhood. Such theories might also be helpful in facing issues of authority and dependence, without either naturalizing some categories of people as deserving privilege over others or assuming that mere assertions of equality or metaphors of siblinghood constitute an adequate feminist theory of authority. Bly is right that men should not be "ashamed of being men" and that they would benefit from social validation of male maturity and responsibility. For the society as a whole to benefit, such a model of mature masculinity must be nonsexist as well, emphasizing growth toward responsible maturity rather than opposition between genders, heeding hooks's desire for a culture that helps "boys become men" and girls become women "wholistically" and Ehrenreich's call to "give new strength and shared meaning to the words we have lost—responsibility, maturity . . . manliness" (hooks, *Killing,* 67; Ehrenreich, "Decline," 182).

NOTES

For support of my project on masculinity in feminist theory, I thank the Institute for the Humanities at the University of Illinois at Chicago, the Rockefeller Foundation for a residency fellowship at Bellagio, Italy, and audiences at conferences of the Modern Language Association, the Radical Philosophy Association, and the American Men's Studies Association.

1. Sedgwick is discussing homosexuality here.

2. Hurston renders Janey's speech as "ode change uh life."

3. Sally Robinson discusses the marking of masculinity in her book, *Marked Men.* Harry Brod, in "Studying Masculinities as Superordinate Studies," this volume, speaks of the usually normative quality of the unmarked categories of whiteness and masculinity. For one recent effort to mark male maturity, see Sheehy, *Understanding.*

4. Unlike the earlier book, Bly's *The Sibling Society* has received modest popular acclaim and little scholarly study. According to a search of the Current Contents and Wilson Humanities Abstracts article databases, there are over three dozen references to the earlier book to about a dozen for the later.

5. Also see Clatterbaugh, "Mythopoetic"; Schwalbe, "Mythopoetic," 202; Seelow, "Loud."

6. This critique of male bonding as adolescent and immature in comparison with heterosexual relationships, especially marriage, may itself be liable to the charge of privileging heteronormativity.

7. At the Million Man March, Louis Farrakhan suggested that African American men adopt youths in jail.

8. I am not denying, however, Clatterbaugh's claim that "the vacuous explanations and permissive moral vision of the mythopoetic movement totally fail to address issues of male power, privilege, and patriarchal supremacy" ("Mythopoetic," 54).

9. The term *teening of America* is mine. For a discussion of one configuration of contemporary American adolescent masculinity, see Gardiner, "*South Park.*"

10. Faludi also describes this perception as common among contemporary men. For a profeminist counterview, see, for example, Stoltenberg.

11. For an analysis of this tendency, see, for example, Clatterbaugh,"Mythopoetic"; Robinson, *Marked Men.*

12. See, for example, Moore and Gillette, *King.* Many of the mythopoetics use Jungian psychologies that see age categories as components of eternal archetypes. However, the differences are not just those between various psychologies and sociologies; see Brod, "Studying."

13. I am developing these ideas in a book in progress, "Masculinity in Feminist Theory."

WORKS CITED

American Association of University Women. *Growing Smart: What's Working for Girls in Schools.* Executive Summary and Action Guide. Researched by Sunny Hansen, Joyce Walker, and Barbara Flom. Washington, D.C., 1995.

Ariès, Phillipe. *Centuries of Childhood: A Social History of Family Life.* Trans. Robert Baldick. New York: Vintage, 1962.

Bem, Sandra Lipsitz. *The Lenses of Gender: Transforming the Debate on Sexual Inequality.* New Haven: Yale University Press, 1993.

Bly, Robert. *Iron John: A Book About Men.* Reading, Mass.: Addison-Wesley, 1990.

———. *The Sibling Society.* Reading, Mass.: Addison-Wesley, 1996.

———. "Thoughts on Reading This Book." In Michael S. Kimmel, *The Politics of Manhood: Profeminist Men Respond to the Mythopoetic Men's Movement (and the Mythopoetic Leaders Answer),* pp. 271–74. Philadelphia: Temple University Press, 1995.

Bordo, Susan. *The Male Body: A New Look at Men in Public and Private.* New York: Farrar, Straus and Giroux, 1999.

Brod, Harry. "The Politics of the Mythopoetic Men's Movement." In Michael S. Kimmel, *The Politics of Manhood: Profeminist Men Respond to the Mytho-*

poetic Men's Movement (and the Mythopoetic Leaders Answer), pp. 89–96. Philadelphia: Temple University Press, 1995.

———. "Studying Masculinities as Superordinate Studies," this volume.

Burke, Phyllis. Gender Shock: Exploding the Myths of Male and Female. New York: Anchor, 1996.

Butler, Judith. Gender Trouble: Feminism and the Subversion of Identity. New York: Routledge, 1990.

Chodorow, Nancy. "The Enemy Outside: Thoughts on the Psychodynamics of Extreme Violence with Special Attention to Men and Masculinity," this volume.

———. Femininities, Masculinities, Sexualities: Freud and Beyond. Lexington: University of Kentucky Press, 1994.

———. "Gender as a Personal and Cultural Construction." Signs 20.3 (1995): 516–44.

———. The Reproduction of Mothering: Psychoanalysis and the Sociology of Gender. Berkeley: University of California Press, 1978.

Clatterbaugh, Kenneth. "Mythopoetic Foundations and New Age Patriarchy." In Michael S. Kimmel, The Politics of Manhood: Profeminist Men Respond to the Mythopoetic Men's Movement (and the Mythopoetic Leaders Answer), pp. 44–63. Philadelphia: Temple University Press, 1995.

Connell, R. W. Masculinities. Berkeley: University of California Press, 1995.

———. "Men at Bay: The 'Men's Movement' and Its Newest Best-Sellers." In Michael S. Kimmel, The Politics of Manhood: Profeminist Men Respond to the Mythopoetic Men's Movement (and the Mythopoetic Leaders Answer), pp. 75–88. Philadelphia: Temple University Press, 1995.

Coontz, Stephanie. The Way We Really Are: Coming to Terms with America's Changing Families. New York: Basic, 1997.

Doyle, James and Michele Paludi. Sex and Gender: The Human Experience. 4th ed. Boston: McGraw-Hill, 1998.

Ehrenreich, Barbara. "The Decline of Patriarchy." In Maurice Berger, Brian Wallis, and Simon Watson, eds., Constructing Masculinity. pp. 284–90. New York: Routledge, 1995.

———. The Hearts of Men: American Dreams and the Flight from Commitment. New York: Anchor, 1983.

Erikson, Erik H. Identity: Youth and Crisis. New York: Norton, 1968.

Faludi, Susan. Stiffed: The Betrayal of the American Man. New York: William Morrow, 1999.

Farrakhan, Louis. "Remarks at the Million Man March in Washington, D.C., October 16, 1995." Federal Document Clearing House, America Online Paging.

Farrell, Warren. *The Myth of Male Power.* New York: Berkley, 1996.

Friedan, Betty. *The Feminine Mystique.* New York: Dell, 1963.

Gardiner, Judith Kegan. "*South Park,* Blue Men, Anality, and Market Masculinity." *Men and Masculinities* 2:3 (January 2000), 251–71.

gossett, hattie. "min's movement??? a page drama." In K. L. Hagan, *Women Respond to the Men's Movement: A Feminist Collection,* pp. 19–26. New York: Pandora, 1992.

Gullette, Margery Morganroth. *Declining to Decline: Cultural Combat and the Politics of the Midlife.* Charlottesville: University of Virginia Press, 1997.

Hagan, K. L. *Women Respond to the Men's Movement: A Feminist Collection.* New York: Pandora, 1992.

Hewlett, Sylvia Ann, and Cornel West. *The War Against Parents: What We Can Do for America's Beleaguered Moms and Dads.* Boston: Houghton Mifflin, 1998.

hooks, bell. *Killing Rage: Ending Racism.* New York: Holt, 1995.

Hurston, Zora Neale. *Their Eyes Were Watching God.* Urbana: University of Illinois Press, 1978 [1937].

Kimmel, Michael. S., ed. *The Politics of Manhood: Profeminist Men Respond to the Mythopoetic Men's Movement (and the Mythopoetic Leaders Answer).* Philadelphia: Temple University Press, 1995.

Kimmel, Michael S., and Michael Kaufman. "Weekend Warriors: The New Men's Movement." In Michael S. Kimmel, *The Politics of Manhood: Profeminist Men Respond to the Mythopoetic Men's Movement (and the Mythopoetic Leaders Answer),* pp. 16–43. Philadelphia: Temple University Press, 1995.

Lorber, Judith. *Paradoxes of Gender.* New Haven: Yale University Press, 1994.

MacKinnon, Catherine. *Feminism Unmodified.* Cambridge: Harvard University Press, 1987.

Males, Mike A. *The Scapegoat Generation: America's War on Adolescents.* Monroe, Maine: Common Courage, 1996.

Moore, Robert, and Douglas Gillette. *King, Warrior, Magician, Lover: Rediscovering the Archetypes of the Mature Masculine.* San Francisco: Harper Collins, 1990.

Noddings, Nel. *Caring: A Feminine Approach to Ethics and Moral Education.* Berkeley: University of California Press, 1984.

Pipher, Mary. *Reviving Ophelia: Saving the Selves of Adolescent Girls.* New York: Ballantine, 1994.

Robinson, Sally. *Marked Men: White Masculinity in Crisis.* New York, Columbia University Press, 2000.

———. "Pedagogy of the Opaque: Teaching Masculinity Studies," this volume.

Ross, Marlon. "Race, Rape, Castration: Feminist Theories of Sexual Violence and Masculine Strategies of Black Protest," this volume.

Ruddick, Sara. *Maternal Thinking: Toward a Politics of Peace.* Boston: Beacon, 1989.

Schwalbe, Michael. "Mythopoetic Men's Work as a Search for Communitas." In Michael S. Kimmel, *The Politics of Manhood: Profeminist Men Respond to the Mythopoetic Men's Movement (and the Mythopoetic Leaders Answer),* pp. 186–204. Philadelphia: Temple University Press, 1995.

Sedgwick, Eve Kosofsky. *Tendencies.* Durham: Duke University Press, 1993.

Seelow, David. "Loud Men: The Poetic Visions of Robert Bly, Ice Cube, and Etheridge Knight. *Journal of Men's Studies* 6.2 (1998): 149–68.

Sheehy, Gail. *Understanding Men's Passages: Discovering the New Map of Men's Lives.* New York: Random House, 1998.

Sidel, Ruth. *Keeping Women and Children Last: America's War on the Poor.* New York: Penguin, 1996.

Smith, Gregory. "Dichotomies in the Making of Men." In Christopher McLean, Maggie Carey, and Cheryl White, eds., *Men's Ways of Being,* pp. 29–49. Boulder: Westview/Harper Collins, 1996.

Steinem, Gloria. "Foreword." In K. L. Hagan, *Women Respond to the Men's Movement: A Feminist Collection,* pp. v–ix. New York: Pandora, 1992.

Stoltenberg, John. *The End of Manhood: A Book for Men of Conscience.* New York: Plume, 1994.

———. *Refusing to Be a Man: Essays on Sex and Justice.* Portland: Breitenbush, 1989.

Woodward, Kathleen. *Aging and Its Discontents: Freud and Other Fictions.* Bloomington: Indiana University Press, 1991.

4

GETTING UP THERE WITH TOM: THE POLITICS OF AMERICAN "NICE"

Fred Pfeil

Over the past several years, first in Tania Modelski's *Feminism Without Women* (1991) and continuing on through such works as Susan Jeffords's *Hard Bodies* (1994), my own *White Guys* (1995), Susan Bordo's *Twilight Zones* (1997), and David Savran's *Taking It Like a Man* (1998), the small but hardy band of us who spend our time reading the entrails of American popular culture for what it can tell us of the changing shape, definition, and implication of normative masculinity have produced a pretty substantial critical literature on the outwardly hard-bodied, inwardly anguished, rampaging male as incarnated in the star image of Bruce Willis, Arnold Schwarzenegger, Mel Gibson, and/or Sylvester Stallone. And justly so, as the horrifying continuity between the character of Willis's John McClain in *Die Hard* and Stallone's Rambo on the one hand and the real-life persona of Timothy McVeigh on the other, or the still more striking likeness in the twisted wreck of the corporate tower at the end of the Willis film to the smoky ruins of the Murrah Federal Building in Oklahoma City, make all too plain.

Yet it has come to seem to me that while throughout the late 1980s and 1990s we have been concentrating our anxious attention on the ways the contradictory and complementary features of this rampaging male hero work, in Savran's concise summation, to "eroticiz[e] submission and victimization while trying to retain a certain aggressively virile edge, offering subjects positions that have been marked historically as being both masculine and feminine, white and black,"[1] a quite different but in at least some respects equally disquieting and symptomatic version of masculinity has, in the form of the emphatically soft-bodied Tom Hanks, been taking up more and more room on the cultural landscape. By 1998, in the season of *Saving Private Ryan* and *You've Got Mail,* the evidence of his preeminence was everywhere. "Tom on Top," *Time* crowed in the headline of its August 3, 1998, cover story on the guy they described as "celebrity mensch," just a week or so after *USA Weekend* canonized him as "America's leading man." Even the tatty but tony *New Yorker* got on the bus and into the act, with what passes there these days for a think piece on what it called (and co-created) as "The Tom Hanks Phenomenon" in which he was (re)introduced to us as "our cinematic saint next door, the perfect baby boomer, Hollywood's shining examplar of unpretentious goodness and decency in an age and an industry where nice guys finish closer to last than first."[2]

In one sense, then, the questions this essay will address about Tom Hanks are, as he might say in one of his beguiling interviews, pretty darn simple. What, exactly, are the constituent qualities of Tom Hanks's vaunted "niceness"? What type of "normal" and "ordinary" masculinity does he model and signify? What kinds of "nice" and "normal" does such a purportedly ideal masculinity include—and, just as significantly, foreclose on or omit? And what, finally and not at all simply, are the implications of the construction and promotion of this particular rendition of white masculinity as the increasingly hegemonic alternative and/or complementary version to that of the rampaging "angry white male" victim, for those of us who still care and dare to dream of a world in which both the insidiously covert and brutally explicit coercions and exclusions of race, gender, and class might reasonably be regarded as nightmares of the past? For the earlier, simpler questions, it seems to me, are only worth considering in the light of the frankly utopian project admitted in the latter, more prolix one. Otherwise, what more would we be doing here than adding to all the chatter about Tom Hanks—albeit in our own highly trained, specialized, and self-approvingly ironic way?

I

"I changed into a grownup but I'm really just a kid."
—Josh in *Big* (1988)

Let us begin with the first stretch of Tom Hanks's career, ranging through his roles as Kip in the short-lived TV comedy *Bosom Buddies* at the turn of the seventies and Allan, the mermaid's young lover in his movie breakthrough *Splash* in 1982, to David, the aspiring young adman with a troubled set of parents in the "serious" comedy *Nothing in Common* (1985) and the boy-man Josh in *Big* (1988), the film whose massive success made Hanks a full-fledged star. What recurring features of the various characters Hanks embodies in this TV series and these films will be carried forward through the films to come?

I find three such entwined features lying in wait for us in these texts—though I hasten to add that only in *Big* does the Hanks character fully embody all three of them. First, there is his *boyishness,* and the particular form of homosociality that accompanies it; second, his *sexual passivity,* or *mutedness;* and third, the extent to which he quite literally *plays out* his various roles as a distinctly happy and creative worker within the *professional-managerial class.*

The three, as I have said, are intertwined and mutually overdetermining, but let us see if we can pick them apart in these early Hanks texts nonetheless. The boyishness is, of course, the very premise of *Big,* in which a thirteen-year-old boy who has been magically endowed by a wish-granting genie with the body of a full-grown adult learns to make his dazed yet, as it turns out, splendidly successful way in the adult world. But it is also at the heart of Kip, the character Hanks played in *Bosom Buddies,* who, like Josh, gawks in prepubescent wonder at the women by whom he is surrounded in the "Susan B. Anthony Hotel" in which he and his buddy Henry take up residence by cross-dressing. The joke about the cross-dressing, incidentally, is played out in a slapsticky way that suggests quite the opposite of any actual incorporation of conventionally feminine psychological attributes, as in the case of our simultaneously feminized and hypermasculinized rampagers; the laughs are merely about how utterly unconvincing and uncomfortable the two guys are in wigs and women's clothes. Meanwhile, the title song opening each episode of *Bosom Buddies* goes, in part, like this:

> I'd like a chateau in Paris
> There ain't no doubt about it
> But I can live without it
> If I got a friend like you
> You can try to shake me loose
> You can tell me to go away
> But it doesn't matter what you say
> It ain't any use
> You ain't never gonna shake me loose

Homosocial? You bet. Yet the form and quality of that homosociality are quite distinct from that embodied by, say, Mel Gibson's Riggs and Danny Glover's Murtaugh in their endless series of *Lethal Weapons* films. For Hanks's Kip and Peter Scolari's Henry are both conspicuously depicted as—in the words of one of the female inhabitants of the Susan B. Anthony Hotel in the series' first episode, meeting them in their getups as women—"probably virgins." Loose-limbed, soft-bodied, and comically geeky in their movements and habits, they consistently register as prepubescent pals whose friendship is too childishly virginal to include any of the scarcely repressed eroticism that hides in plain sight in the hard-bodied buddy films of the eighties.

The likeness in just these respects between the *Bosom Buddies* Kip and *Big*'s boy-in-a-man's-body Josh—who in the film's climactic moment chooses to return to his warm and easy prepubescent friendship with his buddy Billy rather than stay in the adult world with his lover Susan—is so great as to require no further comment. Yet a plot twist in the film does nonetheless merit our consideration; for in *Big*, as soon as Hanks surrenders to a sexual relationship with an adult woman, the playful wide-eyed boyishness that is the source of his creativity and vitality begins to fade. The situation is quite otherwise, yet curiously similar for all that, in *Splash*, in which the mermaid the Hanks character comes to call Madison brings to him precisely the sense of open-ended wonder and joie de vivre that his life as Allan, wholesale distributor of fruit and vegetables, so lacked. But as made clear in *Splash*'s introductory sequence, in which the boy Allan sights the mergirl who will eventually become Madison and jumps off the day-touring boat he and his parents are on in an abortive attempt to meet her, the mermaid's subsequent reappearance in his adult life is, in effect, the return of his playful, creative boyhood itself. It is this boyhood, then, to which he returns at the end of the film when, unable himself to swim, he nonetheless kicks off his tuxedo and, holding Madison's hand, escapes from New York City and his encumbered adult life there for a childhood in perpetuity beneath the waves. (Indeed, *Big* in many ways is no more than a reworking of *Splash*—with the undersocialized Josh/Hanks in the mermaid's role).

Yet before we leave these two films, there is something else to say about the way both of them, and *Bosom Buddies* as well, model the relationships between their male protagonists and the women who become their love interests. In *Bosom Buddies,* the person who most aggressively and unabashedly exhibits sexual desire is a woman (albeit one who is interested in Henry, not Kip). The same is true of Darryl Hannah's mermaid in *Splash,* and Josh's fellow employee Susan in *Big;* both aggressively come on to a Hanks protagonist who is initially quite befuddled by their advances. Following *Splash*'s introductory sequence, and near the beginning of its present-day narrative, we do learn that Allan has just ended an unsatisfactory relationship with a woman we never see; likewise, soon afterward, at a wedding reception for an employee of Allan's, we hear him giving a drunken speech about the love he would like to have above all else. So you might be tempted to conclude that *Splash*'s Allan has a degree of sexual interest and experience that render him qualitatively different from *Big*'s boy-man Josh. But let us listen more closely to that speech:

Do I expect too much out of life? . . . I don't ask that much, do I? I don't ask to be famous, I don't ask to be rich, I don't ask to play center field for the New York Yankees or anything. I just want to meet a woman. I want to meet a woman, and I want to fall in love, and I wanna get married, and I wanna have a kid, and I wanna go see him play a toot [?!] in the school play. It's not much, but—but I'm kidding myself. I'm gonna grow old and I'm gonna grow lonely, and I'm gonna die.

This, I want to say, is a quintessentially Hanksian moment, to which we will have occasion to refer again. For now, let us merely take note of how markedly uninterested, even indifferent the character who utters it is to erotic love. This indifference is, moreover, further emphasized by the context surrounding the speech. For, as he delivers it, the drunkenly awkward Allan first unintentionally ruins an attempt between the man and woman seated at the bar next to him to hook up with each other for the night, while all the while he is muttering we are kept aware that his hopelessly lecherous brother Freddy (John Candy) is merrily slapping the make on two other women at a nearby table.

Tom Hanks I thus emerges precisely *not* as a full-grown man with an—implicitly shallow, crassly predatory—sexual desire of his own but as the goofy, geeky boy-man who *New York*'s David Denby praised as "infantilism incarnate" in *Big*.[3] What little sexual desire this Hanks is capable of must, moreover, be assiduously kindled by an aggressively persistent woman. Yet the Hanks character will remain attached to her only if and insofar as her presence in his life does not prevent him from remaining a child (as Susan's relationship with Josh does in *Big*) and rather reinforces and legitimates his arrested development (as Madison's relationship with Allan does in *Splash*).

The third possibility, hinted at in the speech just quoted, that women might be necessary only insofar as they allow the Hanks figure to become or remain a father to a son, will be more fully elaborated in Hanks's later films. Before moving on to Hanks II, however, I want to say a few words about the third feature of Hanks I, i.e., Hanks's satisfyingly playful location within the professional/managerial class (or PMC). Only in *Splash* does he play a character who, as co-owner with his brother of a wholesale fruit and vegetable distributorship, is arguably more petit bourgeois than professional; yet even as Allan the wholesale produce man, he is nonetheless somehow able to afford to live in an incredibly roomy apartment in a doorman-attended building somewhere on the Upper East Side of New York. In fact, notwithstanding Hanks's soon-to-arrive reputation as our vox populi, the "ordinary man in extraordinary circumstances," he has never played a character whose class location or financial situation poses any difficulty for him.

What is, instead, at issue in a few of these early films, is rather whether the playful boy-man Hanks will be free to give full vent to his ludic, creative junior high self. In *Nothing In Common,* for example, where Hanks works in an ad agency as he did in *Bosom Buddies,* though now as a young ad executive, as David Edelstein of the *Village Voice* noted, "Hanks embodies everything we love and hate about the eighties sense of humor: its lack of conviction, its irreverence, its frank self-interest."4 But, actually, *Nothing in Common* invites us quite unambiguously to cherish that sense of humor in Hanks's David, by depicting it as part and parcel of a creative vitality that is in danger of being squelched by the self-mutilating masquerade he must put himself through to win a new big account for the firm. To get that account and thereby keep his job, he must befriend and impress a quintessentially masculinist, tough-talking, hard-bitten, patriarchal-productivist father named Woolrich, and in the course of nearly doing so David/Hanks also nearly leaves his old high school girlfriend (an artistic type to boot) for Woolrich's daughter, an ambitious hard driver who is nearly as aggressively masculinist as her old man.

Nothing in Common also works out a virtually separate story line concerning David/Hanks's relationships with his two troubled biological parents, played by Jackie Gleason and Eva Marie Saint.5 For our discussion of Hanks's star image, however, what counts most is the story of the boyish, non-Phallic creativity Hanks's David nearly has to give up to win over a preeminently patriarchal-Phallic father—and of how, when David balks at the sacrifice, he is saved and supported by a third and altogether better father figure than either the biological or the punitively patriarchal one. This third and best father is David's boss, Charlie (Hector Elizondo), who, when David revolts against Woolrich's demand that he leave his sick *biological* father (Jackie Gleason) unattended in favor of tending to the Woolrich account, pulls a turnabout, simultaneously backing his "boy" and singlehandedly rescuing the endangered account. In this reversal and rescue, and in his nurturant attention to David throughout the film, Elizondo's Charlie in *Nothing in Common* is akin to the benevolent and playful head of the toy company who becomes Hanks's/Josh's boss (Robert Loggia) in *Big,* protecting him against the attacks of his hard-driven, ambitious, and chronically anxious competitor, Paul (whom, significantly enough, Susan also deserts to become Josh's girlfriend/lover), and enthusiastically backing his creative ideas for new toys.

II

"I'm not at all threatening to anyone."
"I don't want to play pussies anymore."
—Tom Hanks (1993)[6]

As we move on now to Hanks II, in which he appears before us both as a full-fledged star and, increasingly, as the ideal white male adult both on-screen and off, we will see that this star image simultaneously retains and supplements key elements of his initial image. No longer simply a sexually nonthreatening geeky boy, he nonetheless continues to be largely shy of sexuality, to need and deserve the protection of nurturant father figures, and ultimately to live for the sake of being father to the boyhood he simultaneously embodies and sires. It is at this stage, moreover, and around this figure of Hanks as "a safe, new prototype of heroic virtue"[7] that the Hanks publicity machine goes into high gear, proposing both Hanks himself and his various protagonists in *Philadelphia* (1993), *Sleepless in Seattle* (1993), and *Forrest Gump* (1994) as the "extraordinary, ordinary man," the "ordinary man in an extraordinary circumstance," simultaneously "Hollywood's Last Decent Man" and "an intelligent guy who wants to make sense out of the chaos of his life," "your best self having your worst day."[8] I've suggested that many of the elements of this "best" white male "self" we are invited to endorse, admire, and emulate are already present in Hanks I. So let us take a look at how, and with what new additions and inflections, these elements show up in his three smashing successes of the early 1990s. How, and to what effect, has Tom Hanks "changed into an adult" while remaining really "just a kid"? And what is the meaning of his assertion that "I don't want to play pussies anymore"?

Let us begin with *Philadelphia*—for there, surprisingly enough, given the extent to which the film has been promoted as an especially brave departure for Hanks, we will find in his incarnation of the AIDS victim Andy Becket the greatest degree of continuity with his earlier roles. What, for starters, from the perspective of Hanks I, makes the injustice of Jason Robards and the other senior partners of the law firm that discharges him for having AIDS so very outrageous, if not the counterexample of those other maternal business-fathers in *Nothing in Common* and *Big* who gave the Hanks manchild the loving support his loyal, playful, creative self needs and deserves? And who is Denzel Washington's Joe Miller, if not the compensatory paternal defender who rides to Hanks's rescue in their stead?

That Hanks's Andy Becket is depicted less as a gay man in *Philadelphia* than as a son is likewise strongly suggested by the extended sequence near the center of the film in which he returns to the bosom of his healthy, loving, solidly upper-middle-class family on the occasion of his parents' fortieth anniversary—and, as well, by the film's close, in which at the memorial gathering for the now-deceased AIDS victim, we gather with Andy's friends and family to watch home movies of the lovely boy-child he was and will now ever remain, albeit only on film. To arrive at this latter sequence, however, *Philadelphia* has had to negotiate its way around some difficult issues that threaten to destabilize or damage precisely the image Hanks brought to it: that of someone, in Hanks's own words, who is "not threatening to anyone."9 And *Philadelphia*'s special way of simultaneously raising and muting the subject of AIDS as a political issue cues us in to the extent to which that lack of threat includes not only Hanks's charmingly arrested boyishness but the Hanks persona's equally consistent indifference and disinclination to any politics as well.

Those who have followed Hanks's career all along have already been treated, in *Splash,* to the sight of that disinterest, as Hanks's Allan, with mermaid Madison, makes his way blithely past a bevy of catcalling, poster-waving demonstraters to attend a fund-raising dinner with the president of the United States. That film, however, was able, in effect, to redouble Hanks/Allan's disregard by itself rendering the protestors' signs illegible, their cries a roaring indecipherable blur. In *Philadelphia,* no such option was available; the right-wing homophobes and the lesbigay activists outside the courtroom must be seen and heard as such. But Hanks's Andy Becket (or is it Andy Becket's Hanks?) can still refuse to identify himself with any political camp; and that, of course, is just what he does when the reporters' microphones are shoved in his face. "I am not political," he says. "I just want what is fair and what is right."

Such an eschewal of the presumably shrill and sordid actions attendant on political citizenship will be, of course, an even more important constituent of true decency as defined by Hanks's Forrest Gump a few years hence, in a film that renders the politics and history of the past forty years into a senseless, trivialized hash laced with occasional random violence and that punishes unto death (by AIDS, in fact, or so it is hinted) the one character who is so psychologically damaged and deluded as to have taken the notion of her political and sexual liberation seriously. For Tom Hanks, as Gump or gay man alike, sexuality and politics are somewhere between beneath notice and out of bounds. Yet, obviously enough, just as it was not possible to make *Philadelphia* about a protagonist with AIDS without the political issues surrounding AIDS somehow coming up, so it is impossible to make that protagonist a gay man with AIDS without somehow suggesting that that character must have, or, at any rate, have had, some interest at least once in having sex. How, then, does *Philadelphia* handle the hot potato of characterizing Tom Hanks as a sexual being—gay *or* straight? Not, as we know, by representing his relationship with Antonio Banderas's Miguel as at all erotic; for their few moments of physical affection in the film are entirely chaste. Instead the film chooses to reveal Hanks's/Andrew's sexuality only in the displaced and oblique form of his love for opera in general and a Maria Callas aria in particular. The scene occurs when only he and his lawyer, Denzel Washington's Joe Miller, are left at the end of a party thrown by Andrew, and consists of a feverish commentary on the aria, declaimed by a wobbling Hanks/Andrew bathed in a lurid, not to say hellish, orange light. Translating the lines of the aria for his nurturant paternal defender and providing a running commentary on them, Hanks/Andrew is, in effect, providing a secondary translation of his own passion—which itself, moreover, is depicted in the aria Callas sings as "the god that come[s] down from the heavens to the earth," i.e., precisely not an intrinsic quality of Hanks's/Andrew's character but rather an outside force by which he is (and, by implication, was on at least one occasion) possessed.

Yet these extreme measures of distancing and projection are still not enough to expunge the taint; an actively sexual Hanks is a scandal that must be removed—leaving, as we have seen, the innocent son he once was in his place. Likewise in *Sleepless in Seattle* and *Forrest Gump* alike, where though the Hanks protagonist is hetero, the only pretext or warrant for straight desire is for the sake of the kid—specifically the boy—so to speak "to come." Already, in the speech I quoted earlier from

Splash, you will have noted that for Hanks's Allan romantic love is not an end in itself but rather a stage of a desiring narrative whose proper end is that of fatherhood to a male child. In its depiction of a protagonist who makes love just once with his lifelong object of chaste desire, who duly conceives and bears a male offspring and then conveniently dies, *Gump* follows out this program to the letter. And a good deal of *Sleepless in Seattle* is legible as a variation on the same pattern, beginning with (looking backward from *Gump*) the suspicious familiarity of the enabling situation from which its story takes off—yet another instance of a lover-wife who, having given Hanks his boy-child, has sadly (or is it conveniently?) departed this earthly plane. The film labors mightily to persuade us that Hanks's Sam is choked with grief (which Hanks conveys primarily by delivering his lines in a hollow, affectless deadpan), just as it insists we swallow the premise that not only Meg Ryan's Annie but the entire national audience of female radio listeners has been sent into swooning transports by the plight of the widower whose sorrow and need have been broadcast to the world by his cute, smart son Jonah's calls to "Network America." Strip away these insistences, though, and what is left? A story about a boy who puts out a call for a new wife for his father and makes the proper selection from those who respond, crossed, countered, and completed by a story about the woman who throws her previous personal and professional life prospects out the window to pursue the mystically romantic, magically right union the boy engineers between her and his romantically near-inert dad.

In this second phase of the Hanks star image, then, even when he himself is no longer a grown-up child (as he remains, notoriously and perpetually, in *Forrest Gump*), Hanks remains *identified* with the winsome, pure boy-children he has grown out of and/or spawned in turn. It is, we might say, practically as though at least in *Gump* and *Seattle* he himself has become something like the maternal father who provided support and indulgent, loving nurturance to the boy-men of Hanks I. In any case, this exclusively male parent-child axis is the central focus of the on-screen image of Hanks II; so much so, indeed, that it is precisely that focus, and the complementary sexual diffidence or downright indifference to heterosexual romance that comes with it, which in turn women both off- and on-screen are, perversely enough, invited to find attractive. When Hanks II tells us he doesn't "want to play pussies any more," he does not mean he wants to be taken as a full-fledged sexual subject and/or object but rather primarily as father to his own boy-child; as for "pussy" as a contemptuous term for women, of course we know Hanks has never come close to meaning anything like that.

III

> Ryan (*as old man, tearfully*): Tell me I'm a good man.
> Mrs. Ryan (*gently, sympathetically*): You are.
> —*Saving Private Ryan* (1998)

It remains for us only to note how in all these early nineties films our Hanks protagonists remain quite blithely economically enabled—the architect in *Sleepless* can move to a new well-paying job whenever and wherever he likes, as readily as the idiot Gump can good-guy his way through to become the multimillionaire head of a company; neither *Philadelphia*'s Andy Becket nor anyone else in the film expresses any concern over what in real life would be the monumental cost of his treatment and final hospitalization—and our image is more or less complete. Undisturbed by political concerns, unencumbered by economic constraints, and largely ungripped by erotic desire of any kind, Hanks II exists instead more or less exclusively for the sake of either the boy who remains inside him (*Philadelphia, Forrest Gump*), or the boy he has now, with the help of an otherwise expendable woman, externalized in the form of a son (*Forrest Gump, Sleepless*): in either and any case, as a preeminently desexualized, casually apolitical kind of guy whose intrinsic narcissism is both expressed and disguised by the recurrent father/son motif. It will not surprise us, then, that Hanks has gone on to precisely the kinds of male roles little boys are said to imagine they would like to take up when they are grown: as the voice of a cowboy in *Toy Story* (1996), as an astronaut in *Apollo 13* (1995), and as Captain Miller the soldier in *Saving Private Ryan* (1998)—nor that in the romantic comedy *You've Got Mail* (1999), in which Hanks does not play some such role, he is himself, despite his age, a son instead.

As in the shift from Hanks I to Hanks II, then, so in the shift from II to III what we discern is less a break with earlier meanings than a new layer of inscriptions atop the older ones in Hanks's star-image palimpsest. And the decisive element to be noted in these new inscriptions is that of Hanks's full induction and legitimation in a hierarchical order of adult male power and authority. In *You've Got Mail,* as the scion of the Fox family, he is in charge of the construction and promotion of the Borders- and Barnes-and-Noble-style megabook store that puts his email girlfiriend Meg Ryan's "Shop Around the Corner" out of business. In *Apollo 13,* his Jim Lovell is both in charge of the crew on their aborted space mission and himself under the control of the all-male flight control crew back on Earth. As Captain Miller in *Saving Private Ryan,* he is likewise both in charge of his own men and emphatically located within a chain of male authority and transmission, which, in running back and up from Miller in Normandy to General Marshall in Washington and beyond Marshall back to Abraham Lincoln, as well as forward and down from Miller himself to the aged paterfamilias Ryan—the boy Miller saved now grown old, kneeling at the grave of his redeemer as his wife and children stand a respectful distance away— altogether transcends historical space and time.

Our aging Tom in these films faithfully leads his men and executes his orders without question or complaint in a cold and inhospitable world—outer space, war-torn France, the cut-throat world of contemporary capitalism—marked by the threat of extinction. (Even in *You've Got Mail,* where that threat is primarily economic, and is, moreover, visited on Meg Ryan's Annie rather than on Hanks, his Joe Fox briefly but significantly faces the possibility of his physical demise when he finds himself stuck on an elevator in the plush condominium building where he lives.) From these bleak landscapes, moreover, women are absent. They reside, in *Private Ryan,* a world away back in the States (and could it be accidental or, at any rate, without significance, that both Miller and the other soldiers under his command who speak with respectful attention of their wives and mothers all die, whereas those who tell misogynist stories, like Private Ryan's comic tale of the ugly slut Alice Jardine, survive?).[10] So too in *Apollo 13,* where the almost impossible distance between gendered worlds is most concisely suggested by the impossible shot/reverse-shot near the film's climax, which cuts from a close-up of Hanks's Jim Lovell looking down at Earth from the frozen window of his stricken lunar module to a mid-shot of his wife Marilyn looking up at the sky from the backyard of their house. And the warm, cluttered, woody interior of the bookstore Meg Ryan's Annie and her mostly female staff scheme desperately to save in *You've Got Mail* is likewise a world away from the gray-blue office high in some corporate tower in which, together with his father and grandfather, Hanks's Joe Fox oversees the process that will lead to her store's demise.

The masculine duty that the Hanks III character both epitomizes and executes in these films is that which simultaneously prevents him from (re)connecting with the maternally defined woman from whom he is so decisively separate and that which must be done as part of the longed for return. *Apollo 13* rehearses this thoroughly oedipal logic in its simplest form by insisting that Jim Lovell and his fellow astronauts must go up to come down, *You've Got Mail* in its most perverse, by insisting that Hanks's Joe Fox must complete Annie's economic ruin before he can reveal himself as her email boyfriend and win her love. And *Private Ryan* spells out the contradictions of such logic most explicitly when Miller first confesses, "I wonder if I've changed so much my wife won't recognize me," only to assert in the following scene that "if finding Ryan helps me get home to my wife, I'll do it."

In a universe in which a boy's safe return to his mother is supposed to enable a man's return to his wife, the two, in effect, compose a slant rhyme with each other. Male heterosexuality, in other words, is emphatically hetero- , that is, directed toward a femininity defined by its absolutely separate otherness, yet at the same time it is less erotically focused on an adult sexual partner than filially driven toward the safety and comfort of the mother waiting for her boy-man to come home. But as Miller's dying injunction to Ryan implies, boys have to "earn it": that is, earn the right to come home to Mom by constraining the boy within and taking one's place in the hierarchy of dutiful, responsible, rule-observant, self-repressing men. Having grown up, and, indeed, grown old with Tom through all these years, we understand that at the moment in *Private Ryan* when, overwhelmed by all the brutality he has seen and participated in, Hanks's Captain Miller allows the tremoring that afflicts him throughout the film to take over his body, and, discreetly apart from the younger men he commands, gives way to tears, there is nothing womanish in this moment of collapse and release. It is, rather, continuous with the moment in *Big*, eleven years before, when the boy Josh, stuck in a lurid flophouse on the evening of his first day as a grown man, breaks down and cries for his Mom.

This point is worth stressing, since it is a central feature distinguishing the masculinity Hanks's image has come to embody from that of the rampaging Sylvester, Mel, and Bruce. For the latter, as Savran, Modleski, and I in our various ways have each and all explored, is strikingly defined by its *preoedipal* character—which is to say, by its raging, obsessive, and never fully successful attempts to assert and defend its boundaries, not least against the fear of an abject femininity within, which it both displays and mortifies (indeed, displays by its mortification). In Lacanian shorthand, we could say that lacking the Phallus, that is, full accession to the Symbolic Order of authorized masculinity, these disenfranchised wild men can only act out; whereas our fully incorporated, oedipalized Hanks III, incarnating the Law of the Fathers, dutifully and effectively executes that Law's provisions, thereby ensuring that the boy within (in *Apollo 13* and *You've Got Mail*) or without (in *Private Ryan*) can return to the mother/woman/home to which his efficacious actions have now fully "earned" access.

In retrospect, then, Tom Hanks's long career takes on a rather startling teleology, as nothing less than a protracted reconstruction and rehabilitation of a fully empowered, oedipal masculinity for our time. In Hanks's more recent films, that masculinity is warranted and legitimized, I want to say, by our prior acquaintance with and acceptance of the boy-man we know from *Big, Forrest Gump, Philadelphia* and other films starring Hanks I and Hanks II. Such conviction, carried forward from the accreted meanings of Hanks's previous incarnations, is especially crucial to the success of *You've Got Mail,* in which, for example, Joe Fox's deliberate display of naked greed in eating all the caviar at the publishing party even as he mocks and insults Annie's claims to petit-bourgeois entrepeneurial virtue would very likely come off as inexcusable cruelty did it not carry the trace memory of Josh's charmingly unself-conscious gorging at the corporate party in *Big*. So too, more generally, and crucially, in the brutally casual efficacy with which he engineers the success of his all-male family company's newest store and the downfall and destruction of the store that is Annie's sole inheritance from her mother. At the risk of sounding like the shills that pass for movie reviewers these days, we could almost say that only Tom Hanks could pull off the feat of convincing us that the same man who destroys Annie's livelihood is the right man for her to love. For no matter how grimly or brutally effective his actions, no matter how inexpressive his face, no matter how constrained his movements in *Apollo 13, Saving Private Ryan,* and *You've Got Mail* alike, the trace images we retain of our Tom keep us convinced that not only beyond but *thanks to* all the missions unquestioningly accomplished and underneath all that middle-aged body armor, a limber, winsome, rubber-faced, thoroughly lovable boy lives on.

IV

> It is not permissible that the authors of devastation should also be innocent. It is the innocence which constitutes the crime.
> —James Baldwin, *The Fire Next Time* (1963)

By now, offscreen as well, even when Hanks's domestic life and innermost self are described as a "gated community," and Hanks himself uncomplainingly describes his public persona as "some brand of commodity . . . a package,"[11] what takes the chill off both the notion of Hanks's personhood as heavily fortified private property and the idea of his stardom as a thing for sale is our assumption of the irrevocably innocent boy-child wrapped up safely inside both. Step aside from that assumption, however, and something not so "nice" begins to emerge about the nature and function of that innocence and the masculinity it legitimates. I want to end now by describing how, as he gets "up there" in age, reputation, and implied social status alike, the masculinity Tom Hanks has come to model abets what I consider a very ominous cultural-political project indeed. But my way to that description leads through a few final summary observations on the Hanks star image, which in turn will help bring that larger project into view.

The first of these concerns a symptomatic paradox at the heart of Hanks's image as our *national* nice guy—which, notwithstanding his acknowledged support for the Clinton presidency and recent murmurs of vague interest in a political career, is that image's civic indifference. In

Saving Private Ryan, Captain Miller and the boy-men he commands and tries to save may be fighting the Good War—and the entire movie is bookended by the worn and faded American flag that flaps at the film's opening and furls at the end. But as the film depicts these characters, each comes out to be pretty much just what the anonymous soldier described himself as being in the letter from Vietnam read out at the end of an earlier and very different film, Frederick Wiseman's *High School* (1968), "just a body doing a job." In *Ryan,* those bodies need to do that job so those who inhabit them can resume real life in the asocial interpersonal world where Ryan can be reunited with his mom and Captain Miller with his wife. To save Private Ryan is, then, to engage in the squalid public sphere merely in order to recuperate and reinvest in the Private. So, too, far more obviously, with Hanks's Joe Fox, who merely does his job to increase his family's bookchain's volume and profit, so that he can then be about the business of winning the love of the woman whose livelihood he has ruined. Hanks's Miller is not out to defeat the Nazis: he's just trying to get home to his wife. Likewise, his Joe Fox in *You've Got Mail* is not an incarnation of the leveling and homogenizing tendencies of consumer capitalism in an age of rampant deregulation: he's a guy in love. Or, conversely, with Hanks's Forrest Gump and Jim Lovell, who serve the nation best and most iconically simply by doing whatever they feel like doing—going to the moon, starting a business, running across the country—for themselves. Either way, there are no larger purposes or higher values in the world in which Hanks's masculinity is normative than that of accomplishing whatever mission you happen to be given—and/or, insofar as you are still a boy-man, doing as you please: no other instructions for dealing with the world than the complementary alternatives of Do What You're Told and Whatever You Want.

And there is yet another sense in which, though the hero of our time, Hanks is emphatically not a man of the people. Even in his second most populist role, in *Private Ryan,* his Captain Miller is still the former English teacher who, alone in his squadron, has the cultural capital required to recognize Edith Piaf when he hears a record of her singing in the devastation. And in the adulation that greeted his performance as Gump, man of the people par excellence, there is a doubled note of class condescension insofar as that film not only encourages its mass audience to embrace an emphatically apolitical simpleton as its ideal national character but, together with its accompanying publicity, invites us to marvel at the spectacle of a guy as smart and witty as we know our Tom to be stooping down to portray such a sweethearted feeb. More commonly, as we have seen, our Tom is situated in an urban landscape saturated with material ease and privilege, a world that ranges narrowly from the upper reaches of petit-bourgeois entrepeneur at the bottom to CEO at the top—an idyll, in short, of the PMC, from which all traces of poverty and most nonwhite people have been unproblematically erased.

You've Got Mail (1999) is perhaps especially exemplary here, given the frequency with which Hanks is said to be our Jimmy Stewart. Nora Ephron's script is an acknowledged rewrite of the 1940 Ernst Lubitsch comedy in which Stewart starred; yet, while much has been made of the technological upgrade involved in moving from pseudonymous written letters to email as the vehicle through which the lovers find each other, even as in real life they meet as antagonists, no one to my knowledge has cared to remark on the socioeconomic upgrade involved in translating what in The Shop Around the Corner are two dueling clerks in a specialty gift shop separated only by a slight difference in rank to a bookstore owner—Meg Ryan's Annie—and a pampered, privileged corporate scion, Tom Hanks's Joe Fox. It is, I want to say, as though Hanks and Ryan, singly and together, are simply unimaginable any farther down the socioeconomic ladder, or as though no mass audience nowadays could be expected to care about a romance between a couple of service employees. And between such alternatives, of course, we do not have to choose.

So, for all those who have come to view the on- and offscreen images of the lower-class white rampager with alarm, here is Hollywood's alternative: this reinvigorated oedipality devoid of any impulse toward citizenship, this upscale straight man untarnished by desire and devoid of any race or gender ambiguity, this goofy but pointedly unwild boy-man who smoothly negotiates the potentially competing needs to buckle down and do what he's told and to kick back and do what he likes. What matters, what counts, what shows up for this nice guy to deal with are personal problems, issues regarding interpersonal relationships, in comparison with which all that is more widely social or fully political melts into air. When and where a larger polity—the nation, say—is concerned, it is conceived and represented rather as the opening credit sequence of *Sleepless in Seattle* would have it, as an untotalizable array of little starlights winking and twinkling all across the map of the United States, each representing yet another private life, another individual looking for happiness in his or her own personal sphere. And it is precisely this inattentiveness to the larger social issues at stake, this offhanded adherence to the rules of whatever background game is being played, this exclusive concern with private life and personal relations that constellates Hanks's normative identity as an innocent, nice, American white man.

"In the patriotically-permeated pseudopublic sphere of the present tense," Lauren Berlant has brilliantly, urgently argued,

> national politics does not involve starting with a view of the nation as a space of struggle violently separated by racial, sexual, and economic inequalities that cut across every imaginable kind of social location. Instead, the dominant idea . . . is of a core nation whose survival depends on personal acts and identities performed in the intimate domain of the quotidian.[12]

If such a sanitized, depoliticized, airbrushed country is indeed the hegemonic conception of the United States today, Tom Hanks must be its poster boy, the de facto president of its "intimate domain of the quotidian," a.k.a. the "Intimate Public Sphere." By contrast to him and others like him, "only the abjected, degraded *lower* citizens of the United States will see themselves as sustained by public, coalitional, non-kin affiliations."[13] And conversely: those who engage in political activity, who seek coalition, advocate for or dissent from public policy measures, attempt to construct and nurture "non-kin affiliations" with others of their various kinds, from rampaging white males to unruly people of color, strident feminists to militantly queer lesbians and gays, not to mention members of the actual working classes and the poor—all these must be labeled "abject and degraded" if not outright criminalized (over two million behind bars as I write these words, with women the fastest growing segment now that "welfare reform" has done its work) and held back, at all costs, from the gated communitywhere the nice folks face the issues that matter in the only lives worth knowing about.

It's not that hard to spot the noxious politics to which the Bruce or Mel or Sylvester may lend support; much more insidiously, *symptomati-*

cally difficult to discern and trace the line connecting Tom Hanks's virtuous, innocent white masculinity to New York mayor Rudy Giuliani's Tactical Police Units, the burgeoning prison-industrial complex, and all the voices raised to argue, incessantly and in chorus, that in an era of neoliberalism at home and abroad, "special interest politics," affirmative action programs, aid to families with dependent children, and the like are things of the past, and redistribution projects (those, that is, that direct the flow of funds downward instead of up) beyond the pale.[14] Yet like many an earlier model of white straight masculinity, the innocence of the norm now incarnated by Tom Hanks pays tribute to these activities on which it depends by denying their existence and disavowing any connection whatsoever with them. That, indeed, as my Baldwin epigraph suggests, is precisely what constitutes Tom Hanks's perpetually innocent niceness as itself "the crime": its complicity with a project of reactionary national redefinition and restructuring that obliterates the very level or register of the polis, terminates with extreme prejudice any notion of community larger than that of the nuclear family or, at most, a bunch of *Friends*-style yuppies networked by their dating interests, and stigmatizes, demonizes, and criminalizes all those whose unprivileged life circumstances might lead them to think and behave otherwise.

How stunningly appropriate, then, that in his newest film, *The Green Mile* (1999), Tom Hanks should play a prison guard with an especially sensitive relationship to the wrongly convicted Christ-like African American giant whose execution by the state he nonetheless declines to contest. From such a spectacle of Clintonian neoliberal racism, in which, paradigmatically, we are simultaneously invited to beweep and to enjoy the unjust pain we are shown, even mainstream reviewers recoiled in spasms of equally symptomatic disavowal.[15] Yet Hanks's Paul Edgecombe, even more than *You've Got Mail*'s Joe Fox, epitomizes precisely the ideal postcitizen subject the project of domestic American neoliberalism requires and rewards today and the endpoint and apex of Tom Hanks's long trajectory. Let this newest incarnation of our aging boy-man stand, then, as the point at which this analysis can and should come to a halt as well: or, rather, and more hopefully, to lead on, first, to further and more direct exploration of the sociopolitical project to which both Hanks's privileged oedipality and the lower-class preoedipal white rampager who constitutes its obverse lend support and, ultimately, to the goal of bringing that project to a halt, putting a more just and collectively liberating one in its stead.[16]

NOTES

Thanks to Virginia Blum and the rest of the gang at the University of Kentucky; and a special thanks to Chris Walters, for his research skills, keen insights, and sharp phraseology.

1. David Savran, *Taking It Like a Man: White Masculinity, Masochism, and Contemporary American Culture* (Princeton: Princeton University Press, 1998), pp. 4, 9.

2. Kurt Andersen, "The Tom Hanks Phenomenon," *New Yorker* December 7 and 14, 1998, pp. 104.

3. Quoted in Lee Pfeiffer and Michael Lewis, *The Films of Tom Hanks* (Secaucus, N.J.: Citadel, 1996), p. 87.

4. Quoted in Pfeiffer and Lewis, *Films of Tom Hanks*, p. 63.

5. For a more complete reading of *Nothing in Common* on which I have gratefully drawn for my argument here, see Elizabeth Traube's fine study, *Dreaming Identities: Class, Gender, and Generation in 1980s Hollywood Movies* (Boulder: Westview, 1992), pp. 81–85.

6. Jennet Conant, "Tom Hanks Wipes That Grin Off His Face," *Esquire*, December 1993, pp. 78, 82.

7. Brian D. Johnson, "Peaking Tom," *Maclean's*, July 11, 1994, p. 52.

8. The first, third, fourth, and fifth phrase are from Richard Corliss, "Hollywood's Last Decent Man," *Time*, July 11, 1994, p. 58. The second may have originated with Hanks himself, in a interview promoting *Turner and Hooch*, quoted in Pfeiffer and Lewis, *Films of Tom Hanks*, p. 105, in which he goes on to claim that it is "not the usual type I've played." Interestingly enough, then, when the phrase reappears, in the 1993 *Esquire* article (see note 6), it is on the heels of his remark that he doesn't " 'want to play pussies anymore' "—doesn't want, that is, to play that "ordinary guy in extraordinary circumstances" who, according to *Time*, he continues to incarnate and model nonetheless.

9. Conant, "Tom Hanks," p. 78.

10. For that matter, can it merely a coincidence that the woman who is the butt of this savagely misogynist tale bears the same name as a contemporary feminist poststructuralist critic and theorist?

11. Richard Corliss and Cathy Booth, "The Film of the Year: A Perky New Comedy," *Time*, December 21, 1998, pp. 70; " 'It Is Our Responsibility to Do Right,' " interview with Jonathan Alter, *USA Weekend*, July 24–26, 1998, p. 4.

12. Lauren Berlant, *The Queen of America Goes to Washington City* (Durham: Duke University Press, 1997), p. 4.

13. Berlant, *Queen of America*, p. 185.

14. I know of no one text that provides a comprehensive description of the overall clearing and decontamination of the commons that is underway in the U.S. today—unless not until Matt Ruben's groundbreaking dissertation on American culture in the age of neoliberalism is completed and published. Meanwhile, to triangulate and thereby map the dimensions of this comprehensive project of deterritorialization/reterritorialization, I recommend Donald Bartlett and James Steele's now somewhat outdated but still useful *America: What Went Wrong?* (Kansas City, Mo.: Andrews and McMeel, 1992); the publications of United for a Fair Economy, including Chuck Collins, Betsy Leondar-Wright, and Holly Sklar, *Shifting Fortunes: The Perils of the Growing American Wealth Gap* (Boston: UFE, 1999); James Heintz, Nancy Folbre, and the Center for Popular Economics, *New Field Guide to the U.S. Economy* (New York: New, 2000); and the invaluable information available at the UFE website at <www.stw.org>; and, last but by no means least, Elliott Currie's *Crime and Punishment in America* (New York: Holt, 1998); and Christian Parenti's *Lockdown America: Police and Prisons in the Age of Crisis* (New York and London: Verso, 1999).

15. See, for example, David Ansen's "The Executioner's Song," *Newsweek*, December 13, 1999, p. 86, or David Denby, "San Fernando Aria," *New Yorker*, December 20, 1999, p. 103.

16. For aid and companionship in this exploration, see the works by Berlant and Ruben (notes 12 and 14 repectively), and Paul Smith, *Millenial Dreams: Contemporary Culture and Capital in the North* (New York and London: Verso, 1997), especially pp. 188–264.

PEDAGOGY OF THE OPAQUE: TEACHING MASCULINITY STUDIES

Sally Robinson

It is the second week of the semester, and a student in my class on recodings of masculinity in contemporary American culture raises his hand and, in response to some feminist theoretical material or other, asks, "What does masculinity have to do with feminism?" This has happened each time I've taught this course, and while it always surprises me, the question is in fact at the heart of this pedagogical enterprise: What *does* feminism have to do with masculinity, and how does a feminist teacher negotiate the set of conflicting expectations of what it means for students to take a course on (in?) masculinity? In this essay, I theorize from my experience of teaching courses in masculinity over the past five years in order to offer some insight about the future of masculinity studies within feminism.[1] I suggest that some of the problems that emerge in the classroom are versions of the problems that have emerged within feminist analyses of masculinity on the academic scene. My aim is to push the study of masculinity forward by underlining the complex emotional as well as political roadblocks to the feminist agenda of reconstructing masculinity. By no means do I exempt myself from my own criticism; in fact, much of what I have to say here I have learned from my efforts to "teach masculinity."

The difficulty of teaching and doing masculinity studies from a feminist perspective stems from the odd relationship of masculinity studies to the oppressor/oppressed paradigm that has long governed study of gender, race, and ethnicity. The oppressor/oppressed paradigm limits what can be learned about masculinity because it sets up a binary relation between the empowered and the disempowered that reproduces the same narrative regardless of historical or cultural context. As a way out of this binary, students and scholars seek to fragment masculinity by opposing "traditional" to "alternative" models of male identity. But this strategy produces a new binary, in which a "good," alternative, and often more "feminine" masculinity is posed against a "bad," traditional, and unreconstructed masculinity. Reading the history of masculinity as the struggle between good and bad kinds of masculinity makes it difficult to understand the construction of masculinities as an ongoing process within specific historical contexts. In our own historical moment, for instance, public discussion of masculinity and "expert" diagnoses of what ails men suggest that it is the "traditional," not the "alternative," that is under siege, a scenario that dissolves the difference between these constructs and points to their inadequacy as theoretical or historical categories. The institutional contexts in which masculinity studies finds its home further entrench this binary model, predisposing students to rate men and representations as either oppressive purveyors of the gender system or the innocent victims oppressed by it. This either/or binary model dominates public discourse on gender and, while many women's studies faculty work to complicate it, its roots are deep and tenacious. The problem with lumping masculinity studies in with women's studies or ethnic studies is that masculinity—unlike femininity or blackness—already equates with power, so the empowerment model of women's or ethnic studies is almost embarrassingly inappropriate.

The wide acceptance of this model and the problems with assimilating masculinity studies to it account for a good deal of the emotional and political turmoil that can circulate in the masculinity studies classroom, where many male students come to feel that, for feminism, the only way to reconstruct masculinity is to destroy it altogether. Understanding that masculinity is in some sense a "problem" to be studied, students imagine that such a course might offer a cure for what ails men, but, as anyone who attends to the growing American concern with the problem of masculinity can attest, there is a great deal of disagreement about whether feminism is the cure or part of the disease. Within this historical context, the institutional placement of masculinity studies within "oppression" studies can easily work against the feminist project that such studies should, in my view, serve. This is a complex dilemma and one that needs to be addressed not only in the classroom but in the scholarship as well. As a number of feminists have recently argued, the focus of gender studies on men and masculinity risks leveling structures of power by granting to men's studies an equal and complementary place to women's studies. Or, as Tania Modleski puts it, studies devoted to the problem of men and feminism can "tacitly assume and promote a liberal notion of the formal equality of men and women, whose viewpoints are structurally accorded equal weight"; such work, which draws heavily on the notion of the "dialogic," Modleski continues, invokes " 'dialogue'—a concept that in eliding the question of power asymmetry has rather conservative implications" (*Feminism*, 6). In the classroom, the feminist aim of disempowering dominant masculinity can clash with the aims of students who, hearing much about the current "crisis" in masculinity, want to find a cure for this crisis, if not a way to reempower men.

My courses, taught within the English department (always crosslisted with women's studies and often with American culture), have been organized somewhat differently over the years, but they always focus on post-1968 American popular and/or middlebrow culture. We read novels by John Updike, Walter Mosely, Leonard Michaels, and John Irving, among others, and watch some seventies "art" films and some later Hollywood blockbusters. During some semesters, we've focused on wounded white men (the subject of my own current research), while during others we've focused on issues around/about the male body and embodiment. I learned quickly to stay away from the "easy" texts, films like *Fatal Attraction* that are so obviously antifeminist that we can't see masculinity for the vividness of its portrayal of pathological femininity. Instead, I direct attention to complex representations *not* of normative masculinity but of beleaguered, put-upon, wounded masculinity, as in this latest version (see appendix):

In this course, we will investigate changing representations of masculinity in contemporary American culture and ask the question: Is masculinity in crisis? In order to focus our investigation into this fertile field of inquiry, we will concentrate on texts which represent literal and metaphorical woundings of masculine selves and male bodies, and ask: How do representations of male bodies in pain point to a wide cultural and social gender "trauma" in the post-'60s U.S.? In what ways have male writers and directors "cashed in" on the current American romance with the figure of the victim? Do representations of disempowered men offer pleasure as well as pain to men as well as to women?

Some texts I assigned dwell on literal, physical, or emotional wounds suffered by men, while others represent more symbolic wounds—wounds to social position and to entitlements. In focusing on atypical (as opposed to stereotypical) masculinities, my aim is to arrive at an understanding of how normative masculinity constrains men and hurts women and of how the fictions of masculinity serve the interests of an abstract concept of male power or masculinity but few individual men.

This last point is convincing enough theoretically (and is a basic tenet of masculinity studies), and students can readily see that individual men who don't "measure up" not only suffer the consequences but are often seen as "gender traitors."[2] Attention to the conflicts *within* masculinity helps to complicate the women versus men model of gender studies, but it can also form a new binary: my students want to resolve the contradictions within representations of masculinity by posing a stable "traditional" against an insurgent "alternative." While we can learn a great deal from identifying what masculinities are hegemonic at a particular historical moment, and what emergent masculinities challenge that hegemony, a reliance on the traditional/alternative dyad actually blinds us to those historical specificities. "Traditional" masculinity always means distant, cold, insensitive and/or violent masculinity; "alternative" means anything and everything else. I suspect that the ahistorical character of such determinations stems from their source in psychoanalytic theories of masculinity and femininity, ideas to which we are so habituated we understand as "common sense" claims that are at best arguable and at worst complicit in the perpetuation of male dominance. We might ask, for instance, what purposes are served by automatically accepting the psychological truism that male identity functions by erecting rigid ego boundaries, or the one that holds men incapable of expressing emotion. There are countless analyses of literary and filmic texts that reinforce these truisms, perpetuate the alternative versus traditional conflict, and see violations of dominant masculinity as feminizations. It is a challenge to avoid the comforting fiction of a gender continuum; but we will never truly rethink masculinity if we insist on seeing any deviations from the masculine norm as "feminizations" or if we continue to see the traditional and the alternative as the only two ways to articulate the range of available masculinities within any given historical moment.

The pitfalls of the alternative versus traditional model of masculinity have become particularly clear in studying Peter Weir's seductive film, *Dead Poets Society*. Teaching this film is difficult in this context, since the students tend to be emotionally invested in its nostalgic representations of a recent period in their own personal histories. Although students whose experience is quite unlike that represented in the film (whose isn't?) do not fully identify with the privileged young protagonists whose stories it tells, the film appears to exercise some kind of deeper pull. Its melodramatic conventions and seductive visual style both add to the film's appeal, and my students have not reacted very well to what they perceive as my desire to "trash" the film and thus deprive them of their innocent pleasures in it. But this bothers my students less than one might think; they are accustomed to the deconstructive moves of feminist and nonfeminist teachers and expect to find their "naive" pleasures challenged. What bothered them more is that the film appears to espouse the very kind of sensitive masculinity that might serve as an alternative to traditional masculinity. The "they" who are most irritated with my reading of the film are the straight, white, middle-class male students who, understandably, have different investments in the film's representation of masculinity than do the women and other men. Instead of addressing why the students expected their feminist masculinity teacher to applaud the film's representation of "good" masculinity—antiauthoritarian, nonconformist, poetic, sensitive—I foregrounded the conflicts between the students, and posed the question: Do men respond differently to the film than women? While this provoked an interesting discussion, it served to further polarize gender, for it made the great divide between men and women seem natural. Thus, instead of working to *break out* of the binary model that produces traditional versus alternative masculinities, I steered the students right back into it.

What I should have done was to use this moment to deflect student expectations to make the point that masculinity isn't something "owned" by individuals, a character trait that can be evaluated as good or bad. I might draw attention away from the characters' possession of good or bad masculinity and onto the entrenchments of elite white male dominance furthered by the film's positioning of privileged white men as rebels just at the moment when the white man's "others" are about to erupt in rebellions of their own. In other words, the film reconstructs masculinity in order to head off the challenges to the very male authority it seems, on first glance, to be invested in deauthorizing. What my students' responses to the film show is that the alternative masculinity paradigm is inadequate for understanding what works to uphold hegemonic masculinity and what doesn't, and that, in fact, the alternative model may work toward emotional management complicit with the dominant, the traditional masculinity against which the alternative is posed. *Dead Poets Society* can be used to underline the problems of the attack/applaud mode that accompanies the impulse to categorize forms of masculinity as "good" or "bad," for the film ends by reinforcing the very kinds of "bad" masculinity it begins by criticizing, and it does so by elegizing the "good" masculinity as too impossibly good for this world. The suicide of Neil, the sensitive boy, has the effect of consolidating traditional masculinity by containing the threat posed to it by alternative masculinity: the "fairy" dies, and his death enables the "softening" of an authoritative masculinity whose authority nevertheless remains secure.[3]

Such a discussion would have worked to complicate the traditional/alternative paradigm central to the scholarship on masculinity. I find it telling that so many articles and books on masculinity focus on alternative masculinities and nondominant, nonhegemonic, masochistic, wounded, and/or "castrated" men, as if we could pull apart the fabric of male dominance by yanking at its loosest, most vulnerable threads. So much is clear in the most popular texts (such as Robert Bly's *Iron John*) and the most scholarly (such as Kaja Silverman's *Male Subjectivity on the Margins*). Focusing on men who embody alternatives to the dominant construct of masculinity will help us to pluralize masculinities; but does such a strategy actually work to abolish male privilege? Multiplying masculinities does not necessarily fragment the hegemonic and can often do the opposite: relegitimize the hegemonic by cordoning off difference, safely containing it within the "alternative."[4] Such an approach leaves dominant masculinity free of scrutiny and still defining the field of the masculine. It is for this reason scholars interested in deconstructing *dominant* masculinity—straight, white, middle-class masculinity— have recently begun to argue that by making hegemonic masculinity visible we begin to erode its power. The logic of this position is that while over the past three decades scholars have focused attention on women, femininity, and female sexuality, little attention has been paid to men, masculinity, and male sexuality as constructs and contingent historical fictions. This freedom from scrutiny has enabled the white, middle-class, masculine norm to remain invisible, natural, and thus unchallenged. This is a good way to begin initial discussions of masculinity in the classroom, for students quickly flesh out this claim by noting that while they have been studying men and masculinity all their academic lives (in the guise of literature, political science, history courses about humans in general), they have rarely if ever studied men as such. Yet, as I've argued elsewhere,[5] it is not, strictly speaking, accurate to say that men and masculinity have remained invisible, for the very existence of "masculinity studies" and, indeed, of the current "crisis" in masculinity, attests to the relentless making visible of masculinity, male privilege, and male sexuality orchestrated by feminism.

We might say, in fact, that the true subject of masculinity studies (if not men's studies) is how men have responded to feminist constructions of masculinity. Even when such studies focus on prefeminist eras (such as the very good historical work being done on turn-of-the-century American culture), they spring from the critique of masculinity that originates in second-wave feminism. Such responses are sometimes covert, oblique, or unconscious, but the reason we study masculinity at all—or, in a different vein, the reason that others mourn the death of "true" masculinity, or seek to recover a lost male essence—is that feminist critiques of masculinity have deeply infiltrated academic and cultural life. Any discussion of masculinity that begins from the premise that men enjoy unearned privileges in society or that male subjectivity emerges from within a position of dominance, is a discussion of the masculinity constructed by feminism. The "masculinity" that is lately subject to so much scrutiny is the *ground* of so much feminist theory that the answer to the question "What has masculinity to do with feminism?" must be, "Everything."[6] Feminist thinking has created this masculinity that we now study, deconstruct, and work to reconstruct, and *this* masculinity is anything but invisible.

Because feminist-inspired masculinity studies (as opposed to what Michael Kimmel calls "save the male" approaches to masculinity)[7] begin from the premise that there's something wrong with masculinity, students might indeed ask, "What has masculinity to do with feminism?" They *know* what feminism has to say about masculinity, especially if they've taken a women's studies course, for although women's studies is nominally and substantially devoted to the study of women, a strong subtext about men is always present. Students might reasonably expect something different from a course that is nominally and substantially about men. What that "something" might be is circumscribed by the seemingly natural reliance on the oppressor/oppressed paradigm in gender studies, with its tendency to narrativize history as the struggle between victims and victimizers and its somewhat simplistic understanding of how power operates. The problem is augmented by the institutional context that promotes student expectations about the conceptualization of "difference" within gender studies classes. That conceptualization equates difference with oppression and frames the study of that difference as a rehearsal of the historical wounds suffered by minority groups. At the University of Michigan, where I have done most of my teaching on masculinity, students are required to take a course satisfying the "race and ethnicity" requirement, and the description of the requirement makes clear that these courses must focus on "intolerance," "racism," and/or "discrimination."[8] While I won't debate the merits of such requirements here, it's clear that the concept of difference institutionalized by them precludes an understanding of racial (or gender) difference as residing in whiteness (or masculinity). With a great awareness of such requirements, and often a good deal of resentment against them, students who sign up for a course on masculinity might reasonably expect such a course to frame men as the oppressed, just as women's studies frames women as the oppressed. These expectations govern the study of difference not only within the classroom but also within what has now come under attack as "identity politics" in scholarly work. Within these contexts, the rationale for studying any group as a group seems to be the victimization of that group. Are we studying masculinity in order to show that men, too, are oppressed? Or, are we studying masculinity in order to demonstrate the oppressions committed in the name of men and masculinity? Are these the only two possibilities?

This institutionalized concept of difference poses problems for the feminist teacher of masculinity studies, who often finds herself caught between two ideological positions: men are oppressors, men are oppressed. The teaching moment that crystallized this conflict came toward the end of a class entitled "Masculinity in Crisis?" I had framed the syllabus with what I hoped would be a fruitful symmetry: we began with John Updike's 1971 *Rabbit Redux,* a novel of white male angst in relation to the radical movements of the sixties, and ended with his 1990 *Rabbit at Rest,* a novel that announces the demise of white masculinity as a dominant in American culture. Students hate *Rabbit Redux* for the naked racism and sexism that Updike both inscribes and subverts within it,[9] but *Rabbit at Rest* is a more seductive book, a perhaps kinder and gentler picture of a white masculinity in decline. The discussion of this book at the end of the semester became the catalyst for an explosion of suppressed student displeasure. Some students resented my seeming complicity with the racial and sexual ideologies espoused by Updike, while others resented what they saw as my continuous attack on white masculinity, culminating in my lack of compassion for an aging white male literary character about to die from a massive coronary. Had I somehow become two people? Had these two groups of students spent twelve weeks in the same classroom?

What was happening in this classroom was a version of what Fred Pfeil describes as his (leftist) friends' responses to his study of white masculinity:

> To the extent that one—man or woman—does choose to write about constructions of white straight masculinity, folks in my circles tend to assume that you're either gonna whomp 'em or join 'em. . . . The corollary to the notion that white straight masculinity is a single monolithic category here is, obviously enough, that it is simply, unambiguously, essentially evil as well: shot through with violence, megalomania, instrumental rationality, and the obsessive desire for recognition and definition through conquest. (vii)

Here Pfeil caricatures the construction of masculinity produced by three decades of feminist thinking, and he worries that his own book might be misread either as an attack on feminism or as a celebration of "white guys" as victims. His book, of course, is neither of these things; but the tricky thing in studying and teaching about dominant masculinity is that its odd relationship to an oppression model of gender studies exercises a seemingly irresistible pull in opposite directions: we do, somehow, always end up "whomping 'em" or "joining 'em." In my classes, the emotional and political tension often comes from the fact that some students do, in fact, want to eradicate what they take to be a dominant masculinity shot through with violence and power; others want to find an alternative masculinity they can live with; still others end up becoming defensive because they feel that they are being coerced either into a kind a self-hatred for embodying the traditional or into taking up an alternative position that borders on a "feminization." These different responses are conditioned upon individual students' sense of their own relation to the dominant fictions of masculinity—whether they are men or women and, if men, whether they feel included within the category of the masculine or excluded from it.

It is this last point that makes it difficult for me to acquiesce to Pfeil's suggestion that the gender of the writer, reader, or teacher is merely theoretical, his confident claim that "man *or* woman" would provoke the same response. In my classes, it is almost always *men* who complain about the tendency to "whomp" masculinity, and it is *women* who seem most happy to do so. Similarly, male-authored studies of masculinity often exhibit an implicit protest against the kind of overgeneralizations that have marked patriarchal attitudes toward women: "Not *all* men lord it over all women and not *all* expressions of masculinity give equal access to power and prestige." But such protests ignore the important point that masculinity *is a category,* and, like any category, works by erasing differences and specificities. Just as women have been lumped into a marked category—while men, or at least straight, white, middle-class men, have escaped categorization by being identified as the norm or the unmarked individual—so, too, does masculinity studies *mark* men. And it is the experience of this marking that is, perhaps, new to male students and scholars. Both in the classroom and in the scholarship on masculinity, the gender of the speaker *does* matter, for women and men, even if ambiguously gendered, come to the study of masculinity with differing relations to gender as a system and as an epistemological grid through which to approach the world. It is true, as Harry Brod argues in this volume, that gender is a relationship of hierarchy and power among individuals and *not* the property of separate individuals. But it is also true that men and masculinity, experience and theory, feelings and politics, get all mixed up together because patriarchal cultures function precisely by conflating these categories. When I nervously remind my students not to conflate "masculinity" with "men," I do so because I don't want to scare my male students away from a project that requires their consent in order to succeed. But there is always some truth in the suspicion that feminist study of masculinity means attacking men; in my classes, the novels and films we study rarely portray men as heroic fighters against oppression or as selfless beings who willingly renounce their power and privilege in the name of gender equality. And there's a good reason for this: studying masculinity means studying the rewards men reap for reproducing the dominant fictions and the punishments they suffer for violating them. While it is certainly the case that a large number of men—maybe even most—feel that they suffer such punishments, it is also the case that the survival of a *dominant* fiction of masculinity means that *some* people are reproducing, acting out, performing it. Although individual men never easily measure up to an impossible standard of pure masculinity, dominant masculinity nevertheless keeps reproducing itself. It is the individualist approach to gender—ruled by the assumption that people possess masculinity or femininity—that both hampers our understanding of masculinity as a coercive construct *and* causes individual men to feel attacked by the discussion of it.

What is so seductive about an individualist approach to gender is that it underwrites the traditional/alternative model and feeds our young students' desires for a postfeminist future, in which all human beings will have the freedom to be "alternative" and in which the "traditional" will disappear like the dinosaur it is. But we can't easily or productively assimilate masculinity studies to the institutionalized model of difference that understands history as a struggle between winners and losers, the simply empowered and the simply unempowered. The traditional/alternative model is not, in other words, a way out of the oppressor/oppressed paradigm. To study masculinity, and to study it in relation to systems of power, requires that we develop a more nuanced and sophisticated conceptualization of complicity and resistance. How to think complicity and resistance together—*not* from the position of women, but from the position of men? At what moments, with what effects, do men actively resist performing the dominant fictions of masculinity, and does this resistance necessarily mean that men opt out of male empowerment? Can complicity in the perpetuation of male dominance become a force for its demise? Substituting the terms of complicity and resistance for those of oppressor and oppressed might lead us out of the impasse I have often experienced in my masculinity studies classes, and women's studies, too, might benefit from disassociating itself from "oppression" studies: understanding women, also, as variably resistant to and complicit with social inequalities. Those of us who teach in women's studies or gender studies might use our courses on masculinity to underline the problems with the oppressor/oppressed paradigm not only for our students but also for administrators. This is important not only because it would make the job of teaching masculinity studies easier but because the oppression/oppressed model is the dominant model for thinking about gender and racial difference at all levels of American culture. The assumption that gender belongs to women—and race belongs to people of culture—is so deeply rooted in American culture that students who sign up for a course on masculinity sometimes even assume that that course will not be about gender. The student who asks "What has masculinity to do with feminism?" might as well be asking, "What has masculinity to do with *gender*?" For, not only is masculinity assumed to be the opposite of feminism, for the reasons that I outlined above, but gender is assumed to be the property of women and the subject of feminism. If I advertised my courses as "Feminist Approaches to Masculinity," I suspect that I would attract fewer male students than I currently do.

Masculinity studies—or, what Harry Brod terms "superordinate studies"—*can* work to complicate binary thinking about gender, but only if we foreground how and why women's studies and masculinity studies are *not* parallel or complementary enterprises. On the simplest level, there is a basic difference in aim between masculinity studies and women's studies: while women's studies aims to empower women, masculinity studies must come to terms with the fact that masculinity already equates with power. The work driven by the claim that masculinity retains its power by remaining invisible aims to reimagine the workings of power and to break out of a simplistic oppressor/oppressed paradigm. Yet, perhaps because of the seemingly irresistible American romance with the figure of the victim—institutionalized through identity politics and its academic outlets—the visibility thesis can easily reinstall the paradigm it was meant to disrupt: men can now be seen as the victims of the feminist critique of masculinity. The visibility thesis both underestimates the effect of feminist thinking about masculinity over the past three decades and overestimates the progressive political effects of making masculinity visible. Men have become visible, first as the enemies of feminism and more lately as the victims of feminism. And, despite the feminist critique and the mainstream backlash against it, men are still in power. Dominant masculinity always manages to reassert itself, and attempts to restructure patriarchy move at a glacial pace. The feminist critique of dominant masculinity has certainly worked to make masculinity visible, but if this effort has eroded male privilege, it has also prepared the ground for retrenchments of that privilege. While it is useful to ask questions about men's pain, along with men's pleasure, and to focus on nonhegemonic forms or performances of masculinity, it is also risky: how to acknowledge men's pain, and the wounds caused by what Tracy Karner calls a "toxic masculinity," without resorting to simplistic claims that men are just as hurt by patriarchy as women? Oddly, feminism and patriarchy can be seen to work hand in hand, both limiting the possibilities available to men who are forced to adhere to oppressive gender scripts. Men have, in fact, become the newest victims—witness the newsworthiness of Christina Hoff Sommers's *The War Against Boys: How Misguided Feminism Is Harming Our Young Men* and the far more subtle *Stiffed,* by Susan Faludi. While my own work has convinced me that many American men do in fact see themselves as victims of feminism, I worry that feminist stances such as mine can be misunderstood in the current postfeminist (and post–affirmative action) context as arguing that men are oppressed as a group *because they are men.*

Masculinity studies *can* provide a feminist way out of the gender binary, but they can also too easily be assimilated to a postfeminist project that aims to level the fields of power and see all differences as equal. The figure of the white male victim is the emblem of this assimilation, and it is crucial that we resist the urge to institutionalize this figure as the subject of masculinity studies. New kinds of white male power can and do emerge out of victimization, even as the new visibility of dominant masculinity promises to make male power seems less natural and inevitable. Feminists occasionally feel that all this attention to masculinity masks a new ruse of patriarchy, an attempt to keep men in the center; scholars invested in reconstructing, and thus "saving" masculinity, occasionally feel such attention merely serves to rehearse the same old truths about the essential negativity of the masculine. What I have learned in the masculinity studies classroom is that these are not idle complaints; the question whether masculinity studies is to be complicit with, or resistant to, the maintenance of male dominance is at the heart of the theoretical and pedagogical enterprise of masculinity studies. But, just as important is the question whether feminist theory—as it circulates in academic venues and in the classroom—can come to terms with the fact that it has leaned against an essentially negative construction of masculinity. Masculinity studies, in my view, takes off from the deeply felt conviction—on the part of male and female scholars and teachers— not only that masculinity must be deconstructed as a cultural construct but that men, too, must be convinced to distance themselves from the dominant fictions of masculinity that do, more often than not, procure rewards within patriarchal culture. The challenge is not to distance men from *feminism* in the process and not to distance feminism from women.

APPENDIX: SYLLABUS

Professor Sally Robinson
Senior Seminar: American Masculinities

I. Theorizing Masculinity in Post-Sixties America

Michael Kimmel, "The Masculine Mystique" and "Wimps, Whiners, and Weekend Warriors," from *Manhood in America* (secondary)

Lynne Segal, "The Manly Ideal" and "Competing Masculinities: Black Masculinity and the White Man's Black Man," from *Slow Motion: Changing Masculinity,* Changing Men (secondary)

II. Displaced and Disempowered White Men: Surviving the Sixties?

John Updike, *Rabbit Redux* (1971)

John Boorman, dir., *Deliverance* (1972)

Marc Feigen Fasteau, "Violence: The Primal Test," from *The Male Machine* (primary)

Susan Bordo, "Reading the Male Body" (secondary)

Leonard Michaels, *The Men's Club* (1978)

Paul Newman, dir., *Sometimes a Great Notion* (1977)

Richard Lemon, from *The Troubled American* (primary)

Glenn Bucher, "The Enemy: He is Us" and "Confessions," from *Straight/ White/Male* (primary)

Barbara Ehrenreich, "The Androgynous Drift: Counterculture versus Masculine Culture" (secondary)

II. Psychic, Emotional and Physical Wounds: War, Male Sensibility, and the Reinvention of Masculinity

Pat Conroy, *The Prince of Tides* (1986)

Peter Weir, dir., *Dead Poets Society* (1989)

Mike Hammond, "The Historical and Hysterical: Melodrama, War and Masculinity in *Dead Poets Society*" (secondary)

Hal Ashby, dir., *Coming Home* (1978)

Tracy Karner, "Fathers, Sons, and Vietnam: Masculinity and Betrayal in the Life Narratives of Vietnam Veterans with Post Traumatic Stress Disorder" (primary)

Tim O'Brien, *The Things They Carried* (1990)

IV. Dangerous Masculinities and Endangered Men: Male Anxieties, Urban Realities and New Crises

John Singleton, dir., *Boyz N the Hood* (1991)

Robin D. G. Kelley, "Kickin' Reality, Kickin' Ballistics: 'Gangsta Rap' and Post-industrial Los Angeles" (secondary)

Michele Wallace, from *Black Macho and the Myth of the Superwoman* (primary)

Walter Mosley, *Black Betty* (1994)

Fred Pfeil, beginning of "Soft-Boiled Dicks" (secondary)

James William Gibson, "Introduction: Post-Vietnam Blues" and "Old Warriors, New Warriors" (secondary)

Joel Schumacher, dir., *Falling Down* (1993)

Fred Pfeil, "Chips Off the Old Block" (secondary)

NOTES

1. I use *masculinity studies* instead of *men's studies* because *men's studies* can describe a less feminist study of men and masculinity than what I am addressing here. I do realize that others will disagree with me on this question, but in my experience *men's studies* as a term has been contaminated by the ideologies of the highly visible men's movement (and its recent offshoots, the less-than-feminist Promise Keepers and other widely publicized men's groups/meetings). While I can't imagine the point of a masculinity studies that isn't feminist, I can imagine (and in fact have seen) a men's studies that is not.

2. As Harry Brod argues in this volume, an individualistic approach to gender obscures the ways in which the very notion of individualism is a *gendered* construct masquerading as a neutral one. In other words, while talk about "masculin*ities*" is meant to deconstruct a monolithic, singular construct of the masculine in part by individualizing expressions or performances of masculinity, it can have the effect of obscuring the systemic and institutional manueverings of male power by measuring the relative power of specific individuals. It is worth noting here that masculinity *as a category* functions primarily to police the boundaries of the normative, keeping some individuals inside, while the vast majority remain excluded. The primary articulation of that "inside" in American culture is through the concept of the (unmarked) individual; thus, a focus on individualism and individual masculinities perpetuates the very problem it is meant to solve.

3. See also Tania Modleski's reading of the film (*Feminism,* 137–40) and my own in *Marked Men.* Mike Hammond has criticized the film's ideological presuppositions on slightly different grounds, and he begins his essay by questioning why it is that progressive academic men are so enamoured of it ("Historical").

4. Ross Chambers makes the important point that the dominant (whiteness or masculinity) functions in part by claiming a singularity opposed to the heterogeneity of the "other."

> Like the difference between white and non-white, that between masculine and non-masculine, or metropolitan and non-metropolitan (notice I don't say white and black, or masculine and feminine, or metropolitan and colonial) is the difference between an incomparable singular and a plural—the plural of "colors" and "ethnicities," of straight women/lesbians/gay men, of the different kinds of colonies, "client states" and provinces—whose members are eminently subject to comparison among themselves. Thus gay men are "like women" and so on. ("Unexamined," 143)

I read here a caution against reading multiplicity (in masculinities, for instance) as necessarily dangerous to the dominance of what both Chambers and I call the "unmarked."

5. See my *Marked Men*, particularly the introduction.

6. Fred Pfeil, quite rightly, I think, notes that a monolithic, essentially negative "masculinity" has been necessary to much of feminist analysis, even if I find in his tone an intriguing confession of his own wounds vis-à-vis feminism: "It has at least occasionally seemed to me in my readings, experiences and encounters with left-feminist culture over the past decade or so that [various] 'others' are dependent for their sense of affiliation and equivalence with one another, and all the more so for their self-approving understandings of their own lability, fluidity, and positionality, on the founding assumption of their opposition to another tribe whose mode of being is essentially immobile, oppressive, and unchanging; and that, accordingly, such others have little interest in interrogating the folkways or representations of that other tribe for any evidence that it, or any members within it, might be changing or moving around" (*White*, ix–x). This is a perfect example of the lament often barely audible in some male-authored studies of masculinity that I will address later.

7. See Kimmel's chapter on 1990s versions of men's liberation ideologies in *Manhood*, 291–328.

8. The text of the requirement, as distributed among faculty, reads: "All LS&A students are required to take a course in race and ethnicity before graduating. If you are planning to offer such a course, please take a moment to indicate its relation to the requirement. Does your course:

1. discuss the meaning of race, ethnicity, and racism?

2. discuss racial and ethnic intolerance and resulting inequality?

3. compare discrimination based on race, ethnicity, religion, social class, or gender?

"Every one course satisfying the Race and Ethnicity Requirement must devote substantial, but not necessarily exclusive, attention to the required content. For some courses, an annotated copy of the syllabus may be enough the show that the conditions are met. For others, the syllabus will need to be supplemented with brief explanations."

The description of the requirement written for students is essentially the same, with the focus on studying oppression rather than, say, cultural contributions or comparative race studies. The idea that one might study *whiteness* as a racial category is more or less prohibited by the terms of the requirement. These descriptions are available at <http://www.lsa.umich.edu>.

9. This may be an illusion on my part, one fostered by the generally tolerant student population at Michigan. In my experience, students are no longer accustomed to such bald, apparently unapologetic articulations of racism and sexism. Needless to say, the climate of "political correctness," and the loud critique of it mounted by the Right in the late 1980s, both contribute to this discomfort. One of the hardest things for me in teaching such texts has been my not always successful attempts to nudge students toward a different mode of evaluation. I want them to see *Rabbit Redux* as a historical document, a *representation* of a particular mode of white masculinity in a particular context. But teaching this book always risks reinforcing its racism and sexism.

WORKS CITED

Bordo, Susan. "Reading the Male Body." *Michigan Quarterly Review* 32.4 (Fall 1993): 696–737.

Brod, Harry, ed. *The Making of Masculinities: The New Men's Studies.* Cambridge: Unwin Hyman, 1987.

Bucher, Glenn, ed. *Straight/White/Male.* Philadelphia: Fortress, 1976.

Carrigan, Tim, Bob Connell, and John Lee. "Toward a New Sociology of Masculinity." In Harry Brod, ed., *The Making of Masculinities: The New Men's Studies,* pp. 63–100. Cambridge: Unwin Hyman, 1987.

Chambers, Ross. "The Unexamined." *Minnesota Review* 47 (Fall 1996): 141–56.

Conroy, Pat. *The Prince of Tides.* New York: Bantam: 1976.

Ehrenreich, Barbara. *The Hearts of Men: American Dreams and the Flight from Commitment.* New York: Anchor, 1983.

Faludi, Susan. *Stiffed: The Betrayal of the American Man.* New York: William Morrow, 1999.

Farrell, Warren. *The Myth of Male Power: Why Men Are the Disposable Sex.* New York: Simon and Schuster, 1993.

Fasteau, Marc Feigen. *The Male Machine.* New York: McGraw Hill, 1974.

Gibson, James William. *Warrior Dreams: Violence and Manhood in Post-Vietnam America.* New York: Hill and Wang, 1994.

Hammond, Mike. "The Historical and the Hysterical: Melodrama, War, and Masculinity in *Dead Poets Society.*" In Pat Kirkham and Janet Thumim, eds., *You, Tarzan: Masculinity, Movies, and Men.* pp. 52–65. New York: St. Martin's, 1993.

Jeffords, Susan. *The Remasculinization of America: Gender and the Vietnam War.* Bloomington: Indiana University Press, 1989.

Karner, Tracy. "Fathers, Sons, and Vietnam: Masculinity and Betrayal in the Life Narratives of Vietnam Veterans with Post Traumatic Stress Disorder." *American Studies* 37.1 (Spring 1996): 63–94.

Kelley, Robin D. G. "Kickin' Reality, Kickin' Ballistics: 'Gangsta Rap,' and Postindustrial Los Angeles." In *Race Rebels: Culture, Politics, and the Black Working Class,* pp. 183–227. New York: Free, 1994.

Kimmel, Michael S. *Manhood in America: A Cultural History.* New York: Free, 1996.

Lemon, Richard. *The Troubled American.* New York: Simon and Schuster, 1969.

Michaels, Leonard. *The Men's Club.* Expanded ed. San Francisco: Mercury House, 1993 [1978].

Modleski, Tania. *Feminism Without Women: Culture and Criticism in a "Postfeminist" Age.* New York and London: Routledge, 1991.

Pfeil, Frank. *White Guys: Studies in Postmodern Domination and Difference.* New York and London: Verso, 1995.

Pleck, Joseph. "The Theory of Male Sex-Role Identity: Its Rise and Fall, 1936 to the Present." In Harry Brod, ed., *The Making of Masculinities: The New Men's Studies.* pp. 21–38. Cambridge: Unwin Hyman, 1987.

Robinson, Sally. *Marked Men: White Masculinity in Crisis* New York: Columbia University Press, 2000.

Segal, Lynne. *Slow Motion: Changing Masculinities, Changing Men.* New Brunswick, N.J.: Rutgers University Press, 1990.

Silverman, Kaja. *Male Subjectivity at the Margins.* New York and London: Routledge, 1992.

Sommers, Christina Hoff. *The War Against Boys: How Misguided Feminism Is Harming Our Young Men.* New York: Simon and Schuster, 2000.

Updike, John. *Rabbit at Rest.* New York: Knopf, 1990.

———. *Rabbit Redux.* New York: Fawcett Crest, 1971.

Wallace, Michele. *Black Macho and the Myth of the Superwoman.* New York and London: Verso, 1995 [1978].

STUDYING MASCULINITIES AS SUPERORDINATE STUDIES

Harry Brod

T he guys don't read that far in the course catalog; they don't get to women's studies."

That was one explanation why there were so few men given by the female students in my "Men and Masculinities" course. Only two out of fifteen, to be precise. There have been more women than men in the course every time I've taught it, both this year and last year as a women's studies course at the University of Pennsylvania as well as every other time I've taught it over the years, previously at UCLA, Antioch University at Los Angeles, Kenyon College, or originally at the University of Southern California. The course averages from around 20 to 40 percent men. Through what seems to be just the luck of the draw, this year's numbers are particularly skewed.

I make that a subject of discussion the first day of every course. Why do you think, I ask my students, that there are more women than men in a class on men? The answers they give end up falling into what I eventually classify as two categories—the more psychological and the more sociological explanations.

Psychologically, part of the content of contemporary mainstream male roles is to show competence and knowledge. As sociologist Michael Kimmel puts it, "Real men don't study gender." By this standard, he goes on to explain, for a man to admit that he has questions about masculinity is already to admit that he has failed at masculinity. Why, then, would one take a course on what one already knows, when the mere act of taking such a course seems to signal that one does not know what one is already supposed to know?

Supposed here carries two meanings. One is "supposed" to know about masculinity in the empirical sense that one's friends and acquaintances will normally "suppose," i.e., "assume," that one knows it. One wishes not to call this assumption into question because of the other, normative meaning of *supposed,* i.e., one "should" already know this. (If the difference is not clear, an example might help. If I enjoy eating food of a certain cuisine, my friends may suppose that I also know something about cooking in that tradition. But if their supposition turns out to be wrong, my stature does not necessarily diminish in their eyes, because this is not knowledge that I am necessarily "supposed" to have. In contrast, my traditionally minded male friends will normally "suppose" that I know about masculinity because this is knowledge that I am "supposed" to have, and if I do not have it I will have violated the requisite codes of masculinity that we are "supposed"—in both senses—to share).

Some of the students volunteer more sociological answers to the question of the relative absence of men in the classroom. These answers look not at the psychology of individual men but at power relations among groups, specifically between men and women. From this perspective, one would expect that questions about a system of power, in this case gender, would more reliably come from those who are disadvantaged by the system. I make a point of noting, however, that even though such questions come more reliably from those receiving the short end of the stick, they do not come solely from that quarter. Thus, questions about race will more reliably, though not exclusively, come from people of color than from white people. And, as we see by the gender demographics of this class on men and masculinities, questions about gender will more reliably come from women than from men, even, or perhaps especially, when the gender in question is that of men. Men, as do whites, have a vested interest in not asking questions about the sources of their privileges. Any form of oppression maintains itself in power in part by masking how it operates, making its structure as invisible as possible. To shed light on masculinity is therefore at least potentially to threaten patriarchy. Men who are willing to question masculinity to the extent of devoting a semester to examining it therefore pose a threat to their own and other men's power. As implicit and inchoate as that knowledge may be in men who might consider taking such a course, it is not too far fetched to suppose that at some level the imperatives of patriarchy do operate in the processes of course selection.

To this mix of reasons for the dearth of men in the course I add another factor, if it has not already been brought into the conversation by the students. This additional factor is heterosexism, or homophobia. I explain that this functions as a kind of glue or cement that holds sexism in place (Pharr, *Homophobia*). I do not depart from my traditional sex role, given a heterosexist society, lest I be taken for one of "them," in which case I can expect various aspects of heterosexist oppression to descend upon me in all too quick condemnation. This provides powerful incentive for not raising questions about gender.

For all these reasons, then, I tell my students that I believe it important to validate the courage of men who are willing to come through the door of a class on "Men and Masculinities," for they are resisting a good deal of social pressure in doing so.

All this being said, we also address another question of student motivation vis-à-vis this course. We discuss not only why men are not present but also why women are. The question why women would take a course on men becomes more pointed once one realizes that many of these women are women's studies majors or minors. In that context, haven't they learned that academia as a whole already constitutes one grand course in "men's studies?" Why, then, take *another* course on men?

Here, too, one can discern more psychological and more sociological perspectives. For some women, the course promises an opportunity to get inside the heads of the guys they know. What is really going on in there? They think of their boyfriends and their male friends, their fathers and brothers, and are curious about what makes them tick. Other women are less concerned with the psychology of men they know than with acquiring knowledge of men as a group, men they do not know personally. Recognizing the degree to which it is still a man's world and recognizing that knowledge is power, they want to gain knowledge of how the other half lives, thinks, and feels in order to move more effectively in that world. These interests produce a more sociological orientation to the course.

My own orientation to the subject matter of the course is primarily sociological, as is, not surprisingly, my core textbook in the course, Michael S. Kimmel and Michael A. Messner's edited anthology, *Men's Lives,* which is the most widely used text in such courses. The lead article in the volume is Michael Kaufman's "The Construction of Masculinity and the Triad of Men's Violence," which very usefully frames the relationship between these two frameworks that emerge from our opening discussions, a more psychological, individualist approach to the study of masculinities and a more sociological, collectivist approach. While we attempt in the course to be true to the internal subjective experience of men, we also attempt to situate that experience in the context of the social construction of masculinities. The latter provides a critical perspective on the former. Bringing the insights of the latter to bear can bring an awareness that people in certain social situations with certain degrees of access to social resources may, by virtue of such situatedness, find themselves wearing systematic filters or blinders that prevent them from seeing various aspects of what they are experiencing. To give one crucial example, as Kaufman explains, men's subjective experience of themselves as lacking power, especially vis-à-vis women, may not be the last word in a more objective analysis of the social realities in which they find themselves.

Gender is not the only axis of social power with which we are concerned in the course. Other dimensions of our lives, such as race, ethnicity, class, sexual orientation, religion, age, and other factors are also in play. While the course focuses on gender, I explain to the students that this focus does not imply a hierarchy of oppressions or any claim that the category of gender is intrinsically more important than any of these other categories. One must simply choose to highlight one or a few factors at a time. I present as a (hopefully) creative tension in the course this tension between needing to foreground gender in our conversations and holding to the analytical principle that one cannot isolate a dimension such as gender from other dimensions such as race, class, sexual orientation, etc., without oversimplifying and perhaps even falsifying what one is attempting to analyze.

Even focusing on one side of the gender question, the male side, risks violating one of the analytical principles from which I teach. For I believe that gender is not an attribute of individuals at all, but a relational category. That is to say, it is a theoretical mistake to think that one can analyze women's lives and men's lives separately and then simply synthesize the results of these analyses into an analysis of gender. This sort of "separate spheres" model of gender misses precisely the core of the reality of gender, that gender is a socially constructed category formed precisely in and through the interplay of the genders. Though it is legitimate, and perhaps even at some points necessary, for analytical, heuristic, or pedagogic reasons to focus on one gender at a time, this should not blind us to the fact that this practice is also a falsification, a necessary pedagogic evil in which we will inevitably miss or distort some important truths, analogous to the necessary pedagogic evil of isolating gender from other social hierarchies and categories.

For example, this past year when I asked for their final overview of the course, several of my female students complained that one topic in which they were interested had fallen through the cracks. Our text divides things up in a way that has become typical of masculinity studies. It focuses on men's relationships with other men in one chapter titled "Men with Men: Friendships and Fear," which includes essays on friendships among men of varying sexual orientations and on the subject of homophobia and heterosexism; it discusses men's relationships with women in a chapter titled "Men with Women: Intimacy and Power," which includes essays on consensual heterosexual relationships and on rape and other acts of violence against women. Thus the essays on men's relationships with men include both sexual and nonsexual relationships, but the essays on men's relationships with women discuss only issues related to sexuality. What is missing here is any discussion of nonsexual male-female relationships. But many of the women come to the course motivated precisely by a desire to understand better their relationships with their male peers with whom they are friends. They notice that both they and their male friends act differently in these cross-gender friendships than they do in their same-sex friendships, and they wish to understand these differences. But with the academic turf divided between women's studies and men's studies as it has been, this topic of cross-gender friendships has been at home on neither side of the divide.

For the students, this omission is a casualty of our not yet having reached a more fully inclusive way of teaching about gender.

Focusing a course on gender on the superordinate instead of the subordinate group, as does a course on men and masculinities, produces a paradigm shift that can illuminate both sides of the gender divide in new and informative ways. For example, much has been said and written about the feminization of poverty. But, as I point out to my students, the logically necessary corollary to the feminization of poverty is the masculinization of wealth. Very little is said or written about that. Putting it that way, however, shifts the focus, and works to preclude the inappropriate framing of the question in terms of what women may or may not be doing wrong that prevents them from getting their fair share of available wealth, and points us instead to the more appropriate question of what men are doing to garner more than their fair share.

Put most simply, I want my students to understand that men are gendered too. To study "gender" is not just to study women, who are marked as gendered by their oppression (traditionally, women are "*the sex*"). To let the study of gender be equivalent to the study of women is to leave men as unmarked by gender and hence normatively human. But the unmarkedness of the superordinate is precisely the mark of their dominance, as we saw with relation to discussions of the feminization of poverty. In contrast to this patriarchal paradigm in which men are seen as generically and normatively human, the study of masculinities sees men as specifically gendered beings. So, to look at another example, we might question what "fathering" a child might mean or might come to mean as a social activity distinct from the biological act of siring a child and distinct as well from both the gendered social activity of "mothering" and from the ostensibly gender neutral activity of "parenting." Is there, or might there come to be, if we in the final analysis deem it desirable, a male gender specific way of parenting, and, if so, what would it look like? As a society, we have hardly investigated what fathering really means. Numerous studies give us voluminous information about working mothers: when they return to paid work, how they experience role strain, the ages of their children, etc. But similar information on working fathers is extremely rare and difficult to come by.

The paradigm shift of superordinate studies regarding gender paves the way for students to make analogous shifts when thinking about other categories of social hierarchy (Brod, "Case"). Once they have internalized this model, a study of race, for example, can no longer be mistaken solely for a study of people of color. Students will now come to see whites as being raced as well. Further, as I develop this perspective with my students, they come to see that the commonly posed question "What causes homosexuality?" has no answer, not because we do not have the empirical data we need to answer it, but because it is in principle unanswerable, because it takes as norm and leaves uninterrogated the dominant category of heterosexuality. The question that might one day be answered is not "What causes homosexuality?" but rather "What causes sexual orientation?" Questioning the category itself, rather than just the subordinate group marked by it, is in principle the only possible route toward the requisite knowledge.

To stress the socially constructed nature of social categories, I ask my students to consider how each category is part of the reciprocal constitution of itself and the other. Various opportunities for extended social analysis then present themselves. For example, to what extent are masculine identities forged by struggles to avoid the stigma of femininity? And if gender is a role or an enactment, who exactly is the audience for this performance: one's own gender, the other gender, oneself, society at large? Further, what did James Baldwin really mean when he claimed that Europeans did not know they were white until they came to the United States and confronted African Americans here? How is homophobia implicated in the construction of the masculinities of straight men?

In my course the shift from looking at the subordinate to looking at the superordinate goes hand in hand with the shift already discussed from a more psychological emphasis on the attributes or character traits of individuals to a more sociological emphasis on the social construction of group identities, identities constructed largely through differing relative degrees of access to social power available to different social groups. There are several positive effects of the students coming to understand their gender identities as the internalization of social structures rather than adhering to the individualist perspective that sees social structures as individual identities writ large. Especially noteworthy is how this removes the stigma of "male-bashing" that men especially, but women as well, are worried they will get in the course. Students associated with the campus "Greek" systems of fraternities and sororities are especially wary of anything that seems to blame men, and particularly "fraternity guys," for problems of sexism and especially for problems of sexual assault on college campuses. In this regard I have found the essays on fraternity culture in *Men's Lives* particularly useful, for they not only deal with the substantive issues but also contain methodological sections that highlight how these essays are engaged in sociological analysis of fraternities as social institutions, not psychological analysis of fraternity men as deviant individuals (Boswell and Spade, "Fraternities"; O'Sullivan, "Fraternities"). The emphasis is on how institutions and their cultures tend to elicit certain types of behaviors, not on how certain types of men band together in order to gang up on women. Emphasizing these methodological issues in class seems to free students to participate in the discussion by releasing them from fears that they will just be "trashing" their friends. I emphasize that when we discuss sexism (by whatever name, e.g., *patriarchy, male dominance,* or whatever related terms they will read and hear) we are not thereby declaring men to be evil. We are not engaged in a project of pointing our fingers at individual males in order to assign blame but are rather analyzing how societies and social groups function.

For at least some men, moving away from being personally blamed for sexism facilitates moving toward taking personal responsibility for it. It is difficult, if not impossible, to take effective steps toward positive personal and political change if one imagines oneself thereby to be taking steps in opposition to oneself. But if I see that my target is not myself but rather social forces and what they have done to me, I find such steps become not only possible but desirable. Making men's profeminist political activism part of the content of the course, as I do, which includes bringing in local activists as guest speakers, then gives men some ideas for concrete steps they might take. I have seen several male students embark or move further along on an activist path at least in part because of the course.

Attention to how the perspectives of the course relate to the personal and political empowerment of the students is crucial in such a course (and indeed in any course). One reason for paying particular attention to this in a course on gender is that many of our students have a deeply distorted understanding of the relationship between feminism and the goals of empowerment. Many of them have, in varying degrees, accepted the contemporary right-wing criticism that women's studies and feminism more broadly teach women to think of themselves as "victims" and thereby make women less powerful and independent than they can and should be. To those, like myself, who came of age with the pioneering women's studies generation that emerged from the 1960s, this charge is bizarre indeed. To us, it is clear that women's studies and feminism are about empowering women, and it is the antifeminist right that works to disempower them. Nonetheless, this right-wing calumny, propagated through the mainstream media, has influenced many of the students who come to our classes. This mischaracterization of feminism serves the conservative agenda of dismantling whatever is left of the social safety net provided by the state. For, according to the logic of this extreme conservative and individualist position, to accept help from the state is to declare one's dependence on handouts from the state, thereby declaring oneself a "victim." On this view, to escape from victimhood one must stand up for oneself and insist that one will make it on one's own, without assistance from the welfare state. Thus, neoconservatives argue that it is they who really respect and assist women and racial minorities, because it is they who wish to dismantle the liberal welfare state that condescendingly infantalizes them.

This conservative antifeminist rhetoric to which many of our students have been relentlessly exposed, often through the medium of ubiquitous talk shows, has made them hostile to feminism, or at least the term *feminism,* given what they believe it means. To them, feminism embodies a disparaging view of women as victims, i.e., dependent, lacking individual initiative, and disempowered. Young college students are particularly vulnerable to this rhetoric, for it appeals not only to the deeply seated individualism of U.S. culture generally but also to specific issues they face as young adults who need confidence that the world is theirs for the taking. Many young women, especially, resist identifying with feminism because they think that taking on feminist beliefs means taking on a view of themselves as less personally empowered.

Pedagogically, improving their understanding of the issues requires first of all respecting the validity of their point of view. For if this were indeed what feminism stood for, they would be quite right to resist it. Fortunately, this has never been what feminism meant by describing

women as victims of sexism or patriarchy, and it is furthermore fortunately not difficult to clarify this. What is required here is a distinction
between a psychological and a sociological sense of victimhood. The
deeply apolitical, and therefore conservative, individualism of U.S. culture leads our students habitually to translate terms of political analysis into psychological categories. Thus, they readily understand feminism's claims that women are victims of patriarchy to mean that feminism claims that women have adopted a victim's personality profile that
is dependent and helpless. But by describing women as victims, feminism never meant to make this claim about women's psychological
makeup. Feminism always understood this as a sociological claim about
the unjust allocation of social resources between and among groups. To
say that women are victims of patriarchy has always meant to feminists
that, compared to men, women have less than their proportionate share
of socially allocated resources.

I use various analogies to make the point clear to my students. Given
a society set up predominantly to further men's interests, when men act
in their own interests they are "going with the flow," and their personal
efforts are enforced and amplified by the social currents already at work.
Often they need do no more than just tread water to stay afloat, and the
mainstream malestream social currents will carry them forward. But
when women act to advance their interests in such a society, they are
swimming upstream, against the current. Thus, even if they are as personally powerful as men, they will not get as much mileage out of their
efforts. It is in this social sense that women are victims. But, as feminism
has always insisted, they have been victims who have also vigorously resisted the social currents against which they must swim, and they should
not be considered less powerful just because the social currents push
against them such that their efforts bring them fewer social rewards
than do the equivalent efforts of men.

Building on this metaphor, viewing society as a stream helps students
to see that social forces are at work that have a certain direction and
power. This helps to break down the overly static and simplistic view
they tend to have of society, which appears to them to be a neutral background for the exercise of individual agency. The various dimensions of
privilege carried by those in the superordinate group still seem normal
to most of them, a natural and naturalized state to which the oppressed

will automatically rise once the burdens of oppression have been removed. The fortunes of the superordinate appear simply as merited
natural entitlement rather than as fortunes extracted from the misfor-
tunes of the oppressed. But in reality the superordinate have a built-in
advantage simply because all of us are immersed in the same stream,
whose currents favor some over others. Those in the dominant group
need not have any intention to discriminate against or take advantage of
anyone to benefit from being in the mainstream. Typical of these benefits, for example, is how men's voices tend to be heard more clearly and
register as more rational than women's. For if one speaks in harmony
with the established order, one's voice blends smoothly into the chorus,
but if one's speech is out of sync with that order, it grates on the ears of
those who remain in sync. Because of this built-in advantage, men need
not be deliberately trying to outshout or overpower women's voices, but
their voices will nonetheless drown out women's voices if they just speak
in their normal register.

This perspective undercuts the myth of social neutrality that many
people hold very deeply and dearly, according to which if someone is
floundering because of the weight of oppression bearing down on them
all that is required is for the weight to be removed so that they may float
freely like the rest of us, who supposedly swim on our own in a neutral
social sea. But seeing the social setting as a flowing stream, inherently fa-
voring some over others, rather than as a static sea on which all float
equally, makes them realize there is no neutral resting point. If the
ability of some to pursue their interests is made more difficult by the direction in which social forces flow, then the abilities of others to pursue
their interests is equivalently made easier by those same forces. On the
scales of injustice, the same weight that pulls one side down pulls necessarily the other side up.

Probably the most direct application to a contemporary controversy
of the shift in perceptions that adopting this new perspective can bring
about is that it enables students to see that affirmative action in favor of
the oppressed is not a case of reverse discrimination, as conservative
critics would have it, but is rather simply a leveling of the playing field.
Contrary to what many of them have heard and believe, affirmative action is not in opposition to the principles of equal opportunity that they
support; it rather embodies them. It is not just that women face a glass

ceiling that hinders their advancement, while men need to walk up the stairs on their own. Rather, men are on a glass escalator that propels them through that ceiling (Williams, "Glass"). While it is true that a talented and energetic woman may be able to break through the ceiling, it is equally true that a man need only be average to move upward on the escalator. It is not just that some of us are oppressed; it is also and necessarily equally the case that some of us are privileged. Indeed, privilege and oppression are just two ways of speaking of the same thing. To speak of racism is to speak of white privilege, and to speak of sexism is to speak of male privilege. Any course on gender, whether focusing on men or women, is therefore necessarily a course on patriarchy.

Studying the institutional advantages of the superordinate means that in addition to understanding how the personal is political and vice versa, a guiding insight of the women's movement, students must also come to understand how the personal is different from the political. If upper-class men, for example, appear to be personally more genteel, "kinder and gentler" than working-class men, this is only because those who have institutional power can afford to let the institutions do their dirty work for them, while they need not dirty their hands. But those who lack social privilege and have only their personal power to exercise end up with their struggles and prejudices showing more in their personal behavior, with their rough edges all too painfully visible.

Becoming more aware of society as an active force in the lives of individuals, with inherent tendencies to move in directions that favor some over others, helps to render the dynamics of privilege more visible. While many have learned to see oppression, far fewer have learned to see privilege equally clearly. For example, while "gay bashing" readily comes to their minds as an example of heterosexism, the ability to be physically demonstrative in public with one's heterosexual partner comes much less readily to their minds as an example of the heterosexual privilege many of them take for granted. And while they immediately and passionately denounce stereotyping as oppressive, it is striking and sometimes disturbing to them to see not being stereotyped, i.e., being seen as an "individual," as "who they really are," as privilege rather than as simple natural right. In class I tell them that although I may be worried that they think I'm stupid, I am not worried that they will then walk out of the class also believing that white men are stupid. I get to be seen as representing only myself. But if I were a woman of color I might well worry that if I appeared stupid to them I would reinforce stereotypes about women and/or people of color. Such inequalities fuel a self-perpetuating oppressive cycle. With part of my attention taken up by worrying about the effects of my performance on my group, a burden those from the dominant group do not have to carry, I therefore have fewer available resources to devote to the task at hand, which then unfairly becomes that much more difficult for me.

The difference between being seen as an individual and being seen as a member of a group is essential in enabling my students to think more effectively in sociological terms. Given their deep commitments to individualism, they tend to resist any categorization of people into groups, seeming to feel it to be almost a violation of individual rights to be so grouped, which resistance then makes it impossible to grasp how social forces operate. They react as if sociological thought necessarily engages in stereotyping simply by virtue of considering people as members of groups. Having been taught the evils of stereotyping, they therefore do not want to engage in it. I develop at some length a distinction between a stereotype and a generalization because I find that the distinction helps them feel entitled to make sociological generalizations without worrying that they are thereby guilty of stereotyping. A generalization, I explain, may be held to be valid about a group as a general matter without assuming that it applies to any or all particular individuals within the group. It is appropriate, and indeed necessary, to be aware of valid generalizations about social groups, but one must be conscious that they are valid only at the level of general analysis. While they may well be operative in any individual case, they may not be. For example, as a teacher I am aware of research that shows "different ways of knowing" to be prevalent among males and females. Armed with this knowledge, I adjust my teaching to try to reach the diverse range of learning styles I assume to be present in the mixed gender room, but without making any gendered assumptions about any individual present. Based on this research, I have, for example, adopted a practice of regularly embedding points within a narrative of how I acquired this knowledge, in an attempt to demystify and humanize for the students my own process of knowledge acquisition. I have learned that the all too typically male and white style of pronouncements from on high of knowledge obtained in a seeming social vacuum often leaves those from groups without a history of access to higher education, such as women and various racial minority groups, alienated from the process of knowledge acquisition. I view my amended teaching style as an empowering use of generalizations. Were I, however, to change the way I teach or speak depending on whom I was addressing solely according to the gender or race of the individual, I would be practicing sexist or racist stereotyping.

I develop a further example of the difference between generalization and stereotyping from my own background. As a Jew, I know and appreciate that in my culture a certain kind of intellectual, book-centered learning is greatly valued. But if someone upon learning that I am Jewish says to me, "Oh, you must like books," I experience that as anti-Semitism, despite the fact that it is factually true that I do like books. For in learning that I am Jewish this person assumes that they have thereby automatically learned something about me. They have not left room for individual difference, for the possibility that I have a different relationship to my own culture than does its mainstream. They have not seen me, but simply the mark of "Jew" on me. It is as if upon meeting an African American I as white said, "Oh, you must really be a great dancer; you people sure have a natural rhythm." The racism there would be clear, even though I had said nothing I intended as negative; indeed I may have been greatly admiring and envying what I saw as this wonderful inherited black musical ability. While the oppressed are continually subject to being invisible as themselves, to being seen by the dominant society only as marked by the stamp of their oppression, those in dominant groups carry the privilege of being unmarked, and they are therefore available to be seen as individuals. It is eye-opening for those of my students who come from backgrounds that carry one or another dimension of privilege to be challenged by the assertion that the way in which they view themselves and their friends as "individuals," the way in which they proudly ascribe to themselves individualistic identities that cannot be captured by any group identification, is not their natural right, nor is it an accurate assessment of themselves and their world, but it rather is a mark of their privilege and the blindness to broader social contexts that privilege tends to produce.

For all these reasons, it is my experience and conviction that studies of masculinities are best carried out as a subset of superordinate studies,

studies that insistently put the unmasking and overthrowing of the workings of privilege at the heart of their enterprise.

NOTE

I would like to thank Karen Mitchell and Cooper Thompson for helpful comments on an earlier version of this essay.

WORKS CITED

Boswell, A. Ayres, and Joan Z. Spade. "Fraternities and Collegiate Rape Culture: Why Are Some Fraternities More Dangerous Places for Women." In Michael S. Kimmel and Michael A. Messner, eds., *Men's Lives,* pp. 182–93. 4th ed. Boston: Allyn and Bacon, 1995.

Brod, Harry. "The Case for Superordinate Studies." *Transformations* 8.2 (Fall 1997): 55–65.

Heller, Scott. "Scholars Debunk the Marlboro Man." *Chronicle of Higher Education* 2 (February 1993): A6.

Kimmel, Michael S., and Michael A. Messner. *Men's Lives.* 4th ed. Boston: Allyn and Bacon, 1995.

O'Sullivan, Chris. "Fraternities and Rape Culture." In Michael S. Kimmel and Michael A. Messner, eds., *Men's Lives,* pp. 354–57. 3d ed. Boston: Allyn and Bacon, 1995.

Pharr, Suzanne. *Homophobia: A Weapon of Sexism.* Little Rock: Chardon, 1988.

Williams, Christine L. "The Glass Escalator: Hidden Advantages for Men in the 'Female' Professions." In Michael S. Kimmel and Michael A. Messner, eds., *Men's Lives,* pp. 285–99. 4th ed. Boston: Allyn and Bacon, 1995.

7

MASCULINITY STUDIES: THE LONGED FOR PROFEMINIST MOVEMENT FOR ACADEMIC MEN?

Judith Newton

Having been engaged for the last five years in studying projects like Promise Keepers and the Million Man March, I have had regular occasion to reflect upon the phenomenon in the latter part of the twentieth century of U.S. men's movements—white, black, and mixed race—and to contemplate the global developments that have helped produce the very "crisis" over masculinity to which men's movements contribute and respond. Although elite men do control more resources and exercise more power than thirty years before, the profound economic and social changes that have attended the further development of transnational capitalism and economic restructuring—corporate downsizing, the reduction of well-paid unionized jobs, the fall in men's wages, the growing necessity of dual-income families, cuts in worker safety nets, the further racialization of poverty, and the growing division between the rich and the middle-class and poor—are profoundly changing the meanings of manhood for nonelite white men and men of color both. A widely shared, if unevenly achieved, equation of male breadwinning with U.S. manhood, for example, has been eroded. At the same time, female feminisms have radically challenged the moral authority of patriarchy and the myth of male gender superiority, while gay and queer movements have challenged the foundational position of heterosexuality in masculine identities for men.

Popular movements for, or led by, men have, of course, made uneven attempts to retain traditional forms of male identity, authority, and power, but their patriarchal longings must be read as only one set of currents in their variously organized efforts, involving millions of men in the 1990s alone, to invent new forms of male subjectivity, which are often less selfish and less individualistic, more empathetic, and more giving, than masculinities of the past, and, from varying political perspectives, more attuned to (selected) issues of social inequality as well. These efforts to improve manhood deserve our careful attention and, often, our critical respect. There have been several moments during my four-year sojourn at popular mass meetings for men, in fact, when I have had the somewhat envious thought that everyone *else's* men were organizing to work on their masculinities but not *"mine,"* not *"ours."* Where is, I have sometimes wondered, the large-scale men's movement for progressive academic men? Where is it and shouldn't it be doing better than the movements I have seen?

Although masculinity is not confined to men, and although masculinity studies rightly operate as a multigendered set of conversations, masculinity studies continue, at the same time, to share some of the characteristics and functions that I have come to associate with popular movements for men. (Any social formation, of course, may have multiple, overlapping, communities and effects.) These characteristics and functions, I would suggest, help account for the dramatic movement of men onto the masculinities frontier, have shaped its contributions to feminist theory, and are relevant to its political potential.

"IN THE COMPANY OF MEN"[1]

Like men's movements, for example, masculinity studies function as an imagined community and as a specific set of networks in which there are far more men than women. The 631 titles listed under the subject heading "masculinity" on amazon.com, for example, showed us that in 1999 Amazon's male-authored and edited books outnumbered female-authored and edited books about three to one. Masculinity studies as a field, moreover, has rapidly expanded over the last ten years. The reference system on my own campus, University of California at Davis, tells me that the number of new books catalogued each year with the title words masculinity, masculinities, manhood, men and feminism, and men's movements increased seven times between 1989 and 1998. (New books catalogued numbered 3 in 1989, 23 in 1995, and 20 in 1998.) Between 1989 and 1995, the list of new scholarly essays with these title words multiplied five times over—there were 40 new essays in 1989 and 121 in 1995—while the number of articles in popular magazines multiplied by more than a factor of ten, from 10 in 1988 to 102 in 1995. By the mid 1990s, a boom in masculinities was on.

"SAFE PLACES"

Like popular men's movements, masculinity studies are often imagined to provide a space for men in which it is relatively "safe" to reflect upon themselves—safe, that is, from the overriding presence of female and feminist critique (Schwalbe, *Unlocking*, 117). This sense of having space for, and safety in, self-reflection is one of the key attractions offered to participants in popular movements for men, and it may partially account for the growing involvement of men in masculinity studies as well. At any rate, feminist censure did play a significant role in regulating the pace at which academic men first introduced gender analysis into their published work. In a series of oral histories that formed the basis for a collaborative study of the way in which straight-identified, progressive, academic men, now in their late forties and late fifties, viewed the history of their relationship to feminist politics and theory, many of the men we interviewed acknowledged avoiding critical gender work in their published scholarship until the late 1980s (Newton and Stacey, "Men"). Some of the most often frequently cited reasons for this "delay," by white men and men of color both, were their reluctance to act the part of "tourist" or fall into the trap of speaking "for" women, their conviction that in the eyes of female feminists they could never "get it right," and their (well-placed) fear that they would offend feminist women by seeming to poach upon their territory. Not incidentally, the "damned if you do and damned if you don't" conundrum that feminism often posed in relation to male-authored gender analysis prompted some men to conclude that it was "easier to be damned if you didn't."

By the late 1980s, however, masculinity studies would offer the prospect of a profeminist "separate sphere" for men. In three anthologies published in 1987, which marked a transition from the "men's studies" of the past to the "new men's studies" or masculinity studies of the future, and in many contemporary anthologies and monographs as well, masculinity studies have often been conceived of as a project separate from, though cooperative with, that of female-authored feminist theory and scholarship (Brod; Jardine and Smith, *Men;* Kimmel). In 1987, for example, Harry Brod envisioned mens' studies as a "necessary complement to women's studies, needed to bring to completion the feminist project which motivates both" (Brod, "Toward," 264). Insofar as masculinity studies *is* imagined as a complement to feminist theory, seen within this model as a project by and for women, it offers a certain imagined freedom from authoritative female feminist critique.

This freedom, moreover, is only partly imaginary. Being involved more continuously than most women in the performance of, or resistance to, masculine ideals or codes, men *are* often construed, even by female feminists, as persons who may have something to tell us that we may not know. Many female feminists, I believe, would own up, if pressed, to the slight perversity of inviting men to tell us what we do not know ("We, as feminists, need your work"), but on the terms that we alone dictate (Jardine, "Men," 61). As with men's movements, I suspect, the relative freedom of masculinity studies as an imagined community has been a major part of its appeal. Indeed, it may be key to the further involvement of male colleagues in critical gender work and to their production of insights that female feminists need, though in some cases may not want, to hear.

"MAN AS A MORAL IDENTITY"

Men studying masculinities, like the participants of almost every actual men's movement that I know, often reclaim the identity "men" as something to affirm without automatic shame or guilt (Schwalbe, *Unlocking,* 102). In contrast to participants in the most popular men's movements, however, male scholars in masculinity studies often conduct this reclamation in the conscious service of profeminist politics. More than one profeminist scholar/activist has testified to the futility of embracing self-hatred or outright rejection of masculinity as a basis for long-term profeminist work. Michael Awkward, for example, suggests that "rather than seeing a black male feminism necessarily as an impossibility or as a subtle new manifestation of and attempt at an-drocentric domination," it is possible to see certain instances of Afrocen-tric feminism as providing African American men "with an invaluable means of rewriting, of *re-vis(ion)ing* ourselves, our historical and liter-ary traditions, and our future" (Awkward, "Black," 152).

Harry Brod also argues against the view that "insofar as men can do feminism or be feminists, they must leave their masculinity behind" (Brod, "To Be," 197). Such a position, he contended in 1998, fails to pro-vide a basis on which men can sustain the energy for profeminist poli-tics over "the necessary long haul." Rather than painting a "bleak picture of male beings incapable of change," a concept that situates itself in "deeply conservative terrain," Brod argues that "what enables men to do feminism effectively is a vision of men and feminism in which their feminism is inseparably linked to their positive vision of themselves as men" (Brod, "To Be" 199, 201, 198).

"IDENTITY WORK"

As with all men's movements I can name, the project of some work on masculinities by men is not just to reenchant the cate-gory "men" by, in this case, theorizing its general compatibility with feminist politics, but to invent specific subjectivities for men that are more responsive than before to at least some female feminist demands (Schwalbe, *Unlocking,* 102). One new ideal, for example, is that of the "generative father," a man who takes on housework and physical and emotional care of children not as "a reluctant personal sacrifice of privi-lege for the sake of social justice" but as an essential part of his own personal growth (Hawkins et al., "Rethinking," 542). Involving men in family work on these grounds, proponents of generative fathering argue, may be a more pragmatic course for changing men's lives within fami-lies than the "painful emotional work" required by many men's move-

ments or than the defense-provoking strategies of much feminist critique: "people are less likely to change from a position of imposed guilt
and defensiveness" than from a "personal vision of a better way and a
sense of empowerment" (Hawkins and Dollahite, "Beyond," 12). African
American theorists, moreover, have extended the political significance of
generative fathering by pointing to the ways in which its emphasis upon
"agency over victimhood" and "empowerment through love and nurture" may be harnessed to community development and antiracist politics (Allen and Connor, "African," 65, 68).

Other scholars of masculinity propose a model of manhood
based primarily on the struggle for social justice. Gary Lemons's "pro-
womanist" man, or "black (male) feminist positionality," for example,
offers a "transformed vision of black manhood" by "demystifying black
men's relation to feminism and reclaiming the history of black male
support of woman suffrage." Reviving the prowoman legacy of such
men as Frederick Douglass and W. E. B. Dubois, who "moved decisively,"
if unevenly at times, "to empower themselves as *black men* in feminist
terms," Lemons argues, could be a "powerful means to engage contemporary black men in dialogue about the viability of feminist movement
focused on the liberation of all black people" (Lemons, "New," 280, 281).
By the same token, Michael Kimmel advocates a "democratic manhood"
that would embrace differences between men and a "gender politics of
inclusion" and would ground masculinity upon "standing up for justice
and equality instead of running away from commitment and engagement"(Kimmel, *Manhood*, 333).

"IDENTITY WORK" AS THE WORK OF FEMINIST THEORY

These reclamations of the category "men" and these rein-
ventions of new masculine ideals—along with the proliferation of local
and specific studies of different masculinities across time, bodies, and
cultures—constitute one of the most significant contributions masculinity studies make to feminist theory: masculinity studies, that is, make
a profound intervention in the tendency of feminist theory to celebrate
the diversity and fluidity of femininities and women while overunifying
and sometimes demonizing the categories masculinity and men. A cen-

tral project of several recent books on white masculinity, indeed, was to demonstrate that "white guys" are not homogeneous, not everywhere and everytime the same, and to counter the " 'it couldn't have been otherwise' logic . . . of those within feminism and/or among the left who have come to take it for granted that the white male imaginary is not only Bad—racist, sexist, domineering, exploitative, individualistic, oedipal—by definition, but that it must be statically, monolithically so" (Pfeil, *White*, 32).[2]

Men of color, both straight and gay, have also challenged such monolithic categories as "black," "Latino," and "Asian American" masculinity, along with "gay identity" and "gay community," that have informed men's studies in the past. Alfredo Mirandé, for example, emphasized the multiplicity of Chicano/Latino masculinities and the multiple meanings of the concept *macho* in three Chicano/Latino communities in northern and southern California and San Antonio, concluding that Chicano/Latino masculinities are "as complex and varied as Euro-American masculinities" (*Hombre*, 147). Matthew Gutmann challenged the notion of a unified "Mexican masculinity," as well, by exploring the ways in which male identity not only "means different things to different people at different times" but "different things to the same person at the same time" (*Meanings*, 27). Other studies have deconstructed the monolithic masculinities offered by different forms of cultural nationalisms. Phillip Brian Harper, for example, has examined the ways in which black power constructed urban, lower-class, and heterosexual masculinity as representative of authentic black masculinity and indeed authentic black identity as a whole, while also tracing the social consequences of maintaining silence about black gay masculinity in communities beset by AIDS. Scholars such as Damien Ridge, Amos Hee, and Victor Minichiello, finally, have challenged monolithic concepts of "Asian" men, of gayness, and of gay community (" 'Asian,' " 43–45).

"EMOTIONAL SOLIDARITY"

Like other *profeminist* men's movements in the past, masculinity studies, while open to and involving women, has also created networks of men who give permission to and validate other men in embracing profeminist perspectives. Masculinity studies, that is, affords men some of the "pleasure and camaraderie" that females have long enjoyed in being feminist together and that men repeatedly testify to finding in popular movements for men. Such networks address the question raised by Alice Jardine and Paul Smith in 1987 over what "pleasure" men might actually get from being feminist—"well actually, very little," Smith was to observe then (Jardine and Smith, *Men,* 261, 262). The pleasures of collectivity, I believe, which are now more widely available to men in the various and sometimes conflicting networks of masculinity studies, are key to sustaining progressive political activity of all kinds. As Belinda Robnett observed, in her book on African American women in the struggle for civil rights, "interpersonal relations," "intimacy," and the "emotional work" needed to produce them are integral to social movements in all their facets (*How Long?* 192, 193).

"EMOTIONAL SOLIDARITY" AND THE CHILLY CLIMATE FOR FEMINIST THEORY AND RESEARCH

That some academic men are now "making alliances amongst themselves in order to contest sexism and support feminism," moreover, suggests a key shift in academic culture, a shift that works toward promoting feminist theory and research by further warming the chilly climate in which they are still too often produced (Jardine and Smith, *Men,* 261). In our oral histories of fifty-something progressive, academic men, for example, fear of women's anger or disapproval was only one factor in what men saw as their sustained hesitation to do critical gender analysis in their published work. For white men, a more major barrier was other white men, whose judgments controlled the reward system by which academic culture operated. The work-identified men we interviewed, for example, reported that in 1970s academic culture there had been no "discursive slots" for being antisexist men, although there were such slots for being antiracist or anti-Western. While most of the men we interviewed made early accommodations to feminism in personal relations, in classrooms (often at the insistence of feminist graduate students), and in departmental politics, when it came to what mattered most, to where they lived and where they grounded their identity as men—their published work—few were moved to serious engagement with feminist theory. Reflecting the keenly competitive, hierarchal realm of academic scholarship, the norms of which were, and are still, largely set by men, some white subjects recorded anxieties about "fucking up," of not being "expert," of "losing one's edge," if they attempted gender critique, while others expressed fear of not being seen as "serious" by other men, or of being perceived as "soft" on feminism.

The men of color we interviewed did not express anxieties over being "expert" or over losing their critical edge, in part, I believe, because their values were profoundly shaped by more collective projects, such as cultural nationalisms and race liberation struggles in the 1970s, and in part because the academy of the 1970s did not offer them the same openings to status and advancement as it did to white men. One man of color, however, did report that cultural nationalist male colleagues expressed displeasure or distress when he occasionally raised questions about gender in the context of race. Despite the fact, moreover, that he himself read women of color doing feminist work, he reported that he had engaged in "compartmentalization," a process that continued when he "started getting much more into race." When it came to sexism, he recalled, in a moment of genuine openness and self-reflection, he had felt "tremendous pressure" and a division of "head and heart," but when it came to racism he "never felt that same kind of contradiction" because "your head and heart generally merge around . . . issues, where you feel you are in effect a victim . . . as opposed to victimizer."

By the late 1980s, however, most of the men we interviewed had begun to include critical perspectives on gender in their published work. Several external developments had contributed to this change. Feminisms, for one thing, had become institutionalized in the academy and therefore in our subjects' most immediate "public spheres." Women's studies courses and programs, along with feminist courses within ethnic studies programs, were now a norm.[3] Feminist colleagues had multiplied, were directing dissertations, and sitting on tenure reviews. Theorizing by feminists of color, moreover, and by white feminists as well, had contributed to a "theory revolution" in which many feminists and progressive men would meet on newly common theoretical ground— one that now posited multiple identities and politics and the possiblity of alliance across suspect categories. By the late 1980s, as a consequence, feminist theorizing had become a respectable resource in the tool kits of many progressive, theoretically inclined, men.

This shift in theorization, moreover, entered into men's studies too, opening up the field to more inclusive work on men and to more work informed by feminism on masculinities. Men's studies in the 1970s and 1980s, for example, had been dominated by "role theory," which, in producing two fairly homogeneous categories, tended to exaggerate difference between women and men and to downplay race, class, and sexual and national differences between masculinities. Since sex roles were often theorized as the primary source of gender oppression, moreover, sex-role theory also tended to obscure structural power relations and men's domination of women. Indeed, men's equal oppression by sex roles was a central theme of 1970s books on white men. In the late 1980s, however, the theoretical positions of these networks began to change. Masculini*ty* became masculini*ties*, inviting more comparative and inclusive work on men, and role theory was giving way to a more feminist emphasis on the realities of structural inequalities and unequal power.

By the late 1980s, finally, masculinity studies were drawing upon younger generations of men who were accustomed to having female feminist teachers and peers, not to mention feminist sisters and feminist moms. Many of the younger men we interviewed in the early 1990s, for example—men of color and white men both—testified to the influence of feminist teachers and feminists peers in shaping their engagement with gender issues. This generation of men, moreover, was already contributing to an expansion of profeminist networks, to the production of antisexist "discursive slots," and to the generation of a climate within which men might put gender at the center of their work and be increasingly taken "seriously" by other men. For the men who did not grow up with feminist teachers and feminist peers, and perhaps for some who did, men authorize profeminist analysis for other men as I believe most female feminists cannot, not even now. Larry May, for example, has this to say about male profeminist critique of other men: "Men cannot easily dismiss the criticism since it emanates from a position where it is assumed that male experience is taken seriously. For these reasons, criticism of male behavior will sometimes be more believable if it is issued by men rather than by women" (May, "Progressive," 348).

"MEN'S WORK"

In contrast to the organized profeminist men's movement, which has remained quite small and which, unfortunately, continues to diminish, masculinity studies, in its partial function as a movement for progressive academic men, has the potential at least for substantial growth and impact both within the academy and without. Profeminist movements, for example, like other popular movements for men, have had to rely on men's willingness to devote their leisure time to conferences, task forces, small groups, and other activities. Masculinity studies, however, opens up the intriguing possibility of turning the work-related energies of academic men (which, like those of academic women, are considerable) to the process of profeminist analysis and reflection. Certainly, the conditions for such a turn are there.

Popular male-led movements and events, for example, from cultural nationalisms to the men's liberation movement, the Mythopoetics, the Christian Promise Keepers, and the Million Man March, have produced a wealth of topics about men and masculinity and, thereby, a wealth of articles and dissertations to be written and authored by both men and women. At the same time, gender has become one of the most popular subfields in academic job descriptions. According to informal surveys of the academic positions advertised in the Modern Language Association Job Information List, the American Sociological Bulletin, and SPECTRA, the newsletter for the Speech Communication Association, in 1996 and again in 1998, gender, feminist theory, and the like ranked second after comparative race analysis as desirable subspecialities. Economic restructuring, in the meantime, which helped fuel the "crisis" over masculinity and the popularity of the various men's movements and events that often constitute the subjects on which masculinity scholars now write, has reached the academy as well, where it has had negative impact on the employment chances of men as well as women. For all these reasons, writing profeminist work on masculinity may now be compatible with and even good for men's careers.

"MEN'S WORK" AND THE POLITICAL EFFICACY OF FEMINIST THEORY AND RESEARCH

Despite some reasonable feminist fears that men will now take gender-related jobs that would have gone to women, and despite equally reasonable fears that men's voices will now dominate in the study of gender, in its coconstruction with race, class, sexuality, and the rest, there are some significant benefits to be had from men's profeminist work. As with generative fathering, for example, the process of performing these new forms of labor may create profeminist investments and capacities in men that they did not possess before. In our publication-driven culture, after all, what one writes on one reads about and comes to value. To the degree, moreover, that masculinity studies retains a profeminist emphasis, and to the degree that profeminist men deign to write for audiences beyond the narrow realm of academe, they have the potential power to speak to and to intervene in current mass movements for men, perhaps moving them in more progressive directions.

Thus, while progressive men actually *do* have something to learn from popular men's movements—how to be rigorous, for example, in *practicing* rather than merely *theorizing* new modes of self-transformation, new ways of laboring on behalf of others, progressive academic men have an important role to play in popular movements as well. They might do much, for example, in situating popular identity work for men in the context of the unequal structures of gender, race, sexuality, and class that popular men's movements often bracket and/or support. They might help push men's movements, in the words of Michael Schwalbe, to turn men's "feelings of grief, of outrage, of affection for each other, and of longing for lives richer in meaning . . . toward riskier social action and farther-reaching change" (*Unlocking,* 245). Since even Promise Keepers read and cite profeminist writing by other men, accessible profeminist work by academic men could potentially contribute to the political effectivity of feminist theory and research.

THE LIMITS OF MOVEMENTS FOR MEN

As with mass men's movements, nonetheless, masculinity studies, in their function as a loose, internally conflicted movement for academic men, are also in danger of leaving women out, of obscuring their role as social actors. Women's daily work in creating culture, for example, as workers, political leaders, as mothers, as wives, as volunteers, is only fleetingly visible in some otherwise excellent work on masculinities and men. The irony, moreover, is that a profeminist foregrounding of men's domination of women is a contributing cause. By the same token, profeminist male scholars have done major work in re-creating fathers, but few have sought to create new models for the husband, lover, political ally, or best friend. The one striking exception, in my experience, is that of many African American scholars, both male and female, who are constituting what would seem to be a relationship frontier.[4]

Masculinity studies, finally, to the degree that they do function as a movement, or as a set of overlapping and conflicting networks for men, run the risk of deradicalization, of failing to work toward structural alterations in men's privilege and power. From R. W. Connell's perspective, indeed, there cannot be a mass movement of men against sexism because "the project of social justice in gender relations is directed *against* the interest they share" (*Masculinities,* 236). Communities of men on the masculinities frontier do indeed threaten to produce that "narcissistic solipsism," as Joy James calls it, that has often characterized popular movements led by men—and, unfortunately, movements led by women too ("AntiRacist," 252). For women's work on femininity and women has had its own sets of distortions.

NEW DIRECTIONS IN MASCULINITY STUDIES

I am not ready, nonetheless, to write off popular or academic movements for men. Although the gender politics of popular movements range from pro- , to antifeminist, to lovingly paternal, often within the same formation, many of them critique the individualistic, materialistic, and even racist values of the "self-made man," along with his accompanying suppression of compassion and care, and his defensive, sometimes violent, inability to face his own vulnerabilities. On the level of personal transformation, therefore, these movements work against identities, values, and "habits of the heart" that currently sustain the productivist, runaway, racist, and violent nature of globalization from above. Such movements, moreover, encourage men to use their own and other men's energies to be "born again" as somewhat better men than they were before. For the latter reason alone I do not think that masculinity studies should cease all functions as a partial profeminist movement for academic men. Feminist women have too many projects as it is to attempt to preside at second births.

It is essential, however, that women continue to work on masculinities, not just to maintain a crucial critical dialogue with men but to understand women, gender in its coconstructions, and themselves. Writing on men, for example, has consistently revealed new aspects of myself, of other women, and of feminisms as well, not all of which have been flattering. In the end, moreover, it may take deeply cooperative projects to clarify the troubling dynamics that inform men and women's personal, not necessarily heterosexual, or domestic relations. These dynamics, I believe, still significantly impede effective cross-gender alliances.

Connell is hopeful that "a fresh politics of masculinity will develop in new arenas," and he speculates that it will involve both men and women, that it will center on "alliance work rather than 'men's groups,'" and that it will contest "globalization from above," as do other democratic movements (*Masculinities,* 243). It is this kind of politics that is articulated by bell hooks and Cornel West in their 1991 *Breaking Bread,* where they contested "the redistribution of wealth from bottom to top," called for a "conversion" from consumerism and privatism to lives of "service and risk and sacrifice," and yearned for a transformation of "our notions of how and why we bond." This "crucial work in gender relations which has not been done" is essential to movement building and political effectivity, they argued, and would require "humility" and "vulnerability" for women (8, 14, 19, 126).

The mid nineties have seen many calls for, and some formations of, the kind of progressive political coalition that hooks and West envisioned in 1991.[5] These new "politics of feeling" have insisted that any serious strategies for meeting economic and social crises must involve a new ethos of "compassion, community, and civility," to be anchored in the repair of *"damaged solidarities,"* on the level of individual, familial, workplace, and community relations (Wallis, *Who Speaks,* 36; Giddens, *Beyond,* 253). At the heart of this politics, as a deeply implied but often unnamed project, is the massive reconstruction of dominant masculine behaviors and ideals—economic individualism, the obsessive pursuit of winning and success, the suppression of tenderness and nurturing, and the continuing evasion of that time-consuming and lowly labor of doing for others and of building relationships of trust and care in domestic, academic, and political spheres. Could masculinity studies, which in overlapping and contradictory fashion, also constitute a political community of women and men, further shape itself as such a coalition, not just through the study but through the active dismantling of these traditionally masculine, and often cross-gender, "habits of the heart"? That is one, among many, possible new directions for the field.

NOTES

1. All subheadings are taken from Schwalbe, *Unlocking.*
2. Other recent studies include Beneke, *Proving;* Connell, *Masculinities;* Kimmel, *Manhood;* and Schwalbe, *Unlocking.*
3. Such at least was the case in California when I returned in 1989.
4. See, for example, Awkward, "Black"; hooks and West, *Breaking;* Lemons, "New"; James, "AntiRacist"; and McDowell, "Pecs."
5. See Giddens, *Beyond;* Wallis, *Soul,* and *Who Speaks?;* and Lerner, *Politics.* Several of these works drew insights from an earlier book, Bellah et al., *Habits,* a study of individualism and of community in American life, which was originally published in 1985 and then reissued with a new introduction in 1996.

WORKS CITED

Allen, William D., and Michael Connor. "An African American Perspective on Generative Fathering." In Alan J. Hawkins and David C. Dollahite, eds., *Generative Fathering,* pp. 52–70. Thousand Oaks, Cal.: Sage, 1997.

Awkward, Michael. "A Black Man's Place in Black Feminist Criticism." In Tom Digby, ed., *Men Doing Feminism*, pp. 147–70. New York: Routledge, 1998.

Bellah, Robert N., Richard Madsen, William M. Sullivan, Ann Swidler, Steven N. Tipton. *Habits of the Heart: Individualism and Commitment in American Life.* Berkeley: University of California Press, 1996.

Beneke, Timothy. *Proving Manhood: Reflections on Men and Sexism.* Berkeley: University of California Press, 1997.

Brod, Harry. "To Be a Man or Not to Be a Man—That Is the Feminist Question," In Tom Digby, ed., *Men Doing Feminism*, pp. 197–212. New York: Routledge, 1998.

———. "Toward Men's Studies." In Michael S. Kimmel, ed., *Changing Men: New Directions in Research on Men and Masculinity*, pp. 263–77. Newbury Park, Cal.: Sage, 1987.

Brod, Harry, ed. *The Making of Masculinities: The New Men's Studies.* Boston: Allen and Unwin, 1987.

Connell, R. W. *Masculinities.* Berkeley: University of California Press, 1995.

Giddens, Anthony. *Beyond Left and Right: The Future of Radical Politics.* Cambridge: Polity, 1994.

Gutmann, Matthew C. *The Meanings of Macho: Being a Man in Mexico City.* Berkeley: University of California Press, 1996.

Harper, Phillip Brian. *Are We Not Men? Masculine Anxiety and the Problem of African-American Identity.* New York: Oxford University Press, 1996.

Hawkins, Alan J., and David C. Dollahite. "Beyond the Role-Inadequacy Perspective of Fathering." In Alan J. Hawkins and David C. Dollahite, eds., *Generative Fathering: Beyond Deficit Perspectives.*.Thousand Oaks, Cal.: Sage, 1997.

Hawkins, Alan J., Shawn L. Christiansen, Kathryn Pond Sargent, and E. Jeffrey Hill. "Rethinking Father's Involvement in Child Care." *Journal of Family Issues* 14.4 (1993): 531–49.

hooks, bell, and Cornell West. *Breaking Bread: Insurgent Black Intellectual Life.* Boston: South End, 1991.

James, Joy. "AntiRacist (Pro)Feminisms and Coalition Politics: 'No Justice, No Peace.' " In Tom Digby, ed., *Men Doing Feminism*, pp. 237–54. New York: Routledge, 1998.

Jardine, Alice, and Paul Smith, eds. *Men in Feminism.* New York: Methuen, 1987.

Kimmel, Michael S. *Manhood in America: A Cultural History.* New York: Free, 1996.

Kimmel, Michael S., ed. *Changing Men: New Directions in Research on Men and Masculinity.* Newbury Park, Cal.: Sage, 1987.

Lemons, Gary. "A New Response to 'Angry Black (Anti)Feminists: Reclaiming Feminist Forefathers, Becoming Womanist Sons." In Tom Digby, ed., *Men Doing Feminism*, pp. 275–90. New York: Routledge, 1998.

Lerner, Michael. *The Politics of Meaning: Restoring Hope and Possibility in an Age of Cynicism.* Reading, Mass.: Addison-Wesley, 1996.

McDowell, Deborah E. "Pecs and Reps: Muscling in on Race and the Subject of Masculinities." In Harry Stecopoulos and Michael Uebel, eds., *Race and the Subject of Masculinities,* pp. 361–86. Durham: Duke University Press, 1997.

May, Larry. "A Progressive Male Standpoint." In Tom Digby, ed., *Men Doing Feminism*, pp. 337–54. New York: Routledge, 1998.

Mirandé, Alfredo. *Hombre y Machos: Masculinity and Latino Culture.* Boulder: Westview, 1997.

Newton, Judith, and Judith Stacey. "The Men We Left Behind Us: Narratives Around and About Feminism in the Lives and Works of White, Radical Academic Men." In Elizabeth Long, ed., *Sociology and Cultural Studies,* pp. 426–51. London: Blackwell's, 1997.

Pfeil, Fred. *White Guys: Studies in Postmodern Domination and Difference.* London: Verso, 1995.

Ridge, Damien, Amos Hee, and Victor Minichiello. " 'Asian' Men on the Scene: Challenges to 'Gay Communities.' " *Journal of Homosexuality* 36.3–4 (1999): 43–45.

Robnett, Belinda. *How Long? How Long? African-American Women in the Struggle for Civil Rights.* New York: Oxford, 1997.

Schwalbe, Michael. *Unlocking the Iron Cage: The Men's Movement, Gender, Politics, and American Culture.* New York: Oxford, 1996.

Wallis, Jim. *The Soul of Politics: Beyond "Religious Right" and "Secular Left."* New York: Harcourt, 1994.

———. *Who Speaks for God? An Alternative to the Religious Right—A New Politics of Compassion, Community, and Civility.* New York: Dell, 1996.

8

LONG AND WINDING ROAD: AN OUTSIDER'S VIEW OF U.S. MASCULINITY AND FEMINISM

R. W. Connell

Social theory grows out of the material detail of life as much as it comes from the abstracted conversation of theory makers. And theory must, in the end, return to everyday practice. The project here is to explore the territory from starting points in personal experience.

Being a foreigner and a man, I do not have the experiences of most American feminists. I do have a relationship with their story: American feminism has been important to me and to people with whom I have worked. The narrative frame in which its participants retell their struggle is not available to someone who was not even in the country for most of it. My story is necessarily about intersections, not continuities. Making a virtue of necessity, I have borrowed from Australian author Frank Moorhouse the idea of "discontinuous narrative" and from British authors Carolyn Kay Steedman and David Jackson the idea of an autobiographical documentation of gender that repeatedly opens out a narrative for theoretical inspection.

An outsider nonnarrative is likely to highlight issues different from those of an insider narrative. Two are, for me, unavoidable: the significance of American corporate wealth and cultural power and the personal and public response to feminism by men. Neither is simple; I hope to document some of their crosscurrents.

These issues involve strong emotions, among them humiliation and resentment, fear and admiration, pleasure and solidarity. Barbara Laslett argues convincingly for giving full weight to emotions. But how? The conventions of academic prose are designed to exclude emotions, not convey them. I have therefore drawn freely on other genres and techniques of writing.[1]

The story starts with my first encounter with North American sociology over twenty-five years ago, goes on to Australian universities, the growth of feminism there, and my adventures in a new sociology department, moves to Europe and the international publishing business, and returns to the North American academic world in recent years.

THE PATRIARCH IN THE WOODWORK

The scene is set at the end of the 1960s, at a Famous American University, in the office of a Very Famous Scholar. Enter a young man, just married, just off the plane from a distant country, just done with a Ph.D. thesis. He is about to join the department as an unpaid temporary postdoctoral fellow and find out what sociology is like in one of its world centers. A legacy from a great-aunt has funded an expedition by the couple to this side of the world. The young woman will, as it turns out, keep the ship afloat for a year doing clerical work at a consulate.

The Very Famous Scholar looks up from his correspondence, turns from his desk, smiles, and reaches out his hand. The young man is thrilled to shake it. The wood paneling, the leaded windows, the ghosts of sociologists past frame the moment. The Very Famous Scholar kindly asks about intentions. The young man launches into hopes and plans for the year. About three minutes into the recitation, the Very Famous Scholar reaches a decision, swivels back to his desk, and continues signing his correspondence.

CONFERENCEVILLE

By Greyhound across the continent, to the annual meetings of two associations.[2] In 1970 only working-class people and students travel by bus. The dirt and indifference of Greyhound terminals are memorable. So is the dawn sunlight blazing on the mountains behind Salt Lake City.

Friends among the graduate students have arranged a bed in the city where the conference of the American Sociological Association is being held. So I know one or two people there; and I have an Australian friend to meet who knows his way around the radical student network. But the mass and anonymity of the conference are overpowering. The entire membership of the Sociological Association at home would fit into one of this conference's parallel sessions. The corridors are turbulent, full of business, none of which is my business.

I have bought a spiral-bound notebook and start filling it with field notes. There are so many sociologists that they have to be accommodated like a tourist invasion. So instead of the seedy functionality of university classrooms where Australian conferences are held, this one rejoices in the commercial splendor of a giant hotel.

The busiest place in the conference is an enormous book bazaar. Neatly dressed publishers' representatives stand around in little booths trying to get their texts adopted in the sociologists' courses, while the sociologists try to get the publishers interested in their proposals for books. I get my first picture of the scale of American publishing and the economic stakes in higher education here. Some of the texts are familiar; the publishers also market them at home.

I also get a glimpse of employment practices. In another large room is the meat market. Hundreds of people are undergoing public humiliation, advertising their need for a job, putting their life courses on show in loose-leaf books for anyone to see.

The conference sessions themselves are a continuous display of professional power and status. An interesting paper on a topic close to my Ph.D. is delivered by a woman of about my age to an audience of about seven. A panel including a masculine Name I had heard even in Australia has a larger attendance, though I don't know exactly how big—

I can't get in the room; several hundred people at least are there before me.

COMMENTARY

The Very Famous Scholar, I thought at first, had simply decided I was not going to be part of his clientele. I was neither his student nor a resource for his research program. The insult was certainly a display of academic power.

There was more, of course, not least the hegemony of the United States. The term *hegemony* derives from the classical Greek term for the leading state in a military coalition. At this time, the United States was leading an alliance in Vietnam in which my country was a minor participant, a fact of which the Very Famous Scholar was certainly aware. This hegemony extended deep into academic life. Indeed, that is why I was there and not sitting on a rock in the Blue Mountains evolving an Australian sociology from my own inner consciousness. The Very Famous Scholar was, as Louis Althusser had put it not long before, merely the bearer of a structure.

More exactly, structures—though this took me longer to see. The scene would not have played the same way if the Very Famous Scholar had been a woman. Or, probably, if I had been. The authority on display amid the polished wood, and the way it was exerted, had a lot to do with gender.

So did the collective processes of the annual meeting. The Names competing for prestige were masculine. The profoundly alienated market structure of the conference as an institution—notionally an occasion for the sharing of scientific knowledge—reflected a public world predicated on the gender division of labor and massively dominated by men. I know now that a feminist movement was developing in the ASA, but I did not know it then. The first meeting of Sydney Women's Liberation had been called just before we left on the flight to the United States.

But there was something more, which took even longer to see. If the Very Famous Scholar was bearing a structure that day, so was I. The nervous young man was also a competitor in the struggle for gendered authority, and the Very Famous Scholar was doubtless bright enough to see that and a whole lot more experienced at its moves.

If I was one of seven at my comrade's paper, I was also one of hundreds turning up to hear the Name. Reeling around the carpeted corridors of the Sociology Hilton, I, too, was a beneficiary of the gender order that underpinned its glittering horror. My wife was working for me to be there.

There is truth in Dorothy Smith's account of the academic world as a sector of a patriarchal power structure producing abstracted knowledge through texts that substitute for concrete knowledge. Yet her imagery is all too mild to capture the lunatic divisiveness of that world and the tangled dynamics producing academic masculinities as ways of surviving and operating in it.

My path into academic jobs involved learning certain gendered practices (such as ferocious concentration on writing tasks at the expense of human relationships) and rejecting others (including such conventional masculine items as enthusiasm for sport and sexual aggressiveness). In the context of a higher education boom, I was rapidly appointed to senior positions. The trip to the United States and some publications in American journals were no small part of my qualifications.

Senior appointments gave access to some resources needed by a movement to democratize higher education. We thought of it at the time as creating liberated zones in universities. I was, I think, the first New Left professor (i.e., head of department) in Australia, acutely conscious of being on the establishment's ground and wary of cooptation. Both my access and my resistance were gendered.[3] I was fighting against hegemonic masculinity at the same time that I deployed its techniques. I think this gained me a reputation for eccentricity, if not psychopathology: oddly dressed, long in the hair, humorless, by turns quiet and abrasive. In the mid-1970s this trajectory was complicated, but also clarified, by the growth of Australian feminism.

LEARNING

It is 1974, at the conference of another venerable institution run by men, the Australian and New Zealand Association for the Advancement of Science (ANZAAS). Feminism is gaining footholds in the academic world, and here is one. A program of sessions on "the Australian family" has been organized by Madge Dawson. The topic sounds traditional; the content is not. It includes countercultural, gay, and feminist critiques of the family.

The lineup of speakers is diverse. I am one, equipped with a not-very-diverse paper, a quantitative report on sex differences in adolescence wittily called "You Can't Tell Them Apart Nowadays, Can You?" My statistics echo back off the walls of the University of New South Wales, formerly University of Technology, with architecture to match.

There is no flood of requests for copies. Nevertheless, the paper becomes part of Madge's second coup: a special issue of the ANZAAS journal *Search*, usually packed with geomorphology and rabbit virology. Not only does the symposium turn into a special issue but also the special issue turns into a book. Interest in gender questions is building.

Madge is one of a group of women, older than the women's liberation activists, who have been very important in getting feminist concerns onto academic agendas. Madge published the first study of the position of women vis-à-vis Australian higher education, *Graduate and Married*. This book was the product of collaborative work by a group of women in Madge's adult education class, a precursor of many later discussions of feminist research methods. I met her through the peace movement and the Labor Party. I learned from her some important lessons about how tolerance and tough-mindedness, good humor and militancy might be combined.

By the early 1980s, feminism was the leading intellectual force in Australian sociology—ignored by some established men, resisted by others, yet plainly the liveliest area of research, publication, and student interest and finding support from women and men in almost every sociology department. The person who probably did most to make this possible was someone not conspicuously a feminist, Jean Martin. She was the best sociologist in the country in the decades when Australian academic sociology was being established, and she set up the largest department. Although her writing was mainly about community and migration, a thread of argument about family relationships and women's influence ran through it from the 1950s onward. Toward the end of her life, she was explicitly researching the social position of women, and she inspired a great deal of research by other women.

I met her only a few times. The earliest was when I was an undergraduate history student. Jean Martin was the first live sociologist I had seen, and I asked her for a list of books to read. I thought that, unlike the history I was learning, sociology might say something of relevance. I don't have her list any more, but I remember that it emphasized field research and was mostly American.

THE PATRIARCH IN THE ABATTOIR

With the new chair, which I took up in 1976, some resources could be expected from the university's normal staffing processes. Several feminist courses had recently started in other departments on campus, mostly operating on a shoestring budget. Resources for feminist teaching and research would leap if we directed some of sociology's expected growth into the area of sexual politics. The question was how best to do it.

So perhaps twenty-five people sat around the walls of an upstairs meeting room in the behavioural sciences building, newest of the concrete bunkers from which Australian higher education defied the world. From one window we could see the Harbour Bridge across seven miles and a thousand gum trees, from another we could see a big wattle tree that exploded each year in golden flower. Amid this patriotic riot we—mostly women, both students and academic staff from half a dozen departments—debated with a good deal of vigor and humor the options of a broader interdisciplinary program or a narrower but deeper concentration within the sociology discipline. We eventually decided to put our new resources into the latter. A decisive argument came from women in other departments who did not want the men in their areas, beginning to feel pressure to include material about women in their "mainstream" courses, to be let off the hook.

So gender and sexuality were defined as one of the core areas for the new sociology program, and I drafted up course proposals and staffing requests. Which in good academic time were approved. Within a few years a group of academics concerned with gender and sexuality had formed. There were a research program, a group of graduate students, and a flow of publications.

The irony of a male head of department pursuing a feminist agenda was not lost on my fellow patriarchs in the professoriate, or on my colleagues in the department, or on the students. For the most part, the situation was a source of energy; I felt supported, and I was able to support. But there were built-in tensions. It was not a happy coincidence that I was assigned by the departmental meeting to teach the course that centered on feminist theories of patriarchy (its usual convenor being on leave) at the time a separatist current was strengthening in Australian feminism. I tried to run the course as a lectureless, self-managed forum where ideas could be pooled, joint research and reading planned, and conceptions of patriarchy debated, without an agenda predestined by me. The department at that time made regular staff-student reviews of each course after it had run. We sat in a dark downstairs room, and for the two meetings and several hours we spent reviewing my course, the place felt like an abattoir. Some (at least) of the students said that they had been let down by course. Some said its structurelessness involved an abuse of power. It is generally difficult for students to criticize the professor, and when I argued against the criticisms, it seemed like further abuse. I don't pretend to give an impartial account of this; the memory is very painful. Perhaps the most interesting criticism was that by not giving a course of lectures, I had withheld knowledge and thus preserved patriarchal power. For my part, I felt that certain things being said were false, others distorted. I felt for the first time under factional attack, and it seemed as if in the final analysis I was being carved up for being the wrong gender. The other academic members of the department were divided by conflicting commitments and loyalties. Some put a lot of energy and kindness into trying to mend the situation. The aftertaste was still bitter for me. An agreement was reached, then not fully observed. In following years, the department made sure I was not called on to chair that course again. And I don't think I have ever taken such risks again in teaching.

Some of my students in another course at about this time decided that for their collective research project they would interview men in their lives and around campus. It was the first research project on masculinity I had anything to do with, maybe the first in the country. All members of the group were women.

COMMENTARY

Other feminist scholars have spoken of their pioneers and mentors (see Laslett and Thorne, *Feminist*). Older women serve as models and mentors not only for younger women. In a paper about young men involved in Green politics who were trying to reform masculinity, I remarked that most of them had formative encounters with women's strength, and I guess I was unconsciously referring to myself as well (Connell, "Whole").

The point may apply more broadly. The current strength of feminism in Australian sociology is partly an outcome of the alliances women have been able to make. These historically were partly determined by the influence on men of women such as Jean Martin, Madge Dawson, and Jean Blackburn, an architect of Australian education reform.

Such alliances may not be comfortable for either side. Being a male friend of feminism (in Australia, unlike the United States, one does not speak of men as feminists) is a contradictory situation; tension can be expected. As a minor example, a man in this situation gets to hear many expressions of casual, and sometimes not so casual, hostility toward men in general, including the penis jokes mentioned by Gary Dowsett ("I'll Show"). The clash that developed around my teaching was not exceptional, though, of course, it had its specific local causes. Difficulties of that kind, with a fair chance of emotional injury, can be expected whenever there is sustained involvement of men with feminist projects.

Nor is there a simple way around or through these contradictions—except giving up the attempt to make an alliance work. The pleasures of separatism for men have now been discovered by the followers of Robert Bly, the author of *Iron John,* and other leaders of the masculinity cults that developed in the 1980s out of men's consciousness-raising groups, New Age culture, and Jungian therapy. All-male gatherings, "warrior weekends," and reconstituted initiation rituals among men are central to their search for the "deep masculine"—an entity that, however powerful and shaggy, seems too shy to emerge in the presence of women.[4]

Engagement is much more demanding, but it is possible. Alliances can be sustained, despite the inevitable tensions and injuries, wherever there are shared commitments. Such commitments most commonly rest on principles with a certain universality—the cause of humanity, the principle of justice, the goal of equality.

Ironically, radical theory over the last thirty years has put a lot of energy into dismantling principles of this kind: from the Althusserian denunciation of humanism, to the postmodern scorn for grand narratives and the poststructuralist valorization of difference. Radical identity politics hopes to overcome division by generating coalitions, and rainbow coalitions have certainly been formed. But what will hold people in those coalitions when they meet rocks in the road? We will need unconditional commitments. We will need theorizing that moves across boundaries and between standpoints and even finds, like Pauline Johnson's *Feminism as Radical Humanism,* unexpected common ground.

THE MATERIALITY OF THEORY

I am sitting in a small room at the back of a brick house in south London, looking at a row of brick houses across a row of backyards, some with dogs that do not observe curfew. We are living with a close friend who has been fighting for women's interests in British trade unions, a long and grinding struggle. For globe-trotting intellectuals, London is the place to be in 1984: a woman prime minister is in power; the miners are on strike. It is the year of George Orwell, the year our daughter is born, the year of writing *Gender and Power.*

Literally writing, with a pen. I have a sensuous relationship with the text flowing slowly onto the page, not just a cerebral one; a relationship compounded of body, clothes, chair, ink, paper spread on the table, stillness of the room, light falling from the window, scurries in the backyards. These physical matters seem to be part of the way ideas solidify and sharpen, the way prose gets shaped.

The baby is involved with this text making, sharing a lot of it asleep in a carry cot on the floor behind me. She gradually swims up to the top end and gets stuck with her head in a corner, at which point her grunts and gurgles change tone, I get up and lift her back to the bottom, and she starts the journey again. Sometimes the grunts turn to grousing, a familiar aroma steals across the room, and it is time for a paragraph break.

I mostly do the midnight feed, which gives Pam the chance of a solid sleep and me an excuse to be up late. I like writing at midnight. With the house still, and no lights on but the desk lamp (bad for the eyes), I seem to be in the middle of a vast, dark space stretching out in all directions to the stars and nebulae. The only things sounding in it are the words I write and the grunted comments of the next generation.

MEN'S STUDIES

The world turns; *Gender and Power* is published; other comments appear. There are twenty-seven reviews that I know of, from New Zealand to Finland. What is most striking is the difficulty many journals and reviewers have in categorizing the book. Can't be social theory because it's not about Marx and Weber. Can't be women's studies because it's written by a man. Must be jelly 'cause jam don't shake like that.

Seven journals work out a solution that completely throws me when I see the first reviews. Because it's about gender, and because it's by a man, it must be men's studies. (True, it does contain three pages setting out a condensed model of masculinity.) So *Gender and Power* is rolled into review essays covering a bunch of Books About Men, or samples of TNMS (The New Men's Studies), as a sardonic feminist reviewer puts it (Griffin, Review). I have not felt so firmly positioned since the days when reviewers decided that because I wrote about class I must be a Marxist.

Feminist teachers prove to be more interested than feminist editors. The book comes to be used as a text in a number of courses, and the publishers have recently shown me the list to help me in thinking about a second edition. Most are in women's studies programs.

COMMENTARY

Although men come to support feminism for a great variety of reasons, in most cases of which I know, personal relationships with women have been important. Few men, gay or straight, have no close ties to women. Often men have dense networks of ties to mothers, daughters, wives, lovers, sisters, grandmothers, nieces, coworkers, neighbors, and friends. There are interests and motives in abundance here. For instance, I have a fairly close relationship with our daughter, and however well or badly I manage it, this relationship defines a political interest. I want a world that will give her the respect and resources it will give the sons of our friends living across the road. To produce that world means supporting feminism. The arithmetic is not very difficult.

As with a good many other Australian intellectuals, my earliest political commitment was to the labor movement and socialism. The kind of socialism I learned from my mother and father, from Labor Party members such as Madge Dawson, and from reading (George Orwell's *Homage to Catalonia* especially) was about equality, courtesy, respect, and human solidarity rather than about modes of production and commentaries on *Capital*. It still seems to me that a commitment to equality is the litmus test in politics. Given this beginning, it is not hard to see the next step when the facts of gender inequality and the abuse of women are, to use a title of Orwell's, "In Front of Your Nose." [6] They were in front of my nose because I loved, lived with, and worked with feminist women. I have done my best to put the same facts in front of a lot of other men's noses.

The proboscis theory of men's support for feminism has one great flaw: it presupposes that they are willing to read. Orwell's point was precisely that people often are not. Hegemonic masculinity and patriarchal ideology provide a whole repertoire of routines for evading the obvious in gender relations. Here are a few: declaring gender inequality a fact of nature (helped on by sociobiologists), exaggerating the gains made by women (helped on by "PC" backlash campaigns), exaggerating the woes of men (helped on by Bly), mobilizing homophobia (on the principle that any man who sympathizes with women must be a fag— note how the Religious Right, in retreat on abortion, is targeting gays with new vigor), projecting onto minorities (helped on by racists—the current demonizing of immigrants and "violent criminals" in the United States is striking).

In this field of ideological struggle, there is plenty of work for men as well as for women. No applicant will be turned away.

The success of patriarchal ideology depends not only on how vigorously it is contested in public but also on how receptive or resistant people are in their personal lives. I doubt we will ever see capitalist patriarchy overthrown by revolutionary masses led by drag queens in quite the way projected by Italian gay theorist Mario Mieli. But we do need to look closely at the fissures, tensions, and contradictions in gender and at the occasions and potentials they offer for political action.

So far as concerns men, this is now happening in the research on masculinity that has multiplied, and strikingly improved in quality, in the last few years. I have put energy into this work and have done my best to help other men, and women, engaged in it. This research has begun to feed into practice, for instance, in work against rape and domestic violence, in education, and in relation to AIDS. The applications are still on a small scale, but the demand for ideas is certainly there, and I think this activity will grow. The need is so clear that I have grown a little more sympathetic to the idea of "men's studies"—which at first appalled me and still worries me—to the extent that it provides a venue for this kind of strategic research.

BACK IN THE ASA

Another tourist palace, glittering even harder as we approach the end of Reagan's administration. This time I am present by official invitation, to take part in a thematic session about gender in American sociology. I am not exactly a Name, but at least an Object of Interest, possessor of a strange accent and exotic footnotes as well as being a man doing gender. I feel like an Ambassador from Mars. This is silly. A number of people here are familiar with my work, and that is why I have been invited.

The room where the panel is to speak seems dark (all my memories of ASA annual meetings seem to involve dark interior spaces; Erik Erikson would love them). It is full to overflowing; I hear that sex and gender is the most buoyant area of the ASA's membership, and this certainly looks like it. About nine-tenths of those in the room are women.

The presentations are followed closely by the audience. I do my bit about American sociology and my bit for Australian sociology, passing out reading lists of Australian work in the area and inviting people to get in touch to be networked. The session ends, the people swirl out into the corridor, and this time I am full of business.

Later in the conference, as a thematic session presenter and foreign guest, I am invited to a presidential reception in a hospitality suite of the hotel. I sit on the bed in my room on the fourteenth-floor-that-is-really-the-thirteenth, looking out over the urban core of Atlanta (a cluster of high-rise banks and hotels oddly resembling a fleet of spaceships), and have a crisis of my New Left conscience. Should I go? Do I join the Names and finally abandon the People? Is this my final sell-out—not even for thirty pieces of silver, just eighteen pages in the presidential Book of the Conference? Well after the time for the reception to start, I convince myself I ought to go, if only to be Ambassador from Mars. So I set off, dressed as little like a banker as possible.

The reception is in another dark place. The room seems to shimmer with a gray mist. Through it I can make out Names in silvery suits, scores of them, and they are the same Names as twenty years ago, but somehow changed, paler and more lined. They all seem to know each other and are talking quietly but determinedly. Most of the women present are wearing another kind of costume, move deftly through the mist, and offer drugs to all who come. I am courteously introduced to the association's senior officers, inquire about its finances, am waltzed into a technical discussion of conference fund-raising behind the cheese plate. The mist thickens, the voices rise. My panic threshold is reached, and I shake hands and run for it.

BOARDROOMS

The paper did appear in the Book of the Conference (Connell "Wrong"). I admired the president then and admire him still. Not all of the people at the reception were Names; not all of them were men. Most of the academic women did, however, wear suits, in semiotic opposition to the maids.

Months after that reception, I sat in an elegant room in another American city at a lunchtime feminist seminar where a considerable weight of jewelry was present. Its main element was gold.

COMMENTARY

American sociology has declined in size, and perhaps in influence, since the 1970s, but it remains the most wealthy and powerful body of sociologists in the world.[7] My second conference experience was as clear on that point as the first. Sociology is better entrenched institutionally in the United States than in countries like Australia. And it is far more settled in its ways, fully equipped with origin myths, heroes, sacred sites, canonical texts, and ritual disputes. Feminist revolutionaries face a tougher proposition here than in many other places.

The feminist presence at this annual meeting, then, registers a considerable success. Women are much more visible in the organization, every major publisher's booth has its women's studies list, and the conference agenda gives ample space to gender and sexual politics. Sociology here and now is a venue for women's experiences, for truths about sexuality and inequality, in a way it certainly was not a generation ago. Moreover, the success of American academic feminism becomes a resource in other countries. The cultural and economic power of the United States helps legitimate feminist work there; American feminism means literature, models, and sometimes direct personal support for feminism in other parts of the world.

Intellectual influence on the men in the metropole, however, is more elusive. In this respect the revolution is still missing. Most men attending the annual meeting do not come to the sessions on gender. Most theory sessions trundle down the old tracks. American sociology long ago found it could deflect critique by defining each criticism as a new specialty. This mechanism is clearly operating to contain feminism.

Perhaps, too, the seductions of power operate more intensely here in the imperial center than in a small university system in the colonies. As American feminism has won battles, accumulated resources, and pressed on into the academic establishment, it has begun to take on more of the coloration of the American ruling class. Beyond radical and liberal and socialist and cultural feminisms, we seem to be getting corporate feminism.

Listening to the gold jewelry, I realized I was now sitting square in the middle of the privilege that the labor movement had been formed to fight against. Twenty years ago I was demonstrating in the streets against this. Other people in that room had done the same. I do wonder about the meaning of the current turn of theory away from material inequalities and toward complexities of language, relativist epistemologies, and issues of identity, as the movement enters the house of power.

NOTES

This essay is adapted from a chapter in Laslett and Thorne, Feminist, *on life histories of feminist sociologists.*

1. Among my sources are "memory work," in Crawford et al., *Emotion,* and prose techniques borrowed (with trepidation) from James Joyce and Patrick White.

2. The title of this section is with a tip of the Akubra hat to Frank Moorhouse.

3. My access also involved class and ethnic privilege; I came from the Australian-born Anglophone professional bourgeoisie, had an elite education, and had enough money to launch the trip to the United States.

4. For fuller discussion of this movement and its context in masculinity politics, see Connell, *Masculinities.*

5. I am not implying that Orwell was any supporter of feminism! Quite the reverse was true.

6. Enrollment statistics for undergraduate majors and Ph.D.s are compiled by the national office of the ASA.

WORKS CITED

Blackburn, Jean, and Ted Jackson. *Australian Wives Today.* Melbourne: Victorian Fabian Society, 1963.

———. *Girls, School, and Society.* Canberra: Australian Schools Commission, 1975.

Bly, Robert. *Iron John: A Book About Men.* Reading, Mass.: Addison-Wesley, 1990.

Connell, R. W. *Gender and Power: Society, the Person, and Sexual Politics.* Stanford: Stanford University Press, 1987.

———. *Masculinities.* Berkeley: University of California Press, 1995.

———. "Notes on American Sociology and American Power." In Herbert J. Gans, ed., *Sociology in America,* 265–271. Newbury Park, Cal.: Sage, 1990.

———. "A Whole New World: Remaking Masculinity in the Context of the Environmental Movement." *Gender and Society* 4 (1990): 461.

———. "The Wrong Stuff: Reflections on the Place of Gender in American

Sociology." In Herbert J. Gans, ed., *Sociology in America*, pp. 155–166. Newbury Park, Cal.: Sage, 1990.

Crawford, June, Susan Kippax, Jenny Onyx, Una Gault, and Pam Benton. *Emotion and Gender: Constructing Meaning from Memory*. London: Sage, 1992.

Dawson, Madge, ed. *Australian Families*. Australian and New Zealand Association for the Advancement of Science, 1975.

——. *Graduate and Married*. Sydney: Department of Adult Education, University of Sydney, 1965.

Dowsett, Gary. "I'll Show You Mine, If You'll Show Me Yours: Gay Men, Masculinity Research, Men's Studies, and Sex." *Theory and Society* 22 (1993): 70.

Griffin, Christine. Review of *The Making of Masculinities, Changing Men,* and *Gender and Power*. *Feminist Review* 33 (1989): 103–5.

Jackson, David. *Unmasking Masculinity: A Critical Autobiography*. London: Unwin Hyman, 1990.

Johnson, Pauline. *Feminism as Radical Humanism*. Sydney: Allen and Unwin, 1994.

Laslett, Barbara, and Barrie Thorne, eds. *Feminist Sociology: Life Histories of a Movement*. Newark, N.J.: Rutgers University Press, 1997.

Martin, Jean I. *Refugee Settlers*. Canberra: Australian National University Press, 1965.

Mieli, Mario. *Homosexuality and Liberation: Elements of a Gay Critique*. London: Gay Men's, 1980.

Moorhouse, Frank. *The Americans, Baby: A Discontinuous Narrative of Stories and Fragments*. Sydney: Angus and Robertson, 1972.

——. *Conference-Ville*. Sydney: Angus and Robertson, 1976.

Orwell, George. "In Front of Your Nose." In *Collected Essays: Journalism and Letters,* 4:150–54. Harmondsworth: Penguin, 1970.

Smith, Dorothy E. *The Conceptual Practices of Power: A Feminist Sociology of Knowledge*. Boston: Northeastern University Press, 1990.

Steedman, Carolyn Kay. *Landscape for a Good Woman: A Story of Two Lives*. London: Virago, 1986.

9

MASCULINITY AND THE (M)OTHER: TOWARD A SYNTHESIS OF FEMINIST MOTHERING THEORY AND PSYCHOANALYTIC THEORIES OF NARCISSISM

Isaac D. Balbus

In this essay I derive an an account of masculine identity formation from a partial synthesis of the feminist mothering theory of Dorothy Dinnerstein (*Mermaid*), Nancy J. Chodorow (*Reproduction*), and Jessica Benjamin (*Bonds*), on the one hand, and the psychoanalytic theories of narcissism of Heinz Kohut (*Analysis, Restoration*), Otto Kernberg (*Borderline*), and James Masterson (*Narcissistic*), on the other. In the next section, I summarize the competing assumptions of these two bodies of psychoanalytic theory and argue that it is both necessary and possible to resolve the opposition between them. Since each raises key questions about the sources of the (masculine sense of) self for which the other can provide no answer, a theoretical synthesis would enable us to answer more important questions about "masculinity" than either of the theories on which that synthesis was based. In the third section I work toward that synthesis by evaluating the diametrically opposite arguments of Christopher Lasch (*Minimal*) and Ilene Philipson ("Heterosexual," "Gender") on the relationship between gender and narcissism. This evaluation sets the stage for my effort in the fourth section of this essay to set forth (the beginnings of) a synthesis that incorporates the merits and overcomes the limits of these polar positions. In the fifth and final section, I demonstrate that Chodorow's recent reformulations (*Feminism, Femininities,* "Gender") of her original version of feminist mothering theory do not render this synthesis superfluous but rather underscore its necessity.

STRUCTURE OR PRACTICE: FEMINIST MOTHERING THEORY VERSUS PSYCHOANALYTIC THEORIES OF NARCISSISM

Feminist mothering theory starts from the assumptions a) that there is a *gendered* sense of self and b) that this gendered sense of self is produced by the "mother-monopolized" *structure* within which parenting takes place. Dorothy Dinnerstein, Nancy Chodorow, and Jessica Benjamin all argue that under these conditions there are fundamental differences in the object relations of men and women—their sense of themselves in relation to others—and that these differences are the inevitable outcome of an inherent difference in their early relationship with the mother. Because boys must define themselves in opposition to their mothers in order to become "men," mother-raised men will develop a disproportionately "oppositional" orientation within which connection with the other will be sacrificed to separation from the other. Because the relationship of girls with their mothers, in contrast, is not an obstacle to but rather the source of their feminine sense of self, mother-raised women will develop a "relational" orientation within which separation from the other will be subordinated to connection with him or her.

Thus neither men nor women will be able to combine connection with separation until the end to the female monopoly on mothering, i.e., until fathers join mothers as equal partners in the early care of their male and female children. Under coparenting, boys would also be closely identified with a primary caregiver of the same sex and men would thus become less afraid of connection than exclusively mother-raised men. Under coparenting, girls would also be closely identified with a primary caregiver of the opposite sex and thus coparented women would be less fearful of separation than exclusively mother-raised girls. In sum, the consequences of this transformation in the *structure* of child rearing would be that men would become more like women and women more like men, each absorbing the best that the other presently has to offer.

Thus feminist mothering theory ignores differences in the *quality* of parenting practice under the prevailing, mother-dominated structure of child rearing as well as differences in parenting that might outlive the transformation of that structure in the direction of coparenting.[1] It thereby also ignores the problem of the difference in the object relations of children of both genders that these differences in parenting might make.

These are precisely the differences with which psychoanalytic theories of narcissism are preoccupied. The defining assumptions of these theories are a) that the sense of self is *not gendered* and b) that the sense of self is produced by the quality of parenting *practice*. Kernberg, Kohut, and Masterson all assume that differences in the object relations of individuals result (at least in part) from differences in the quality of the maternal care they experience in their earliest years. Masterson connects those differences in object relations more clearly than Kernberg and Kohut to the way in which the mother responds to the "rapprochement crisis" of her child, i.e., to the way she handles her or his effort to negotiate the increasingly intense, conflicting claims of connection and separation during the second year of her or his life (*Narcissistic*, 12–14, 25–27, 102–7, 133).

If mothers suppress the separation and over-reward the merger of their little boys and girls, then they will grow up to be men and women who privilege connection over separation. If mothers suppress the merger and over-reward the separation of their little girls and boys, then they will grow up to become women and men who privilege separation over connection. Both women and men will be able to combine connection and separation if, in contrast, they have been fortunate enough to have had a mother—a "good enough mother"—who was able to encourage each equally during their early period of rapprochement.

Thus narcissism theorists take for granted the mother-dominated structure of parenting and do not explore the way in which this structure inhibits the formation of "good enough" object relations in both women and men. They likewise tend to ignore any connection between

gender and sense of self that might result from that structure.[2] Consequently they neglect as well any changes in that connection that might
result from the transformation of that structure.

Each of these theories, it should be clear, is the exact obverse of the
other. Feminist mothering theory assumes the complete dominance of
structure over practice and of gender over sense of self. It thereby ignores the *relative autonomy* of practice from structure and sense of self
from gender. Narcissism theory, in contrast, insists on the complete autonomy of practice from structure and of sense of self from gender. It
necessarily neglects in the process the *influence of structure* over practice
and gender over sense of self. In order to preserve the merits and overcome the limits of both theories it is therefore necessary to grasp what
neither theory is able to grasp, namely, the *relationship of connection and
separation between structure and practice and between gender and sense of
self.*

This is what I shall attempt to do in the fourth section of this essay.
But first I will take up two recent efforts to understand the relationship
between narcissism and gender: one that privileges practice over structure and sense of self over gender, the other that privileges structure
over practice and gender over sense of self. My critique of these efforts
should serve to clarify some of the criteria that a more adequate understanding would have to satisfy.

RECENT REFLECTIONS ON GENDER AND NARCISSISM

Christopher Lasch's Critique of Feminist Mothering Theory

In *The Minimal Self,* Christopher Lasch relies on Otto
Kernberg, as well as other psychoanalytic theorists of narcissism, for a
depth-psychological diagnosis of the discontents of modern capitalism.
He argues that capitalist culture "tends to favor regressive solutions . . .
to the [universal] problem of separation" (194) of individuals from their
maternal origin, specifically, that it encourages omnipotent fantasies of
either symbiotic fusion with or grandiose independence from the world
that both reflect and reinforce the narcissistic defenses of children who
have not been able to achieve a "state of being in relation to the mother

as something outside and separate" (Winnicott, *Playing*, 14). This is a provocative and, to my mind, persuasive argument about the reciprocal relationship between narcissism and contemporary capitalism.

Far less persuasive, however, is Lasch's bold claim that "narcissism has nothing to do with femininity or masculinity" (20). This claim is intended as a rejoinder to feminist mothering theorists like Chodorow who have associated "relatedness" or "feminine mutuality" with a woman's never entirely renounced wish for merger with her mother, on the one hand, and a "radically autonomous" sense of self with a man's enduring denial of his dependence on his mother, on the other. According to Lasch, that kind of argument

dissolves the contradiction held in tension by the psychoanalytic theory of narcissism: namely, that all of us, men and women alike, experience the pain of separation and simultaneously long for a restoration of the original sense of union. Narcissism originates in the infant's symbiotic fusion with the mother, but the desire to return to this blissful state cannot be identified with "feminine mutuality" without obscuring both its universality and the illusions of "radical autonomy" to which it also gives rise, in women as well as men. The desire for complete self-sufficiency is just as much a legacy of primary narcissism as the desire for mutuality and relatedness. Because narcissism knows no distinction between the self and others, it expresses itself in later life both in the desire for ecstatic union with others, as in romantic love, and in the desire for absolute independence from others, by means of which we seek to revive the original illusion of omnipotence and to deny our dependence on external sources of nourishment and gratification. . . . Since both [fantasies] spring from the same source . . . it can only cause confusion to call the dream of [absolute independence] a masculine obsession, while extolling the hope of [ecstatic union] as a characteristically feminine preoccupation. (245–46; see also 20, 184)

Thus Lasch's claim that narcissism has nothing to do with femininity or masculinity is based on the argument that the fantasies of absolute independence and absolute fusion cannot be considered gender based since both these fantasies stem from the same source, namely, the "pain of separation" from and the longing for "the restoration of the original union" with the mother that "all of us, men and women alike," have experienced. But this argument is simply a non sequitur. From the premise that the *source* of narcissistic fantasies is gender neutral, we cannot infer that the fantasies *themselves* are necessarily gender neutral; although the pain of separation and the longing to undo it may be common to both female and male infants, the way in which boys and girls, and thus men and women, come to *defend against* this pain and longing may be very different. Lasch arbitrarily assumes, in other words, that the narcissistic fantasies that defend against the separation anxiety of boys and girls have nothing to do with the fantasies by means of which their gender identity is constructed. Consequently, he is able to conclude, equally arbitrarily, that the differences in the girl's and the boy's "preoedipal" relationship with the mother that shape their respective gender identities have no effect on their narcissistic fantasies.

There are good reasons to reject this conclusion. Masterson argues, as we have seen, that narcissism is the child's defense against the mother's failure adequately to respond to her or his rapprochement crisis during the second year of life. It is precisely at this point, according to Robert Stoller, that the child begins to become aware of his or her "core gender identity" as well as the identity or difference between that identity and the gender identity of his or her mother (*Presentations*, 10–24; Mahler et al., *Psychological*, 104–6). Thus the peak of children's "pain of separation" from their mother is likely to coincide with the onset of their concern about whether they are either the same as or different from her. Does it not seem probable that the way in which they come to defend against that pain will depend decisively on their answer to that question? More specifically, should we not expect that a child, whose longing "for a restoration of [his] original union" with his mother is complicated by fear that this union threatens his emerging gender identity, is particularly prone to fall prey to the "illusion of radical autonomy," and thus that—contrary to Lasch's claim—boys are far more likely than girls to succumb to the grandiose narcissism of "complete self-sufficiency"?

Essentially the same point can be made with respect to Kohut's account of the origins of the narcissism of the "grandiose self." According to this account, a child whose self-esteem is not confirmed by a mother who "mirrors [his or her] exhibitionistic display" will defend against this maternal deficit by "concentrating perfection and power upon the self . . . and turning away disdainfully from an outside to which all imperfections have been assigned" (Kohut, *Analysis*, 116, 106). This account, in other words, is based on the assumption that any child will feel affirmed if he or she is adequately mirrored by his or her mother. But this assumption is called into question by feminist mothering theory. As Jessica Benjamin has argued (echoing a similar, earlier argument of Dorothy Dinnerstein),

> The need to sever the identification with the mother in order to be confirmed both as a separate person and as a male person . . . often prevents the boy from recognizing his mother. She is not seen as an independent person (another subject) but as something other—as nature, as an instrument or an object, as less than human. The premise of this independence is to say, "I am nothing like the one who cares for me." In breaking this identification with . . . mother, the boy is in danger of losing his capacity for mutual recognition altogether. (Benjamin, *Bonds*, 76; see also Dinnerstein, *Mermaid*, 91–114)

If, following Hegel, we assume that all self-affirming recognition must be mutual (Hegel, *Phenomenology*, 229–31), then the fact the boy is in "danger of losing his capacity for mutual recognition" means there is no guarantee that he *will* feel self-affirmed by the recognition he receives from his mother. To the contrary: a boy who refuses to recognize a mother who mirrors him will be unable to recognize himself in her mirror, and therefore will be unable to take pride in being recognized by her.[3] Thus he is likely to be far more vulnerable than his sister to omnipotent fantasies that unrealistically inflate his pride. In short, under the maternal mode of child rearing, boys are more likely than girls to suffer from the narcissism of the "grandiose self."

Feminist mothering theory can also explain why girls are much more likely to suffer from what Kohut calls the narcissism of the "ideal object" or to defend against the anxiety of separation from the mother with what Lasch calls fantasies of "ecstatic union" with the other. Because the intimate preoedipal relationship with her mother is the source of rather than an obstacle to the girl's gendered sense of self, according to Chodorow, "girls come to experience themselves as less separate than boys, as having more permeable ego boundaries . . . [and] come to define themselves more in relation to others." The others in relation to whom girls define their self often become others to whom that self is sacrificed: "There is a tendency in women toward boundary confusion and a lack of sense of separateness from the world." This tendency will be particularly pronounced in the case of women whose preoedipal relationship with their mothers was marked by the "prolonged symbiosis and narcissistic overidentification" that are often characteristic of that relationship (*Reproduction*, 93, 110, 104).

Chodorow's clinically based inferences are confirmed by empirical observations of the different ways in which boys and girls negotiate the difficulties of their rapprochement stage. Margaret Mahler and her colleagues report that just when boys were

> beginning to enjoy their functioning in the widening world, girls seemed to be more engrossed with mother . . . and were more persistently enmeshed in the ambivalent aspects of the relationship. . . . The task of becoming a separate individual seemed . . . to be generally more difficult for girls than for boys. (*Psychological*, 102, 106; see also Abelin, "Triangulation," 151–69; Levenson, "Intimacy," 529–44; and Flax, "Conflict" 171–89)

The girl's task of individuation is more difficult than the boy's, according to Chodorow, because she "does not have something different and desirable [a penis] with which to oppose maternal omnipotence" (*Reproduction*, 122). Unlike the boy, the girl cannot rely on any obvious physical difference to help disentangle herself from a relationship with her mother that is even more overwhelming than his. What she *can*—and usually does—do (at least within intact nuclear families) is to "transfer to the father . . . much of the weight of her positive feelings [toward her mother], while leaving the negative ones mainly attached to their original object." In this way, the girl "gains a less equivocal focus for her feeling of pure love, and feels freer to express her grievances against her mother without fear of being cut off altogether from . . . a magic, animally loved, parental being." But the price she eventually pays for this overidealization of her father is a "worshipful, dependent stance toward men" (Dinnerstein, *Mermaid*, 51–53) to whom she will sacrifice her agency in order to repudiate her mother's.

According to Kohut, narcissists of the idealizing type defend against the loss of infantile omnipotence by "giving over the previous perfection to an admired, omnipotent . . . self-object: *the idealized parent imago.*" Their central defense mechanism, in effect, is the fantasy that "you are perfect, but I am part of you" (*Analysis,* 25, 27). This description of the narcissist who defends against separation by basking in the reflected glow of the overidealized other clearly dovetails with Chodorow's and Dinnerstein's descriptions of women who live their lives through the men with whom they seek "ecstatic union."

Their account of the origins of this tendency toward female self-subordination is also consistent with Kohut's (rather sparse) reflections on the etiology of this type of narcissism:

> Under . . . favorable circumstances, the idealized parent imago . . . becomes integrated into the adult personality. Introjected as our idealized superego, it becomes an important component of our psychic organization by holding up to us the guiding leadership of its ideals. . . . If the child, however, *suffers . . . traumatic disappointments in the admired adult,* then the idealized parent imago . . . is retained in its unaltered form [and] is not transformed into a tension-regulating psychic structure. (*Analysis,* 28; emphasis added)

"Traumatic disappointments in the admired adult"—in the admired mother—are precisely what, according to feminist mothering theory, most mother-raised girls experience as they turn from their mothers to embrace their fathers. Thus feminist mothering theory is able to explain what neither Kohut nor Lasch is even able to recognize, namely, the disproportionate tendency of women to defend against what Lasch calls the "pain of separation" and the longing for a "restoration of the original sense of union" by privileging "union" over "separation."

Thus from feminist mothering theory it is possible to derive the generalizations that a) "grandiose" narcissists are more likely to be men than women and b) "idealizing" narcissists are more likely to be women than men. These generalizations are confirmed by careful consideration of the case material that Kernberg, Kohut, and Masterson present in their major works. Ilene Philipson has noted that among the "29 cases presented as exemplary of . . . narcissistic disorders [of the grandiose variety]" in Kernberg's *Borderline Conditions and Pathological Narcissism* and Kohut's *The Analysis of the Self* and *The Restoration of the Self* "only five depict women" ("Gender," 215). My own count of the cases in Kernberg's book revealed an even stronger correlation between gender and type of narcissism: I found only one woman among the fourteen grandiose narcissists, but sixteen women among the twenty-four idealizing narcissists (who are called borderline by Kernberg). My count of the cases in Masterson's *The Narcissistic and Borderline Disorders* revealed a strikingly similar result: all four grandiose narcissists were men and seventeen out of twenty-four idealizing narcissists (also called borderline by Masterson) were women.

Thus the gender composition of the clinical cases of the psychoanalytic theorists of narcissism on whom Christopher Lasch relies confirms the connections between gender and narcissism that feminist mothering theory would predict. We can conclude, then, that feminist mothering theory is well able to withstand his critique.

Ilene Philipson's "Gender and Narcissism"

However, another look at the gender composition of Kernberg and Masterson's cases reveals something that feminist mothering theory is *not* able to explain. Although all but one of their grandiose narcissists were men, and although all but one of their female patients were idealizing narcissists, *seven out of Masterson's twenty-four idealizing narcissists and eight out of Kernberg's twenty-four idealizing narcissists were men.* To state these findings another way: whereas the combined ratio of male to female grandiose narcissists is seventeen to one, the combined ratio of female to male idealizing narcissist is barely more than two to one. These results are an anomaly for feminist mothering theory.

We have seen that from the assumptions of feminist mothering theory it is possible to derive the hypothesis that it is the daughter's difficulty in disentangling herself from her mother that accounts for the narcissistically idealizing woman. It would therefore seem to follow that we should expect that narcissistically idealizing men would have similar difficulties in extricating themselves from their preoedipal relationship with their mothers. *But this inference is excluded by the assumptions of feminist mothering theory.* This becomes clear when we examine a recent account of gender and narcissism that is based on those assumptions.

In "Gender and Narcissism" and "Heterosexual Antagonisms and the

Politics of Mothering," Ilene Philipson draws on feminist mothering theory in order to criticize Kohut's gender-neutral account of narcissism and to claim that "it is men who are more likely [than women] to display feelings of grandiosity and extreme self-centeredness, and to need the admiration of others." She also argues that the way in which the female narcissist "deal[s] with low self-esteem appears to be quite different from the grandiosity . . . of men," and typically entails the fantasy that the "male love partners [are] part of the woman's self" ("Gender," 224–25). The following passage nicely sums up her conclusions concerning the connection between gender and narcissism:

> For men . . . women partners do not become parts of the self; in fact, they are used to admire and esteem the defensively autonomous and tenuously maintained self. Women admire men's grandiosity, while male partners are constitutive of women's sense of worth. Women esteem men, while men are the vehicles through which women frequently attempt to find their self-esteem. ("Heterosexual," 70)

To reach this conclusion, Philipson relies on many of the same Chodorowian arguments that I have independently adduced in my critique of Christopher Lasch.[4] But she also emphasizes one that I did not. Philipson argues that the asymmetries in the boy's and girl's preoedipal relationship with the mother are compounded by the tendency of the mother to *treat them differently:* "Sons are most likely to be seen [by insufficiently empathic mothers] as husbands, fathers, and brothers, while daughters are seen as women's mothers or as extensions of themselves" ("Gender," 220). The passages from Chodorow's *The Reproduction of Mothering* that this claim references are worth reproducing in detail:

> Because they are the same gender as their daughters and have been girls, mothers of daughters tend not to experience [their] infant daughters as separate from them in the same way as do mothers of infant sons. In both cases, a mother is likely to experience a sense of oneness and continuity with her infant. However, this sense is stronger, and lasts longer, vis-à-vis daughters. Primary identification and symbiosis with daughters tends to be stronger and cathexis of daughters is more likely to retain narcissistic elements, that is, to be based on experiencing a daughter as an extension or double of a mother

herself, with cathexis of the daughter as a sexual other usually remaining a weak, less significant theme. (109)

Mothers tend to experience their daughters as more like, and continuous with, themselves. Correspondingly, girls tend to remain part of the dyadic primary mother-child relationship itself. This means that a girl continues to experience herself as involved in issues of merging and separation, and in an attachment characterized by primary identification and the fusion of identification and object-choice. By contrast, mothers experience their sons as a male opposite. Boys are more likely to have been pushed out of the pre-oedpial relationship, and to have had to curtail their primary love and sense of empathic tie with their mother. A boy has . . . been required to engage . . . in a more emphatic individuation and a more defensive firming of experienced ego boundaries (166–67).

Thus Chodorow assumes that girls will find it difficult to separate from their mothers not only because they do not experience themselves as different from their mothers but also because their mothers do not experience them as different from themselves; this identity leads mothers to treat their daughters as extensions of themselves and thus to discourage their separation. Boys, in contrast, will separate from their mothers far more easily, both because of the *internal pull* toward separation that results from the boy's experience of an opposition between his gender and hers and because this internal pull will be complemented by an *external push* toward separation that results from her experience of him as a "male opposite." Thus it is Chodorow's assumption of a necessarily complementary, mutually reinforcing push-pull toward separation that leads Philipson to her conclusion that "it is men who are . . . likely to display feelings of grandiosity and extreme self-centeredness," i.e., to associate men exclusively with narcissism of the grandiose self.

It is precisely this assumption, then, that makes it impossible to account for men who are idealizing narcissists. Such men, I have suggested, must have difficulties with separation that are, at least in certain respects, similar to the difficulties of narcissistically idealizing women. If these men have similar difficulties with separation, this can only be because their separation was similarly discouraged by their mothers. But Chodorow's assumption that mothers experience their sons as "opposites" and thus push them toward separation effectively denies the existence of men whose separation has been suppressed by their mothers.[5] To make room for these men it is therefore necessary to call that assumption into question. We must challenge the claim that mothers necessarily treat their little boys in a way that is fundamentally different from the way that they treat their little girls.

Miriam Johnson has already done so. In *Strong Mothers, Weak Wives*, she summarizes an impressive array of empirical studies that contest Chodorow's claim of significant, gender-based differences in the maternal care of young children. According to Johnson, very "few of these [studies] find differences in the way in which mothers interact with male and female children." Most report that there are "no differences on the part of mothers in the amount of affectionate contact between mother and male and female infants" and that "the degree of early attachment to the mother appears to be remarkably the same for both genders." Thus she concludes that "mothers do not differentiate appreciably between males and females in the amount of nurturance they provide" (136, 109).

Although Johnson's insistence on exonerating mothering from any blame leads her to interpret this evidence as a refutation of Chodorow's claim that many mothers are narcissistically overinvested in their daughters, a less idealist interpretation of this evidence would culminate in the conclusion that many (mother-raised) mothers are also likely to be narcissistically overinvested in their sons. Such mothers, pace Chodorow, will not "experience [their sons] as separate from them," will not "experience [them] as a male opposite," and will not "push them out of [their] preoedipal relationship." Instead, we should expect that they will strive to suppress their sons' separation every bit as strenuously as they attempt to discourage their daughters.'

TOWARD A SYNTHESIS

Chodorow fails to anticipate this possibility because she infers from the *fact* that their sons are in some sense their gender "opposites" the conclusion that mothers will necessarily *experience* their sons as "opposites," and act accordingly. But the evidence suggests that this inference is an unwarranted form of gender determinism. Mothers who, in the words of Donald Winnicott, treat their children as "projective entities" rather than "entities in their own right"(*Playing*, 89) may be just as likely to experience their sons as mothers who exist to take care of them as husbands who exist to fulfill them. If they experience their sons as mothers, they will treat them as mothers in spite of the "obvious" physical difference between them. The relative indifference of fantasy to reality thus makes it *impossible directly to derive parenting practice from the structure of parenting.*

Neither can the sense of self be directly derived from gender. If the structure of parenting does not guarantee that mothers will encourage the separation of their sons, it follows that it does not ensure, pace Chodorow once again, that "the basic masculine sense of self is separate" (*Reproduction*, 169). This claim, it seems to me, only applies to the boy who has been both *pushed and pulled away* from his mother. Having received, as it were, a consistent set of messages about the dangers of connection, it is he who becomes a man who consistently privileges separation from over connection with the others he encounters. It is he, in other words, who will suffer from the narcissism of the grandiose self.

The boy who has, in contrast, been simultaneously *pulled toward and away from* his mother has received an inconsistent set of messages about the meaning of separation. He learns, in effect, that separation from the (m)other is both incompatible with and essential to the survival of his self.

Having been overprotected by his mother, he (like his overprotected sister) will defend against the anxiety he associates with separation by seeking out relationships with overidealized others to whom he can cling. In this respect *his* sense of self is anything *but* separate, and in this respect his narcissism duplicates the idealizing narcissism of his female counterpart.

But the very symbiosis he seeks necessarily negates the masculinity that he must maintain. In order to transcend this double bind, the narcissistically idealizing man is likely to seek the safest possible connections with others, connections within which his need for others takes the form of a *need to take care of them*. Thus the idealizing man is both similar to and different from the grandiose man. Both need to control others in order to shore up their selves. But the grandiose man tries to control others by proving that *he* does not depend on *them*, while the idealizing man tries to control others by proving that *they* depend on *him.* Thus he differs from his narcissistically idealizing female counterpart by virtue of what might be considered his grandiose defense against an underlying overdependence on his others.[6]

This theoretical synthesis is far from complete. It seems clear that the type of mothering that girls and boys experience is a necessary but insufficient explanation for the type of women and men they in fact become. A more comprehensive account of the variations on the theme of masculine and feminine identity would have to consider the kind of relationship that boys and girls establish—or fail to establish—with their *fathers.*

Thus John Munder Ross emphasizes the crucial role of the father in "determining . . . a son's readiness or not to tender love" and whether his "urges towards generativity and the reality of his gender identity [will] coalesce" (Ross "Towards," 342, 345). According to Ross's account, "In their nurturing and teaching roles [fathers] may provide possibilities for their sons to include in their definitions of masculinity capacities first learned in identification with their mothers" (Fast, *Gender,* 101).[7] Thus a friendly father is necessary for the incorporation of maternal propensities into a masculine identity. Ross's reasoning leads to the conclusion that maternally overprotected boys who identify with relatively nurturing fathers will become different kinds of men from maternally overprotected boys who do not. My sense is that only the former will wind up to be narcissistically idealizing "good boys" who try to take care of others, while the latter will lean toward the nastier narcissism of a hypermasculine misogyny. Whereas the overprotected and father-identified boy can defend against his frighteningly powerful need for his mother by telling himself, "Because I am a man like my father who takes care of my mother, I will one day be able to take care of a woman who is like my mother," the overprotected boy with an absent or distant father is only able to defend against his fearsome fusion with his mother by trashing the women who represent her and thus assiduously avoiding long-term, emotionally intimate relationships with them. Similarly, maternally underprotected boys who are able to identify with their fathers will grow up to be different kinds of men from maternally underprotected boys who are not. Both boys will defend against premature separation from their mother with fantasies of exercising omnipotent control over her, but the grandiosity of the boy who confronts and then internalizes his father's prohibitions is repressed, while the grandiosity of the boy who does not encounter, and therefore never identifies with, paternal authority is given free reign. Only the latter become men "who feel they have the right to control and possess others and to exploit them without guilt feelings" (Kernberg, *Borderline*, 228), while the former will develop the strong superego of the inhibited, "inner-directed" man. Although psychoanalysis typically contrasts the neurosis of the "Guilty Man" with the narcissism of the "Tragic Man" (Kohut, *Restoration*, 171–248), Jessica Benjamin has argued, persuasively, that the repressed (and therefore never really relinquished) narcissism of the Guilty Man inevitably returns in the form an "aspiration to omnipotence that is nowhere more clearly evident than in the rape of nature" ("Oedipal," 216). Thus it would be more accurate to distinguish between what might be called the "neurotic narcissism" of the underprotected but father-identified man and the grandiose narcissism of the underprotected and not father-identified man.

My synthesis has even less to say about variations on the theme of feminine identity. In treating idealizing narcissism as a disproportionately female phenomenon, I have offered no explanation at all for the (apparently) relatively rare instances of grandiosely narcissistic girls. It would follow from my theoretical assumptions that their preoedipal merger with their mothers must have been prematurely curtailed, and that the combination of this external push away from and their internal (gender-based) pull toward their mothers would lead them to defend grandiosely against their own tendency toward self-denigration. But I have no explanantion as to *why* they would have been pushed away from their mothers.

Given my assumptions, it would be reasonable to speculate that paternal control over maternal practices might be part of the answer. But Miriam Johnson argues that "*fathers differentiate more than mothers* between their male and female children" (*Strong*, 128) and that we should not expect a girl to be treated nearly as harshly by her father as a boy. Even the most underprotective father will be far less threatened by the dependence of "Daddy's little girl" than by the dependence of his "big strong boy." But if this is the case, then paternal control over maternal practices is not likely to be a satisfactory explanation for a mother's disdain for her daughter's dependence. What *would* be a satisfactory explanation remains an entirely open question.

So too is the question of the difference that different daddies would make. Maternally underprotected girls who are able to identify with their fathers are likely to grow up to be very different women from maternally underprotected girls who are not. Perhaps only the latter become the cold female counterparts of guiltlessly grandiose men. It also follows that maternally *over*protected girls who are father-identified will become different kinds of women from maternally overprotected girls who are not. Perhaps only the mother-fusion fantasies of the former culminate in an idealization of men, while the mother-fusion fantasies of the latter will be focused more exclusively on their children.

In this concluding section, I consider whether the "uwarranted gender determinism" that I have attributed to Chodorow's *The Reproduction of Mothering* continues to apply to her more recent reflections. There are, of course, definite differences between the position of Chodorow in her by now classic work of 1978 and the positions she developed over the next two decades. *Feminism and Psychoanalytic Theory* was published in 1989 and included articles and essays written between 1979 and 1987. In this book, Chodorow called for a "melding of object-relations feminism and recent psychoanalysis" that would treat the "self as . . . separate from but related to gender identity" (197, 189). Thus at first glance it would appear that by 1987 she was already committed to a synthesis similar to the one I have outlined above. But a careful reading of *Feminism and Psychoanalytic Theory* as well as her subsequent writings reveals that she does not make good on that commitment.

On the one hand, in *Feminism and Psychoanalytic Theory* Chodorow relies on psychoanalysts like Winnicott to understand the way in which the child's sense of self is shaped by the quality of the practice of his or her parents:

> The integration of a "true self" that feels alive and whole . . . is fostered by caretakers who do not project experiences or feelings onto the child and who do not let the environment impinge indiscriminately. It is evoked by em-

pathic caretakers who understand and validate the infant as a self in its own right, and the infant's experience as real. (106)

Thus my claim above that Chodorow "ignores differences in the *quality* of parenting practice under the . . . mother-dominated structure of child rearing as well as . . . the problem of the difference in the object relations of children of both genders that these differences in parenting might make" does not in fact apply to her post-*Reproduction* reflections.

On the other hand, in *Feminism and Psychoanalytic Theory* this new-found focus on the impact of parenting practice on the formation of the self is in no way integrated with her longstanding and reaffirmed recognition of the impact of parenting structure on the formation of gender. At one point, in fact, Chodorow appears to preclude the very possibility of such an integration when she argues (in an essay originally published in 1979, to be fair) that "problems [in object relations] are [not] bound up with questions of gender; rather they are bound up with questions of self" (*Feminism*, 110). Here Chodorow seems to reject her claim that "questions of self [are] separate from but related to gender identity" in favor of the claim that they are *entirely* separate. But this latter claim is an exact echo of Christopher Lasch's argument that narcissism and gender are entirely unrelated and is therefore vulnerable to my critique of that argument.

At another point, however, Chodorow comes to a diametrically opposed conclusion. In the same essay in which she insists that questions of self and questions of gender are "separate but related" she also *effectively eliminates* the distinction between them, reiterating the structural claims of *The Reproduction of Mothering* that as a result of being parented primarily by a woman "the basic feminine sense of self is connected to the world [while] the basic masculine sense of self is separate" (*Feminism*, 169). And, in the same 1979 essay in which she insists on the opposition between "questions of gender" and "questions of the self," she also reaffirms her 1978 claim that one (of the two) reasons why the masculine sense of self is more separate than the feminine is that "a mother unconsciously and often consciously experiences her son as more of an 'other' than her daughter" (110). But, as we have seen, that is exactly the claim that makes it impossible to account for the difference between the idealizing "good boy" and the grandiose "macho man" or, more generally, for any significant differences in the sense of self of different men.

Thus a close reading of *Feminism and Psychoanalytic Theory* reveals that Chodorow does not work out a synthesis between structure and practice, or gender and sense of self, but rather waivers between *an insistence on their absolute separation and a complete collapse of difference between them.* Caught between these contradictory claims, she is not able to grasp what (as I argue above) it is necessary to grasp, "namely, *the relationship of connection and separation between structure and practice and between gender and sense of self.*"

Nor does she come any closer to grasping this connection in her subsequent work. In *Femininities, Masculinities, Sexualities,* Chodorow is once again divided against herself. But this time the division is different. Whereas the question that confounds her in 1989 was "What is the relationship between gender-identity and the sense of self?" the problem that plagues her now is whether it is possible to speak of any (unitary) "gender identity" at all.

One answer seems to be "no." Embracing the postmodern feminist "wariness . . . of generalizations about gender differences" (89; as well as what she has learned as a therapist about the particularity of her patients) Chodorow cautions that "though each person's gender is centrally important to him or her, it does not follow that we can contrast all women, or most women, with all or most men" (90). Gender identity is, instead, as multiple as the plurals in her title proclaim. Indeed, Chodorow concludes her book with the claim that "to understand femininity and masculinity . . . requires that we understand how any particular woman or man creates her or his own cultural and personal gender" (92), which sounds very much like the claim that there can be as many different gender identities as there are different people. Chodorow's conclusion that gender is an individual *creation* thus appears to rule out the very possibility of a structural account, and seems instead to point in the direction of (an individualistic version of) what postmodernists like Judith Butler have called a "performative" account of gender.[8] But Chodorow's concession to postmodernism is called into question by her reaffirmation of the utility of the very gender generalizations that are anathema to the postmodernist feminists. Chodorow

argues that such narratives or "patterns help give meaning to and interpretively situate particularity" and reminds the reader that "I have written about gender differences, and I take the usefulness of these insights
for granted" (89). Indeed, she recirculates *exactly the same* insights or
gender generalizations that she first formulated in *The Reproduction of
Mothering*. Whereas

> most girls seek to create in love relationships an internal emotional dialogue
> with the mother . . . those aspects of men's love that grow out of their rela-
> tionship to their mothers are more likely . . . to be intertwined . . . with
> [their] sense of . . . masculinity. Subjective gendering for men means that
> such love defines itself negatively in relation to the mother as well as in terms
> of positive . . . attachment. (82–84)

There it is: mother-raised women are relational while mother-raised
men are oppositional. The more things change, the more they stay the
same. And they remain the same in "Gender As a Personal and Cultural
Construction," published in *Signs* in 1995, where Chodorow not only re-
peats this generalization but also reiterates one of the reasons why it
holds: "Typically, mothers unconsciously as well as consciously experience . . . sons and daughters differently, because of their gender simi-
larity or otherness" (522). Thus she reaffirms the very structural account
of gender that the title of her article would appear to call into question.

In principle, of course, there is no inherent opposition between a
structural and a constructionist theory of gender. It is always possible to
argue that the structure accounts for the commonalities *across* different
men and *across* different women and that the construction accounts for
the differences *within* each gender. A generous reading of Chodorow's
search for "patterns [that] help give meaning to and interpretively situate particularity" might suggest that this is exactly the case that she is
trying to make. But the problem is that she fails to make that case, because her structural account of "patterns" *eliminates* rather than illumi-
nates the "particularity" to which her constructionist account is committed. It does not seem possible simultaneously to sustain the claim
that "the basic masculine sense of self is separate" and to make the case
that the relational "good boy" and the oppositional "macho man" are
two separate but equal variations on the theme of masculine identity.

To accommodate this particularity it would be necessary to contest rather than reaffirm Chodorow's gender generalization about "the basic masculine sense of self." And, as I show above, to contest that generalization it would be necessary as well to challenge the unwarranted gender determinism that underlies it, namely, the assumption that mothers necessarily experience their sons as "others" rather than "mothers" and will therefore push them away rather than reel them back in. But Chodorow continues to chain herself to precisely that assumption.

It is not clear why she does. In *Feminism and Psychoanalytic Theory,* Chodorow approvingly cites Miriam Johnson's finding that fathers are far more likely to sex-type their children than mothers (109). But her assumption that mothers treat their male infants fundamentally differently from the way they treat their female infants is entirely inconsistent with that finding. This assumption is also inconsistent with Chodorow's emphasis in "Gender As a Personal and Cultural Construction" on the centrality of "processes of transference"—and the process of projection in particular—in the construction of gender identity. She argues that in "projection we accord an emotional and fantasy meaning to others . . . because of intrapsychic processes or we project fantasied or experienced aspects of ourselves into aspects of these others" (520). But if projection is so central to the formation of gender identity then there is no reason to assume that a mother wouldn't fantasize her son as a mother to take care of her just because his body is "objectively" different from hers.

In short, my conclusion is that Chodorow's work still suffers from a literalism that prevents her from theorizing the difference between the mother who encourages and the mother who suppresses the separation of her son. The consequence of her inability to theorize this difference in parenting practice, in turn, is that rather too much of the variance in masculine identity is treated as a purely personal construction and rather too little as the result of that difference in parenting practice. Thus Chodorow's overly voluntaristic constructionist account of gender identity and her overly deterministic structural account of gender identity are merely two sides of the same theoretical coin.

NOTES

I would like to express my appreciation to Judith Kegan Gardiner for helping to kindle my interest in Kohut. Many years ago she was kind enough to let me read a draft of her "Self Psychology as Feminist Theory," subsequently published in Signs *12.4 (Summer 1987): 761–80.*

1. Strictly speaking, Chodorow does not entirely ignore differences in maternal practice under the prevailing structure, but these differences in practice, as we shall see, are treated—inadequately—as the automatic result of the structure.

2. Masterson is a partial exception to this generalization. In *The Narcissistic and Borderline Disorders,* he suggests that narcissistic disorders (of the "grandiose" type, in which separation is privileged over connection) may result from a "wholesale [transfer of] the symbiotic relationship with the mother onto the father in order to deal with [the child's] abandonment depression" and speculates that "since this turn to the father occurs earlier and more harmoniously in boys than in girls . . . narcissistic disorders [of the grandiose type] may be more common in boys than girls, which seems to agree with clinical experience" (13–14). But this passing two-page reference to the connection between gender and types of narcissism is not developed further, and it is, in fact, the only such reference in a book of almost 250 pages. References to that connection are entirely absent in Kernberg's *Borderline Conditions and Pathological Narcissism* and Kohut's *The Analysis of the Self* and his *The Restoration of the Self.*

3. Of course it makes a difference—as my friend Michael Mitsoglu pointed out to me some years ago—whether nor not a mother adequately mirrors her son prior to the point at which he becomes aware of the opposition between her gender identity and his own and thus prior to the point at which the boy repudiates his "mirror." The narcissism of the boy who is inadequately mirrored prior to this point is likely to be even more grandiose than narcissism of the boy who is lucky enough to have a "good enough" mother. But the point is that even this more fortunate son is likely to exhibit grandiose tendencies.

4. Only after working out that critique did I encounter Philipson's articles.

5. To avoid misunderstanding, I want to stress that my claim is not that Chodorow is unaware of the existence of such boys. Indeed in *The Reproduction of Mothering* (184–89) she specifically refers to them. My claim is rather that their existence cannot be squared with her *assumption that "mothers experience*

their sons as male opposites" and that *"boys are [therefore] more likely to have been pushed out of the preoedipal relationship"* than girls.

6. On the concept of a grandiosely narcissistic defense against an idealizing overdependence on the other, see Masterson, *Narcissistic*, 32–37, and *Emerging*, 16–17.

7. Fast relies on Ross, among others, to buttress her claims that "it is not necessary . . . for the boy to dis-identify with the mother" (*Gender*, 72) and that "dis-identification . . . signals failure in optimum development of masculinity" (73). It seems to me that the second claim is correct but the first claim is not. Fast herself acknowledges that the fact that "boys [in contrast to girls] must recognize their difference from their primary caregiver . . . may make it more difficult for boys than girls to move from sharply dichotomous notions of what it is to be masculine and feminine" (104). This admission undermines her claim that the boy's "dis-identification" from his mother is unnecessary under "mother-monopolized" child rearing and suggests that the "optimum development of masculinity" to which she is committed is far more dependent on coparenting than she realizes.

8. For a critique of Butler's position see my *Emotional Rescue,* chapter 14.

WORKS CITED

Abelin, Ernest. "Triangulation, the Role of the Father, and the Origins of Core Gender Identity." In Ruth Lax, Sheldon Bach, and J. Alexis Burland, eds., *Rapprochement: The Critical Subphase of Separation-Individuation*. New York: Aronson, 1980.

Balbus, Isaac D. *Emotional Rescue: The Theory and Practice of a Feminist Father.* New York: Routledge, 1998.

Benjamin, Jessica. *The Bonds of Love: Psychoanalysis, Feminism, and the Problem of Domination.* New York: Pantheon, 1988.

———. "The Oedipal Riddle: Authority, Autonomy, and the New Narcissism." In Mark E. Kahn, ed., *The Problem of Authority in America.* Philadelphia: Temple University Press, 1981.

Bernstein, Paula. "Panel on Gender Identity Disorder in Boys." *Journal of the American Psychoanalytic Association* 41 (1993): 729–42.

Butler, Judith. *Bodies That Matter.* New York: Routledge, 1993.

————. *Gender Trouble: Feminism and the Subversion of Identity.* New York: Routledge, 1990.

————. "Gender Trouble, Feminist Theory, and Psychoanalytic Discourse." In Linda Nicholson, ed., *Feminism/Postmodernism,* pp. 324–40. New York: Routledge, 1990.

Chodorow, Nancy J. *Femininities, Masculinities, Sexualities: Freud and Beyond.* Lexington: University Press of Kentucky, 1994.

————. *Feminism and Psychoanalytic Theory.* New Haven: Yale University Press, 1989.

————. "Gender As a Personal and Cultural Construction." *Signs* 20 (1995): 516–44.

————. *The Reproduction of Mothering.* Berkeley: University of California Press, 1978.

Dinnerstein, Dorothy. *The Mermaid and the Minotaur: Sexual Arrangements and Human Malaise.* New York: Harper and Row, 1976.

Fast, Irene. *Gender Identity: A Differentiation Model.* Hillsdale, N.J.: Lawrence Erlbaum, 1984.

Flax, Jane. "The Conflict Between Nurturance and Autonomy in Mother-Daughter Relationships and Within Feminism." *Feminist Studies* 4 (1978): 171–89.

Hegel, G. W. F. *The Phenomenology of Mind.* New York: Harper andd Row, 1967.

Johnson, Miriam. *Strong Mothers, Weak Wives.* Berkeley: University of California Press, 1988.

Kernberg, Otto. *Borderline Conditions and Pathological Narcissism.* New York: Aronson, 1975.

Kohut, Heinz. *The Analysis of the Self.* New York: International Universities Press, 1971.

————. *The Restoration of the Self.* New York: International Universities Press, 1977.

Lasch, Christopher. *The Minimal Self: Psychic Survival in Troubled Times.* New York: Norton, 1984.

Levenson, Ricki. "Intimacy, Autonomy, and Gender: Developmental Differences and Their Reflections in Adult Relationships." *Journal of the American Academy of Psychoanalysis* 12 (1984): 529–44.

Mahler, Margaret, Fred Pine, and Anni Bergman. *The Psychological Birth of the Human Infant.* New York: Basic, 1975.

Masterson, James F. *The Emerging Self.* New York: Brunner/Mazel, 1993.

———. *The Narcissistic and Borderline Disorders: An Integrated Approach.* New York: Brunner/Mazel, 1981.

Philipson, Ilene. "Heterosexual Antagonisms and the Politics of Mothering." *Socialist Review* 66 (1982): 55–77.

———. "Gender and Narcissism." *Psychology of Women Quarterly* 9 (1985): 213–28.

Ricoeur, Paul. *Freud and Philosophy.* New Haven: Yale University Press, 1970.

Ross, John Munder. "Towards Fatherhood: The Epigenesis of Paternal Identification During a Boy's First Decade." *International Review of Psycho-Analysis* 4 (1977): 327–47.

Stoller, Robert. *Presentations of Gender.* New Haven: Yale University Press, 1985.

Winnicott, D. W. *Playing and Reality.* New York: Basic, 1971.

10

THE ENEMY OUTSIDE: THOUGHTS ON THE PSYCHODYNAMICS OF EXTREME VIOLENCE WITH SPECIAL ATTENTION TO MEN AND MASCULINITY

Nancy J. Chodorow

Men who share an ethnic area, a historical era, or an economic pursuit are guided by common images of good and evil. Infinitely varied, these images reflect the elusive nature of historical change; yet in the form of contemporary social models, of compelling prototypes of good and evil, they assume decisive concreteness in every individual's ego development.
—Erikson, "Ego Development and Historical Change"

It is to moments of humiliation such as these that we owe men like Robespierre.
—Stendhal, *The Red and the Black*

What do we make today of Freud's arguments in *Civilization and Its Discontents* about the genesis and inevitability of aggression? How do current psychoanalytic understandings help us understand extreme aggression and cultural violence? Is there some linkage between cultural violence and aggression and masculinity? These are the questions addressed in this essay. I suggest that Freud's arguments, though rhetorically and intuitively powerful, need much amendment, that we can draw upon alternative theories and clinical experience for greater understanding of extreme violence, and that there is a complex link between violence-aggression and gender. My thinking is tentative, and, like Freud's, speculative.

Psychoanalytic thinking about violence, necessarily beginning with a reconsideration of *Civilization and Its Discontents,* must concern itself not only with "ordinary," normative, collective violence and aggression but also with the extremes of widespread vicious violence, often tied in some way to nationalism and its (tribal, ethnic, racial) equivalents, that we witness today and witnessed throughout the twentieth century.[1] Fifty years after the Holocaust, which still stands as the ultimate standard against which collective cruelty, brutality, killing, and torture can be assessed, we confront death squads, ethnic cleansing, and political rage expressed through torture, murder, and rape, genocidal murders of indigenous populations, and ethnocidal tribal warfare, not to mention widespread gang violence and gang wars in many parts of the urban world. At least, these are the kinds of violence and aggression that are in my preconscious as I write this paper.

Civilization and Its Discontents, Freud's remarkable attempt to explain the role of aggression in the psyche and in culture, must stand as one of the great social theories (whose review in any completeness is beyond the scope of my project here). Freud elegantly weaves together an account of the human psyche with an account of civilization or culture, showing both how basic cultural processes depend upon transformations of the sexual and death-aggressive drives and how, without these cultural processes, people, literally, could not survive. Drives, the most basic components of psychic life, are incompatible with society per se— with group life, interpersonal commitments, families, and economic cooperation—as well as with civilization and "high" culture—religion, art, and politics. Freud's project seems twofold. On the one side, there is the general spirit of his argument, his "pessimism": Freud's sense of the inevitability of conflict, aggression, and unhappiness in human life. On the other, there is a specific, elaborated psychological argument based on the dual-drive theory that Freud has developed in *Beyond the Pleasure Principle* and the structural theory that he develops in *The Ego and the Id. Civilization and Its Discontents* makes strong claims for the inevitability of aggression:

> The element of truth behind all this, which people are so ready to disavow, is that men are not gentle creatures who want to be loved, and who at the most can defend themselves if they are attacked; they are, on the contrary, creatures among whose instinctual endowments is to be reckoned a powerful

share of aggressiveness. As a result, their neighbour is for them not only a potential helper or sexual object, but also someone who tempts them to satisfy
their aggressiveness on him, to exploit his capacity for work without com-
pensation, to use him sexually without his consent, to seize his possessions, to
humiliate him, to cause him pain, to torture and to kill him. Homo homini
lupus. (111)

Freud notes that whereas this innately propelled aggression usually waits
for an excuse for provocation, it sometimes just emerges at will: "When
the mental counter-forces which ordinarily inhibit it are out of action, it
also manifests itself spontaneously and reveals man as a savage beast to
whom consideration towards his own kind is something alien" (112). He
lists examples very much in the national-ethnic-racial realm: "the atrocities committed during the racial migrations or the invasions of the
Huns, or by the people known as Mongols under Jenghiz Khan and
Tamerlane, or at the capture of Jerusalem by pious Crusaders, or even,
indeed, the horrors of the recent World War [the war that some commentators think provided one proximate cause of Freud's rethinking of
the drive theory]" (112). Freud continues to elaborate upon the national-
ethnic-racial question, pointing to "the narcissism of minor differences"
that rationalizes aggressive tendencies and leads neighbors like the English and the Scots, or the North and South Germans, to fight. He
notices the ease with which larger cultural groups latch onto smaller
groups or groups seen as social intruders as foci for the expression of innate aggression, and he with rueful irony (and tragic prescience) recognizes especially how the Jews have, historically, "rendered most useful
services" (114) throughout European history and across the European
continent by being outsiders and potential collective targets of violent
aggression.

This account of aggression is what I mean by the spirit of Freud's argument. Who can contest his observations of widespread violence, torture, and hatred? Who would want to ignore it? Freud captures our interest and attention by boldly taking on this central problem of human
interaction and of actual, physical, human and cultural survival. Yet, in
spite of his powerful, and (we would have to say) empirically accurate if
not adequately theorized account of cultural violence and aggression,
Freud's attention in *Civilization and Its Discontents,* his "pessimistic"

conclusions about the origins of human misery, in fact stem from a different source. He is less concerned with the actual destructive violence that he finds inevitable and (not surprisingly) more with psychic costs: his book, finally, is about the problem of guilt, of aggression turned not outward but inward. Repression, rather than action, is the threat that concerns him. He reviews his project: "My intention to represent the sense of guilt as the most important problem in the development of civilization and to show that the price we pay for our advance in civilization is a loss of happiness through the heightening of the sense of guilt" (134).

We have to ask, I think, whether the specific psychodynamic argument Freud makes adequately addresses either the question of guilt as a civilizing force or the question of aggression. Freud assumes, I believe, that in the normal course of events guilt works, that the superego as he has described it institutes repression and holds the drives that threaten civilization in check. That is, Freud does not need continually to concern himself with unmitigated aggression as a threat to civilization. In this view, when unbridled aggression erupts, it has two sources, both in the weakening of the superego. First, by definition, either adequate superego formation and internal guilt did not develop in the first place, or the aggressive drives that have been turned inward as guilt are redirected outward (the libidinal drives can also be directed inward or outward; moreover, aggressive drives turned inward can, rather than constituting a benign and appropriate superego, instigate punitive attacks on the self and what analysts call primitive guilt). But there is a another element in superego formation: the superego holds moral standards against which it measures the desires of the id, and these standards are formed through the internalization of parental, and thence societal, norms. Thus, second, a failure of morality and ethics, in addition to the reexternalization of aggression, enables excessive violence.

I think there is a problem with both of these claims. I will say more below about current psychoanalytic understandings of aggression as a drive, but here I want to point to a problem with the notion of a weakening or failure of superego standards. Sagan (*Freud*) persuasively argues my case. He notes that Freud's account (in *Civilization and Its Discontents* and "Lecture XXXI" of the *New Introductory Lectures*) describes a superego that is in some ways largely id. It is an expression of cruelty and violent condemnation, not of conscience, morality, empathy, or kindness. Moreover, the superego has no innate morality or ethical standards; rather, its standards and behavioral dictates come entirely from without. Thus, there is nothing—as the concept of "identification with the aggressor" makes clear—in the development of internalized guilt or in superego formation that in itself would prevent expressions of extreme violence and aggression, as long as that violence and aggression were in accord with or sanctioned by societal standards, nothing that "by itself, can make a judgment between a moral and an immoral value" (Sagan, "Cultural," 12). Sagan notes that "the Nazis used all the trappings of the superego to promote genocide: purifying, healing, curing, oath, community, the Volk, social usefulness, ideal society, sacrifice and dedication, ideology, idealism, and morality" (12).[2]

Thus, although I find *Civilization and Its Discontents* moving and evocative, I do not think we can turn to it for a psychodynamic explanation of cultural or individual violence. Nor do I think that the structural theory, with its underlying drive-repression dynamic, its focus on the Oedipus complex, and its assumptions about the constraining influence of the superego, is the most useful theory we have of psychic functioning. Accordingly, I also do not think that concepts like identification with the aggressor are adequate, unless we can explain the unconscious motivations that lead to such identification. Otherwise, we have to ask what made the aggressor himself aggress, find the answer in his identification with the aggressor, and so on through the generations.

Within post-Freudian psychoanalysis, the status of aggression, even more than sexuality, became an arena of contention. Klein agreed with Freud that innate destructiveness fuels psychic life, describing how the infant's fantasy of destroying with hatred and aggression the good breast/object leads to persecutory anxiety about being destroyed by the bad breast/object, and then attempts to reconstitute a good self and good breast, cyclically leading to further defensive splitting, projection, and persecutory anxiety. Managing fantasied aggression toward the self and the object is perhaps the major Kleinian psychodynamic goal; without such management a whole self and whole other cannot emerge, and the psyche is overwhelmed by intolerable anxiety. For Klein as for Freud, aggression does not in the first instance need explanation. It is a push from within, and explanations for its invocation are post hoc justifications for what emerges on its own. On the other side, neo-Freudians like Fromm as well as British Independents like Fairbairn and Guntrip argued strongly, drawing upon clinical evidence, that aggression is a reaction to environmental intrusion, danger, frustration, failure of fit, depressive affect, or anxiety.

In the contemporary period, many analysts hold a middle ground. Mitchell puts the case clearly ("Aggression"; see also Fonagy, Moran and Target, "Aggression"). He wants to hold onto both the drive-side perspective (that aggression must be biologically hardwired, is universal, is driven from within when experienced, and has dynamic depth and centrality for the individual) and the environmental side (that aggression, rather than being an innate, destructive, antilibidinal force driving independently and without proximate cause for release, emerges as a response under particular environmental or constitutional conditions or in particular relational contexts). Clinically, whether or not they believe theoretically in an innate aggressive or death drive, most analysts focus on what seem to be the immediate internal contexts in which aggression emerges. Much as Balint argued, against primary narcissism and for primary love, that clinically, whenever we find narcissism we explain it developmentally in the individual case, so also, Mitchell and others note, when we find aggression we look for its history and psychodynamic meaning to the individual rather than assuming that it simply expresses an innate drive. I think we could claim that even in Klein's writings, as well as in the work of contemporary Kleinians, developmental and clinical descriptions of paranoid-schizoid splitting and projection and unconscious aggressive and destructive fantasies do not require a theory of innate death or aggressive drives.

In what follows, I point to formulations that I find particularly useful in thinking about extreme aggression.[3] As I noted earlier, management of aggression is central to Kleinian accounts of psychic functioning. In Klein's view, cycles of splitting that keep separate good and bad internal objects and good and bad self, projection of aggression into bad objects, and persecutory anxiety define paranoid-schizoid functioning. Depressive position functioning arrives when a whole object (breast) can be seen to have good and bad aspects, enabling reciprocally a sense of good and bad whole self to emerge. Guilt for having previously harmed what is now seen as a whole object with feelings develops, leading to the wish to make reparation for one's destructiveness.

A Kleinian perspective would suggest that extremes of destructive aggression reflect paranoid-schizoid functioning, when the other is seen as a part rather than a whole object and the self is also fragmented. In paranoid-schizoid fantasy, the paranoid element involves persecutory anxiety—feeling attacked by the object and wanting to retaliate or attack first. The schizoid element involves the splitting of different aspects of self and object so that neither self nor object is whole. Such splitting may also include a derealization—an absence of depth of feeling in oneself and in one's perception of the other, so that neither seems real and alive. In paranoid-schizoid fantasy, it is important to keep good and bad objects very separate in order to keep good and bad aspects of the self separate and to protect the good aspects of object and self. This makes the bad aspects of self seem worse and further demonizes the object world, as bad elements of the self are evacuated and put into that world.

Other psychoanalytic accounts also focus on the implication of selfhood in aggression, claiming that aggression appears when the psychological self feels threatened. Mitchell ("Aggression," 366–67) points to the many ways that infants may experience threats and dangers (lack of attunement, separation, parental anxiety, environmental impingement, unresponded to hunger or other physiological distress). He suggests, more or less following Klein, that these sufferings tend to be experienced as intended. They are projectively experienced as coming from without (or they may indeed come from without); therefore, the ensuing suffering is intended by an external agent (or a projectively externalized agent). The belief that one's suffering is intended by another is found also prevalently in adults. As a result, suffering becomes unconsciously hooked up with feelings of being attacked, endangered, and threatened by another, and defensive retaliatory aggressive feelings ensue. Some people's internal world becomes centrally organized around these feelings of threat and danger (those with punitive superegos would be one example here), so that their unconscious fantasy life revolves around aggression and attack, and they are likely projectively to experience the world as attacking and threatening and to respond accordingly. A patient says, "I'm always vigilant to keep bad things from happening, and I feel threatened by people who aren't." Mitchell stresses that the observed actuality of danger and threat here is not important. Subjectively, the person feels endangered, and these "threats to the integrity of the self, as subjectively defined, tend to generate powerful, deeply aggressive reactions" (368). He sums up a widely accepted psychoanalytic perspective, although he is careful, following Klein, to make clear that he is talking not only about actual threats to the self (as might, say, Kohut) but also about internal fantasy and projective-introjective spirals of attack and defense.

Several developmental accounts describe the emergence of the kinds of self likely to enact destructive aggression. These accounts begin from the developing child's need for intersubjective recognition (see Benjamin, *Bonds* and *Like Subjects*). In order to develop a psychological self—a depressive position self capable of seeing self and other in terms of internal mental states, feelings, beliefs, intentions, desires, and so forth—the developing child needs parental reflection of her thoughts and feelings (Winnicott, for example, in *Playing*, writes in this context of holding, Bion, "Theory," of containment: a container for, and someone who returns in more integrated form, the child's frightening, fragmented, projections). According to Fonagy, and colleagues ("Aggression" and "Understanding"), if a young child's self-expression is either ignored or interpreted as aggression, a psychological self cannot develop. When there is an inability to experience oneself in the mental domain, thoughts, beliefs and desires will be expressed and managed physically. At this paranoid-schizoid level, lacking whole, alive, reflective objects, aggression may eventually become fused with self-expression. In such a case, extreme destructiveness becomes an attempt to express an inadequate, defective self-structure when confronted by other human beings who are themselves seen as inanimate, nonreflective selves or dangerous objects. Moreover, insofar as they are seen as without feelings or thoughts, other people are perceived to be without the capacity to suffer, so that inhibitions against aggression may be further reduced (Benjamin, *Bonds,* describes the contrary case, when the other's suffering at the hands of the self recognizes the self and affirms the self's existence). Fonagy, Moran, and Target describe the boy, David, who exhibited "uncertainty about his identity except when angry and fighting"

("Aggression," 477), for whom "meaningful emotional experience had been replaced by mindless aggression" (478).[4]

Aggression, then, is not an innate drive needing expression and gratification. It seems to emerge from a variety of situated psychodynamics that in the most general sense seem connected to self and other, selfhood and object status. It emerges as a defense against an endangered self (the sense of danger being physiological, a fantasied or perceived threat of physical or emotional attack, punitive guilt, shame and humiliation, a threat of fragmentation—and danger can be felt to come from within or from without) or in an attempt to express a self in a situation of internal paranoid-schizoid fragmentation, lack of internal wholeness, and lack of mentalization, in which the person relies more on the body for expression (and perhaps sees others also more as bodies than as whole minds). Projective constructions of the object as well as the self can also lead to aggression: Kleinians point to the unconscious fantasy that the object is aggressive and threatens the ego (originally, that the bad breast threatens the infant-self), leading to the fantasy of retaliation and destruction of the object, as well as to envious feelings toward the good breast, leading to the desire to destroy its goodness. They also point to the preference for hatred of a bad object over envy of a good one: it is better to destroy something seen as bad and therefore hateful than good and therefore hateful (see Klein, "Envy"). (With envy, in the Kleinian view, we are certainly on the terrain of innate aggression, but, whatever its origins, we often see clinically the power and terror of destructive fantasies toward goodness that is envied.)

I have tried to focus on psychoanalytic conceptions that might be generative for an understanding of destructive aggression and violence, but such an inquiry, focused as it is on the individual, only gets us part way to cultural violence and aggression. Here we run into similar problems to those we face in any cultural psychoanalytic inquiry. Can we see cultural practices and processes as individuals writ large? Can peoples be reduced to or equated with individuals? Do we want to explain cultural violence on the basis of collective child-rearing practices or infantile experiences of failures in recognition and intersubjectivity? And so forth. Many cultural commentators have documented persuasively the complexity and difficulty of tying the individual psyche to culture or society and the reductionist dangers in so doing, and we can see this complexity and difficulty clearly in psychodynamic analyses of rituals, myths, culturally laden dreams, beliefs about sexuality, etc. In these cases, we expect and find complex symbolization, mediation, transformations, and condensations of themes, themes that also have a cultural and historical life of their own, even as a psychodynamic account helps us further to understand them. This would be true to some extent, I imagine, of ritual or culturally normative violence.

In my view, however, there is something peculiar about the psychodynamic case of extreme cultural violence and aggression. To begin, the behavior itself—rape, killing, torturing—seems directly, physically, aggressive: we may also be talking about paranoid-schizoid interchanges inside the head, but we are certainly talking about how this internal world is enacted. Furthermore, and perhaps more important, the consciously articulated cultural ideologies that tend to justify such behavior often seem directly, and without much symbolic transformation or elaboration, to express exactly what psychoanalysts describe as the individual unconscious motivations and internal constructions that lead to aggression. That is, several of these ideologies seem particularly expressive of unconscious life. In this sense, they may well serve as a kind of personal symbol or transitional concept, linking what comes psychodynamically from within the individual to a similar formulation that comes culturally from without.

Almost definitionally, contemporary violence seems to organize itself around identity. Erikson (*Childhood,* "Ego"), of course, theorized more than any other analyst the importance of identity to psychic health, and he also provided many clinical vignettes as well as psychocultural analyses of ethnic, national, and racial identity (ironically, his account of Hitler's motivations—based on his relations with his mother and father and the problem of paternal authority in Germany more generally—has less to say about German identity than his accounts of almost every other national-ethnic group). He makes an incontrovertible case for the centrality of ethnicity to many people's identity and sense of self, though when he describes disrupted, spoiled, or subjected identities (Native American, African American, immigrant), these do not in his case accounts lead to rage and aggression but rather to depression and despair. What we take from Erikson, however, is an argument for identity as a primary motivational force (insofar as identity for Erikson is linked to basic trust and directly tied to being recognized for who you are, with history, continuity, and a place in the world, his theory is closely tied to Winnicott, Kohut, Benjamin, and others who make recognition central).

Culturally also, identity seems to be one of the concepts that consolidates and justifies genocide, ethnic cleansing, and similar practices. The psychological here is not simply a displacement or rationalization for political and economic causes (nor, of course, would we say that social factors and forces are simply displacements of the psychological). However, if ethnicity is ego identity on a social scale, or the social equivalent of psychic selfhood, with the same deep roots and centrality to a sense of being recognized and being whole, then we can begin to understand how it could drive collective violence, just as threats to the self generate aggression in the individual—how, under particular conditions, violence becomes a way to affirm collective selfhood and identity as much as it affirms individual selfhood.

These particular conditions resonate directly with psychodynamic accounts. Just as narcissistic threats, humiliation and shame, trauma, or being unrecognized lead on the individual level to an aggressive response, so these are the terms in which collectivities often describe the reasons for their violence. Analysts locate hate-filled violence on the paranoid-schizoid level, focusing on splitting and the projection of hatred and aggression; similarly, national-ethnic-racial violence is justified in split, projective terms, in terms of the objective evil, destructiveness, and badness of the group that is being attacked or eliminated (Erikson's "common images of good and evil").

It is relatively easy here for individuals to bring personal psychodynamics to cultural symbols. Many accounts of the rise of Nazism point to the humiliating defeat at Versailles in 1918, and Hitler certainly appealed to the German shame; Serbian language has repeatedly focused on the humiliation and defeat of Serbia over the centuries, as does the language of both Israelis and Palestinians. Moreover, if questions of identity and selfhood are central to extreme violence, it is also clearer why the enemy is found close to hand rather than far away or in the nonhuman environment. An object fantasied to be like the self is more likely to threaten the self's integrity and sense of difference, and it is also the object most easily introjected and set up as an internal persecutory object.

We can sometimes see mediating developmental psychodynamics as well. Loewenberg ("Psychohistorical") argues that a confluence of factors in a particular generation growing up during and after World War I in Germany and Austria—prolonged or permanent father absence followed by the return of individually defeated fathers to a collapsed economy, psychically and nutritionally unavailable mothers, extreme hunger and privation, along with national defeat, humiliation, and political-social collapse—generated on an individual level intense, destructive oral rage, intolerable anxiety, and a lack of internal ability to modulate and control intense emotions. This individual anxiety-laden, hate-filled fragmentation met a polity filled with anger and potential violence.

We may be able to find a meshing between developmental outcomes and political outcomes in other cases of extreme cultural violence, but I would not necessarily expect so. What I think more likely is that in this realm, for some reason (and I am very hesitant to suggest this), we can really see social processes to some extent as a sum of or homologous with individual processes: individuals themselves feel humiliated, endangered, and attacked, and their individual feelings resonate directly, in the manner of a personal symbol, with collective ideologies and claims. Language on an ideological level reflects what analysts describe psychodynamically, explaining violent expansionism, racism, and ethnocide as a reaction to humiliation and defeat.

Other dynamic elements may not seem as directly available to collective or individual subjectivity, though they are nonetheless part of unconscious fantasy. I am speaking particularly of the paranoid-schizoid level of functioning on which extreme collective violence, like individual pathological aggressive fantasies and actual aggression, seems to take place. It appears that social disintegration, in polities that did not provide previously for adequate mentalization, illusion, and psychosocial depressive-level integration, leads to collective psychic disintegration expressed in splitting, projection, and violent acting out of projective fantasies. Just as analysts find in someone who feels endangered and who has not been able previously to develop a reflective self (whose potential container has not provided meaning) a flooding fragmentation and dissolution of boundaries intertwined with reactive aggression, so the breakdown of a totalitarian state or a state symbolized in one leader, like the Soviet Union or Yugoslavia, or the sudden withdrawal of a colonial power, may lead to violent lawlessness, ethnic war, and brutal ethnic cleansing. There is a connection here between a sense of meaning (on the psychological level, a subject who contains projections and reflects and integrates subjectivity for the developing self; on the social level, a society and polity not founded on aggression and social repression) and a sense of identity, on both individual and collective levels (I find myself tempted to return to some of the earliest and globalized psychological-anthropological accounts, to think, as might have Benedict, of paranoid-schizoid societies).

We can also see such paranoid-schizoid disintegration in polities that, although systematically racist, we might consider more benign. Israel, for example, operates more or less as a civil democracy (I do not mean to minimize the anti-Mizrachi sentiments and practices nor anti-Palestinian policies, but I do distinguish Israel from the Soviet Union or the previous Eastern European dictatorships), but when there is a Palestinian suicide bombing, or an attack or uprising in the West Bank, we find both the rhetoric and the behavior becoming suddenly more militaristic and the imagery of Palestinians becoming extensively demonized. By complement, when Rabin was assassinated, there was no psychic space in the Israeli collective consciousness for normal splitting, given that the assassin was also a Jew. (To take a personal example, I found myself, shortly after hearing about Peres's defeat in 1996, wrathfully thinking that if the Palestinians stepped up bombing and violence the Israelis would be getting what they deserved.)

I note here that a more classical psychodynamic explanation would concern the decline of a paternal authority (the Soviet state, Tito, the colonialist British raj, or Palestinian protectorate) able to rein in aggression, identification with the aggressor, or group psychological identification with a leader. I do not think these accounts are entirely wrong. Especially, we cannot rule out either the loss of capacity for displacement of both self-sustaining idealizations and hatred of racial-ethnic others onto an oppressive leader or identification with the aggressor while that aggressor is in power—an identification, moreover, that can defend against personal humiliation (see Fanon, *Wretched*). But I think these explanations do not adequately describe even on the individual level the kind of fragmentation and hate-filled destruction let loose that a more object-relational account of disintegration and its consequences can account for.

We can see paranoid-schizoid functioning also on the level of symbolization. The swastika, for example, seems to have become a nonsymbolic symbol: it can be and stand only for itself rather than having many purposes and meanings.[5] This kind of symbol is what Klein ("Importance") and Segal ("Notes") call a concrete symbol, or symbolic equation, in which the ego does not differentiate between the symbol and the thing symbolized, so that there can be no elaborations and transformations of the symbol in relation to other symbols. National-ethnic-racial politics often organizes itself around such symbols, in terms of nation or ethnos, of historical events, of the land itself (Judea and Samaria, Greater Serbia). By contrast, true symbols are felt to be created by the ego, and therefore can be modified, entered into connection with other objects and symbols, and transformed into other symbols. As Segal puts it, "The symbols, created internally, can then be re-projected into the external world, endowing it with symbolic meaning" (167).[6]

I find, then, that I am focusing on two general arenas involving challenges to the collective self. First, on a more articulated level of unconscious fantasy that finds expression and reflection in conscious collective fantasies and ideologies, humiliation and shame seem to generate extreme violence (e.g., Germany was humiliated in World War I). I imagine that defeat takes different forms depending on how it is put into collective fantasy, such that the sense of humiliation linked to defeat leads to more narcissistic retaliatory rage, while "defeat with honor" leads to less. Second, on a less articulated level of psychic and social functioning, social disintegration seems to generate similar paranoid-schizoid fantasies to psychic disintegration (e.g., Yugoslavia disintegrates and there is no longer a—however disturbed—protective container). I expect that we also need to differentiate between enemies (or victims), and that this differentiation, based on whether victims are more or less dehumanized, may bear some (not direct and simple) relation to humiliation or paranoid-schizoid and identity fantasies respectively. On the one side, to what extent are enemies thought to feel and suffer, so that there is also identificatory joy in torture or rape, in the case of sadistic retaliatory violence for humiliation (Stoller's work is apt here; see *Sex and Gender*)? On the other, to what extent are enemies (as Fonagy and colleagues suggest) thought of as not having thoughts or feelings but as bad part objects who are expelled and destroyed, in the identity case? Finally, I speculate that grief and loss in themselves do not lead to pathological collective violence, and, in that sense, I am not sure how to draw from psychoanalytic conceptualizations of mourning. It is, rather, mediating dynamics—when loss and grief become connected to a sense of injury and rage—that signify (for an individual and cultural case, see Rosaldo, "Grief"). One of my patients tells an anecdote about an Irishman at the negotiating table with the British: he is offered one thing after another (the return of Northern Ireland, unification, economic help) and finally gets up, saying, "I'd rather have my grievance."

In spite of this persuasive isomorphism, which I do not dismiss, I also think we cannot without evidence assume that these cultural claims—however straight out of a psychoanalytic text they might be—are also what motivate individuals to act aggressively in cultural situations. As Erikson puts it, we need to show how collective historical processes "assume decisive concreteness in every individual." It is likely that in many particular cases when cultural violence becomes personally psychodynamically animated and constructed as a result of individual life histories, this personal animation is not a replica of the social claim. For example, many projective ideologies (of nationalism, xenophobia, racial-ethnic hatred, and so forth) clearly support the view that identity is a psychosocial as well as an individual issue. Nonetheless, if we were to analyze those individuals engaged in ethnic violence, we might well find that their individual unconscious fantasies involved not threats to selfhood, but, for instance, reparative wishes toward a parent, survivor guilt, separation fears, depressive anxiety, homosexual panic, defensive masculinity, identification with a soldier father, manic denial of survival, triumphant elation at survival, mourning a loss, or any number of other fantasies. Annihilation anxiety, or anxiety about impingement, might be involved for an individual participating in collective violence conceptualized ideologically as a reaction to national humiliation, whereas personal humiliation and a sense of narcissistic injury might fuel participation in ethnic warfare organized around questions of ethnic survival and identity. Ideologies and politics, even when cast in language consonant with psychodynamic explanations, themselves have their own history, and participation in politics can also only be understood on the individual level, in terms of personal psychodynamic meaning.

Thus, on a cultural level, there are processes similar to those on the individual level: cultures have identity questions, feel persecuted, symbolize racial-ethnic others in terms of pollution, engage in paranoid projection and splitting, all of which form the ideologies that justify violence and aggression. Cultures may also have individual ideologies (of manhood, whiteness, Aryanness, Serbness) that lead to violence, either culturally sanctioned individual violence (ritualized warfare, ambushing, head taking) or group violence (mass rape or murder). Finally, there are individual psychodynamic reasons for adherence to a cultural process or belief system.

Counterexamples, of course, would help to turn descriptions into explanations. We know, and can observe both clinically and historically, that identity and selfhood seem dynamically important on both individual and cultural levels. We know that projection and splitting are prevalent ways that individuals and cultures create selfhood and peoplehood. We know that this projection and splitting link up intrapsychically in fantasy with aggression and destruction and that they can do so behaviorally as well. We know something about how integration works for the individual level: paranoid-schizoid functioning can be replaced by depressive functioning and desires for reparation toward rather than destruction of the other; holding and containing help development; potential space and the realm of illusion foster creativity and playfulness in the individual and intersubjective cultural creativity between people. What we know less about is how to describe such conditions on a political, social, or cultural level. It is striking, for example, that although there has certainly been serious political, racial, and ethnic violence in postapartheid South Africa, this violence is not at the level of ethnic cleansing and has not meant the deaths of millions. Volkan's notion of "chosen trauma" ("Chosen") seems important: there seems to be something not only of what the traumatic experience has been but of how it is subjectively conceptualized, and how and whether a response has been developed that enables some resolution and hope. Various issues are involved: is identity able to be reconstituted in an integrated way that does not involve rigid boundaries and projective splitting off of hated aspects of self into a collective other? Does the trauma involve humiliation, which seems so potent a predictor of retaliation, and is there a clearly defined projective other who inflicted the humiliation? Alternatively, is there a more complex ideological picture of what happened, with a sense of differentiated and connected forces that make it harder to divide the world into good and bad? Or is there someone, or a new set of laws or pactices, that is seen as a benevolent protective intervener in the trauma?[7]

As should be clear, I have found it impossible to rethink *Civilization and Its Discontents* directly in relation to gender. Here, I replicate Freud. Although he implicitly links in this text superego formation, aggression, aggression turned inward, identification with parents, and the childhood need for protection to gender (paternal protection is what's needed and also, indirectly, protection from the father who, after all, threatens castration and leads the boy to turn aggression inward in superego formation), Freud does not specify that he is talking about gendered dynamics. Similarly, I have written about threats to the self, flooding and disintegration, narcissistic injury, humiliation, and paranoid-schizoid fantasies as if these involve (and they do) humanity in general. We find an asymmetry in which psychoanalytic writing notices dynamics found predominantly in women (for Freud, narcissism and masochism), whereas dynamics that predominantly characterize men (aggression) are discussed in generic human terms. My impression (I have not surveyed the literature) is that with the exception of Stoller's extensive work on perversions, which describes feelings of humiliation and rage and the desire to humiliate and aggress against the other (*Perversions*), psychoanalytic books about masculinity barely mention aggression except to suggest that it can be positive and normal, and they never discuss masculine violence. They focus, rather, on questions of sexuality, homosexuality and heterosexuality, fathers and father absence, disidentification from mother, castration fears, feelings about women, gender in the transference, and so forth.

I do not want to replicate Freud's scotoma nor the scotoma in psychoanalytic thinking. Men, after all, are directly responsible for and engage in the vast majority of both individual violence and rape as well as collective violence. Historically and cross-culturally, they make war. Men are soldiers and, as politicians and generals, those who instigate and lead the fighting. Men also engage in extreme violence: they are (mainly) the concentration camp guards, the SS, those who perpetrate genocide, mass ethnic rape, pogroms, torture, and the murder of children and old people. Hormones, the structure of masculine personality, and/or the social and political organization of gender, male bonding, and male dominance, all lead many men to react to threats with violence and aggression in a way that most women do not. Men find themselves and organize themselves into groups whose goal is extreme violence, and perhaps they get pleasure from extreme violence and aggression. The military in all societies is by definition masculine, and descriptions of military training always note how such training involves the invocation of ideologies of aggressive masculinity and explicit, often sexualized deprecation of women. Women, by contrast, tend not to be fighters, and many feminists (Ruddick, *Maternal*, following writers like Vera Brittain, Olive Schreiner, and Virginia Woolf) think women might have a special relationship to peace and pacifism. Historically, we find the Women's Peace Party in World War I, the Women's Strike for Peace, alliances between Protestant and Catholic women in Northern Ireland, Russian mothers pulling their sons out of the army. There seems to be an almost natural link between violence-aggression and men.

Yet such observations take us only so far. We cannot contrast men's universal aggression with women's universal nonaggression. Aggression is found and develops in nonpathological ways in both sexes; not all men are violent, not all women are peaceful. Many women support torturers, ethnic murderers, and rapists; many men are peacemakers and revolted by the extreme violence of our last century. Moreover, unlike the connection of dynamics of self to threats to social selfhood, I do not think we are talking in the case of masculinity and violence about psychology writ large in culture and society. We cannot minimize the social and political organization of gender and male dominance that feminists have described so extensively and that any social scientist must see as having its own historicity and sociocultural level of functioning. I do note, however, that one early definition of male dominance (Hartmann, "Patriarchy") insists that it is a mistake to see such dominance solely in terms of men's power over women. Male dominance involves alliances and hierarchies among men that enable and enforce dominance over women. These alliances and hierarchies do not rest solely on relations and institutions of violence and aggression, but the cross-cultural and historical record makes clear that they often include such relations and institutions.

For our purposes, however, I want to put these sociocultural observations aside. What can we see in masculine psychology that might account for men's participation in extreme violence? We are talking about reactions to humiliation, threats to identity and selfhood, and propensities to the enactment of paranoid-schizoid fantasies. Here, also, psyche meets culture. It is certainly not the case that men operate more on the paranoid-schizoid level than women. We are looking at what leads, or allows, men to enact aggression. Cultural constructions of masculinity must play a part, constructions that foster or make understandable individual and collective male aggression and the expression of anger.

First, I note an important mediating link. Men are the perpetrators and enactors of extreme violence, so that it would seem that such behavior and the psychodynamics that underlie it are related to masculinity. However, the identity involved in much of this violence is national-ethnic-racial. I suggested earlier that this national ethnicity or peoplehood can be experienced psychodynamically as cultural selfhood, and that, as such, threats to it are experienced directly as threats to the self. Gendering in this context comes in only secondarily, as the language of ethnic hatred is often cast in gendered and sexualized terms. (Much of the unconscious fantasy of ethnic hatred is also cast in gendered and sexualized terms, but it is a psychodynamically reductionist mistake to think that gender and sexuality are more primary here. As Erikson and occasionally Freud show, ethnic identity and its conflicts can be basic to psychic functioning.) As my earlier work suggests (*Reproduction,* "Gender, Relation"), issues of selfhood tend to differentiate men and women. Seeing the self as not the other, defining the self in opposition, does not seem generally as important to women as to men, nor does merging seem as threatening. Insofar as a cultural politics of identity is involved, and if the male's self (I am not talking about his sense of masculinity here) is indeed more defensive, then it makes some sense that women would not feel as endangered by threats to cultural selfhood. Of course, the unconscious intertwining of ethnicity and otherness with gender would further reinforce the felt danger of men, whose sense of masculinity is also generally more fragile than women's sense of femininity.

Humiliation may also in some way adhere more to men than to women (I am not talking universals here; of my patients, the women most prone to feeling humiliated are also those most liable to outbursts of rage). We could expect this from classical Freudian accounts of challenges to phallic narcissism and from descriptions of the humiliation of being a little boy in relation to grown men or women (for a cultural case study, see Slater's still powerful *The Glory of Hera;* for a psychodynamic case in the cultural arena, see Zwigoff's movie *Crumb,* which documents R Crumb's relentless, deadened, aggressive treatment of women as bodily part objects in a way that makes transparently clear his paranoid-schizoid functioning and his retaliation for feelings of having been humiliated).

In the cases of both identity and humiliation, fathers must enter the picture. My guess is that the experience of a humiliated father alone does not generate cultural or individual male violence; identification with such a father would rather tend to lead to submissiveness (a complaint brought by Freud against his own father). But a humiliated father who turns on his son in rage would especially lead that son to his own violent reaction to feeling humiliated (there is much documentation of irrational authoritarian absolutism and punitiveness in German fathers; a review quotes James Gilligan's *Violence:* "The most dangerous men on earth are those who are afraid that they are wimps"). Similarly, although in the normal family case recognition, mutuality, depressive guilt, and reparation to a mother with subjectivity form a primary container for the development of an integrated selfhood in both boys and girls (Benjamin, *Bonds,* best documents the way that the breakdown of mother-son mutuality and intersubjective recognition leads to masculine sadism and violence), many analytic accounts also describe the potential role of a paternal third (we have to acknowledge that in the best case, especially for the boy, this third should be male). The paternal third helps children to move to an observer's position vis-à-vis the mother-child dyad, provides another image of subjectivity and intersubjectivity, and allows "space to think . . . capacity to present the child with a reflection of his place in relationships" (Fonagy, Moran, and Target, "Aggression," 497). In the absence of a paternal third, moreover, when boys may experience intersubjectivity as a female-male (mother-child) affair, they may split off intersubjectivity from relations with other men and feel driven to fall back on less mentalized externalizations.

Fonagy, Moran, and Target make a related point ("Aggression"). They note that men and women both engage in violence when mentalization is not available, but men are more likely to direct hostility toward others, whereas women engage more in self-mutilation. In both cases, the attempt is to get rid of intolerable fantasies of the thoughts in someone else's (originally, the fantasied parent's) mind. Identification with the same-sex parent may feel more painful and inescapable, so that the wish will be more to attack the thinking of the same-sex parent. If, for both girls and boys (as Chodorow, *Reproduction,* would predict), the mother's thoughts about the child are intersubjectively experienced earlier and represented more as within, whereas the father's thoughts are experienced more as coming from without, then we would expect a woman to attempt to destroy an internal object (herself), whereas men would be more likely to engage in external violence against an object experienced as being without. The girl or woman tries to rid herself of the mother in her mind; the boy or man tries to rid himself of the father out there.[8]

It is as if the experiences of humiliation, of identity and selfhood, and indeed of masculinity and manhood themselves, have two potential components (divided for heuristic purposes only). For some men, and in some cultures, masculinity is cast as an adult-child dichotomy: being an adult man versus being a little boy, being humiliated by other men. For Freud, becoming a man has to do with identification with the aggressive father, so that the dynamics of masculine identity are centrally about aggression or aggressivity (activity). Oedipal identification with the father casts heterosexuality as a matter of male dominance (see Chodorow, *Femininities*). For Stoller, by contrast, becoming a man has to do with not being a woman (*Perversion*), and my own previous work (Chodorow, *Reproduction,* "Gender") links this further to becoming a self.

My guess is that political challenges may similarly be cast predominantly in one of these two ways. Hertz describes cases from French nineteenth-century history, cast as male-female, in which threats to political authority were experienced as Medusa-like challenges to organized masculinity, including ways that disheveled, sexualized, evil women came to symbolize Socialist disrule and order-challenging chaos ("Medusa's"). "Ordinary" war, by contrast, seems to be a male-male affair, and the threat is of being defeated or humiliated by other men. However, it seems that in the Holocaust and other genocides, in Serbian ethnic cleansing, mass rape of women and murder of men and boys, in the extensive, often sexualized torture by rightist dictatorships, these two components of masculinity both operate. In this situation, challenges to ethnicity and nation threaten individual or collective selfhood, and the close developmental and experiential interlinking of selfhood and gender mean that masculinity is also threatened. Humiliation from men (the man-boy dichotomy) becomes linked with fears of feminization (the male-female dichotomy).

In this overdetermined situation, we find extreme masculine violence. Paranoid-schizoid gender, based projectively on split off images of repudiated women and feminized or boylike men, fuses with paranoid-schizoid splitting of good self and hated bad object. The enemies are constructed as part objects without subjectivity; at the same time, destroying their subjectivity helps provide the sadistic pleasure of violence. This rigid, projective splitting and expulsion, both of bad objects and bad aspects of gender identity at the same time, seem to involve a disintegrative flooding of self-object boundaries and drives, so that the projected object and threatened aggression not only return in paranoid fantasy but also threaten to meld and fuse with the self. Affects and drives overwhelm the subject and lose their linkage to organized fantasy. When social wholes fracture, and identity, via conscious and unconscious concepts of peoplehood, nation, or ethnos, is threatened, for men, especially, gender identity seems to fracture along similar lines. This reinforces the threat to selfhood and leads to reactive, hate-filled violence.

NOTES

This paper was originally prepared for presentation at the conference, "Civilization and Its Enduring Discontents: Violence and Aggression in Psychoanalytic and Anthropological Perspective," September 2–6, 1996, Bellagio, Italy. It has been edited only to remove direct references to the conference and, in reprinting, to acknowledge the new century. I am extremely grateful to the Guggen-

heim Foundation and the National Endowment for the Humanities for support during the year in which it was written. My thinking has been influenced by presentations at the 1992 Meetings of the University of California Interdisciplinary Psychoanalytic Consortium by Robert Pynoos on children, trauma, and violence and by Robert Nemiroff and Marcelo Suarez-Orozco on the psychodynamics of violence and torture, by the conference, "Psychoanalytic Perspectives on Neo-Fascism and Anti-Immigration Politics" at the University of California, Berkeley, in 1995, and by conversations with E. Victor Wolfenstein.

1. Perhaps there has always been collective violence with similar motivations and ideologies, so that what makes the twentieth century stand out is the larger weapons of destruction and worldwide communication.

2. Apropos gender, Sagan argues that innate ethical standards—conscience, morality, empathy and ultimate human values—arise from the early mother-child connection, formed, in the desirable case, around nurturing, recognition, and attentiveness to the needs of the other ("Cultural"). Infant observers describe children's desires to reciprocate nurturance, their growing intersubjective capacities for recognizing the other, and their identification with caretaking behavior. Children may well aggress against an other and identify with an aggressor, but even very little children may also identify with victims or those who seem unhappy and attempt to comfort them.

Benjamin (*Bonds*) makes related arguments. In her appraisal of the Frankfurt School's analysis of society without the father and the decline of the internalization of paternal authority, she notes that paternal authority itself represented the very oppressive bourgeois values and society that the Frankfurt School otherwise critiques. Like Sagan, Benjamin makes recognition of the other's subjectivity, first learned in relation to the mother, rather than internalization of paternal authority, central to ethical human development.

3. Winnicott, in "The Use of An Object" (*Playing*, 86–94, and " 'Use' ") points out that aggression—destroying the object in fantasy—is not only inevitable but necessary to development, and Benjamin, *Like Subjects,* elaborates his point. But it is important to note that Winnicott here is talking about destruction in the internal world, not actual destruction. The point, as Benjamin also makes clear, is that the external object survives—is actually psychodynamically created as external through the internal destruction—thereby making her ruthless aggression not terrifying to the child. The same could be said, I believe, about Klein's account of splitting and projection. As Klein notes, especially in "Mourning and

Its Relation to Manic-Depressive States," if there is an actual loss, the inner world threatens to fragment and collapse. Most analysts would agree that aggression is not inherently pathological.

4. In my experience, the relations of aggression and the self can go either way. I have some patients who use aggression and rage to combat feelings of disintegration: expelling feelings outward organizes and focuses their threatened psyche, and they feel bounded and whole when angry. I have other patients for whom the expression of rage, and aggression itself, threatens disintegration, who hold in and deny feelings of anger at all costs. For these patients, a lack of sense of aliveness is worth the flooding disintegration and loss of the object that might ensue from the expression of anger.

5. I am grateful to Hanne Haavind, personal communication, for this formulation and example.

6. For a related argument that creative and imaginative democratic politics operate in the realm of Winnicott's illusion, see Prager, "Politics"; the distinction is also probably related to Obeyesekere's symptom versus symbol (*Work*).

7. Pynoos (presentation at the Meetings of the International Psychoanalytic Association, San Francisco, 1995) finds that children who have been violently traumatized do better when there is an arrest, or with clinical protective intervention, both of which seem to help them to move beyond the psychic disintegration that in turn leads to more violence.

8. Fonagy, Moran, and Target, "Aggression," note that men trapped in feelings of maternal engulfment are more likely to turn toward self-mutilation or suicide.

WORKS CITED

Balint, Michael. *Primary Love and Psycho-Analytic Technique.* New York: Liveright, 1965.

Benjamin, Jessica. *The Bonds of Love.* New York: Pantheon, 1988.

———. *Like Subjects, Love Objects.* New Haven: Yale University Press, 1995.

Bion, Wilfred. 1962. "A Theory of Thinking." In Elizabeth Bott Spillius, ed., *Melanie Klein Today.* Vol. 1: *Mainly Theory,* pp. 178–86. London: Routledge, 1988.

Chodorow, Nancy J. *Femininities, Masculinities, Sexualities.* Lexington: University of Kentucky Press and London: Free Association, 1994.

———. "Gender, Relation and Difference in Psychoanalytic Perspective" (1979). In *Feminism and Psychoanalytic Theory*, pp. 99–113. New Haven: Yale University Press and Cambridge: Polity, 1989.

———. *The Reproduction of Mothering*. Berkeley: University of California Press, 1978.

Erikson, Erik. *Childhood and Society*. New York: Norton, 1963.

———. "Ego Development and Historical Change" (1950). In *Identity and the Life Cycle*. New York: International Universities Press, 1959.

Fanon, Frantz. *The Wretched of the Earth*. New York: Grove, 1963.

Fonagy, Peter, George S. Moran, and Mary Target. "Aggression and the Psychological Self." *International Journal of Psycho-Analysis* 74 (1993): 471–85.

Fonagy, Peter, and Mary Target. "Understanding the Violent Patient: The Use of the Body and the Role of the Father." *International Journal of Psycho-Analysis* 76 (1995): 487–501.

Freud, Sigmund. *Beyond the Pleasure Principle*. In *The Standard Edition of the Complete Psychological Works of Sigmund Freud*. Vol. 18. Ed. and trans. James Strachey and Anna Freud. London: Hogarth, 1920.

———. *Civilization and Its Discontents*. In *The Standard Edition of the Complete Psychological Works of Sigmund Freud*, 21:57–145. Ed. and trans. James Strachey and Anna Freud. London: Hogarth, 1929.

———. *The Ego and the Id*. In *The Standard Edition of the Complete Psychological Works of Sigmund Freud*. Vol. 19. Ed. and trans. James Strachey and Anna Freud. London: Hogarth, 1924.

Hartmann, Heidi. "Patriarchy, Capitalism, and Job Segregation by Sex." *Signs* 1.3 (1976): 137–69.

Heilig, Steve. Review of James Gilligan, *Violence*. *San Francisco Chronicle*, May 19, 1996, p. 9.

Hertz, Neil. "Medusa's Head: Male Hysteria Under Political Pressure." *Representations* 4 (1983): 27–54.

Klein, Melanie. "Envy and Gratitude." In *Envy and Gratitude*, pp. 176–235. New York: Dell, 1975.

———. *Love, Guilt, and Reparation and Other Works and Envy and Gratitude and Other Works*. New York: Dell, 1975.

———. "Mourning and Its Relation to Manic-Depressive States." In *Love, Guilt and Reparation*, pp. 344–69. New York: Dell, 1975.

———. "The Importance of Symbol-Formation in the Development of the Ego." In *Love, Guilt and Reparation*, pp. 219–32. New York: Dell, 1975.

Loewenberg, Peter. "The Psychohistorical Origins of the Nazi Youth Cohort." In *Decoding the Past,* pp. 240–83. Berkeley: University of California Press, 1985.

Mitchell, Stephen A. "Aggression and the Endangered Self." *Psychoanalytic Quarterly* 62 (1993): 351–82.

Obeyesekere, Gananath. *The Work of Culture.* Chicago: University of Chicago Press, 1990.

Prager, Jeffrey. "Politics and Illusion: A Psychoanalytic Exploration of Nationalism." *Psychoanalysis and Contemporary Thought* 16 (1993): 561–95.

Rosaldo, Renato. "Grief and a Headhunter's Rage." *Culture and Truth,* pp. 1–21. Boston: Beacon, 1989.

Ruddick, Sara. *Maternal Thinking: Toward a Politics of Peace.* New York: Ballantine, 1989.

Sagan, Eli. "Cultural Diversity and Moral Relativism." Brandeis University Women's Studies Program Working Papers no. 4, 1993.

———. *Freud, Women, and Morality.* New York: Basic, 1988.

Segal, Hanna. "Notes on Symbol Formation" (1957). In Elizabeth Bott Spillius, ed., *Melanie Klein Today.* Vol. 1: *Mainly Theory,* pp. 160–77. London and New York: Routledge, 1988.

Slater, Philip. *The Glory of Hera.* Boston: Beacon, 1967.

Stoller, Robert. *Sex and Gender.* Vol. 1. New York: Science House, 1968.

———. *Sex and Gender.* Vol. 2. London: Hogarth, 1975.

Volkan, Vamik. "On Chosen Trauma." *Mind and Human Interaction* 3.1 (1991): 13–30.

Winnicott, D. W. "On 'The Use of an Object.'" In *Psycho-Analytic Explorations,* pp. 213–46. Cambridge: Harvard University Press, 1989.

———. *Playing and Reality,* pp. 86–94. New York: Basic, 1971.

Zwigoff, Terry, dir. *Crumb.* 1994.

11

ART, SPIRITUALITY, AND THE ETHIC OF CARE:
ALTERNATIVE MASCULINITIES IN CHINESE AMERICAN LITERATURE

King-Kok Cheung

Are we supposed to change the world for our men? What do you want me to do about a culture that says Asian women are beautiful and acceptable and Asian men aren't? . . . Is it so bad that America has a little hang-up about Asian men's masculinity?
—Shawn Wong, *American Knees*

The Asian man is defined by a striking absence down there. And if Asian men have no sexuality, how can we have homosexuality?
—Richard Fung, "Looking for My Penis"

In a recent anthology titled *Q&A: Queer in Asian America,* editors David Eng and Alice Hom urge scholars in queer studies to heed the insights of Third World feminism:

> Feminists of color . . . have alerted us to the fact that one becomes a woman not only in opposition to men—not only through the axis of gender—but also along multiple lines of social and cultural differences. . . . We might also extend the question of the "subject" of feminism to the field of lesbian/gay studies to suggest that one does not become queer merely through sex or sexuality. . . . One may also become a queer in opposition to other queers. (Eng and Hom, 11–12)

These insights are no less crucial to masculinity studies and ethnic studies: one may become a man in opposition to other men or an Asian

American in opposition to other Asian Americans. Both fields must tackle a multiplicity of differences such as race, ethnicity, gender, sexual orientation, class, and national origin. Furthermore, these hierarchical differences, as black feminists have repeatedly demonstrated, are not merely additive but interactive (see Crenshaw, "Demarginalizing"; Davis, *Women;* Harris, "Finding"; hooks, *Feminist;* Spelman, *Inessential*). Michael Awkward similarly cautions in "Black Male Trouble," this volume, against "notions of monolithic masculinity." Examining the matrix of different hierarchies is, I believe, no less important in masculinity studies than in feminist studies.

In the United States, persons who are white and male have always enjoyed a privilege not accorded men of color. For instance, Chinese American men, as Lisa Lowe points out, were historically relegated to a "feminine" status:

> Racialization along the legal axis of definition of citizenship has also ascribed "gender" to the Asian American subject. Up until 1870, American citizenship was granted exclusively to white male persons. In 1870, men of African descent could become naturalized, but the bar to citizenship remained for Asian men until the repeal acts of 1943–1952. Whereas the "masculinity" of the citizen was first inseparable from his "whiteness" . . . Chinese immigrant masculinity had been socially and institutionally marked as different from that of Anglo- and Euro-American "white" citizens. (*Immigrant,* 11)

In addition, laws were in place prohibiting miscegenation and the immigration of Chinese laborers' wives. These laws forced early Chinese immigrants—90 percent of whom were male—to congregate in the "bachelor" communities of various Chinatowns, unable to father a subsequent generation. After the gold rush in California and the completion of the transcontinental railroad, job discrimination meant that these men were employed mostly as restaurant cooks, laundry workers, waiters, or houseboys—jobs traditionally considered "feminine."

This historical legacy has given rise to invidious stereotypes. The skewed representation of Asian men in American popular culture has long been a sore point among Asian Americans. According to Richard Fung, in Hollywood cinema Asian men "have been consigned to one of two categories: the egghead/wimp, or . . . the kung fu master/ninja/samurai. He is sometimes dangerous, sometimes friendly, but almost always characterized by a desexualized Zen asceticism" ("Looking," 148). Renee Tajima similarly observes that not only is the portrayal of love relationships between Asian women and Asian men noticeably lacking in American cinema but "Asian men usually have problems with interracial affairs too—quite often they are cast as rapists or love-struck losers" ("Lotus," 312). In the past, the mainstay of Asian American male images were Fu Manchu (the cunning Chinese criminal) and Charlie Chan (the inscrutable, obsequious, and asexual detective). To this day, Asian American men, as one-half of the "model minority," may be considered intelligent computer scientists or engineers, or impressive martial artists, but not original thinkers, charismatic political leaders, or glamorous TV anchors or movie stars.[1]

Overcoming stereotypes generated by this long history of "emasculation" and redefining Asian American manhood have been major concerns since the inception of Asian American literary studies.[2] In the introduction to *Aiiieeeee! An Anthology of Asian-American Writers,* one of the earliest and the most influential anthologies, the editors observe: "The white stereotype of the acceptable and unacceptable Asian is utterly without manhood. Good or bad, the stereotypical Asian is nothing as a man. At worst, the Asian-American is contemptible because he is womanly, effeminate, devoid of all the traditionally masculine qualities of originality, daring, physical courage, and creativity" (xxx). They believe that the invisibility of Asian American men is due in part to the dearth of Asian American writers at the time and to the "lack of a recognized style of Asian-American manhood" (xxxviii). They see this absence as analogous to castration: "Language is the medium of culture and the people's sensibility. . . . Stunt the tongue and you have lopped off the culture and sensibility. . . . On the simplest level, a man in any culture speaks for himself. Without a language of his own, he no longer is a man" (xlvii–xlviii). In *The Big Aiiieeeee!*—the sequel to *Aiiieeeee!*—the editors attempt to refashion Asian American masculinity by espousing an "Asian heroic tradition," by glorifying the martial heroes featured in classical Chinese and Japanese epics, and by implicitly presenting these heroes for contemporary Asians to emulate. Notwithstanding the editors' masculinist leanings, which have been contested by numerous feminist and gay critics, their arguments concerning the denigration of

Asian men in American popular culture remain valid today. What has changed is the growing number of Asian American male writers who have been reconfiguring the contours of Asian American masculinity. In fact, two of the *Aiiieeeee!* editors—Frank Chin and Shawn Wong—have themselves written novels that refashion Chinese American manhood.

Yet much of the refashioning is, from my point of view as a Chinese American woman, mired in patriarchal notions of manliness, whether of Asian or American origins. In an earlier essay titled "Of Men and Men: Reconstructing Chinese American Masculinity," I sought to demonstrate, through analyzing the work of Frank Chin, Gus Lee, Norman Wong, and David Wong Louie, that the Chinese American male writers have either inverted racist stereotypes by creating pugnacious heroes or internalized the stereotypes by reproducing lovelorn losers. I contended that from both cultural nationalist and feminist standpoints a quest for Chinese American manhood should allow us to engender an alternative cast rather than simply clone Western heroes. I then proposed two alternative models. The first is the traditional *shusheng,* or poet-scholar, a masculine ideal in many Chinese classics and drama. He is seductive because of his gentle demeanor, wit, and poetic or artistic sensibility; he prides himself on being indifferent to wealth and political power and seeks women and men who are his equals in intelligence and integrity. Such a model not only counters the cultural invisibility of Asian Americans but offers a mode of conduct that breaks down the putative dichotomy of gay and straight behavior. The second model is any man who embraces what Nel Noddings, taking her cue from Carol Gilligan, calls the "ethic of care," which she describes as a "feminine approach to ethics" (*Caring*) In shifting Noddings's emphasis from feminine to masculine caring, I focused on men—be they spouses, parents, or social workers who help underprivileged youth in inner cities—who are nurturing or who are attentive to another's need.

In this essay, I resume the search for alternative masculinities through an analysis of three works by Chinese American male writers published within the last decade: Shawn Wong's *American Knees,* Li-Young Lee's *The Winged Seed,* and Russell Leong's "Phoenix Eyes." Like the fiction covered in "Of Men and Men," these works attest to the inextricability of gender, race, ethnicity, and sexuality and the importance of foregrounding what Kimberlé Crenshaw calls "intersectionality"—of highlighting these overlaps—in gender studies and ethnic studies. But unlike the authors discussed in my previous essay, Lee, Leong, and Wong counter the "emasculation" of Asian men without falling into the trap of reinstating hegemonic masculinities. Among their characters are artists, poet-scholars, caring fathers, and men inspired by spirituality—which can be an effective antidote to the pervasive association of masculine power with economic success or physical prowess.

AMERICAN KNEES

Shawn Wong's *American Knees* at once undermines traditional Chinese patriarchy, explodes American mythology about Asian men, and reveals the difficulties faced by a Chinese American in defining his masculinity independently of Chinese filial obligations and American stereotypes. Raymond Ding, the protagonist, recalls how children used to tease him in the schoolyard:

> "What are you—Chinese, Japanese, or American Knees?" they'd chant, slanting the corners of their eyes up and down, displaying a bucktoothed smile, and pointing at their knees. When Raymond, not liking any of the choices, didn't answer, they'd say, "Then you must be dirty knees." (12)

The title thus conveys how Asian Americans have long been subjected to racial slurs in the United States. But "American Knees"—a play on American and Chi*nese*—also captures Raymond's liminal status: he is too American to abide by Chinese patriarchal injunctions, but as an Asian he also cannot be accepted fully as "American" by the dominant culture.

Raymond, who works in the Affirmative Action office of a San Francisco college, finds it difficult to fulfill Chinese expectations of filial piety. When the novel opens he is in the process of divorcing Darleen, his Chinese wife, an event that triggers an internal dialogue with traditional Chinese beliefs, such as the stigma associated with divorce, the taboo against marrying outside one's race, and the responsibility incumbent on male offspring to have children so as to perpetuate the family name. Upon seeing his father, Woodrow (or Wood, as his friends call him), Raymond is conscious of an "ominous unspoken thought" that goes through both their minds: "Raymond would never again marry a Chinese woman and would thus be the first in his thin branch of the family tree not to be married to a Chinese. He was already the first to divorce" (23). While Chinese patriarchy is often equated with male privilege, Wong shows how it also imposes a special burden on male heirs, especially number one sons: "The first son in a Chinese family has certain duties to family as well as to himself, and over time the performance of these filial obligations is a test of patience and tolerance against personal ambition" (32). Darleen, on the other hand, is free from such obligations: "She understood that the power in the family rested on the shoulders of the men. This wasn't the legendary and oppressive Chinese patriarchy at work; it was freedom and the luxury of choice for Darleen" (17). While Wong makes light of sexism here, he brings out the contradictions inherent in Chinese patriarchy—especially the way it afflicts those it supposedly favors.

Through Raymond's appreciation of Wood, Wong undercuts conventional Chinese and American codes of manhood. Wood breaches the code of the stoic and invincible Chinese father when he asks his son to sleep with him two nights after his mother's funeral: "There's too much space there" (28). Raymond considers the voicing of this request—this reaching out to his son for solace and intimacy—to be "the bravest thing his father had ever done" (28), thereby redefining manly courage. Raymond also redefines the paternal ideal to include the ability to relinquish command. Unlike Darleen's father—the typical Chinese patriarch who dictates the lives of all his sons and sons-in-law—Wood gives Raymond "his place in the family by not telling him, by not asking, by not saying what was in his heart. It was the manly way of doing things. This was how Raymond became a man" (31).

Through his protagonist, Wong also overturns American stereotypes about Asian men. Raymond often measures himself against both the ideal Chinese son and the ideal American minority—only to deconstruct the ideal. His racy seduction of a red-haired wine rep is juxtaposed, for instance, against his putative "image": "Raymond was a good Chinese boy who never cut class . . . never tore up a parking ticket, didn't burn his draft card" (18). We later learn that what in fact is a mere semblance to the stereotype is a result of fear and subjugation during his military service in the Vietnam War. All Raymond could remember of the war is "the fear he'd felt when the sergeant had called him a 'gook.' That, and the desire he'd brought back from his few months in the army to be anonymous in the world. There was safety in being Asian American at home in America. *We work hard. We keep quiet. I am the model minority*" (59). The model minority is merely the flip side of a gook: the solution to being treated as enemy alien is to be a member of a docile and invisible minority. Both the laudatory and the derogatory epithets unman the Asian American male.

Wong then proceeds to delineate an alternative masculinity. Raymond's two-year courtship and affair with Aurora Crane, who is half Irish and half Japanese, shows he is far from quiet and invisible and challenges the widespread perception, propagated by the media, about Asian "preference for lovers not of their own race" (40). Being handsome, witty, articulate, and sexy, Raymond bears no resemblance to America's "stereotypical wimpy Asian nerd" (103). Instead he brings to mind the classical Chinese "flirting scholar" (*fengliu caizi*). The most famous classical exemplar, known as Tang Yen or Tang Po-hu, is a gifted poet drawn to women who are not only attractive but also intelligent—and who often outwit him (see Chen, *Tang*; Pan, *Tang*, 23–36). Though Raymond, too, has a few lessons to learn from women, he also disabuses Aurora. On first seeing him at a party, Aurora—who has herself soaked up the stereotype—"searched for the most typically Chinese feature about him, but couldn't find the usual landmarks: cheap haircut with greasy bangs falling across the eyebrows, squarish gold-rimmed glasses, askew because there's no bridge to hold them up, baggy-butt polyester pants" (36). During their initial "long distance phone sex" (47), Raymond further chips away at Aurora's presuppositions about Asian men. Like Tang Yen and his beloved maid, Chiu-hsiang, or Shakespeare's Benedick and Beatrice, their initial courtship is a battle of wits:

"I didn't know forty-year-old Asian men masturbate." . . .

"We can even use the other hand to calculate logarithms on our Hewlett-Packard calculators." . . .

"How big is this golden aura of manhood?"

"How big do you want it to be?"

"Big as a cucumber."

"How about a pickle." (46, 48)

Wong insistently stresses Raymond's verbal felicity. After they become lovers, Raymond spins an erotic tale for Aurora whenever they make love: "In Aurora's bedtime stories Raymond learned to flirt, be romantic, be seductive, and undress her all at once, making love to her in complete sentences and full paragraphs" (47–48).

Part of Raymond's appeal to Aurora is his knowledge and sensitivity about Asian American history: "Their conversation was complementary. She offered information, and he filled in the blanks without asking embarrassing questions" (42). Aurora finds Raymond seductive not because he conforms to dominant masculine ideals but precisely because he differs from matinee idols and pushy adolescents: "She thought about how some men kissed like they had learned to kiss by watching James Bond movies and fishing shows on television, coming at her with their mouths open. . . . Raymond preferred to take turns kissing. . . . His hands applied no pressure on her bare skin. She found herself remembering the teenage boys who had pressed their hands up her skirt or kneaded her breasts or grabbed her hands and forced them into their unzipped flies" (82–83). Raymond's masculine attraction stems from his tenderness, his lack of aggression. What Aurora finds "sexiest" about him is his "patience with women": "I've noticed it's how you flirt with women. You sit and listen. You actually want to be friends" (65). Raymond's eloquence, refinement, and attentiveness align him with classical Chinese poet-scholars rather than with mainstream heroes. Insofar as masculinity in the United States is associated with domination, Raymond exemplifies a refreshing alternative.

But he is not immune from intellectual condescension. Aurora, though drawn to Raymond the romantic poet, soon finds Raymond the didactic ethnic scholar patronizing and tiring: "She hated his instructive tone" (58). Instead of accepting Aurora's biracial status, he tries to raise her Asian quotient: "He thought his ancestry was a gift. Their union was never just love and desire and friendship to him" (54). When Aurora resists his efforts, he reprimands her, "I guess you haven't learned a thing. Don't you know in America skin color is your identity? This is a racist country. You can't be invisible" (55). Aurora retorts, "Not everyone can be a professional affirmative action officer like you. I'm your lover, not a case history" (57). To be fair to Raymond, age difference, gender, and race do account for important differences between the lovers. The political consciousness of Raymond, who is forty-one, has been forged in the crucible of the civil rights movement; Aurora, still in her twenties, is a beneficiary of the movement, which has dismantled the most blatant forms of inequality. The two of them also have different experiences in a "culture that says Asian women are beautiful and acceptable and Asian men aren't"; furthermore, being beautiful and biracial, Aurora is much less susceptible to the sting of racism. It strikes her that "Raymond had become, on a more complicated level, like the people who asked Aurora what she was and where she came from. The ignorant were rude; Raymond was educational" (81). She decides to leave him.

It is perhaps the Raymond as forsaken lover that we find at his most attentive and caring: "In the end, Raymond moved and Aurora stayed in the apartment because he could not bear to see her leave. . . . He couldn't live in the apartment that held the memory of the two of them. . . . His leaving was love . . . his silence was love." No sooner have they separated than they commit a mutual lapse. Aurora calls her (own) apartment to leave a message for him; Raymond, who shouldn't be there, picks up the phone. She invites him for dinner, and he brings her favorite dessert: "It wasn't fair to expect him not to know things about her, not to remember a passion for peach pie or her taste in clothes, not to be able to read her mind, not to know that there was a reason they often said the same things at the same time" (80). His attentiveness and understanding continue to disarm Aurora, though Raymond has now entered into an affair with Betty Nguyen, his coworker.

Where Raymond has tried to shape Aurora's life, to study her as a case history, Betty—a refugee from Vietnam who was cruelly abused by her former husband, to whom she also lost custody of their daughter— refuses to reveal her painful past to Raymond; she does not want him "to bear the responsibility of knowing" (85). Later, in an angry outburst, Betty does speak to Raymond about her daughter, who has been told that her mother is dead. No amount of intellectual analysis and political correctness can fathom or assuage Betty's pain. Raymond learns "to love [her] so completely that [he]'d forget the names of all other women" (189). Aurora has complained to Raymond, "I don't see me anywhere in you" (70); Betty says, "I don't want to be the object and purpose of your life" (189). Realizing that Raymond still loves Aurora, Betty decides to remove herself for good.

When Raymond and Aurora are given the opportunity to meet again over the hospitalization of Wood, who has suffered a brain aneurysm, Aurora notices changes in her former lover:

> He *was* different . . . as if some sudden pain preoccupied him. She sensed the faintest edge of insecurity around him. Perhaps thinking about his father's mortality had made him fragile and uncertain. His eyes were more open, but also less confident, less guarded. They no longer flirted in their familiar way. He looked the way people look when they grieve a lost love. (228)

Aurora is drawn back to a chastened Raymond. It seems that, from having entered another's pain, he has learned his limits and lost his cocksureness and self-possession, not to mention insouciance and insolence. Aurora sees his diffidence and insecurity as strengths, not weaknesses. His care, his grief, and his loss have made him a better person—a better man.

In *American Knees,* Wong succeeds in evoking a form of masculinity that is not of the dominant mold. There are, however, also limits to his attempt at redefining Asian American manhood. Even as the author attempts to overturn stereotypes through his protagonist, he also reinforces them by portraying Raymond as an exception to the rule. After Aurora's initial search "for the most typically Chinese feature about him," she begins "looking for and analyzing the most un-Asian features about him" (36). Implicitly, what Aurora finds attractive in Raymond at first sight is precisely his "most un-Asian features." Raymond, who himself complains that Aurora is "not culturally sensitive enough," describes his Uncle Ted's son as "an undergraduate nerd with a slide rule, on his way to becoming a nerd of a nuclear engineer" (120). His comment echoes one made earlier by Darleen's roommate, who "convinced Darleen that the Asian guys in the public administration program were less nerdy than the ones in the business school" (13). Finally, when Raymond and his friend Jimmy examine the stereotypes of Chinese men in the book *Chinese Girls in Bondage* (apparently a title made up by Shawn Wong), they conclude jokingly that it is "better to be evil and Chinky than sexless and obsequious" (150). The slanted perspectives of the characters demonstrate that stereotypes are not just imposed on Asians by

the dominant culture but also perpetuated by Asian Americans themselves.

Even as the exception, Raymond lends credence to the oppressive
rule. He is so conscious of the stereotype of Asian men as asexual that
he comes across at times as merely a deliberate inversion of the stereotype. He has to be exceptionally good in bed to be good enough, has to
be hyperactive sexually to be considered masculine. Cornel West has
pointed out that "Americans are obsessed with sex and fearful of black
sexuality" (*Race,* 83). And, one may add, oblivious of Asian male sexuality. In magnifying Raymond's sexual prowess and in devoting many
pages of the novel to graphic scenes of lovemaking between Raymond
and Aurora (e.g., 49–52, 81–85), Wong unwittingly subscribes to the
dominant culture's overemphasis on sexual potency as an index of masculinity.

Furthermore, Raymond is an exception only within the Asian community. While he takes "real pride" in being able to date Gretchen, a
white woman, and knows that "other Asian men would be envious"
(108), he remains invisible to non-Asian men:

> Men at airports and in hotels would come right up to Gretchen as if Ray-
> mond weren't there and start talking with her or offer to help her with her
> bags. They assumed Raymond was (a) not with her; (b) a business partner;
> (c) an employee of the hotel; (d) a driver delivering her to the airport, and/or
> (e) someone named Hop Sing. (107)

American Knees offers new ways to think about masculinity, but it also
attests to the ubiquity of the stereotype about Asian men, the continuing
assault on their manhood, and the difficulty of disentangling entirely
from the dominant ideology.

THE WINGED SEED

Li-Young Lee's *The Winged Seed* is a memoir about the
narrator's father—Ba (Chinese vocative for father). According to the
editors of *Aiiieeeee!* "A constant theme in Asian-American literature . . .
is the failure of Asian-American manhood to express itself in its sim-

plest form: fathers and sons. . . . The perpetuation of self-contempt between father and son is an underlying current in virtually every Asian-American work" (xlvi–xlvii). In the last decade, however, the field has witnessed a few memorable father-son relationships: in Peter Bacho's *Dark Blue Suit,* Frank Chin's *Donald Duk,* Chang-rae Lee's *Native Speaker,* and, as described above, in Wong's *American Knees.* Ba, a political prisoner under President Sukarno of Indonesia, stands out as perhaps the most formidable father. After nineteen months in prison, he escapes with his family through many a voyage to the United States, settling in Chicago. The narrator is haunted by him, an ambivalent figure who teeters between saint and taskmaster, magnanimous minister and exacting father, invincible man of God and vulnerable man of flesh, and who falls somewhere between alternative and hegemonic masculinities. Through the narrator's fluctuating emotions toward his father as they move from various Asian countries to the United States, we also witness the ways in which masculinity is inseparable from race and can be bolstered or threatened depending on the environs.

During the family's odyssey, Ba occupies himself by constructing a model of Solomon's Temple. This painstaking achievement illustrates his paternal devotion, artistic talent, and Christian resolve: "What it took a great king seven months to accomplish with stone and three hundred thousand slaves, it took my father nearly four years to complete out of cardboard and paper, a feat of love, or someone serving a sentence" (37). The replica has been intended as a gift for his daughter's eleventh birthday: "And the real genius of the thing was . . . its portability. For each piece could be gently dismantled, unfolded, spread flat, and put into a box to be carried across borders" (38). This labor of love, together with such consummate craftsmanship, "indicating the obsessive and aching hand of a maker whose playfulness was surpassed only by his determination" (40), comes across as a creative expression of masculinity.

Ba's dexterity with his hands is matched by his virtuosity as a preacher: "On the island of Hong Kong he drew crowds in such numbers that rows of folding chairs had to be set up in the very lobbies of the theaters where his revival meetings took place, while loudspeakers were set up outside, where throngs of sweating believers stood for hours in the sun, listening to him speak and pray" (73). His power as a preacher is the more remarkable when set against the frailty of a body ravaged by his long imprisonment, as though the two were inversely proportional, as though his spiritual ascent were propelled by the downward momentum of dying.³

More impressive than what Ba can do with his hands and voice is the way he puts his Christian faith and universal love to practice by attending to the " 'shut-ins,' those who never left their houses, mainly old, infirm, crazy, or dying" (67). One of them is a "frighteningly little bag of bones . . . and you couldn't tell she wasn't a corpse until you heard her wheeze" (71). Ba sincerely cares about everyone in his congregation, which, as the author wryly notes, is made up largely of people who look askance at him: "I think he loved each and every one of them and more than I ever felt they deserved, they who referred to him as their heathen minister, these alcoholic mothers . . . delinquent children, shell-shocked bus-drivers, pedophilic schoolteachers, adulterous barmaids. . . . Perhaps it was my father's calling to love every mangled or lost or refused soul" (82). Ba's ethic of care surely measures up to the model furnished by Noddings and labeled "feminine."

Yet there *is* a difference between Ba's forms of caring and Noddings's model, especially with regard to Ba's own children. Noddings states that "when the attitude of the one-caring bespeaks caring, the cared-for glows, grows stronger, and feels . . . that something has been added to him" (*Caring,* 20). Where his children are concerned, however, Ba seems to take something away from them, as symbolized by the narrator's response as he sketches their portraits: "As his hand moved to make a face or an arm appear on a white tablet . . . I could feel large parts of myself being vanquished by his gaze and his drawing hand, as though, being translated that way to rough page and graphite by my father, there would soon remain nothing of me" (56). Despite a certain paradox suggested by the narrator ("For he was making me go away so completely, I was beginning to arrive" [56]), there is something unsettling about Ba's obliterating strokes. Unlike the relationship between Wood and Raymond in *American Knees,* in which father and son give each other room to grow, Ba overshadows his offspring. Instead of inspiring confidence, Ba elicits fear and longing for recognition in his children, who vie with one another to please their father.

We can better understand the peculiar relationship between father and son by noting the narrator's frequent linkage of the earthly father and the heavenly Father:

> We would fashion our souls to fit the grip of God. . . . [We] who would fashion ourselves thus were earlier than sparrows, though never earlier than our father, who would never have the light find him supine. . . . And our sincerest wish was . . . to be seen, truly seen, seen once and forever, by our father, Ba who was earlier than light and later than the last each night. . . . It was, then, for love, that we got on with it: for love of him who was remote and feared, that we fashioned ourselves. (43–44)

In this conflation of God and Ba, we can divine the narrator's ambivalence toward his father. Ba elicits intense devotion from his children, who, ironically, worship him rather than God. At the same time, his rigorous discipline and supreme standards render him implacable and forever unreachable. His godlike demeanor inspires in his children fear, respect, and love, but not intimacy.[4] On rare occasions he is capable of tenderness, as when he massages the narrator's feet after their prolonged voyage across the Pacific: "By the time we got to America, my feet were tired. My father put down our suitcase, untied my shoes, and rubbed my feet, one at a time and with such deep turns of his wrist. I heard the water in him through my soles. Since then I have listened for him in my steps" (42). The lyrical and almost spiritual manner in which this moment is reminisced suggests its rarity, its preciousness, and its lasting impression on the narrator—who is "never allowed to look . . . straight into his [father's] eyes" (60).

More often, the son is made to follow in his father's footsteps, literally, as when he accompanies Ba on his endless rounds to tend the poor and lost souls on communion Sundays: "We headed out after lunch . . . and . . . we usually got home no sooner than ten o'clock. For me it was a trial" (68). The father is more attentive to his religious duties than to his son's fatigue toward the end of the day: "I was hungry, impatient, my feet freezing, and my trouser legs damp. My father smiled at me and said, 'One more visit . . . then we'll have done a little good.' A glum fourteen, I was not cheered" (70). Besides his physical discomfort, the son is also tormented by the uncertainty as to whether Ba is indeed doing good: "If those communions were difficult, were they empty? . . . Was my father wasting his time?" (73).

The disjuncture between Ba's single-minded devotion to his congregation and his inability to monitor his son's physical and mental distress recalls the classical division of public and private spheres traditionally associated with men. While Ba is admirable in his capacity to "love every mangled or lost or refused soul" (82), he is oblivious to his own children's suffering. His behavior thus remains governed by the traditional code of masculinity, which puts much greater stock in public than in private life. One cannot help but wish that Ba, who has such a magnetic hold over both his congregation and his family, could also step down from the altar to play with his children and harken to their growing pains.

There is, however, another way to interpret the narrator's increasing grudge against his father. As long as Ba is in Asia, his authority as a minister and as a patriarch has never been questioned, notwithstanding his long imprisonment. All that changes when the family arrives in the United States. Just as Raymond's "masculinity" is enviable among Asian men but invisible to white men, Ba, a renowned preacher in Asia, is dubbed a "heathen minister" by the lowest of the low, the pariahs of society in Pennsylvania. The narrator, meanwhile, also has to adjust to the status of a poor and dumb alien. In a painful confession, he recalls feeling "a mixture of sadness and disgust, even shame" when, years later in the United States, he encounters a man who had been a great fan of his father in Hong Kong, who "recollected [Ba's] first testimony and remembered sermons" (75).

Why did I feel disgust? . . . I was almost ready to disavow everything. Why? What makes a person want to disavow his own life? When I was six and learning to speak English, I talked with an accent anyone could hear, and I noticed early on that all accents were not heard alike by the dominant population of American English speakers. . . . More than once I was told I sounded ugly. My mouth was a shame to me. . . . I still remember the feeling of being asked a question in English and, after a brief moment of panic, starting to move my lips . . . only hoping I made sense to my American listeners . . . whose ears were more often so baffled by my confounded din, they winced in annoyance. (75–77)

What are the father's moving testimony and sermons to the son? Ba's eloquence and fame in Asia cannot remove the narrator's speech impediment in America, cannot wipe out the stigma of his "ugly" accent. Perhaps the narrator's diminishing esteem for his father—his movement from awe to something akin to pity and contempt—is closely tied to Ba's "emasculation" in the adopted country and to the narrator's own sense of abjection and rejection. Thus, even in this intensely personal memoir, one still cannot disentangle masculinity, paternal authority, and filial devotion from nationality, race, and place.

Unlike Ba's dexterity, which, analogous to his Solomon's Temple, is eminently portable, his patriarchal sway cannot be transplanted across the Pacific. The question remains as to whether the forms of masculinity that can be so easily stripped away are truly desirable. What do Asian American men mean and want when they try to reclaim their masculinity? Do they seek to (re)occupy positions of dominance or do they envision a world free of domination? What is inalienably masculine and what are merely the trappings of manhood?

"PHOENIX EYES"

Russell Leong's "Phoenix Eyes," which features a gay protagonist, provides perhaps the most radical alternative to hegemonic masculinity. Although debates about gender have been simmering in Asian American studies for almost three decades, discussions around themes of sexual orientation have remained relatively hushed until recently. The cultural nationalist movement designed to give voice to Asian Americans has also repressed (homo)sexual difference. The editors of *The Big Aiiieeeee,* in their preoccupation with manhood as traditionally defined, come close to making homophobic pronouncements: "It is an article of white liberal American faith today that Chinese men, at their best, are effeminate closet queens like Charlie Chan and, at their worst, are homosexual menaces like Fu Manchu. . . . The good Chinese man, at his best, is the fulfillment of white male homosexual fantasy" (xiii). Leong, whose highly elliptical "Rough Notes for Mantos" is included in *Aiiieeeee!* under the pseudonym Wallace Lin, recently told how "in the late 60s and 70s there was simply no room for sexuality that diverged from the conventional, even within Asian American movement

or literary circles" ("Writing," 1). The Asian American gay subject, as Eng
and Hom have pointed out, is also marginalized in queer studies, which
generally casts "the white, European, middle-class gay man as the unac-
knowledged universal subject" and ignores "how other axes of difference
form, inform, and deform the queer subject" (12). Not surprisingly it has
taken a long time for gay Asian American writers to break out of the
closet. Prior to the publication of Leong's *Phoenix Eyes and Other Stories,* the only book-length work by a Chinese American male writer that
contained homosexual themes was Norman Wong's *Cultural Revolution*
(see Cheung, "Of Men," 182–186). While Wong's protagonist, Michael,
takes issues with Chinese patriarchy, he also subscribes to the colonialist
stereotype of the Chinese as the "sick man of the East" and the American image of Asian men as devoid of manhood, thereby blunting the
subversive edge of Wong's literary intervention.

Tackling crisscrossing lines of difference, Leong's articulation of a gay
Asian American male subjectivity in "Phoenix Eyes" disrupts not only
Asian patriarchy and American racial hierarchy but also the unacknowl-
edged universal subjects of Asian American studies and gay studies. The
story follows the career of the narrator—Terence—a college graduate
with a degree in theater arts and business communications. After being
rejected by his parents because of his homosexuality, he lights out for
Asia—Taipei, Hong Kong, and Osaka—where he works as a call boy for
a living.

The title calls attention to the possibilities of seeing outside the
"normal" vision of the white and the Asian (American) heterosexual
male subject. Terence elaborates on the meaning of "Phoenix Eyes"
when he describes his work for the *hung kung hsien,* the international
call line:

> We were all accessories. Whether we were from the country or the city,
> whether pure-blooded Chinese or mixed with Japanese genes. . . . Or
> Malay. It didn't matter. We were beads on a string. A rosary of flesh. . . .
> There was some room for variation, for beauty was in the eye of the be-
> holder. I myself was called *feng yen* or "phoenix eyes" because of the way the
> outer folds of my eyes appeared to curve upward like the tail of the prover-
> bial phoenix. Such eyes were considered seductive in a woman, but a devia-
> tion in a man. Thus, the male phoenix sings by itself, as it dances alone. (135)

Terence's "phoenix eyes" invite various interpretations. As a symbol of rebirth in Western mythology, the phoenix anticipates the theme of reincarnation at the end of the story. In the immediate context, however, "phoenix eyes" call attention to the arbitrariness of societal standards and regulations. That the same shape of eye is seen as desirable in women but deviant in men underlines the vagaries of gender distinctions, of what constitutes feminine and masculine beauty. The synecdoche also hints at Terence's sexual orientation, which deviates from the heterosexual norms. Such norms isolate gay people who, like the male phoenix that dances alone, must keep to themselves. In the light of Terence's profession, in which generic "Oriental" bodies are bought and sold, the phoenix eyes are likewise ornaments—symbols of objectification: one is desired or shunned on account of some accident of phenotype. However, in the context of the narrative as a whole—which is seen from the point of view of those eponymous eyes—the object becomes the subject: the allegedly aberrant eyes of Terence look critically at Chinese patriarchy and the Orientalism of his white and Asian patrons. Through these eyes, Leong also provides us with glimpses of alternative masculinities.[5]

Leong has observed elsewhere, building on Dana Takagi's argument, that "the domain of the Asian American 'home' is usually kept separate from the desire of the sexual and emotional 'body' " ("Introduction," 5). Like Raymond in *American Knees,* Terence chafes under Chinese patriarchal mores. He is banished by his parents after he reveals his intention to remain single: "Ba and Ma had high hopes of me, of a wife and children soon. . . . When I told them I would never marry, they threatened to disown me. . . . It was as if I, the offending branch, had been pruned from the family tree" (130). Since traditional Chinese filial piety is defined partly as the obligation to produce offspring, to ensure the continuing growth of the family tree, Terence's refusal to marry and procreate is tantamount to betrayal of the family.[6]

In addition to confronting Chinese patriarchy, Terence also faces racism in the United States, where Asians are cast as hyperfeminine, designed for the white male's consumption. He notes that when he was a student in the United States, "Asian men going together was considered 'incestuous' " (131), as though it were a perversion for Asians to be attracted to one another.[7] But unlike the protagonist in N. Wong's *Cultural*

Revolution, who internalizes the stereotype, Terence sees through the objectification and exploitation of Asian bodies. Instead of worshiping white men, he is drawn to Asian males who are sexually, intellectually, and spiritually appealing. His preference for Asians may be attributed in part to his being where Asians are the majority, with no stigma attached to their race. Where Ba in *The Winged Seed* is disempowered by his immigration to the United States, Terence is empowered by his sojourn in Asia.

Terence's phoenix eyes are not merely an object of the Orientalist gaze; they also stare back at the Orientalists and register their folly. One of the most insidious aspects of Orientalism—the equation of human bodies with art objects, or as props to bolster aesthetic appreciation—is embodied by Otto, a Swiss manufacturer of cookware who has a predilection for "slender Asians in their twenties, and important antiques" (135). No less vexing are those who view Oriental beauty as frozen in the past and who use the natives to enhance their admiration of classical art or poetry: "A certain Ivy League professor known for his translations of Sung poetry loved to shop at the boutique whenever he was in Taipei and have Wan [Terence's coworker] undress and dress for him" (133). Terence is told that these "horny American sinologists . . . were suitable for conversation and culture . . . but not for their allure or their dollars. They were the orientalist tightwads of the Orient" (133).

Orientalism is not confined to whites. Asians—especially wealthy males and females—also participate in the objectification of Asian bodies. A Chinese art connoisseur in Hong Kong has an eye for old Chinese paintings and young male bodies: "At the same time that he could appreciate esoteric old masters, however, his sensual tastes ran to young, unschooled hairdressers and bartenders with thick hair and bright eyes" (137). Businessmen's wives who are betrayed by their unfaithful husbands pay for the spectacle and service of younger men: "We would set up parties for these *tai-tais,* who paid well for good-looking men. Struggling (but handsome) students, and out-of-season soccer players were my specialty. Women, we found, went for the strong thighs and tanned calves of the players, which performed more diligently than the listless limbs of their pale husbands" (137). Physical attributes such as "strong thighs" and "tanned calves" are putative accoutrements of manhood. Yet the ways in which these masculine athletic bodies are being dished out to rich elderly women and men ("We gave up our youth to those who desired youth" [135]) are palpably emasculating.

Ironically, it is when Terence encounters an armless artist who paints with his toes and mouth that he has an epiphany about virility: "I looked at the crayfish emerging as his toes deftly controlled the bamboo brush. . . . [Then] he bent over, inserting the brush into his mouth. . . . The green carapace of a grasshopper emerged. . . . How did he bathe or cook or make love. Despite his lack of arms, he seemed to have a part that I lacked" (139–40).[8] The "part" that Terence—a dilettante in love and art—lacks may be a sense of purpose, commitment, or transcendence. But the phrase, coming right after the query about lovemaking, suggests above all that the lack is akin to castration.[9] Up against an artist whose spiritual determination transcends his physical handicap, Terence feels inadequate. In portraying this artist who uses his defective body to create beauty—against young men who sell their beautiful bodies—as the most potent figure in "Phoenix Eyes," Leong redefines masculinity as inner resources rather than physical endowments. The question, Leong implies, is not "how big is this golden aura of manhood" (to borrow Aurora's words), but how deep.

Two other episodes from the story stand out against the ubiquitous commerce of flesh and redefine Asian masculinity. The first is a sexual encounter between Terence and a Chinese waiter. The scene is, as far as I know, one of the first portrayals of passionate sex between two Asian men. Like the lovemaking between Raymond and Aurora and between Raymond and Betty, it is an unabashed violation and refutation of the pervasive belief in the United States that Asians are not sexually attracted to one another. That it is in Taiwan where Terence has his first uninhibited flings with Asian men is therefore not a coincidence. Furthermore, Terence and the waiter are far removed from the effete Asian men on American movie screens: "We pulled out the table from between two red vinyl banquettes, then pushed the upholstered seats together. We lay on the slick vinyl, sweating and breathing hard. . . . In the darkness, I fumbled for the glass jar on the table . . . sesame oil . . . steadily working the oil and sweat between his legs" (136). The next day the waiter asks Terence whether he can find him some—specifically American—"friends," as he has to pay for his brother's tuition. Terence immediately pulls out $50 for him, but the waiter vehemently refuses:

"No. . . . Brother, you are Chinese. We look the same. . . . *I ch'uang t'ung meng*—though we sleep in different beds, we have the same dreams!" (137). The needy waiter has more compunction than either Terence's rich clients—who do not hesitate to exploit fellow Asians—or even Terence himself. At the same time, it is important to note that although Terence is of Chinese descent he is an American citizen. His ready acceptance by the waiter as being "the same" by virtue of his race bears critical comparison with the primacy of race in determining whether one is granted or denied acceptance in the United States, where European immigrants are readily accepted, because they "look the same," but Americans of Asian descent are regarded as perpetually foreign.

The second episode also involves a bonding between a Chinese American (Terence) and a Chinese—P., the man who introduces Terence to the call line. If the armless artist makes us rethink the often superficial attributes associated with masculinity, the loving friendship between Terence and P. belies the common representation of gay relationships as driven primarily by sex and incapable of lasting love. Terence first meets P. at the National Palace Museum in Taipei—another repository of art and artifacts. Yet the repartee between the two knowingly parodies class cleavages and the objectification of human bodies: " 'You'd have been a good model for a stable boy.' . . . I retorted: 'And you are a Tang prince waiting to mount the horse?' " (132). Although P. and Terence come from different economic backgrounds, both of them work as call boys, Terence for a living and P. for pocket change: "Sometimes, after double-dating with clients . . . P. and I would fall asleep on the same bed, feeling safer in each other's arms" (134). During a visit to a lotus pond, P. tells Terence about his grandmother:

Upon seeing [the white lotuses], he began to tremble. I put my arm around his shoulder. His grandmother, who had raised him, had always looked forward to . . . the blooming of lotuses. . . . She had the lowest status in the large household . . . because she could not produce a male heir. Yet she had raised P. as her own son. . . . Each year, during the two or three weeks that lotuses were in full bloom, she would just before dusk, pour clean water onto the bulb of each pale flower. At dawn, she would, with a tiny spoon, transfer what remained on the flowers into a jar. This precious liquid, mixed with morning dew, would make the purest water for tea, enough to brew a single cup, which she would sip with him. (134)

Embedded in the passage, in which we are told that the grandmother's inability to produce a male heir accounts for her humble status, is another condemnation of Chinese patriarchy, which marginalizes son-less mothers, daughters, and gay men. But the passage also adumbrates a tender moment between P. and Terence. Analogous to the white lotuses that "pushed themselves up to reach the sun" from "the depths of mud and dark water" (134), the friendship between P. and Terence rises above the sordid commerce that is their quotidian occupation. Like the grandmother sharing a special cup of tea in a manner reminiscent of communion, P. shares his precious past with Terence. The grandmother's ethic of care also anticipates the mutual caring of the two men, whose sensibility recalls that of poet-scholars.

Leong resumes his attack on Chinese patriarchy when he discloses the homophobia in Chinese families. Terence returns to the United States, settling in Los Angeles. He receives a foreboding postcard from P., who has moved to San Francisco. Three days later he learns about P.'s death:

No funeral services were held in the States. His family. . . were not alone in their desire not to see or hear about AIDS. In Asian families, you would just disappear. . . . They simply could not call AIDS by its proper name: any other name would do—cancer, tuberculosis, leukemia. Better handle it yourself, keep it within the family. Out of earshot. (143)

Worse than being objectified is being treated as a cipher. For a man to contract AIDS in a homophobic culture is perhaps the ultimate "emasculation." If many Asian gay sons and lesbian daughters already feel ostracized in their familial homes, those who are afflicted with AIDS are further quarantined and "shut up." Leong subverts this imposed silence not only by having Terence name his comrade at the end: "Only now I can say his name, because now it doesn't matter. Peter Hsieh, the beloved grandson of the general" (143). He also gives P. another life by putting this sensual and sensuous tale inside a Buddhist narrative frame. "Phoenix Eyes" opens in a Buddhist temple where P. and Terence used to go. Terence is listening to the five Buddhist precepts, saying "yes" to all but the last: "Do not have improper sexual relations" (130). The rest of the story is told, while Terence stalls for time, as a flashback of his life in Asia and the United States. After P.'s death, Terence reflects: "I thought that I was prepared to accept the news of his death. But I wasn't. Rereading his card, I began to tremble from the fear and beauty of his words, 'A new birthday in a new month.' Being nominally Buddhist, he believed in rebirth, and in good or bad karma begetting similar karma" (144). Terence's tremor recalls P.'s reaction at the sight of the lotus flowers. Just as the lovely flowers—a Chinese symbol of purity and a Buddhist symbol of immortality—prompt P. to recall his grandmother's loving gestures, P.'s beautiful words evoke memories of the now deceased speaker. The two incidents not only illustrate that those who have passed away continue to live in the memories of those who love them but also imply, through the Buddhist allusions, that the beloved will live again in another life. By the end of the story, the narrator, who has been balking at the fifth precept, finally says "yes": "I could sense his presence nearby. He was not the one whom my eyes had sought and loved, or the one who had already lived and died. He was another—the one still waiting to be born" (144). It is possible that Terence, in answering affirmatively, has decided to abstain from same-sex love. Yet the palpable presence of P. suggests a different interpretation: Terence does not consider homosexuality to be "improper." In this deliciously ambiguous ending, Terence is saying "yes" simultaneously to the Buddhist precept against "improper sex" and to same-sex desire and love, thereby validating P.'s life and his own.[10]

Leong's "Phoenix Eyes" thus gives voice to perhaps the most silenced of all men: Asian American AIDS victims. It also reclaims same-sex love among Asian men and exposes Orientalist exploitation of Asian bodies. Like other subversive texts, however, it at times risks reverse stereotyping. The scathing portrayals of white characters such as Otto and the American literary scholar may come across as caricatures. The Chinese waiter's willingness to fleece non-Chinese exclusively is, as noted earlier, also a form of racism. Nevertheless, by setting the first part of his story in Taipei, in which whites are the foreigners, and thereby reversing the Orientalist gaze and the racial hierarchy, Leong defamiliarizes the racism against Asians and the stereotyping imposed on them in the United States. Unlike the "typical" Oriental courtesan in French and English literature who, in Edward Said's words, "never spoke of herself . . . never represented her emotions, presence, or history" (6), the Chinese hustler in Leong's story is the one who gets to speak about and to represent the "Occidental" clients. More important, in speaking out against the heterosexual mandate of Chinese patriarchy, which makes AIDS unspeakable and its victims invisible and inaudible, and in memorializing an AIDS victim, Leong makes room for an alternative masculinity in sickness, and restores dignity to those afflicted, and the dying.[11]

It is perhaps an odd choice for a feminist scholar to play fast and loose with a flirting scholar, an evangelical preacher, and gay hustlers. Part of my intention is to decouple masculinity from paramountcy or invincibility—traditional burdens of manhood. What Leong says of P.'s family in "Phoenix Eyes" is also true of many men: they are not willing "to admit at all that the myth of . . . invulnerability is simply a myth" (143). It would be both presumptuous and counterproductive to present "perfect" models, who probably do not exist and, if they do, may not prove desirable. The figure who most approximates a godhead in the works I have analyzed is Ba, who is also the most chilling figure. Despite his wide sympathy, he strikes his children (and the reader) as remote and elusive. By contrast, Wood—Raymond's father—is deemed heroic by his son precisely because he has the courage to reveal his susceptibilities.

The three works covered all succeed in unsettling patriarchal mores, undermining stereotypes about Asian men, revealing the crosscutting vectors that bear on manhood, and furnishing alternative examples of masculinity. The narrator in *The Winged Seed,* much as he venerates his father, critiques the conventional patriarch in him. Both Raymond in *American Knees* and Terence in "Phoenix Eyes" resist their filial duty to marry and procreate; Terence further condemns the compulsory heterosexuality that excommunicates and exiles gay offspring. Raymond and Terence also redefine Asian sexuality. Eloquent, seductive, and sensitive, they belie the stereotype of Asian men as asexual nerds. In being attractive to Asians and non-Asians, female and male, they also challenge the distorted representation of Hollywood movies, in which Asian men are almost never presented as desirable partners—neither for Caucasian women and men nor women and men of color.

The three works further illuminate how manhood is inflected by various determinants, which are often interactive rather than additive. The difference in age, gender, and racial makeup between Raymond and Aurora accounts for their varying degree of "political correctness" and self-esteem. Though male privilege pervades both United States and Chinese cultures, men of Asian descent in the United States are actually subject to more negative stereotypes and greater social rejection than their female counterparts. Location is thus also crucial. Terence, who finds it awkward to go out with Asians in the United States, has no trouble consorting with Asian men in Taipei, where he prefers Asian to Caucasian lovers. Ba, a famous preacher in Hong Kong, becomes a "heathen minister" in the United States. Perceptions about masculinity can also fluctuate within the same country depending on the surroundings. Raymond, whose physical appearance arouses envy among Asian men, is invisible to white men; Ba, an impeccable and constantly available minister in public, can sometimes be a tantalizing and forbidding father to his own children. Sexual orientations, above all, can play havoc with masculine prerogatives. Leong illustrates that the discrimination faced by gay Chinese men is not a sum total of their oppressions as gay men and as men of color. As gay Asians they are outside the definitions of manhood altogether. Putative Chinese male privilege does not extend to gay sons; AIDS victims, according to Leong, are often marooned and silenced in Chinese families.

Finally, while the characters in these works are far from paragons, they all subvert hegemonic masculine ideals and exemplify alternative forms of strength. Instead of being males who dominate others by physical, economic, or political power, they define their masculinity through art, spirituality, and the ethic of care. Art takes the form of Raymond's bedtime stories, of Ba's handicraft and sketches, and of the armless artist's paintings. Spirituality takes the form of Ba's Christian pursuits and of Terence's Buddhist quest. The ethic of care is embodied in Raymond's small acts of love toward Aurora and Betty, Ba's indefatigable ministration to the needy, and the reciprocal solicitude of Terence and P. Lest the reader think that I merely want men to become more "feminine," I wish to reiterate that engagements such as caring, serving, and dedication to intricate handicraft need not come over as traditionally feminine, and certainly not as "emasculating." In questioning received patriarchal values and invoking alternative strengths, the three authors prompt us to entertain other manly possibilities.

NOTES

Research for this essay was facilitated by an Academic Senate grant and a grant from the Asian American Studies Center, UCLA. An earlier version of this essay was delivered at the Association for Asian American Studies Conference at Scottsdale, Arizona, May 27, 2000. I thank Russell Leong, Gerard Maré, and Rosalind Melis for their helpful comments.

1. The current popularity of Hong Kong actors Jackie Chan and Jet Li, like Bruce Lee in the past, may seem an exception to this rule. It is important to note, however, that both Chan and Li are Chinese rather than Chinese American and that all three actors achieve their fame through martial arts. Having martial artists as the only positive Asian male images in Hollywood cinema reinforces the patriarchal association of masculinity and physical aggression.

2. I am aware that the trope of "emasculation," which implicitly acknowledges masculine superiority, is problematic. But I share Jinqi Ling's view that despite its "complicity with patriarchal prejudices," it is important to "examine its usage within specific social and political formations" ("Identity," 313).

3. In an interview, Li-Young Lee discusses the opposite yet connected momentum of dying and making art: "The momentum of dying and the act of making art are opposing forces. Making art opposes dying, but at the same time it gets all its energy from this downward momentum, this art into the abyss that all of us are a part of, that's the tension we feel in art that we enjoy" (*Winged*, 274).

4. One is reminded of the Buddhist father in Hisaye Yamamoto's "The Legend of Miss Sasagawara":

> This man was certainly noble. The world was doubtless enriched by his presence. But say that someone else, someone sensitive, someone admiring, someone who had not achieved this sublime condition and who did not wish to, were somehow called to companion such a man. Was it not likely that the saint, blissfully bent on cleansing from his already radiant soul the last imperceptible blemishes . . . would be deaf and blind to the human passions

rising, subsiding, and again rising, perhaps in anguished silence, within the selfsame room? ("*Seventeen*," 33)

5. I am indebted to Leong's conference paper, "Writing Sexuality, Death, and Rebirth in the Gay Diaspora," for the term *aberrant eye* and for several insights regarding the significance of "Phoenix Eyes."

6. According to a Chinese proverb, "There are three ways of being unfilial, the worst being childlessness" (my translation).

7. David Henry Hwang makes a similar observation in the afterword of *M. Butterfly:*

> Gay friends have told me of a derogatory term used in their community: "Rice Queen"—a gay Caucasian man primarily attracted to Asians. In these relationships, the Asian virtually always plays the role of the "woman"; the Rice Queen, culturally and sexually, is the "man." This pattern of relationships had become so codified that, until recently, it was considered unnatural for gay Asians to date one another. Such men would be taunted with a phrase which implied they were lesbians. (98)

8. This portrait is based on an actual artist Leong encountered in Chongqing, China. See "Memories," 9.

9. The association of the armless artist with sexual potency is later made explicit when Terence induces the ejaculation of a Japanese businessman without using his arms or hands: "Flexing my calves and thighs, I pressed my feet together until finally he could not contain himself. At that moment, in my mind, I could see the painter" (Leong, *Phoenix*, 141).

10. Departing from the traditional Buddhist belief that desire leads only to attachment and suffering, Leong holds that desire "is inclusive of suffering, sexuality, and joy" and urges us "to overcome the split, fractured ways in which we analyze our nature" ("Writing").

11. Leong has addressed this theme earlier in his poem, "The Country of Dreams and Dust" (*Country*).

WORKS CITED

Chan, Jeffrey Paul, Frank Chin, Lawson Fusao Inada, and Shawn Wong, eds. *The Big Aiiieeeee! An Anthology of Asian American Writers.* New York: New American Library/Meridian, 1991.

Chen, Chih-shen, ed. *Tang Po-hu tien Chiu-hsiang/yuan chu kao Pa-chih.* Taipei: Kai Hui, 1981.

Cheung, King-Kok. "Of Men and Men: Reconstructing Chinese American Masculinity." In Sandra Kumamoto Stanley, ed., *Other Sisterhoods: Literary Theory and U.S. Women of Color,* pp. 173–99. Urbana: University of Illinois Press, 1998.

——. "The Woman Warrior Versus the Chinaman Pacific: Must a Chinese American Critic Choose between Feminism and Heroism?" In Marianne Hirsch and Evelyn Fox Keller, eds., *Conflicts in Feminism,* pp. 234–51. New York: Routledge, 1990.

Chin, Frank, Jeffrey Paul Chan, Lawson Fusao Inada, and Shawn Wong, eds. *Aiiieeeee! An Anthology of Asian American Writers.* Washington, D.C.: Howard University Press, 1983 [1974].

Crenshaw, Kimberlé. "Demarginalizing the Intersection of Race and Sex: A Black Feminist Critique of Antidiscrimination Doctrine, Feminist Theory, and Antiracist Politics." *University of Chicago Legal Forum* (1989): 139–67.

Davis, Angela Y. *Women, Race, and Class.* New York: Vintage, 1983.

Eng, David L., and Alice Y. Hom, eds. *Q & A: Queer in Asian America.* Philadelphia: Temple University Press, 1998.

Fung, Richard. "Looking for My Penis: The Eroticized Asian in Gay Video Porn." In Bad Object-Choices, eds., *How Do I Look? Queer Film and Video,* pp. 145–68. Seattle: Bay, 1991.

Harris, Cheryl I. "Finding Sojourner's Truth: Race, Gender, and the Institution of Property." *Cardozo Law Review* 18.2 (1996): 309–409.

hooks, bell. *Feminist Theory from Margin to Center.* Boston: South End, 1984.

Hwang, David Henry. *M. Butterfly.* New York: Plume/Penguin, 1989.

Lee, James Kyung-Jin. "Li-Young Lee: Interview by James Kyung-Jin Lee." In King-Kok Cheung, ed., *Words Matter: Conversations with Asian American Writers,* pp. 270–80. Honolulu: University of Hawai'i Press, 2000.

Lee, Li-Young. *The Winged Seed: A Remembrance.* New York: Simon and Schuster, 1995.

Ling, Jinqi. "Identity Crisis and Gender Politics: Reappropriating Asian American Masculinity." In King-Kok Cheung, ed., *An Interethnic Companion to Asian American Literature,* pp. 312–37. New York: Cambridge University Press, 1996.

Leong, Russell. *The Country of Dreams and Dust.* Albuquerque: West End, 1993.

——. "Memories of Stone Places." *Emergence* 9.1 (1999): 149–62.

————. *Phoenix Eyes and Other Stories*. Seattle: University of Washington Press, 2000.

————."Writing Sexuality, Death, and Rebirth in the Gay Diaspora: Chinese American Desire in 'Phoenix Eyes.' " Paper delivered at Remapping Chinese America: An International Conference, Academia Sinica, Taipei, June 12–13, 1999.

Leong, Russell, ed. "Introduction: Home Bodies and Boy Politic." In Russell Leong, ed., *Asian American Sexualities: Dimensions of the Gay and Lesbian Experience*, pp. 1–18. New York: Routledge, 1996.

Lowe, Lisa. *Immigrant Acts: On Asian American Cultural Politics*. Durham: Duke University Press, 1996.

Noddings, Nel. *Caring: A Feminine Approach to Ethics and Moral Education*. Berkeley: University of California Press, 1984.

Palumbo-Liu, David. *Asian American: Historical Crossings of a Racial Frontier*. Stanford: Stanford University Press, 1999.

Pan Chun Ming, ed. *Tang Po Hu Wai Chuan*. Chiang-su [China]: Ku wu hsuan chu pan she, 1993.

Said, Edward. *Orientalism*. New York: Vintage, 1979.

Spelman, Elizabeth V. *Inessential Women: Problems of Exclusion in Feminist Thought*. Boston: Beacon, 1988.

Tajima, Renee E. "Lotus Blossoms Don't Bleed: Images of Asian Women." In Asian Women United of California, eds., *Making Waves: An Anthology of Writings by and About Asian American Women*, pp. 308–17. Boston: Beacon, 1989.

Takagi, Dana Y. "Maiden Voyage: Excursion in Sexuality and Identity Politics in Asian America." In Russell Leong, ed., *Asian American Sexualities: Dimensions of the Gay and Lesbian Experience*, pp. 21–35. New York: Routledge, 1996.

West, Cornel. *Race Matters*. Boston: Beacon, 1993.

Wong, Norman. *Cultural Revolution*. New York: Persea, 1994.

Wong, Shawn. *American Knees*. New York: Simon and Schuster, 1995.

Yamamoto, Hisaye. *"Seventeen Syllables" and Other Stories*. Latham, N.Y.: Kitchen Table/Women of Color, 1998.

12

BLACK MALE TROUBLE: THE CHALLENGES OF RETHINKING MASCULINE DIFFERENCES

Michael Awkward

In their introduction to *Male Trouble,* Constance Penley and Sharon Willis consider the advisability of trends in feminist social and cultural analysis toward exploring the complexity of male subjectivities. Penley and Willis ask:

> Wasn't there a danger that a theoretically sophisticated study of masculinity, which would necessarily involve positing male subjectivity as nonmonolithic and even capable of positive or utopian moments, could entail a significant digression from a feminist project that remains underdeveloped in its attention to differences among women? (vii)

What, indeed, are the stakes—and the "danger[s]"—for "a theoretically sophisticated" feminism in acknowledging—and seeking to chart the manifestations and implications of—male differences? What has happened to feminism, and the institutional and larger social worlds in which it is produced, to permit, perhaps even to necessitate, public articulations of what, to echo the formulations of perhaps the most influential theorist of postmodernity, we might call an incredulity toward the metanarrative of monolithic masculine subjectivity?

Obviously, we might use notions such as generational shifts and progression toward ideational perfection to help to account for such developments, but, in this context, such notions would encourage us to bracket the strategic, context-specific nature of ideological choices. Notwithstanding the possibility—indeed, the certainty—that feminism has helped to produce behavioral differences in males that currently make the *articulation* of theories of monolithic masculinity less tenable than they appeared two decades ago, to argue that we see male differences that earlier feminists could not both underestimates their interpretive capacities and overestimates our own in ways that seem to me utterly self-serving. A more useful starting point for a feminist study of such changes in perspective might be to ask what kept earlier generations from placing such interrogations at the center of their interpretive practice. The answers we are able to generate in response to that question may help us to understand what to make of the fact that, as even a cursory survey of contemporary feminist interrogations of masculinity will attest, nonmonolithic masculinity has emerged as one of the new centers of humanistic critical inquiry.

While their work evinces at points a keen awareness of the fact that gendered subjectivities, including masculinity, were nonmonolithic, American academic feminist pioneers who were engaged in literary and cultural study in the 1970s insisted on highlighting commonality. These scholars emphasized gendered similarities even when they recognized that doing so seemed to many to confirm beliefs that feminism placed a transgressive middle-class white womanhood at its center and thus normalized that class's struggles and aspirations. They did so even when they became aware that black women like Alice Walker and Barbara Smith believed that that emphasis marginalized and, in some cases, pathologized other female realities and responses to social conditions.

A crucial governing notion of mainstream feminism has been that the personal is political. But from our current vantage point in the academy, where the proliferation of autobiographical criticism, autobiographies, and autocritographies—which feminism encouraged—has altered our sense of the possibilities of critical self-disclosure, texts like *The New Feminist Criticism*, perhaps the most representative collection of pioneering American feminist literary criticism and theory, surprise us because their authors were, indeed, so reticent in dealing with aspects of their own lives. At the very least, given, for instance, Sandra Gilbert's heart-wrenching disclosures in her recent memoir, *Uneaseful Death*, concerning her deceased husband's encouragement of her career pursuits, we cannot help but be struck by the fact that supportive relationships with men—including male colleagues—failed to inform their perspectives on patriarchy. Gilbert argues in "What Do Feminist Critics Want?" her 1980 address to the Association of Departments of English, that "many of our male colleagues and students . . . seem indifferent to the crucial questions that concern us feminist critics" and were "scornful of the excitement our enterprise has generated" (36). Still, as she confesses, Gilbert has "a number of male colleagues who not only support and encourage my work . . . but engage in what I would call feminist criticism themselves." However, those "male colleagues" proved to be exceptions at that still early institutional moment, before feminism's establishment at the center of the academic humanistic enterprise.

Academic feminism's primary goal during the period in which Gilbert wrote these remarks was to gain institutional power by emphasizing and legitimizing the perceptiveness of its critical take on the cumulative, debilitating impact of patriarchy on women and the cultures in which they lived, produced, and reproduced. Hence, its leading practitioners publicly associated masculinity not with the behaviors of sympathetic males and/or men who found patriarchy's rigid rules of masculine—and feminine—being difficult, if not impossible, with which to live in accordance. Instead, feminism, when it dealt with male subjectivity, argued that the male psyche that is formed under patriarchy inevitably reproduces, in its social, cultural, and political manifestations, that historically oppressive sociopolitical regime's misogynistic behaviors, attitudes, and structures of female oppression. Consequently, those sympathetic "male colleagues" were, for earlier versions of post–civil rights feminism, not "men" like the department chair with whom Gilbert interviewed in 1970 who "quite unexpectedly confided . . . that he was alarmed by the demands of some female graduate students" who seemed to "want to throw out a thousand years of Western culture" (31). The precise nature of their gendered subjectivities, however, did not greatly concern that group of scholars whom Elaine Showalter dubbed "New Feminist Critics."

This separation of public and private, of work and home, characterized the articulations of many white feminists of this period, enabling them to represent masculinity as a monolithic entity to which all men had unproblematic access while at least some of them went home to men who were, indeed, quite supportive of their careers. Such separation, however, appeared to have been less feasible for many black women during this period, whose political awakening in most cases resulted from their participation in radical 1960s racial politics. Indeed, many critics have suggested that a key issue mainstream 1970s feminism failed sufficiently to address was the complexity of black women's relationships with black men, with whom, as texts like Walker's *Third Life of Grange Copeland* and Toni Cade Bambara's anthology, *The Black Woman,* demonstrated, many black women sympathetic to the antipatriarchal thrust of mainstream feminism felt their fates were intertwined as a result of their histories, initiation in integrationist 1950s and radical 1960s racial politics, and shared racial oppression.

If white feminists were able to bracket racial and, often, class and other differences in order to serve what they viewed as women's—and feminism's—greater good, these black women saw race as a significant factor in black women's—and black children's and, also, black men's— social misery. Indeed, the most powerful, or at least most representative, black female-authored literary narratives and critical formulations of the 1970s were concerned with reconstructing aggressively male-centered black communities so that black American women and men could struggle collectively against an omnipotent white force that devalued blackness in all its myriad forms. In 1970s works like Toni Morrison's *The Bluest Eye,* Ntozake Shange's *for colored girls,* and Gayl Jones's *Corregidora* and early 1980s fictions such as Gloria Naylor's *The Women of Brewster Place* and Alice Walker's *The Color Purple,* as well as in influential 1970s critical formulations found in texts like *The Black Woman* and Michele Wallace's *Black Macho and the Myth of the Superwoman,* the lives of black women are depicted as constrained both by racist forms of white patriarchy and by intraracial, that is to say, domestic and black communal, forms of misogyny.

Reflecting that dual concern with racism and black communal sexism, for example, Alice Walker's concept "womanism" is a reaction against the caucacentrism of 1960s and 1970s mainstream feminism and the phallocentrism of black nationalist formulations. Indeed, Walker begins her nonfiction prose collection, *In Search of Our Mothers' Gardens,* by defining *womanist* as "a black feminist or feminist of color," and *womanism* as someone "committed to the survival and wholeness of an entire people, male and female. Not separatist, except periodically, for health" (xi). As Walker's and other formulations from the period in question demonstrate, to foreground race as a crucial feature of a self-consciously gendered politics is to recognize that, to some extent, black and other minority men's relatively limited access to power distinguished them from white men struggling to traverse the distance between real and symbolic phallic power. Not only could black men be allies for black feminists/womanists, but the very success of the black feminist project also depended upon their willing, active contributions, on their enthusiastic commitment to recognizing and striving to change the gender politics that inhibited black people's efforts to achieve a "health[y]," truly liberating antiracist stance.

Having presented, in an admittedly encapsulated form, some of the race-conscious challenges black feminism of the 1970s posed for white, mainstream feminism, I want to linger for a moment on Elaine Showalter's formulation of gendered commonality in "Feminist Criticism in the Wilderness" (1981). (I have chosen this essay in part because I found its myriad insights particularly helpful during my own efforts in the mid-1980s to learn to read as and/or like a feminist.) In her advocacy of a "wild zone" of female artistic difference that reflects "the symbolic weight of female consciousness" (262–63), Showalter argues that "the first task of a gynocentric criticism must be to plot the precise cultural locus of female literary identity and to describe the forces that intersect an individual woman writer's cultural field" (264). Such inquiry results from "a cultural theory [that] acknowledges that[, while] there are important differences between women as writers . . . nonetheless, women's culture forms a collective experience within the cultural whole, an experience that binds women writers to each other over time and space" (260).

Her recognition of women's differences notwithstanding, Showalter privileges "collective experience," in large part because she sees it as providing a means of overcoming "the feminist obsession with correcting, modifying, supplementing, revising, humanizing, or even attacking male critical theory[, which] keeps us dependent upon it and retards our progress in solving our own theoretical problems" (247). Similarly, one could argue that positing a male "collective experience" that produced something she identifies as "male critical theory" served feminism's ideological and interpretive ends at the historical moment of "Wilderness's" publication.

For a variety of complex reasons, 1970s feminism needed to see "female" and "male" subjectivities as occupying distinct regions of and, hence, forming distinctive "collective experiences within[,] the cultural whole." But its practitioners' formulations often are now summarily dismissed as mindlessly essentialist by the scholar of subsequent generations who, as film critic Janet Staiger argues, "rereads canonized works not only [to provide] another interpretation, but also, usually, to make one's name with a new methodology." If Staiger is indeed correct that "one applies rigorous analyses of theories and methodologies to indicate fallacious reasoning of predecessors" (203), feminist critics who study nonmonolithic masculinity must think seriously about debts their projects owe not merely to Judith Butler, whose powerful feminist theories of the performative nature of identity helped to reshape our articulations of an understanding of the constitutions of gendered being, but to pioneering 1970s work such as Showalter's, and to black and other minority feminist/womanist conceptualizations that never embraced notions of monolithic masculinity in the first place.

In the absence of such acknowledgments, feminist cultural critics today run the risk of becoming critically ineffectual in some crucial respects. In addition to our concommitant emphases on "coverage," many of us operate under the fallacious assumption that our "rigorous" antiessentialism, our unsentimental "new methodologies," applied to interrogations of, among other things, nonmonolithic masculinity, will have more to tell us about the gendered world in which we live. To exemplify some of these dangers, I want to speak briefly about the study of contemporary Afro-American film, on which a variety of practitioners of modes of cultural inquiry have begun to train their interpretive lenses. Particularly in their efforts to stabilize, albeit provisionally, its representations of black subjectivity, these studies posit black film's connections to their various analytical agendas in ways that sound very much like parodic versions of the putatively mindless essentialism in which subsequent generations of scholars have accused 1970s feminists of engaging.

In the important collection, *Black American Cinema,* editor Manthia Diawara posits that a black cinema aesthetics, as manifested in such films as Spike Lee's *She's Gotta Have It* and Julie Dash's *Daughters of the Dust,* reflects an observable concern

> with the specificity of identity, the empowerment of Black people through mise-en-scene, and the rewriting of American history. Their narratives contain rhythmic and repetitious shots, going back and forth between the past and the present. Their themes involve Black folklore, religion, and the oral traditions which link Black Americans to the African diaspora. (10)

What Diawara seeks to identify here is, if not collective experience, then collectivist representational practices. But for the phrase "black American cinema" to signify meaningfully, he needs to try to identify some of its—and black people's—constitutive qualities. Such a gesture, offered in the service of an analysis of an undertheorized area of study, threatens to stabilize—if not essentialize—black being, to (re)create racialized hierarchies that necessarily construct certain behavioral responses (including those whose styles or points of view appear to owe obvious debts to extant formulations of white culture) as illegitimate or inauthentic. Even if we argue that such gestures reference not essence but culture ("folklore, religion, and . . . oral traditions"), their descriptive veneer renders them just as likely as unproblematized essentialist statements to delimit the range of acceptable and provocative black filmic representation—and blackness—for readers who embrace them uncritically.

If a savvy, theoretically engaged black film critic like Diawara can succumb to the urge to participate in the putatively retrograde search for black constitutiveness, it is impossible to imagine that analyses that utilize contemporary Afro-American cinema within larger rubrics like "feminist film criticism" and "nonmonolithic masculinity" can resist the categorizing impulse. For example, along with black and/or feminist film scholars and cultural critics, feminist film critics who are not black cinema experts have embraced Dash's *Daughters of the Dust* as the quintessential black feminist cinematic achievement.

One feminist critic who speaks appreciatively of Dash's film, B. Ruby Rich, emphasizes in the same essay the capacity of viewers to be "active producers of [filmic] meanings." Rich goes on to argue that "a woman's experiencing of culture under patriarchy is dialectical in a way that a man's can never be: our experience is like that of an exile . . . daily working out . . . cultural oppositions within a single body" ("Name," 35). In addition to praising Dash's film as a work of "lyrical revivalism" that manifests "dream glimpses of a future of a different color, in which aesthetic decisions follow a different history" (44), Rich highlights the contributions of black feminist film critics to efforts to redefine cinema studies by "looking, sometimes for the first time, at the aesthetic foundations of these new works and, just as important, critiquing productions from the brothers (Spike Lee, Luis Valdez) whose films are filling the commercial screens still empty of women" (44–45). But all the admirable qualities attributed to Dash et al.—"a different history," "aesthetic foundations," "critiquing [brothers'] productions"—pivot around rigid assumptions about racial or gendered cultural features that serve Rich's agenda to critique monolithically masculinist film, white and (through Dash et al.) black.

Elsewhere, I have argued that "to recognize difference within the class of males . . . is to acknowledge the existence of various levels and sites of mediation and to position the critical self to contribute to their subtle interrogation" (95). But in addition to creating what I've called "flexible theories of male difference" (96), we need to be cognizant of the ends to which such theories are being put. If, for example, *Daughters of the Dust* or, to choose a more recent film, Kasi Lemmons's wonderful *Eve's Bayou* are to be evaluated in terms of their auteurs' "woman-centered" aesthetics, particularly in the context of their representation of gender, attention must be paid to the fact that both movies offer extremely sympathetic portraits of black masculinity even as they associate black masculinity with violence, sexual and otherwise, and what many would view as a racialized desire for sexual power. In addition, in both films, femininity is defined in part through women's efforts to adapt to such male self-definitions.

Rather than offer yet another take on Dash's justifiably much discussed film, I want to explore the gender politics that emerge in *Eve's Bayou,* a black family drama that the influential film reviewer Roger Ebert regards as the best film of 1997 (*Roger,* 644). A provocative, satisfyingly disturbing representation of how unself-reflective acceptance of patriarchal logic can pervert black family relations, *Eve's Bayou* adapts to the screen themes that animate the work of Toni Morrison, the most influential Afro-American—and, perhaps, the most influential American—writer of the post–civil rights era. Indeed, the film's unmistakable debts to Morrison are clear in the first words uttered in the film in which, like Morrison's *Song of Solomon* and *Beloved,* black familial connections and disconnections are examined through imprecise, but nonetheless constantly pressing, narratives of memory.

The film opens with black-and-white closeup shots of parts of two bodies in motion, motion we are only able to recognize, toward the end of the scene, as the sexualized gropings of a partially disrobed man and woman. As the jumpcutting of the images slows, in fact, to permit the viewer to recognize a woman's gartered leg and stockings and her right arm wrapping itself around a taller man's back, the film lingers on a tight shot of youthful eyes observing this motion, clear, unblinking eyes obviously shocked by the scene they witness. In contrast to the visual fragmentation of the scene of adult passion that initially makes it virtually indecipherable for the film's audience, these eyes' view of the embrace of the two figures is stabilized, rendered clear and immobile, reflecting, it would appear, a shocked certainty concerning the meaning of the events they are witnessing. A woman's voice then interrupts these contrasting representations of lustful motion, serving as a bridge between the shocked witnessing and sweeping camera shots of Bayou swampland vegetation surrounding Eve's childhood home by insisting that "memory's the selection of images, some elusive, others printed indelibly on the brain."

The first words of the speaker—the film's narrator, whom we learn is an adult Eve, traumatized, as a young child, by the sights and sounds of one of her father's acts of infidelity—reflect a concern she shares with Morrison about the subjective nature of personal and historical recollection, with, in other words, the often self-serving, strategic, and ideological uses to which memory and history are put. At the end of her essay,

"Unspeakable Things Unspoken: The Afro-American Presence in American Literature," Morrison offers uniquely informed—yet purposefully not definitive—readings of the "first words" of her first five novels. Speaking, in her discussion of *Song of Solomon* (which, like *Eve's Bayou*, explores personal and familial history's limitations in dramatizations of the motivations for characters' interpretations of traumatic events) of the "spaces" of interpretive undecidability with which she suffuses her work, Morrison insists "that into these spaces should fall the ruminations of the reader and his or her invented or recollected or misunderstood knowingness" (29).

Because of its prefatory ruminations concerning the selectiveness of memory, *Eve's Bayou* can be said to present us with the challenge of self-conscious discernment of the interpretive troubles that result from its introduction of two types of "invented or recollected or misunderstood knowingness": Eve's and the viewer's. Like the film's seeming reliance on polarities between ways of knowing and, hence, of healing the traumatized self and psyche—in particular, that between Eve's father's seemingly rational, medical-school-trained formulations of the causes of cures for physical and emotional maladies and his psychologically unbalanced sister's reliance on black magic and "second sight" to gain knowledge of the unseen and otherwise unseeable for her desperate clients, who seek to devise strategies that will allow them to move beyond their traumatic states—Eve's clear vision and the viewer's distorted perspectives are not wholly incompatible. What Eve has done is to arrive at a "knowing" interpretation, in other words, to stabilize the meanings of the scene she witnesses—the sexual "rubbing" of her father and his childhood friend, Mattie. While not an entirely accurate representation of what she witnesses (in her eyes, her father and his lover are partially unclothed, but when we observe the scene in the story proper, they are fully clothed), this interpretation reflects her engagement in the types of necessarily subjective acts of memory and meaning making that Morrison sanctions.

Certainly, Eve's interpretation can be seen as a legitimate response to her knowledge of her father's serial infidelities, a possible—but certainly not the only—reading of the fragmented scenes of sexual motion the viewer is offered before he or she is confronted by reflections of Eve's traumatized witnessing. But the film disrupts the epistemological cer-

tainties of its characters throughout, including moments when both
Eve's father and her aunt Mozelle, the ostensibly rational Western man
of science and the previously institutionalized advocate of black magic
and second sight, respectively, acknowledge that their healing powers are
greatly overestimated by the members of the community who seek out
their services. While they are on clear display, *Eve's Bayou* doesn't so
much merely expose the doctor's infidelities and other phallocentric
weaknesses as force the viewer, like Eve, to attempt to discern their
myriad causes and consequences. Thus, answers to basic narrative questions concerning what motivates the doctor to behave in ways that trau-
matize Eve and, later, her older sister, Cecily—"why," "what," "how"—
remain as "elusive" as the meanings of the selected images of which an
adult Eve speaks in the beginning of the film.

In a textual atmosphere characterized by at least partial interpretive
undecidability, traditional feminist readings of Eve's philandering father,
Louis—readings that are not black womanist and/or do not reflect what,
following Penley and Willis, we might see as the emergence of theoretically sophisticated studies of nonmonolithic masculinity—are unlikely
to help us explore this provocative film's nuanced investigation of gender and desire. As I have described him, Louis obviously has embraced
many of the attitudes and behaviors that traditionally feminism has associated with the worst forms of patriarchy. He makes house calls, in
part to service his apparently large supply of avoidable sex partners, and
refuses subsequently to try to hide his affairs from his family or the
larger community. (One such "call" occurs when Eve—who he is fully
aware has already been traumatized by his gropings with Mattie in the
carriage house adjacent to his large house—is accompanying him.) Having internalized traditional phallocentric notions of women as either
saints or sluts, as either passionless childbearers or perpetually available
conduits of sexual pleasure, his affairs seem motivated, like slaveowners'
dalliances with slavewomen, by a belief that his wife, whom he tells Eve
is the most "beautiful, perfect" woman he's ever known, a "lady" whom
he'll "always love," cannot either stir or witness displays of his most primal sexual urges. In addition, he dotes on his three children, especially
his two daughters—his son is, in Eve's memories, a virtual absence except in two Freudian scenes of family matters featuring real or toy
snakes, where he is figured as the unworthy inheritor of symbolic phallic

power—but gives very little thought to the lessons that his public philandering will teach them.

In the sexual economy in which he operates, women are valued only
when men see them as sites and sources of pleasure, and both of his
daughters vie, in ways that are at once innocent and perverse, to please
him and to garner his attention. Still, despite behavior and attitudes that
destroy his daughters'—and his wife's—sense of the security and permanence of their materially comfortable home life, he comes across as a
charming, even sympathetic character whom Samuel L. Jackson plays
with more than a hint of remorse and thoughtfulness, which subverts
any possibility that the viewer will see his character as a personification
of masculine evil, as we inevitably regard, for example, the brutal and
incestuous Pa in Steven Spielberg's film, *The Color Purple*.

The question of whether Louis exercises unchecked phallic power is
most powerfully addressed when, after a late-night encounter with her
drunken father, his oldest and "most beloved" child, Cisely, tells her sister Eve—who has already witnessed manifestations of her father's transgressive appetite—that their father has kissed her in an incestuous manner. Before this accusation is leveled, the viewer is made aware that
Cisely, who has just begun to menstruate and is desperate to keep her
family together, has begun to attempt what we might recognize as a
Freudian replacement of her mother in her father's affections. She gets
her hair cut in a mature style, frequently criticizes her mother for,
among other things, condemning her husband's behavior, and generally
displays unconditional support for her wayward father who—as she
later tells Eve—she is afraid will want to "divorce us." Instead of gynocentric ridicule—Louis characterizes his mother, sister, and wife as
whining women who are "always mad" at him about his infidelities, one
of which results in his impregnating a woman whose condition becomes
public knowledge—in both representations of the scene (Cisely's as it is
related to Eve and her father's as he relates it to his sister, Mozelle, in a
letter Eve discovers after her father's murder), his oldest daughter seeks
to have a calming, soothing effect. Cisely massages the shoulders of her
inebriated father after a particularly vicious argument between Louis
and his wife, Roz, fixes him a nightcap, sits on his lap, and kisses him
once, briefly, innocently, on his lips.

In both Cisely's and Louis's versions, they then share an inappropriately passionate kiss. But it is at this point that their representations diverge—each blames the other for introducing sexual passion into the kiss—forcing the viewer to decide whether to believe either an adulterous father who seems uninterested in protecting his family from the effects of his affairs or a daughter who is obviously seeking to make herself attractive to her father physically and to make their household, in which he clearly does not want to be for long periods, a nurturing environment where his vanity and huge ego can be stroked. At any rate, this kiss awakens Louis from his alcohol- and guilt-inspired stupor, causing him to strike his daughter violently either because she has transgressed or because, through an act of transference, he blames her for his own sins. At the very least, because of his infidelities, he has helped to create conditions that lead to an unstable home environment and, in the minds of the females in his house, ready acceptance of Cisely's insistence that incest has become a perversely logical outcome of his sexual transgressiveness and insatiability. Armed with their individualized, incomplete knowledge of his behavior and its motivations, they reason that a man who is having an affair with the wife of a childhood friend who loves him and whom he loves, who impregnates another woman and mocks his mother, sister, and wife for their consternation about his behavior, and who has sex with a perfectly healthy patient while his young daughter accompanies him during his house calls, could indeed assault his maturing older daughter.

The film, however, refuses to let us rest content with such a reading and concludes not only with Louis's written denial addressed to a sister blessed with the power of "second sight" but also with Cisely's own acknowledgment to her sister, who shares her Aunt Mozelle's gifts and who had encouraged both a bitter voodoo woman and a cuckolded professor-husband to kill her father, that she doesn't know on whom to blame the transgressive kiss. Cisely's "I don't know" serves as an appropriate, perhaps even the fullest, manifestation of the veracity of Eve's introductory remarks about the sometimes indecipherable nature of memory and history. Hence, even if we disapprove strongly of his behavior, we are not allowed to view Louis simply as a man who abuses his masculine power, for *Eve's Bayou* is not so much a cautionary tale concerning the dangers of patriarchy as it is what Morrison calls a "rumination" on "invented or recollected or misunderstood knowingness." In essence, the viewer, like Louis's daughters, is forced to "invent" analyses of patriarchy's causes and consequences because the film locates them as at least partially unstable and uncertain.

In a letter to Mozelle in which he tries to clear his name, Louis acknowledges that his adoration of his daughter Cisely—and his encouragement of her adoration of him—was a "sweet indulgence" that, unlike his sexual philandering, did not, until their transgressive kiss, move beyond accepted social boundaries. Neither he nor the film more generally attributes his phallocentrism to a perverse embrace of white patriarchal attitudes, and he certainly does not see himself as victimized by white racism. (Whites make no appearance whatsoever in the film and are only mentioned in Eve's opening narration of the origins of her namesake's lineage.) How, then, do even those of us gifted with the clarity of vision associated with earlier versions of feminism arrive at a simplistically antipatriarchal reading of the film's traumatic scenes, when its female protagonist, whose powers of knowing are profound and otherworldly, recognizes that her sister's uncertainty is the, perhaps, most appropriate—the truest—response? *Eve's Bayou* does not so much delegitimize earlier interpretations of patriarchy's sins as it verifies perspectives that I feel are implicit but repressed aspects even of 1970s mainstream feminist literary-critical inquiry, including the notion driving contemporary study of nonmonolithic masculinity: that "men" were never so easily knowable, so easily reducible, in the first place.

WORKS CITED

Awkward, Michael. *Negotiating Difference: Race, Gender, and the Politics of Positionality.* Chicago: University of Chicago Press, 1995.

Bambara, Toni Cade, ed. *The Black Woman.* New York: Signet, 1970.

Diawara, Manthia. "Black American Cinema: The New Realism." In Manthia Diawara, ed., *Black American Cinema,* pp. 3–25. New York: Routledge, 1993.

Ebert, Roger. *Roger Ebert's Movie Yearbook 1999.* Kansas City, Missouri: Andrews McMeel, 1998.

Gilbert, Sandra. "What Do Feminist Critics Want? A Postcard from the Volcano." In Elaine Showalter, ed., *The New Feminist Criticism,* pp. 29–45. New York: Pantheon, 1985.

————. *Wrongful Death: A Medical Tragedy.* New York: Norton, 1995.

Lyotard, Jean-Francois. *The Postmodern Condition: A Report on Knowledge.* Trans. Geoff Bennington and Brian Massumi. Minneapolis: University of Minnesota Press, 1984.

Morrison, Toni. *The Bluest Eye.* New York: Washington Square Press, 1970.

————. *Song of Solomon.* New York: Signet, 1977.

————. "Unspeakable Things Unspoken: The Afro-American Presence in American Literature." *Michigan Quarterly Review* 28 (Winter 1989): 1–34.

Penley, Constance, and Sharon Willis. "Introduction." In Constance Penley and Sharon Willis, eds., *Male Trouble,* pp. vii–xix. Minneapolis: University of Minnesota Press, 1993.

Rich, B. Ruby. "In the Name of Feminist Criticism." In Diane Carson, Linda Dittmar, R. Welsch, eds., *Multiple Voices in Feminist Film Criticism,* pp. 27–47. Minneapolis: University of Minnesota Press, 1994.

Shange, Ntozake. *for colored girls who have considered suicide when the rainbow is enuf.* New York: Bantam, 1977.

Showalter, Elaine. "Feminist Criticism in the Wilderness." In Elaine Showalter, ed., *The New Feminist Criticism,* pp. 243–70. New York: Pantheon, 1985.

Staiger, Janet. "The Politics of Film Canons." In Diane Carson, Linda Dittmar, R. Welsch, eds., *Multiple Voices in Feminist Film Criticism,* pp. 191–209. Minneapolis: University of Minnesota Press, 1994.

Walker, Alice. *In Search of Our Mothers' Gardens.* San Diego: Harcourt Brace Jovanovich, 1983.

————. *The Third Life of Grange Copeland.* San Diego: Harcourt Brace Jovanovich, 1970.

RACE, RAPE, CASTRATION: FEMINIST THEORIES OF SEXUAL VIOLENCE AND MASCULINE STRATEGIES OF BLACK PROTEST

Marlon B. Ross

Building on the critical work of Blyden Jackson, Trudier Harris discusses the victimized position of black men in Richard Wright's fiction in the familiar terms of black male castration: "To suppress the black man, in this analogy [to castration], is to put him in the feminine position of the sexual act; his manhood is stripped from him; he is 'castrated' (black women presumably join their men in being powerless and oftentimes submissive, but must suffer additionally from the male-oriented analogy)." She then proceeds to label this lynching ritual a form of "communal rape": "There is an ironic reversal in that there is a communal rape of the black man by the crowd which executes him. They violate him by exposing the most private parts of his body and by forcing him, finally, into ultimate submission to them" (*Exorcising*, 109; see also Jackson, *The Waiting*, 129–45). While offering helpful paths, the critics who analogize rape with lynching castration do not follow through with the devious sexual logic that Wright and other protest writers, especially men, exploit in the intrinsically interconnected phenomena of race castration and race rape. What does it mean to label as "rape" a particular historically situated kind of race violence like castration, which itself constitutes one crucial aspect of enslavement and racial lynching? What does it mean to analogize the racial violence of "literal" castration with the sexual violence of rape?

As argued by some feminists, sex in patriarchal culture might be so inextricably tied up with a desire for domination and power that it becomes *theoretically* difficult to separate heterosexual sex in general from various modes of visual, verbal, and physical coercion of women as culturally interrelated acts of sexual violence, from pornography to actual assault. Most famously and comprehensively made by Catharine A. MacKinnon, this argument stresses the continuity between heterosexual sex and rape. "Like heterosexuality," MacKinnon writes, "male supremacy's paradigm of sex, the crime of rape centers on penetration" (*Toward,* 172). Whereas this theory emphasizes how patriarchal sexuality "assumes the sadomasochistic definition of sex" in that "intercourse with force or coercion can be or become consensual" (172), it tends to spotlight the perversity of gender oppression while casting the role of race into the shadows.[1] African American feminists like Angela Davis have placed rape in historical perspective as a matter not only of men's domination over women but also of racial and class domination through sexualized violence from the period of slavery forward (*Women,* 172–201). Influenced by black feminism and revising MacKinnon's theory, Michael Awkward has investigated contemporary mass culture inflections of rape and race to suggest that we cannot ignore questions of how men in subordinate social positions in U.S. culture, particularly African American men, become self-implicated in acts of domination through sexual violence (*Negotiating,* 95–100). Taking these theoretical cues from Davis and Awkward, I want to push the cultural logic of race castration, more symbolically referred to as black men's "emasculation," as it collides with the cultural logic of rape.

Rather than assuming an equal, reciprocal, or analogous relation between rape and castration, however, I want to consider the equivocal imbalances and disruptions operating in this cultural logic, which equates graphic racial violence against black men with an abstraction of men's sexual violence against women. Paradoxically, this process of analogy and abstraction tends to keep the two acts of violence—sexual and racial—bifurcated even as they are united symbolically in the figure of race rape. It tends to construct violence against women as deriving ultimately and/or solely from sexual oppression and violence against black men as deriving necessarily from racial oppression. Sexual violence against black men—and the sexual violence they perpetrate against others—is thus reduced to a matter of racial jousting between men of European and of African descent. Racial violence against African American women then becomes exceptional, rather than symptomatic and explanatory of racial violence itself. As Hazel V. Carby has noted, "The institutionalized rape of black women has never been as powerful a symbol of black oppression as the spectacle of lynching" (*Reconstructing,* 39). Elsa Barkley Brown raises the important question of why black women's experiences of being lynched have not weighed heavier in our cultural representations of racial violence ("Imaging"). Sandra Gunning provides a literary historical answer to this question when she suggests that the story of black men's rape of white women followed by white retaliation through lynching comes to dominate at the turn of the century because it structures for white Americans a "more compelling narrative of their nation in racial danger," despite the fact that "many lynchings . . . aimed to punish African American women and children for any number of petty 'crimes' " (*Race,* 6).[2] I would add that to remember violence against black women as representative of racial struggle would be to interrupt the series of overly determined analogies that constructs races as masculine on the premise that only *men* can be emasculated— that is, only men can be cut off from the social power owed them. As the figure of race rape borrows from the horrific connotations of rape as *the* axiomatic crime against womanhood, it also ironically further marginalizes black women in the discourses on race and rape. Attempting to overcome the erasure of black women's victimization as *both* women *and* black, Catherine Clinton has coined the term *penarchy* as a counterpoint and supplement to patriarchy: "Within penarchy, status is sexualized and inextricably linked to power relationships within society. . . . Penarchy incorporates class and race considerations without privileging gender" (" 'With a Whip,' " 208). Clinton's need to coin a new word indicates the challenge of keeping these terms—race and sex, rape and castration—in dialogue without subordinating one to the ideology immanent in the others.

Many feminists continue to think of rape *first* as an act of sexual violation, despite the fact of its constitutive presence in what Gunning has called narratives of the "nation in racial danger" and despite attempts like Clinton's to find sufficient language. Conversely, many race theorists and black protest writers tend to use the notion of castration to encode *racial* domination, despite the fact that castration, in its most literal sense, is the unsexing of a male body, and thus is most apparently a sexual act. Thus, when rape is referred to in racial contexts, it accrues a curious double life. On the one hand, it summons accusations of black men as inveterate rapists of white women and white men as ancestral rapists of black women. On the other hand, against this rather literal sense of the racial endangerment of women by men of the other race, rape flies off into abstract allusion when it is used metaphorically to connote the psychological vulnerability of black people, and especially of black *men,* under the administration of a racist system. It is as if, when bringing the metaphoric function of rape into view, the materiality of castration as a historical practice of racial torture disappears, and, conversely, when bringing the materiality of rape as a historical practice of racial torture into view, the metaphoric function of castration gets suppressed. Despite our best efforts to understand the *racial* ideology at work in the sexual torture of rape, we seem always at risk of understating the *sexual* ideology of castration as a racial practice. It is true that we are dealing here with the phantom of language, with the way that language seems to make the felt swelter of realities seem both shadowy and fixed. As many others have pointed out, language itself seems to violate reality in attempting to script it. To paraphrase Teresa de Lauretis, in heteronormative culture representation *is* rape.[3] Nonetheless, in addition to the violating deficiencies of linguistic representation, we are also dealing here with the embeddedness of ideological formations in which race can be made manifest only through sexualized characteristics and behaviors.

In much black protest narrative and race theory, rape becomes the symbolic shorthand for indexing both the physicality of black men's tortured condition under slavery and Jim Crow and at the same time the psychological harm that occurs even when physical torture is "merely" threatened rather than actually enacted as lynching castration. We are confronted here with the varying linguistic and conceptual resources available for observing and representing physical pain versus psychological suffering. As Elaine Scarry expresses it, "The rarity with which physical pain is represented in literature is most striking when seen within the framing fact of how consistently art confers visibility on other forms of distress." Constructing a binary between psychological suffering and physical pain, Scarry writes, "*Psychological* suffering, though often difficult for any one person to express, *does* have referential content, *is* susceptible to verbal objectification, and is so habitually depicted in art that . . . there is virtually no piece of literature that is *not* about suffering (*Body*, 11). Actually, rather than a binary between the physical and the psychological, there are at least three potential sites seeking representation in language when racial violence is involved. First, there is the physical wound itself, which can be observed, marked, narrated—just as abolitionist former slaves might display to an audience the scars on their flesh as visible evidence of the cruelties of enslavement. As Scarry points out, although there is a surfeit of language to represent suffering, there is no ready language available for referencing the experience of pain itself. Accordingly, it is difficult to describe or narrate the physical pain that accompanies and results from a whipping, a castration, a rape, or other forms of physical assault, especially when the pains are serially and perpetually experienced under the conditions of enslavement or Jim Crow as opposed to a singular or exceptional event within the life of a person, such as the rape of a woman by a stranger on the street.[4] There is another sphere of experience existing somewhere between the inexpressibility of felt pain and the familiar narratives of psychological suffering. Concurrent with the mark of the physical wound is the felt pain, and accompanying the felt pain is the unmarked and unmarkable "wound" upon the mind and spirit inflicted by the pain. Obviously, I am speaking metaphorically here, given the scarcity of language for expressing "pains" of the mind and spirit. But, for the sake of precision, let's call these mental/spiritual pains *psychological injury* to distinguish them from the less pointed, more prolonged experience of psychological suffering. The affliction of psychological injury results not only from serially experienced pain but also and perhaps more intensely from the trauma of not knowing exactly when or how punishments will be meted out. The administration of a racial system requires the constant threat of torture as a means of managing surveillance and maintaining the ideology of mastery. The unpredictability, the lack of control, the anxiety of constantly anticipating torture may be even more "painful"—at least psychologically—than the physical infliction of torture itself, as Scarry has so reminded us. Just as a ubiquitous threat of rape not only constricts women's physical mobility and access to public spaces but also inflicts a subtle, more generalized psychic toll, so the threat of racial punishment in enslavement and Jim Crow can inflict psychological injury, which, perhaps unlike the subtle anxiety of anticipating rape, is thought to inflict a continually brutalizing impact each time it is reexperienced or reanticipated. Furthermore, this brutalizing impact within the psyche, "social death" as Orlando Patterson and "soul death" as Nell Irvin Painter have called it, is impossible to narrate satisfactorily, perhaps even more so than the aching throbs and piercing thrusts of physical pain itself.

The problem for protest writers and race theorists is how to prevent the psychological injury of racial torture from being reduced to the cliché of generalized suffering. In the first place, who wants their deep psychic scars to be reduced to the comforts of cliché? Second, even the depth imagery of the psychic wound implies the notion of its being buried or hidden away, unlike the visible scars of flesh. In the lingo and logic of Western binaries, the deepness of the psychic harm also implies the capacity for submerging, sublimating, and sabotaging such wounds. A physical cut can be forgotten once it is healed, even when a scar remains to remind us of the pain that once accompanied it. With the psychic cut, we are not so sure. Should the psychic wound possess greater power over us because its workings cannot be visibly traced, or should we be able to overcome it with the stamina and decisiveness of personal willpower because it is so deeply invested in the self? In the third place, suffering comes to us loaded with other troublesome intentions— pagan, Judeo-Christian, and secular—related to the spirit as a higher register of personhood. Suffering is made noble exactly because it calls forth such acts of personal virtue. As we know, and as James Baldwin reminds us in his critique of Wright's protest strategies (*Notes*, 13–45), suffering can too easily become a rationale for complacency, sentimentality, and vacuous pieties. In the fourth place, the register of psychological suffering is troublesome for black male protest writers because its provenance is so laden with passivity, pacification, and selfless passion. To suffer is too easily conflated with choosing to be passive and pacified, with choosing to scapegoat the self for another's agenda. Suffering is properly a feminine affliction best avoided by men even when they want to boast of confronting their anguish face to face. To choose to suffer as black men is to choose not to be proper men. Finally, suffering does not solve the difficulty of how to represent black men's psychological injury because it too quickly reverts to an image of the harms contained *within* the mind, and thus subverts the intention of marking the endangerment to black masculinity as a psychological damage that springs *directly* from the jeopardy of physical mutilation. Paranoia is a predictable theme of black protest because it embodies a defense against the charge of masculine hysteria, whereby *imaging* the harms contained within the mind converts to *imagining* those harms. And, of course, *imaginary* harms—however deeply suffered—cannot muster the sort of embattled self whose hidden profile is always an implicit call to masculine arms. In all these ways, black male protest writers are at pains to avoid falling into the cliché of suffering, which would seem to diminish their claims to the rights and rites of full masculine agency.

Rape operates in the discourse on race and gender, then, both as a sign of the *materiality* of racial torture, its palpable wounding of the flesh, and simultaneously as a sign of the *psychology* of racial torture, the "palpable" cutting of the psyche. Because endangerment to the psyche cannot be marked on or cut into the flesh, writers seek to narrate and thus to mark undetectable psychic wounds with the explosive agency of rape. Instead of rape, why not simply substitute emasculation as a metaphor for castration to signal the unmarked effects of racial discipline on black men? After all, *emasculation* is more precisely related to castration in that etymologically it also means to "out"—that is, to cut out—the male member: "to castrate, to remove the testicles of." As is the habit of words, *emasculation* becomes a metaphor for itself, as it comes to signify any practice that diminishes the potency of men in the family or in society more generally: "to deprive of masculine strength or vigor; to weaken; to make effeminate." Though precise and handy, emasculation, I would suggest, does not go far enough for the black male protest writers and the theorists of race. Emasculation is constantly put forward as a threat to *all* men in U.S. society. As many gender theorists have argued, it is exactly this constant fear of emasculation that indexes the instability of masculinity as a social construct. Emasculation may be too close in meaning to castration to gain the desired affect/effect that rape provides in protest writing.

Although rape is most typically gendered as a man's violation of a woman, castration is formulated in U.S. culture as requiring a tragic male victim, but it can easily script either a female or a male perpetrator.[5] And as the Freudian scenario has made popular, castration in dominant U.S. culture is frequently seen as the improper acts of phallic women (or lesser men) envious of legitimate male power, rather than as the racialized acts of powerful white men. In fact, in Euro-American psychoanalytic, feminist, and cultural theory, castration usually hinges on a merely symbolic threat to (white) men. In *Male Subjectivity at the Margins,* for instance, Kaja Silverman goes so far as to define "conventional masculinity" (*white* heterosexual masculinity?) as "the denial of castration, and hence as a refusal to acknowledge the defining limits of subjectivity" (46). "Indeed," she continues, "traditional masculinity emerges [in Freud's texts] as a fetish for covering over the castration upon which male subjectivity is grounded" (47). Silverman reminds us not to mistake the phallus as a sign of patriarchal power for the penis as a palpable but insufficient claim to such power. She also cautions us to analyze castration as a *projection* intrinsic to dominant masculinity, requiring the (white) male subject to fear his own castration by casting this threat onto lesser others identified by sex, race, class, sexual orientation, age, etc. This reigning theoretical paradigm of castration is deeply problematic, however, in that it transcendentalizes castration into an abstractly symbolic phenomenon that occurs only within the hypothetical psyches of unnameable male subjects. From the viewpoint of race theory and African American history, this reduces castration to an illusory anxiety afflicting transcendent male subjectivity by obscuring the *historical fact* of castration as a systematic instrument of torture and discipline practiced by white men against African Americans from the time of enslavement through the era of Jim Crow. The danger has not been that white men might fall prey to oppressed others' castrating fantasies but instead that truly powerful white men have in fact enforced their rule by castrating, raping, and committing other forms of racial-sexual violence against others as proper objects of violent subordination. Despite its own analogizing (con)fusions, the concept of race rape at least enables us to expose this blindness at the heart of influential Euro-American psychoanalytic, gender, sexuality, and cultural theories.

It may be that for protest writers castration as emasculation alone is not sufficiently peculiar to address the particular sexual nature of racial torture, especially those aspects of psychological harm that remain untraceable except insofar as it can be inferred from observable—and thus narratable—behavior as somehow deviant. Commonly used as a synonym for emasculation in both academic and vernacular discourses, castration has come to operate metaphorically as the mere psychic threat of a sexual wounding that signifies the universal jeopardy of being fully masculine. The threat of being raped, however, is quite different. To suggest that black men are raped by their racial condition—or, more to the point, that they are driven to rape as an emasculated reaction to their racial condition—presents a more throttling spectacle of black manhood dismembered, embarrassed, and dishonored. The black male body, metaphorically raped or literally raping, communicates explosively the deviance from masculinity visited upon black men, physically and psychologically. Unlike the effeminating effects of a psychology of suffering, in which black men might too easily be seen as *choosing* their masculine deprivation, rape powerfully communicates that black men are in constant jeopardy of having their manhood plundered by more powerful men. The extremity of rape consists partly in its allusion to myths of absolute agency. The rapist is a sort of extreme agent, and the target of his rape likewise an extreme object, the very image of agentless abjection, the one thrown down to be torn apart. If not able to meet his rapist with at least as equal a counterforce, a man cast down to this level of feminine abjection stands no chance of recovery. His dismemberment is as good as final. Although the notion of castration as emasculation can communicate that final fear of dismemberment, it utterly fails to capture the steps intervening between the impact of physical assault and the ongoing impact reverberating from a psychological injury of incalculable proportions.

The transferences that occur between rape and castration in the context of race enable race theorists and protest writers to invest castration with the emotional reverberations of rape as an act of violence that is constantly personalized and likewise (less consciously) to politicize rape through its association with racial castration as an act of violence immediately recognized as possessing political implications. The overtly sociopolitical purpose of castration is conceived as the discipline of all black men (and, secondarily, black women) by punishing one black man (and frequently a woman) publicly. Rape, on the other hand, tends to present the pretense of a private, domestic nonpolitical act, one committed out of an excess of sexual confidence and/or insecurity on the part of an individual man, who unconsciously projects an absence of sexual value and autonomy onto women.[6] I should point out how my essay has thus far insisted on a vernacular usage of rape to signify the routine sexual assault of women in heteronormative society, a meaning that in turn implies the exceptionality of men as the victims of rape. It is exactly this exceptionality that betokens, for black male protest, the exceptionality of their case as abject black men. Rape, however, has etymological roots that reveal its less personalized and less sexualized moorings in any act of predation. Originally *to rape* meant simply to seize and take away, especially as it relates to the spoils of warfare: rapine and pillage, raping and pillaging, as the cliché goes. The image of Helen of Troy reminds us, however, to what extent this military signification needs women as a highly desirable target of warriors' acts of invasion and penetration of other men's territory. Just as women mediate the territoriality of warfare by being placed in the position of raped booty in combat, so rape makes some sense as a way of describing the ways in which women, black or white, mediate racial combat by being made the targeted spoils, whether imaginary or real, of the other race's men. Again, the curious thing about race rape is instead the unspoken act of metonymy whereby black men, rather than women, become the improper tokens of the other race's raping desire. I think that I have resisted using rape in this militaristic sense because it seems as though it could easily reproduce the cycle that I've attempted to interrupt—that is, erasing women as the routine targets of rape in order to metaphorize racial violence as the psychological desexing of black men. The militaristic notion of rape, though, may be useful in considering the compulsion to take away body parts—especially men's genital parts—in rituals of racial lynching. More to the point, slavery itself could be seen as a sort of race rape whereby the African body itself is seized and taken away as the spoils of imperial competition. In traditional cultures, captivity often comprised one result of warfare, the tangible body of the captive, male or female, forced to live amidst the victors as a profitable sign of the warring men's pillaging and plundering ventures into enemy territory. This enlarged meaning of rape, however, does not fully particularize the ways in which chattel slavery, Jim Crow, and other forms of racial administration rely on making the captive body a permanent object of the master's *sexualized* torture. As part of military activity, rape is usually not so much a strategy or even a tactic but instead an effect of the warring mentality as reward for the warrior's mettle. This cannot be said about race rape, which is a strategic, indeed a systematic, process in the constitution of the racialized body as a sexual object vulnerable to the mastering desires of the superior race.

In symbolizing racial domination through rape, it is the act of genital dismembering, rather than penetration, that signifies masculine supremacy. Proper manhood is defined not only by the normativity of the impulse toward masculine violence but more subtly by an injunction *not to fear* enacting such violence on others.[7] The male who fears beating up a faggot cannot be truly masculine, must be a faggot himself. The white man who fears lynching a black man risks being identified with the black man as not properly white enough and thus risks being castrated and lynched himself, as some white male liberals were under Jim Crow. Ironically, this inversion of the white man's phallic assault into the black man's phallic deprivation suggests the extent to which a fantasy of (white) masculine control through penetration is necessarily haunted by *penetration panic*. Not only does race rape represent men's proper desire for control as an out-of-control desire to mutilate other men's phallic weapons; it also *implicitly* insinuates within the normal desire for masculine control through penetration a *normalizing fear* of being penetrated by other, lesser men. The injunction to fear penetration is normalized, however, as an unspeakable threat haunting the desire to penetrate as its repressed binary opposition. Even more repressed in dominant discourse on race rape is men's fear that the desire to penetrate might invert into the *desire to be penetrated*, rather than merely the appropriate fear of penetration—the likelihood that just on the other side of aversion is the lure of the forbidden. Robyn Wiegman captures an aspect of this dynamic when she writes, "In the image of white men embracing—with hate, fear, and a chilling form of empowered delight—the same penis they were so overdeterminedly driven to destroy, one encounters a sadistic enactment of the homoerotic at the very moment of its most extreme disavowal" (*American*, 99). Although I would hesitate to label this moment of the white lyncher's grasp of the black castrated

penis "homoerotic"—which seems to recast lynching as an act of violation and violence into an intimate act of caressing and romantic
desire—I do think that Wiegman is right in detecting a same-sexual
logic at work.[8] Because race rape unintentionally calls attention to the
male-male sexual relation buried deep within the heterosexual ideology
of rape, it also exposes, again unintentionally, the reversible dynamic by
which the social norm of aversion can flip into an impulse to attraction,
by which the castrating risk of white male supremacy must provoke a
fantasy of black men's penile supremacy and by which the focus on
touching other men's sex organs, purportedly in order to dismember
them, must turn into a panic over being attracted to male same-
sexuality.

Just as racial ideology requires white male projection of black women
as exotic, forbidden objects of both desire and contempt simultaneously,
so white men's repulsion for, and thus fascination with, black men's
bodies, particularly the size and potency of their penises, serves as a hidden ground for U.S. practices of racial domination. Furthermore, just as
black women are displaced by black men as the proper victims of race
rape, so the taboo threat of male-male penetration is displaced by the
proper, less palpable, less disturbing threat of "emasculation." Although
same-sexuality has been largely repressed in the cultural logic of, and
suppressed in the theoretical discourse on, racial-sexual violence, as
we unravel the seemingly impenetrable clichés of race rape we begin to
observe the liminal positions of same-sexuality, homoeroticism, and
homosexuality in the cultural dynamics of race, rape, and castration.[9]
That is, same-sexuality, homoeroticism, and homosexuality constitute
the threshold beyond which representations of race rape—like representations of masculine rivalry and camaraderie in general—dare not go.
And yet, as a disarticulated limit point, they also provide an obscurely
buried foundation upon which ideas and images of racial-sexual domination constantly, silently articulate themselves. Although race castration historically has been committed by mobs of white males and females, most often it is imaged in literary, historical, and critical texts as
white men's violation of a black man, whose subordination is determined solely by race even as it is marked symbolically *and* materially as
a *sexual* wound. This tends to repress the same-sexual undercurrents
carrying the racial weight of this logic. In speaking of the modes of

sexual and racial violence practiced in the U.S. South during enslave-ment, bell hooks, in a rare instance in which same-sexuality *is* men-tioned in race and feminist theory on sexual violence, even goes so far as to assert the following:

> Racist exploitation of black women as workers either in the fields or domestic household was not as de-humanizing and demoralizing as the sexual ex-ploitation. The sexism of colonial white male patriarchs spared black male slaves the humiliation of homosexual rape and other forms of sexual assault. While institutionalized sexism was a social system that protected black male sexuality, it (socially) legitimized sexual exploitation of black females. The fe-male slave lived in constant awareness of her sexual vulnerability and in per-petual fear that any male, white or black, might single her out to assault and victimize. (*Ain't*, 24)

When a female captive is sexually assaulted by her master, how does she determine whether that assault inflicts racial or sexual violence? Does not the awful social and psychic aggression of the assault consist *in* the interrelatedness of exploiting sexual violation to reenforce racial subordination and simultaneously exploiting racial violence to reenforce sexual subordination? Similarly, how can we know that masters "spared black male slaves the humiliation of homosexual rape and other forms of sexual assault"? Given the lack of historical and textual evidence sur-rounding this question, we can assume that black male rape did not oc-cur only by presuming that it would be unthinkable to masters. Consid-ering how white rulers during enslavement and Jim Crow routinely committed female rape, female mutilation and lynching, castration, burn-ing, and other horrendous dehumanizing acts, why should we presume that they would be so punctilious as to exempt occasional acts of literal male rape?[10] It makes little sense to say that the slave masters' *sexism* spares black male slaves from "the humiliation of homosexual rape and other forms of sexual assault." For it is exactly *sexism* that encourages some *heterosexual*-identified men to assault, sexually and otherwise, other males identified as homosexual or as not fully masculine in other ways. If castration itself is not a form of *sexual* exploitation for the pur-poses of racial discipline, then what is it? What does it mean for a sys-tem of racial oppression to protect "black male sexuality" when it systematically enforces its racial interest by attempting to turn black men into beasts of burden, breeding machines, perpetual boys, eunuchs, uncles, and inveterate rapists all at the same time? By continuing to re-press the same-sexual element inherent to racial violence, we deny the extent to which the *racial* exploitation of men or women always presup-poses the license—and thus the right—to exploit them *sexually*.

Although critics and historians have overlooked the same-sexual im-plications operating in both literal lynching castration and symbolic race rape, black male protest literature itself occasionally probes this same-sexual dynamic—sometimes in oblique ways that seem further to bury the dominant repression of same-sexuality and sometimes in ex-plicit ways that unwittingly challenge that repression.[11] In other words, despite the rigid bifurcation of sexual and racial violence in the protest literature, its obsessive attention to the messy symbolic relation between castration and rape tends to erupt into revealing moments in which racial violence collides with male-male sexuality. By distinguishing be-tween castration, rape, and racial violence more generally, we can unveil the gender-sexual ideology requiring the eruption of racial anger and sexual violence in the climactic moments of protest literature and also encouraging the uneasy binding of race castration to race rape in both feminist theory and race theory. The confusion at work in representa-tions of racial violence in protest literature and later writings that equate castration with rape proves theoretically productive, as it unwittingly helps to reveal a necessary confusion at the heart of cultural norms that attempt to separate masculine from feminine, racial violence from sexual violation, same-sexuality from heterosexuality, and racial from sexual identity.

In Richard Wright's protest fiction, African American men are as much the objects of white men's *sexual* violence as they are its perpetra-tors on women. This ambiguous dynamic places black men in a curious sexual position whose racial identity is determined by its gender am-bivalence, the volatility of being liminal subjects/objects of sexual viola-tion as both victims of emasculation and agents of penetration. This creates for Wright an anomalous situation in which masculine endow-ment without phallic power, on the one hand, subjects black men to the risk of being castrated like dumb animals and, on the other hand, pro-vokes them to savage acts of rape against the "weaker" sex. In both cases, male genitalia become the depriving mark of a forced animality rather than a sign of masculine control and self-control. If male endowment itself cannot serve to mark the right to normal phallic power for black men, then perhaps the black man's penis can only be an embarrassment. In his 1945 autobiography, *Black Boy*, Wright explores this liminal dynamic in two titillating scenes that repress their same-sexual subtext by paradoxically bringing it out in the open. When young Richard is working in Mr. Crane's optical factory, the white workers, Pease and Reynolds, become offended when he asks them to train him as Mr. Crane has instructed them to do. As they seek ways to humiliate Richard, Reynolds settles, in one instance, on his sexual endowment.

> But one day Reynolds called me to his machine.
> "Richard, how long is your thing?" he asked me.
> "What thing?" I asked.
> "You know what I mean," he said. "The thing the bull uses on the cow."
> I turned away from him; I had heard that whites regarded Negroes as animals in sex matters and his words made me angry.
> "I heard that a nigger can stick his prick in the ground and spin around on it like a top," he said, chuckling. "I'd like to see you do that. I'd give you a dime, if you did it." (222–23)

It does not matter whether Reynolds is motivated by sexual aversion or attraction—or both—in his fantasy of watching Richard spinning like a top on an abnormally large penis. Reynolds's penis envy or curiosity or disgust or desire—or whatever it is—can only express itself in feigned admiration that either hides or hides behind racial hostility. The confusing disorder between desire and disgust, admiration and hostility, hiding and exposing within the Jim Crow mentality is prone to penetration panic. Reynolds's fascination with the black boy's penis takes the form of a fantasy about black men's penetration mastery—in this instance, the ability to spin around on the cock like a "top."[12] This fantasy of lesser men's penetration mastery is liable in turn to explode into the kind of castrating acts frequently carried out in Jim Crow lynching rituals.

Whatever remains unspoken and repressed in Reynolds's pornographic suggestion of paying to see Richard play with himself, the young black man can have only one internal, suppressed reaction: anger. He

feels that Reynolds is regarding him as an animal. Because he cannot respond to this insult "like a man" without being treated in fact like an
animal—violated, castrated, and hanged in public view against his
will—he can only suffer in silence "like a woman." The charge of a larger
penis ironically marks the young black boy's *lack* of masculine power
within Jim Crow society. Even when white men's fantasy gaze is turned
onto a black man's admirable endowment, it is the black man who is being emasculated. The white man's sexual joke simultaneously communicates the boy's danger in the face of legitimate white manhood while
masking this castrating threat as erotic play focused on both the black
man's superior penile size and facility and the white man's racial aversion and sexual attraction. Just as Reynolds has every right to expose
young Wright's penis to humorous contempt covered by admiration (or
is it admiration covered by contempt?), so, if the boy responds with any
signal of self-affirmative manliness, Reynolds would have every right to
expose that penis to the white mob's castrating rage. From his response
in the scene, we could say that Richard feels as though he has been
"raped" by the white men's joke, and yet it is a peculiar sort of rape that
pictures apparently awestruck white men speculating the black man's
power of penile penetration to a gargantuan size.

This scene in which the narrator must submit to white men's fascination with his sexual endowment or risk the punishment of castration
must be paired with another scene in which the *Black Boy* narrator observes a very different and yet analogous act of black emasculation. After
moving to Memphis, Richard is even more disturbed when he is forced
to observe a black fellow worker who humiliates himself for the kind of
small change that he himself has implicitly refused to take from
Reynolds in the optical factory. Shorty, "the round, yellow, fat elevator
operator" (267), "was proud of his race and indignant about its wrongs.
But in the presence of whites he would play the role of a clown of the
most debased and degraded type" (268). When Shorty decides that he
needs a quarter for lunch, he engages in a sordid drama to amuse a
white man who has stepped onto the elevator. Shorty does not work the
elevator, but instead whimpers: "I'm hungry, Mister White Man. I'm dying for a quarter" (268). Pretending frustration: " 'Come on, you black
bastard, I got to work,' the white man said, intrigued by the element of
sadism involved, enjoying it" (268).

"What would you do for a quarter?" the white man asked, still gazing off.

"I'll do anything for a quarter," Shorty sang.

"What, for example?" the white man asked.

Shorty giggled, swung around, bent over, and poked out his broad, fleshy ass. (269)

Shorty's sexually suggestive gesture engages him in a game that plays on the sadistic fascination of the white man in relation to the debased black man's body. Implying Shorty's feigned willingness to be "raped," at least symbolically, for a quarter, the interchange elicits the sort of investigation of the confused and confusing relation that sometimes adheres between sadomasochistic sexual pleasure and the sadomasochism required to administer and inhabit a totalizing regime of sexualized racial discipline. Both Shorty and the white men who play this game have clearly established limits in their sadomasochistic ritual, as is the case among those who practice sadomasochistic sex. The limits are defined by Shorty's humorous (tragic to the narrator and reader) delivery of his ass to the white man's whim, and by the white man's assent only to kick it, rather than to take (i.e., *to sexualize*) the act of penetration further. By stressing that Shorty is "round, yellow, fat," Wright effeminizes him as a ready object of sexual violation. Shorty's flesh, in its soft roundness, is not hard enough, just as Shorty himself is not man enough, to withstand Jim Crow without being penetrated, physically and psychically. With his "fleshy" backside offered up, Shorty continues:

"You can kick me for a quarter," he sang, looking impishly at the white man out of the corners of his eyes.

The white man laughed softly, jingled some coins in his pocket, took out one and thumped it to the floor. Shorty stooped to pick it up and the white man bared his teeth and swung his foot into Shorty's rump with all the strength of his body. Shorty let out a howling laugh that echoed up and down the elevator shaft.

"Now, open this door, you goddamn black sonofabitch," the white man said, smiling with tight lips.

"Yeeeess, siiiiir," Shorty sang; but first he picked up the quarter and put it into his mouth. "This monkey's got the peanuts," he chortled. (269)

The narrator points out that this is not a singular event but, instead, that he "witnessed this scene or its variant at least a score of times and I felt no anger or hatred, only disgust and loathing" (269). As a repeated scene of racial sadomasochism, it is a sexualized ritual no less than the scripted lovemaking of sadomasochistic sex, and yet it is *not* homoerotic in any usual meaning of the word, for its complex motivations highlight racial hostility through a structure of same-sexual contact and possession as intimate attack in the same way that rape highlights the mechanics of sexual intimacy and possession without necessarily implicating the erotic as an arena of give-and-take pleasurable consent. Nonetheless, the obligatory ejaculation of "Yeeeess, siiiiir" indicates the demand that this pain-giving-taking regime of desire be consensual: the white man must desire to command as absolutely as Shorty must desire to be commanded by him. The absence of "anger or hatred" on the narrator's part only accentuates the purity of his "disgust and loathing." This ritual is *beneath* his anger and hatred, which at least imply his own desire to match the white men's controlling power with his own emotional explosion. But Shorty, remember, is as "proud of his race and indignant about its wrongs" as the narrator, so "disgust and loathing" are not enough to separate the narrator from Shorty, who, after all, must feel some disgust and loathing himself.

What is so deeply disturbing about this ritual scene of sexualized racial debasement is the nagging question of Shorty's consent, more precisely Shorty's instigation of the game. It is one thing to be forced, another to anticipate, fantasize, and motivate the white man's punishing pleasure. It seems to suggest that Shorty takes some kind of perverse pleasure in it himself. When the narrator once asks, "How in God's name can you do that?" Shorty's response is painfully insufficient.

> "I needed a quarter and I got it," he said soberly, proudly.
> "But a quarter can't pay you for what he did to you," I said.
> "Listen, nigger," he said to me, "my ass is tough and quarters is scarce."
> I never discussed the subject with him after that. (269–70)

Shorty puns on the slang of being "tough-assed," which should mean to be manly, to be willing to fight, to be able to withstand the worst that other men can give without submitting to penetration. The literal meaning reduces Shorty not exactly to the position of a prostituted woman, which is the analogy operating at various levels through the exchange of the quarter that Shorty pops in his mouth. Shorty is more precisely a hustling male, one willing literally to sell his ass to white men for lunch change. What is lost in hastening to an analogy of Shorty as the prostituted black woman—the black man as raped black woman—is exactly the same-sexual intimacy-possession that is both repressed (and thus obscured) and invoked (and thus exposed) as constitutive of this regime of racial command and submission, race emasculation as male "rape." In his leaving the conversation at such an insufficient point, Wright constructs a unique moment in a narrative in which the narrator-hero defines his identity through his unrelenting curiosity. In all other cases, he expresses this "want to drive coldly to the heart of every question and lay it open to the core of suffering I knew I would find there," this "love [of] burrowing into psychology" (118). Richard's "love [of] burrowing" as narrator indexes his potential penetrating power as an exceptional black boy (one not like Shorty) who is prevented by Jim Crow from enacting his rightful power to penetrate. This power of penetration *is* enacted by Wright as master-author directing our disgust and loathing at Shorty. Ironically, however, the narrator cannot peek farther into this psychology of same-sexual, crossracial attraction and hatred, self-humiliation and self-hatred. For Wright's narrator, and Wright himself, it is not so much that same-sexuality is unspeakable as that its pathological manifestation in the scene makes all the more frightening those rumors of surveillance and entrapment, seduction and recruitment, penetration and unmanning violation that spin around homosexuality as one of Western culture's greatest sexual taboos. To go down that dark-assed abyss would be to observe (and reenact) the narrative's final unmanning of itself.

In Wright's radio play, "Man of All Work," from his short story collection *Eight Men* (1961), he literalizes the connection between black male emasculation and race rape. When a black husband, Carl, is unable to find work, and his wife, Lucy, is unable to go to her maid's job because she is recovering from childbirth, he dresses in his wife's clothes, assumes her name and letters of recommendation, and takes a job as a maid. Wright is here embodying the idea that black urban men are emasculated partly because they are disallowed from taking the traditional husbandly role of family provider, while black women are seen to usurp that role due to their access to more reliable forms of domestic labor in the cities. By literally putting the black man in the familiar position of the black female domestic servant who is constantly vulnerable to the untoward sexual advances of the white master of the household, Wright seems to substitute the black man for the black woman as the victim of white men's rapacious behavior. Taking Carl in drag for "Lucy," a characteristically drunk Dave Fairchild, the master of the house, attempts to rape him/her, as he clearly has taken advantage of earlier maids. By putting Carl into desperate drag, Wright seems to bury the same-sexual logic of this assault at the same time that he exposes it, most notably by depicting Dave as being further excited—rather than turned off—by "Lucy"'s masculine rebuffs. "Goddamn, you're as strong as a man. Well, we'll see who's the stronger. I'll set my drink down and test you out, gal," Dave says. "Damn, you've got guts. You're spry, like a spring chicken. Come here" (145). The language of the spry spring chicken is cliché, for it is routinely used to represent how men are turned on by women's determined resistance to their sexual advances. This sadistic idea of finding pleasure in fighting to overcome a woman's rejection easily also insinuates that the assaulting man finds masochistic pleasure in the prospect of a woman who could conceivably fight back and instead force her sexual desire upon him. The desire to penetrate potentially sublimates a desire to be penetrated.

When Dave's wife, Anne, catches her husband in the act, she shoots "Lucy" rather than her own husband. Ironically, this echoes the situation in which a black man is lynched because he is wrongly forced to bear the blame for the white woman who has attempted to seduce him and cried rape at the prospect of being found out. Wright's scenario reverses the roles—whereby black male rape of white female becomes white male rape of black fe/male—but keeps intact the common situation of the white housewife who fires the black maid for the sexual assaults committed against the black woman by the white husband. When the doctor comes to treat Carl/Lucy for his/her wound, he discovers that the maid is a man in drag. Dave immediately comes up with a way out: "This nigger put on a dress to worm his way into my house to rape my wife!" (154). This brings the lynching narrative of black male rape directly into view as a literal reembodiment of the black woman's domestic rape narrative. Dave's idea fails only because Anne, in her frustration with her husband's wrongs, refuses to make the false charge.

By substituting the black man for the black maid, Wright literally makes him the victim of both a white man's potential lynching rage and a white man's rape of black women. In this way, Wright disentangles the double character of race rape as both an act of castration and a displacing act of phallic penetration. Does this displacement—the substitution of Carl in drag for Lucy—mean that Wright has further dismissed violence against black women as representative of racial oppression? Or, by forcing the black man into the physical and psychological position of the black woman, has Wright turned the metaphorical logic of race rape on its head by insisting that black men learn to value black women's heroic resistance to actual rapes? Likewise, has Wright exposed the same-sexual logic of the race rape metaphor, or has he merely bracketed that logic by turning the black man's potential for being literally raped into an almost humorous plot device in a comedy of scandal. The radio play concludes with a comedic resolution, whereby all the confusions of cross-dressing and sexual misalliances are resolved into domestic bliss for Lucy and Carl and the promise of such for Anne and a reformed Dave. As a "man of all work," Carl both exemplifies the emasculated black man as racial rape victim and escapes the ultimate threat of being penetrated by a more powerful (white) man. Out of fear of being exposed to scandal, Dave pays Carl to keep his mouth shut. If the play concludes with a sort of whitemail that prevents the white man from enjoying his sexual license (exacted by Carl in the form of money and by Anne in the form of Dave's promise to reform), this symbolic holdup of white masculinity seems a precarious, cobbled, limited solution that necessarily cannot resolve the systemic problems of racial emasculation and sexual subordination for the long term.

In other well-known and less familiar texts of the mid to late twentieth century by James Baldwin, Chester Himes, Eldridge Cleaver, and many others, race rape and male same-sexuality constitute a theme deeply embedded, though rarely commented on, in the black male protest tradition. Although any one of these texts invites race critique through gender theory of sexual violence, I'd like to focus on a near rape scene in a rarely examined text of this tradition, George Wylie Henderson's *Jule* (1946). Jule, the young Negro growing up in the Jim Crow

Deep South, and Rollo Cage, his white playfellow, represent the inevitable integrationist progress of the next generation biding their time until their respective father figure and father, *Uncle* Alex and *Old* Cage, have given way to dust. When Jule is sixteen, "a gangling boy, all arms and legs," his mother says, "You done growed up, Jule. You is a big boy now. I is proud of you, Son" (49). This moment of manhood transformation is commemorated in the text by two significant, contrasted events representing the potential innocence of an erotic attraction transcending race ruined by the racial and sexual violations of Jim Crow. First, Jule notices the womanly attractiveness of Bertha Mae, the young woman who lives with her mother in a "two-room shack" (69) on the property of Boykin Keye, the white man for whom Jule has begun to do occasional work. Second, Rollo and Jule go on an extended hunting trip. Through this trip they are companionately bonded even more tightly as they share the exclusive sphere of male hunting camaraderie amidst nature. In fact, like the incipient romance signaled by Jule's sudden notice of Bertha Mae, the hunting trip triggers a slightly variant sort of romance, that between two boys on their own, trusted with guns, hunting dogs, very valuable horses and trusted to take care of their own lives in the lush and harsh subtropical wilderness.

Henderson paints, in the initial part of this journey, an unrelieved idyllic innocence and joy in the unself-conscious physical pleasures of the two boys in each other's company. Verging on the homoerotic without going too far over that undetectable line, Henderson provides the classic scene of a spontaneous swim at a waterhole (57). In a sense, Jule and Rollo are twins whose minds are so mirrored that they don't have to talk in order to be understood, or they are nonsexual lovers whose desire is so commensurate and explicit that they don't need sex for it to be consummated. Perhaps due to the narrative expectations set up by black protest naturalism, as readers we are already deeply suspicious of this cross-racial idyll, and we wait for the racial catastrophe that will rend Rollo from Jule, by rending—either literally or metaphorically—Jule's manhood from him. If this racial catastrophe is going to strike, Henderson forestalls it or, rather, displaces it for the moment with a different, literal-minded catastrophe of nature. In the middle of the night, a thunderstorm awakens them and alerts them to the danger of the lightning, but it is already too late. The horses have been struck dead. This violent event ruins the hunting idyll, but it draws them even closer, as Jule helps Rollo regain his nerves, upset not only by the loss of the horses but even more in anticipation of his father's disappointment and/or anger. Hunting in U.S. life and literature conventionally represents an exclusive manhood rite of passage. Such scenes are cast frequently as a bonding struggle between father and son, as the son either fails or succeeds in persuading the father that he is worthy of the masculine obligations of patrilineal inheritance. By replacing Jule, the intimate black friend, for Old Cage, the distant white father, in these hunting scenes, Henderson accentuates not only the trust that Mr. Cage invests in his son but also— more subtly—the trust that he places in the black boy around his son. Henderson demonstrates how Jule is more than worthy of this trust, as Rollo momentarily doubts his worthiness, represented in his loss of hunting nerve. As the boys need to bag some meat to last them for the return journey on foot, the next day they spot some squirrels. Rollo misses, his hands and nerves shaken, his gun dangling then dropped. Later that night, Jule comforts Rollo by giving him other reasons for missing squirrels. Building on the theme of unarticulated trust between men, Henderson binds the two boys in a mythical world of nature's harsh realities. Rather than some racial catastrophe that separates the boys from each other, the boys' crisis seems fully reciprocal. If Rollo is to achieve manhood or be symbolically emasculated by the father for his failure with the horses, Jule will feel equally as hardened and matured or as dangling and stunted.

Significantly, it is Jule who comes to Rollo's aid when they must confront Mr. Cage with the terrible truth (65). Reconfirming the boys' own masculine bond of unarticulated trust, Mr. Cage suppresses his deep emotion and laconically responds with measured but uncalculated words and gestures. "Old Cage choked up. Then: 'It's all right, Son. You did your best.' He put his arm around Rollo's shoulder, gripped it, 'I understand . . .'" (65; ellipsis in original). Intentionally anticlimactic, to us as readers as well as to the boys, Cage's words indicate that what the boys (and we) have taken as a test of manly worthiness is not really so. Mr. Cage himself already beforehand has embraced his son as a budding peer. The emotional current moves from the white father's absolute trust of his son through the absolute trust of the black friend, who has interceded on behalf of the white son, to the white heir's reclaimed confidence in manly trust. This posthunting scene helps to construct, early in the novel, an idealized network of manly trust—a network whose violation threatens constantly to unravel the plot into explosive racial and/or sexual violence.

If, in the hunting scene, nature itself enacts violence where we expect it to be brought about instead through some mode of racial-sexual conflict, it is also the case that the physical violence expected between black and white is forestalled and displaced with the most homoerotic image of the narrative, the scene of Rollo and Jule holding each other amidst the drenching storm in the moment after lightning strikes the horses. "They stood in silence, gripping each other. Rain streamed down their faces. Rain and tears. The dogs howled. It was a weird sound. Jule's flesh crawled. His nails bit into Rollo" (58). In chapter 6, this gentle erotic gripping, as the rain hides their vulnerable tears and the lightning stalks their palpable fear, should be contrasted with the not-too-subtle sexual violation that initiates Jule into heterosexual passion in chapter 8. In a sense, Henderson separates out literal sex (that is, *hetero*sexual sex) as the pursuit of sexual *rights* (that is, his right to possess a woman) from the cross-racial test of manhood *rites* (the hunting scene as reaffirmation of patrilineal descent) and places the former later in the plot, as though each takes place in a different mythic world. Thus, the theme of potential castration through race lynching is plotted along one character axis involving the intrusion of women, alienable and alienated from the natural myth of manhood rites, which constitutes another character axis concerning the commitment of men to each other above race and to their mutual development as men across race. If the hunting scene represents Rollo's test of manhood rites reflected as Jule's own, Jule's heterosexual romance likewise reflects a test of manhood rights back onto Rollo, who is significantly devoid of a female mate throughout the novel. The conventional protest theme of lynching castration as symbolic racial emasculation takes place along this second character axis (Jule–Bertha Mae–Boykin Keye) much more formulaically triangulated as heterosexual sex and cross-racial rivalry over a woman.

Henderson initiates the chapter in which Jule and Bertha Mae have sex for the first time appropriately with reference to Jule's beginning to work for Boykin Keye, who treats Jule as an unusually "smart nigger" (66)—awarding him gifts that seem to be payment for debts that are yet to come, debts that symbolically cannot be repaid. The trusting network of bonds among men whose lives are so differently situated socially but so interdependent has been ominously disturbed. Keye's furtiveness shows itself through his surveillance of Jule and by the hidden thoughts he has about the young man. As Jule burns the field to prepare for the spring seeding, for instance, Keye gazes at him: "Jule's muscles rippled along his shoulders. Boykin Keye sat there, his head cocked to one side, looking at Jule. He thought: 'He's a big buck. A strong buck.' " We know the ensuing protest plot before it gets under way. We know Boykin's furtive, envious looks at Jule's rippling muscles. But how can we know that his gaze is totally void of any sexual attraction? We know the emasculating contempt hidden in the appraising epithet "buck," which seems on the surface to attribute such pure unadulterated maleness—an unbridled animal maleness in need of being gelded. Likewise, we know the hidden meaning of Keye's gazing at Bertha Mae. The discord that emerges with Keye continues into the lovemaking scene between Jule and Bertha Mae.

Like the idyllic scene between Jule and Rollo, the romantic scene between Jule and Bertha Mae occurs outdoors between the spring rows of corn after the couple sneak away from a twilight prayer meeting. Despite their settings away from social institutions, both scenes script, and are scripted by, formulaically romantic cultural understandings of tender heterosexual romance and heroic male friendship. Henderson carefully contrasts the two erotic scenes through three small details: tears, gripping nails, and the image of lightning striking. Amidst the spring corn, Jule's lust is figured as healthy and natural, Bertha Mae's as appropriately fissured between the desire to be good by resisting or the desire to be bad by yielding. Throughout the entire sexual act, she is clearly thinking as much about the prayer meeting that they are missing (she keeps mentioning the singing in the distance), as she is thinking about what is happening to her: " 'Don't, Jule! Don't do it no mo'! . . . It hurts, Jule. It hurts bad! . . . Jes' like—like lightnin' strikin'!.' . . . Tears spilled over her lids and she smothered them against his chest" (73; first ellipses in original). By resisting Jule's lust, and her own, she can at least construct her virtue as wrested from her rather than liberally given away. And yet, we are supposed to understand that the stinginess of her lust results from appropriate moral scruples, not from any lack of passion for Jule.

Like Keye, however, she is positioned in the narrative as a sort of bodily resistance placing limits on the free play of desire beyond race—a resistance not operative in the boys' de/eroticized heroic friendship until *after* Keye threatens Jule with a lynching. Jule's lust for Bertha Mae is direct, forward, unfazed, for it knows no such artificial social, moral, and sexual scruples. However naturalized the setting and however ambivalent Bertha Mae's gestures, Jule's seduction of Bertha Mae leads to what we today would consider rape. I am more interested, for the moment, in the "forced" character of Jule's desire in contrast with the naturalized scene of twinned boyish homoeroticism. In the hunting scene, the boys grip each other, allow themselves to cry in the rain, and experience the lightning as a threat binding both equally. In the contrasting heterosexual scene, the pattern of forcing and yielding is all unidirectional, from Jule's focused thrust toward Bertha Mae's seeming indecision. Repeatedly, she says, "I can't Jule! I jes' can't." His response is firm: "He gripped her and pinned her against the hedgerow" (74). The expression of heterosexual desire through naturally violent language—so familiar as to be easily overlooked, perhaps especially in 1946—seems odd against the previous homoerotic scene. Could it be that Henderson is defamiliarizing and denaturalizing our customary acceptance of the violence usually portrayed in such heterosexual initiation scenes? To some extent, I take this to be the case. However, in the overall sweep of the narrative, such an insight seems to dissipate. The insight makes a full impact only when we place Henderson's narrative in the context of the naturalist conventions of black protest within and against which Henderson is writing.

The fissure between pain and pleasure figured in Jule's drive to tear Bertha Mae's virginal body is quite different from both the shared pain of the hunting catastrophe and from the sadomasochistic game shared between Shorty and the white man. The sexual initiation splits Jule from Bertha Mae as a male's pure pleasure differentiated from a woman's mixed pleasure in pain. If the cultural script of heterosexual romance ordains the joining of two into one forever, this scene subtly disturbs that myth, for it stresses how the female initiate experiences desire at the peril of being a physically split social being. The rural nature setting, the innocent character of their passion, and the highly conventional process of wooing—scripted both before and after the sex scene—remind us that this is just an ordinary young couple in love. There is nothing socially deviant about their desire, and most certainly nothing pathological in the expected mode of black protest fiction, where rape, or some other form of violence, usually interrupts and thus warps the black hero's heterosexual desire. Even the fact that it is sex outside of wedlock helps to determine the scene as naturally blessed, for there is no furtive intention here, either of Jule to abandon her after having exploited her or of Bertha Mae to jilt him after he has revealed his all-consuming desire for her. (Of course, there are forces beyond their control that may bring about this same result in effect despite their intentions.) Nonetheless, furtively lurking in this most normative heterosexual romance, cast in the highly conventional scene of a female's seduced initiation, is also a hint of sadomasochism. Does Jule desire to hurt Bertha Mae in simply desiring to have her? Clearly, as the scene is formulaically scripted, she can desire the pleasure of initiation only by submitting to being hurt. Through this lovemaking scene, Henderson offers a subtle critique of the natural(ist) assumptions of *physical* sexual violation against women and *symbolic* sexual violation against black men so evident in protest fiction.

In fact, if we did not know the context of the scene's final sentence indicating sexual climax (mutual?), we would think that what has occurred is a sexual murder plagiarized from some unrelated raging protest narrative: "He beat her body against the ground until it was still" (74). Bertha Mae's body becomes an objectified "it" beat against the fertile ground of the cornfield in the act of this sexual climax. The odd feeling of a sexual murder is not by mistake, for the scene clearly alludes to Bigger's rape of Bessie in *Native Son*. In Bigger's disposing of Bessie's corpse, we also get the same sense of the stilled woman's body as objectified "it": "The body hit and bumped against the narrow sides of the air-shaft as it went down into blackness. He heard it strike the bottom" (*Native Son*, 276).[13] In a sense, then, Henderson *does* want us to think of the link between heterosexual passion and race lynching as they are entangled in the exploding rage of protest narrative. The differences made apparent through this allusion are intentionally obvious in Henderson's narrative even as *Jule*'s romance plot ultimately averts the overtly violent protest logic. Bertha Mae is not dead. Instead, she is now betrothed to Jule in an unspoken vow assumed in the gentle, teasing lovers' dialogue that follows sex as they rest amidst the corn and look up at the moon. The (fore)shadow(ing) of the protest narrative is subtly embedded in the lovemaking that is both sexual violation and not a rape. Whether literal rape or not, through Henderson's 1946 eyes, the lovemaking scene borrows its undercutting sinister effect obliquely from the *Native Son* scene, which *is* a rape. As James Baldwin suggests in a famous flourish of generalization about African American fiction, "In most of the novels written by Negroes until today . . . there is a great space where sex ought to be; and what usually fills this space is violence" (*Nobody,* 151). If Baldwin had limited his statement to most protest narrative, it would perhaps be more tenable, for this seems to be the point as well of Henderson's allusive treatment of the lovemaking scene. Henderson seems to suggest that there *can* be "normal" love between black men and women, even amidst the most pathologically racist and most sexually violent Jim Crow culture. Given relations between men and women in patriarchal culture, the question remains whether there can be "normal" heterosexual passion without the implication of sexual violence, a question intentionally left open in Henderson's scene. The objective of Henderson's composition becomes to acknowledge the ugly Southern reality of racial tension, sexual constriction, lynching, and castration, but to do so without validating the complex of racial-sexual pathologies dominating African American fiction in 1946 through the reign of protest conventions influenced by Freudian psychoanalysis and Chicago sociology.

Accordingly, it is not racial tension per se that brings the shadow of protest violence into *Jule,* but "normal" heterosexual rivalry. Now betrothed to Jule, Bertha Mae realizes that she must tell her lover that she is owed to another, Boykin Keye, the white master. Keye represents the will to perpetuate the old Jim Crow order, in which the white master's desire is the black girl's (and boy's) command. If there is a hint of sadistic sexual violation in Jule's seduction of Bertha Mae, its tenor seems somewhat diminished by Keye's taking of her as a concubine through the assumption of his manhood rights to ab/use her as a master would a captive. In other words, in the logic of *Jule,* the white supremacist, Keye, is properly the rapist, both literally and symbolically. While retaining the ambiguity of sexual violation on the part of the black male protagonist, Henderson resists the tendency of protest narrative to make that protagonist the actual rapist, in an effort to shock us with the effects of the black man's symbolic race emasculation. Henderson is not pretending that Jule is incapable of literal rape, as the scene makes clear that normative heterosexuality always presupposes the capacity for *socially condoned* sexual violation against women. Jule's capacity for rape in a patriarchal culture based on racial oppression does not stem from some obscure, devious pathological repression caused by his symbolic race castration and embodied in his compulsion to commit a deviant sexual crime so as to release his frustrated desire in a displaced act of ineffectual political protest. Jule's capacity for rape stems from his being a "normal" male involved in a "normal" heterosexual relationship with a "normal" female.

Henderson is anticipating how the logic of race rape in the protest mode can too easily lead to the kind of devious sociosexual psychological rationalizations made by an ersatz political radical like Eldridge Cleaver in *Soul on Ice*. Cleaver claims to have begun a political project of raping random white women as a way of venting racial frustration. To bring about this revenge of white men's symbolic race rape through the actual rape of women, he decides to practice literal rape on black women in his own neighborhood (*Soul on Ice,* 22–27). Cleaver turns the existentialist act of Bigger's murder of Bessie into an "insurrectionary act" with profound political implications for black nationalist politics, and in turn enhances Wright's work with the currency of 1960s radicalism:

> I wanted to send waves of consternation throughout the white race. Recently, I came upon a quotation from one of LeRoi Jones' poems, taken from his book *The Dead Lecturer:*
>   A cult of death need of the simple striking arm under this street lamp. . . . Rape the white girls, Rape their fathers. Cut the mothers' throats.
>   I have lived those lines and I know that if I had not been apprehended I would have slit some white throats. (26)

Citing Baraka (formerly known as Jones) makes clear the male-male rape dynamic that Wright barely averts. Later, Cleaver accuses Baldwin of desiring to be sexually penetrated by white men.[14] To take the offensive in this game of gaining power through symbolic race rape, the black male militant must turn the tables and literally rape first black then white women, which symbolically means raping white men. Cleaver is motivated by the same kind of penetration panic characterizing the *Black Boy*'s Shorty scene, in which the logic of male-male rape lurks furtively in the depth psychology that the texts refuse to plumb due to disgust and loathing specifically projected onto same-sexual penetration.

Cleaver's explosive text seems far away from the spare restraint of Henderson's *Jule*, and yet the ideological spin that *Soul on Ice* puts on race rape links it inextricably to Henderson's critique of the sexual violence of conventional protest anger. Keye's relation to Jule is *structurally* no different from the white master's relation to Bertha Mae. We do not have to read a homoerotic subtext into Keye's spying envy of Jule's rippling muscles to see the structural equation of Jule and Bertha Mae as slaves to the master's whim. Just as he decides to turn Bertha Mae, his sharecropping tenant, into an unwilling concubine, so Keye naturally assumes that he can "use" in whatsoever way he pleases a strong black "buck" dependent on him for work. The assumption of absolute mastering power over a naturally submissive other always presupposes the right of the master's sexual abuse as part of the contract of oppression regardless of the sex anatomy of the master and captive. Likewise, in the heterosexual triangle created by this rivalry, the arrows attaching inferior Jule to Bertha Mae on one side and superior Keye to her on the other must necessarily suggest or suppress the potential for that third line attaching Keye, as tormenting sexual master, to Jule, as unwilling sexual slave. With the sexual rivalry over Bertha Mae, all the formulae of protest naturalism crash obtrusively into the narrative. Mr. Keye becomes the Jim Crow white supremacist full of racial hatred and manhandling lust for the black girl. Jule becomes the symbolically emasculated black male, deprived of his sexual rights and manhood rites. Jule's forceful seduction of Bertha Mae becomes the dark foreshadowing of the white's man own rape of his black servant, a rape that Keye must project onto the strapping black buck. This disturbance cycles out to all the other relationships, including that between Jule and Rollo. Their cross-racial homosocial bond, which we might call *homoracial* bonding, at times so intimate as to verge on the homoerotic, now threatens to revert to merely a patronizing relationship between the privileged white boy and his deprived black charge. At last, the violence of black rage can explode into the narrative and we can rest assured of the final pathological outcome.

What follows in the plot is as close as *Jule* will come to adhering to a protest narrative structure. Having come to visit Jule at his work site, Bertha Mae, in Jule's arms, is trying to make him see her relation to Keye without having to say it aloud: "I don't know how to tell you, Jule" (84). Keye rides up and pulls out his hidden gun. This detail reminds us of the gun that drops from Rollo's hand at the moment of his hunting panic—and how Jule responds by picking it up. Jule knocks the gun out of Keye's hand, and the fight that ensues confirms our expectations. When Jule punches the white man and knocks him to the ground, Keye responds in the formulaic way of protest anger: "Nigger, you ain't going to get away with this! By God, I'm a white man! I'll blow your goddamn brains out if it's the last thing I do!" (85). Henderson, however, is more interested in Jule's leavetaking for the flight northward than in consummating the lynching plot. Ironically, the expected separation of the lovers (Jule and Bertha Mae) before the flight North gets suppressed in the narrative so that the homoracial bond between Jule and Rollo can be elaborated and reaffirmed against the grain of racial loyalties. When Jule goes to explain and say goodbye to Rollo, race suddenly intervenes between them for the first time:

> He looked at Rollo's eyes, china-blue and vivid, at the mop of blond hair that fell over his eyes. Eyes he had seen a thousand times, without seeing them at all. Jule looked at Rollo as though he were seeing him for the first time. Rollo was a white boy.
> "I can't tell you," Jule said. (88)

Rollo forces Jule to reveal what has happened, and to give him the loaded gun, reversing the action of the hunting scene in which Jule lovingly takes a loaded gun from Rollo. This action reaffirms Rollo's misplaced loyalty to Jule in the face of absolute proof that Jule himself has taken a loaded gun from a white man in the middle of a sexual dispute. It is difficult to imagine a more defiant assault of Jim Crow protocol. It is Rollo's turn to protect Jule from the rage of the white fathers at a moment when Jule is deemed, by Jim Crow, as no longer trustworthy to carry a loaded gun. But Rollo does not flinch. He immediately goes to his father, who gives his son a race morality lesson, as Old Cage tells his son that Jule must leave immediately—an act of generosity on Cage's part, considering the seriousness of Jule's racial offense. Rollo refuses to accept the (hetero)sexual logic of racial supremacy, which dictates that Keye has a right to Jule's black woman just because he is a white man. Rollo intuits that such logic also contravenes his homoracial bond with Jule:

> Rollo stared at his father. He said: "If Boykin Keye is white, Dad, I don't want to be white!"
>
> His father flushed. "Rollo, don't ever let me hear you say a thing like that again! Not ever! Not as long as you live! Do you hear me!"
>
> "I don't give a damn, Dad! It's the way I feel! Jule ain't done nothing!" Rollo burst into tears. (89–90)

Rollo's threat to defect into blackness—a defection that has already occurred emotionally and morally—again diverts the potential protest plot into an act of transracial male fantasy. Rollo's unconditional trust and love of Jule are reaffirmed across the now articulated barrier of race— embodied most immediately in the white father's insistence on the white son's submission to an uncrossable racial line. Note, as well, how the father's implicit trust, gestured after the hunting fiasco, is dramatically revoked, as Cage strongly implies that for Rollo to wish defection into blackness is the *one* transgression that can erase the son's worthiness of patrilineal inheritance. To follow his father's command, as he must, is to deny the universality of those manhood rites into which he has been initiated with, and through the generous intervention of, his black friend. Race here trumps the sentimental claims of universal manhood rites.

Once Rollo is persuaded of Jule's need to go, he is then given his father's reluctant blessing to see Jule away. This restored balance, however, requires that Rollo displace the black female lover in the final farewell scene. Henderson also reroutes the narrative focus away from Jule's feelings and toward Rollo's: "Rollo watched the train slip into the night. 'God!' he said, 'it ain't no fun to be a white boy and alone!' He buried his face in his hands. His horse stood waiting" (95). Perhaps it is ironic that the only way Henderson can imagine a way out of the race raping logic of protest fiction is through this de/eroticized bond between a black and white boy. Once we realize, however, that homoerotic love can function *in opposition to* male-male rape, rather than as its penetrating consummation or its punitive double, the novel's homoerotic structure makes some sense. Homoeroticism, like mutual male-female desire, is something other than the penetrating power of the dominant male. Anticipating what Baldwin brings to fruition in 1962 with the publication of *Another Country,* Henderson in 1945 thinks that one way to attempt to disarm the race war between men and its subsidiary logic of raping conquest of women is to turn symbolic race rape into literal (that is, sexual) love between men across race. In order to do so, however, he must also intensify the fraternal bond between men (homosocial contact) into a more intimate homoerotic yearning, however accommodated or suppressed as male camaraderie, vulnerable because it is cross-racial.

At the close of the novel, when he returns to his Southern hometown to retrieve Bertha Mae and thus his manhood rites, Jule finds Rollo unwed and alone, still melancholic, although having taken his rightful place as heir to his father's estate. In the heteronormative logic of the novel, something must be sacrificed for this pairing to be gained. Rollo's singleness—we could say his singularity as a Southern white man who has reached across race—enables the joyful pairing of the black man and woman. Rollo's singleness and singularity, in other words, make possible the antiprotest narrative structure, in which race rape is averted. Rollo is neither a raping threat nor even a marriageable rival. In this novel, it is not so much the black woman who mediates the black man's emasculation. Instead, it is Rollo, the subliminal queer, who mediates by helping to redirect the proper desire of the manly black hero toward chaste black womanhood. And yet, unlike the black female in most black male protest fiction, Rollo as mediator is neither raped nor erased. Rollo occupies the very visibly and queerly privileged position of a gaze without an object, the perfect figure of melancholy, a conventional site of the homoerotic in literature. Rollo plays this role well by serving as a stopgap for the novel: the place where yearning can reach its pure potential. Just as the novel desires a racial coupling without the dangers attendant upon racial ideology, just as it desires a cross-racial vision without being sidetracked by interracial sex, Rollo bears the cross of white desire desexed and thus disarmed of its racial powers. Does this mean that Rollo is also emasculated by his desexed status? I don't think so. In the end, Rollo still has his balls—if I may be so crude in putting it this way—because he still inherits the white father's estate. In avoiding the cliché of black male emasculation as psychological suffering, Henderson ironically falls into another cliché of (un)manly suffering, the homoerotic as a singular site of melancholic yearning.

NOTES

1. Or we could say that they tend to place race in parenthesis, as MacKinnon does in one of the two instances where she mentions it in relation to African American men: "So rape comes to mean a strange (read Black) man who does not know his victim but does know she does not want sex with him, going ahead anyway" (*Toward*, 181).

2. Charlotte Pierce-Baker brings attention to the converse side of this problem. Because African American men have been so long stereotyped as rapists in dominant U.S. culture, the black woman raped by a black man can be made to feel guilty for accusing any black man of rape—a psychological burden that contributes to the patterns of silence surrounding rape within African American communities (*Surviving*, 63–65, 76–77, and 219–24). In an argument that almost equates rape with lower-class black men as "myrmidons" for white male authority, Susan Brownmiller makes an analogous point about white women's racial guilt in charging black men with rape (*Against*, 251–55).

3. See, for instance, the anthology edited by Nancy Armstrong and Leonard Tennenhouse, *The Violence of Representation*, especially Teresa de Lauretis's essay, in which she writes, "Violence is en-gendered in representation" ("Violence," 240).

4. Part of what makes rape a powerful index for the effects of racial oppression on African American men is exactly our sense of its singularity as a rare, life-changing event in the life of a woman. Of course, as feminists have been careful to indicate, rapes occur much more frequently and routinely than our sense of its singularity will allow.

5. Although it is possible for castration to mean the *voluntary* removal of the genitals, as in the case of male-to-female transgender surgery, the word carries such strong negative connotations of violent deprivation that biological males who have undergone such a procedure are commonly seen as absurdly and tragically self-mutilated and self-degraded. Another curious instance in which violence and volition become ambiguous involves the eighteenth-century Italian practice of castrating young boys to retain their soprano register in opera—the falsetto voice of the castrato. On the ambiguous gender signification of castrati, see Wayne Koestenbaum (*Queen's,* 158–69).

6. Much of the theory on heterosexual rape has been constructed to overcome the notion that rape is merely an individual, private, or domestic nonpolitical act. In addition to MacKinnon, *Toward,* see Brownmiller, *Against,* who connects her raised consciousness of rape as a political category to her involvement with civil rights activism in advocating on behalf of black men accused of raping white women, especially 210–55; also see Susan Schecter, *Women,* especially 29–52; and Donat and D'Emilio, "Feminist."

7. Peter Middleton offers a critique of Freudian theory on masculine violence, a critique that draws a similar conclusion: "Freud's methodological reversal of the [Wolf Man's] fear [of being beaten by his father] into a wish [to become the passive sexual partner of his father] is especially evident. . . . How much then does the complex fear of male violence translate into homosexuality and the defence of homophobia against it?" (*Inward,* 98).

8. I hesitate to label lynching homoerotic because the notion carries so much cultural baggage implying a subliminal or repressed *desire for* the full range of homosexual intercourse, including tenderness, romance, and passion. By same-sexuality, I mean to suggest the *structure* of male-male sexual interaction without necessarily connoting any desire for romantic intimacy. The homoerotic is one aspect of same-sexuality, but too frequently potential sexual interactions between men are reduced to either homoeroticism or homosexuality. That men can desire to touch other men out of curiosity, fascination, and even hostility must be kept in mind.

9. One aspect of this problem of the relation between same-sexuality and masculine violence of penetration and castration has been taken up by queer theorists as issues of homophobia, misogyny, and AIDS-phobia. See, for example, Leo Bersani's essay, "Is the Rectum a Grave?" and D. A. Miller's "Anal Rope." Unfortunately, however, such studies in queer theory tend to overlook the racialized dynamic undergirding U.S. notions of violent same-sexuality. In fact,

Bersani is so indebted to an assumption that racial and homosexual identities are totally separate that he can argue that "it is also true that the power of blacks *as a group* in the United States is much greater than that of homosexuals" (204), as though there are no black homosexuals.

10. In another rare instance where male rape is mentioned in this context, Catherine Clinton points out in passing how Toni Morrison implies male rape as torture in her depiction of Paul D.'s experience on the chain gang in the novel *Beloved* (" 'With a Whip,' " 209; *Beloved,* 107–8).

11. In addition to Wiegman, another enlightening instance in which a critic has taken up this issue can be found in Robert Reid-Pharr's provocative interpretation of Martin Delany's novel *Blake* as working toward an image of black male heroism through subliminal scenarios of homosocial and repressed homosexual sadomasochism between white masters and slave boys ("Violent," 89). Although instructive in foregrounding the same-sexual dynamic buried in this fictive representation of racial emasculation, Reid-Pharr's essay stops short of theorizing the racial-sexual operation of same-sexuality in such representations of race emasculation. For other figurations of the black male as sadomasochistic fetish object, see Mercer, *Welcome,* 171–219; Farley, "Sadomasochism"; Smalls, "Public"; Maurice Wallace, "Autochoreography"; and Doy, *Black,* 156–203.

12. The cock-spinning metaphor is actually quite ambivalent. On the one hand, it projects superior size, manipulation, and capacity onto the black boy and places him literally in the position of "top" man. On the other hand, the spinning action and reference to a bull indicate the black boy's mechanical and animalistic lack of control over his own sexuality.

13. Bessie is objectified further when we are aware that, according to Keneth Kinnamon, in Wright's manuscript version Bigger fantasizes about making love to Mary Dalton while he is having sex with Bessie ("Introduction," 14).

14. Cleaver castigates Baldwin ironically to join arms (speaking metaphorically in terms of weaponry but not discounting the erotic pun) with Norman Mailer, who himself portrays black men as the source of unbridled, primal sexuality and white men as desiccated by bureaucratic culture (*Advertisements,* 337–58). The confusions in the sexual politics of *Soul on Ice* are multiplied when Cleaver climaxes the text with love letters to his white female lawyer alongside essays celebrating the beauty of black women; see Jordan, "Cleaver," 13; and Dudley, *My Father's,* 137–65.

WORKS CITED

Armstrong, Nancy, and Leonard Tennenhouse, eds. *The Violence of Representation: Literature and the History of Violence.* London: Routledge, 1989.

Awkward, Michael. *Negotiating Difference: Race, Gender, and the Politics of Positionality.* Chicago: University of Chicago Press, 1995.

Baldwin, James. *Another Country.* New York: Dell, 1960.

———— *Nobody Knows My Name: More Notes of a Native Son.* New York: Dell, 1961.

———— *Notes of a Native Son.* Boston: Beacon, 1955.

Barkley Brown, Elsa. "Imaging Lynching: African American Women, Communities of Struggle, and Collective Memory." In Geneva Smitherman, ed., *African American Women Speak Out on Anita Hill–Clarence Thomas,* pp. 100–24. Wayne State University Press, 1995.

Bersani, Leo. "Is the Rectum a Grave?" *October* 43 (Winter 1987): 197–222.

Brownmiller, Susan. *Against Our Will: Men, Women, and Rape.* New York: Fawcett Columbine, 1993 [1975].

Carby, Hazel V. *Reconstructing Womanhood: The Emergence of the Afro-American Woman Novelist.* New York: Oxford University Press, 1987.

Cleaver, Eldridge. *Soul on Ice.* New York: Deal, 1992 [1968].

Clinton, Catherine. " 'With a Whip in His Hand': Rape, Memory, and African-American Women." In Geneviève Fabre and Robert O'Meally, eds., *History and Memory in African-American Culture,* pp. 205–18. New York: Oxford University Press, 1984.

Davis, Angela. *Women, Race, and Class.* New York: Vintage, 1981.

de Lauretis, Teresa. "The Violence of Rhetoric: Considerations on Representation and Gender." In Nancy Armstrong and Leonard Tennenhouse, eds., *The Violence of Representation: Literature and the History of Violence,* pp. 239–56. London: Routledge, 1989.

Donat, Patricia L. N., and John D'Emilio. "A Feminist Redefinition of Rape and Sexual Assault: Historical Foundations and Change." In *Gender Violence: Interdisciplinary Perspectives,* 184–93. New York: New York University Press, 1997.

Doy, Gen. *Black Visual Culture: Modernity and Postmodernity.* London: Tauris, 2000.

Dudley, David L. *My Father's Shadow: Intergenerational Conflict in African*

American Men's Autobiography. Philadelphia: University of Pennsylvania Press, 1991.

Farley, Anthony Paul. "Sadomasochism and the Colorline: Reflections on the Million Man March." In Devon W. Carbado, ed., *Black Men on Race, Gender, and Sexuality,* pp. 68–84. New York: New York University Press, 1999.

Gunning, Sandra. *Race, Rape, and Lynching: The Red Record of American Literature, 1890–1912.* New York: Oxford University Press, 1996.

Harris, Trudier. *Exorcising Blackness: Historical and Literary Lynching and Burning Rituals.* Bloomington: Indiana University Press, 1984.

Henderson, George Wylie. *Jule.* 1946. Intro. J. Lee Greene. Tuscaloosa: University of Alabama Press, 1989.

hooks, bell. *Ain't I a Woman: Black Women and Feminism.* Boston: South End, 1981.

Jackson, Blyden. *The Waiting Years: Essays on American Negro Literature.* Baton Rouge: Louisiana State University Press, 1976.

Jordan, Jennifer. "Cleaver vs. Baldwin: Icing the White Negro." *Black Books Bulletin* 1 (Winter 1992): 12–15.

Kinnamon, Keneth. "Introduction." In *New Essays on Native Son,* pp. 1–33. Cambridge: Cambridge University Press, 1990.

Koestenbaum, Wayne. *The Queen's Throat: Opera, Homosexuality, and the Mystery of Desire.* New York: Poseidon, 1993.

MacKinnon, Catharine A. *Toward a Feminist Theory of the State.* Cambridge: Harvard University Press, 1989.

Mailer, Norman. *Advertisements for Myself.* Cambridge: Harvard University Press, 1992 [1959].

Mercer, Kobena. *Welcome to the Jungle: New Positions in Black Cultural Studies.* New York: Routledge, 1994.

Middleton, Peter. *The Inward Gaze: Masculinity and Subjectivity in Modern Culture.* New York: Routledge, 1992.

Miller, D. A. "Anal Rope." In Diana Fuss, ed., *Inside/Out: Lesbian Theories, Gay Theories,* pp. 119–41. New York: Routledge, 1991.

Morrison, Toni. *Beloved.* New York: Knopf, 1987.

Painter, Nell Irvin. "Soul Murder and Slavery: Toward a Fully Loaded Cost Accounting." In Linda K. Kerber, Alice Kessler-Harris, and Kathryn Kish Sklar, ed., *U.S. History as Women's History: New Feminist Essays,* pp. 125–46. Chapel Hill: University of North Carolina Press, 1995.

Patterson, Orlando. *Slavery and Social Death*. Cambridge: Harvard University Press, 1982.

Pierce-Baker, Charlotte. *Surviving the Silence: Black Women's Stories of Rape*. New York: Norton, 1998.

Reid-Pharr, Robert. "Violent Ambiguity: Martin Delany, Bourgeois Sado-masochism, and the Production of a Black National Masculinity." In Marcellus Blount and George P. Cunningham, eds., *Representing Black Men*, pp. 73–94. New York: Routledge, 1996.

Scarry, Elaine. *The Body in Pain: The Making and Unmaking of the World*. New York: Oxford University Press, 1985.

Schechter, Susan. *Women and Male Violence: The Visions and Struggles of the Battered Women's Movement*. Boston: South End, 1982.

Silverman, Kaja. *Male Subjectivity at the Margins*. New York: Routledge, 1992.

Smalls, James. "Public Face, Private Thoughts: Fetish, Interracialism, and the Homoerotic in Some Photographs by Carl Van Vechten." In Thomas Foster, Carol Sieger, and Ellen E. Berry, eds., *Sex Positives: The Cultural Politics of Dissident Sexualities*, pp. 144–93. New York: New York University Press, 1997.

Wallace, Maurice. "The Autochoreography of an Ex-Snow Queen: Dance, Desire, and the Black Masculine in Melvin Dixon's *Vanishing Rooms*." In Eve Kosofsky Sedgwick, ed., *Novel Gazing: Queer Readings in Fiction*, pp. 379–400. Durham: Duke University Press, 1997.

Wiegman, Robyn. *American Anatomies: Theorizing Race and Gender*. Durham: Duke University Press, 1995.

Wright, Richard. *Black Boy (American Hunger): A Record of Childhood and Youth*. Intro. Jerry W. Ward Jr. New York: HarperCollins, 1989 [1945].

———. *Eight Men*. Foreword by David Bradley. New York: Thunder's Mouth, 1987.

———. *The Long Dream*. New York: Harper and Row, 1987 [1958].

———. *Native Son and "How 'Bigger' Was Born."* Intro. Arnold Rampersad. New York: HarperCollins, 1993 [1940].

THE GOOD, THE BAD, AND THE UGLY: MEN, WOMEN, AND MASCULINITY

Judith Halberstam

This essay explains the relationships of men and women to dominant and minority forms of masculinity through a discussion of three very different sets of debates. The first debate is about a perceived late-twentieth-century crisis in heterosexuality and dominant masculinity, and I take as my texts a series of films that I call "heterosexual conversion narratives." The second debate is the explicit focus of this volume, namely, the relationship between feminism and masculinity studies. And my final section addresses the topic of female ugliness and the history of the abjection of female masculinity.

In general terms, as we begin the twenty-first century, the minority genders and sexualities that were categorized as pathological at the twentieth century's beginning have come to undermine the authority and authenticity of the genders and sexualities they were supposed to mimic. The early twentieth century's invert has become the model for the constructedness of desire and embodiment. But this does not signal some magical end to homophobia or genderphobia. Rather, to keep pace with changes in the social and political recognition of queers, homophobic response has become ever more subtle and devious. In what follows, I pay particular attention to the history and the fate of minority masculinity—female masculinity in particular—and the special forms of political and cultural animosity that it inspires. While mainstream media acknowledge the existence of queer masculinities, they do so only to reassert the hegemony of white male masculinities. And while masculinity studies as a field has largely been formed in response to a perceived neglect of the topic in feminism, the work produced there has largely and almost exclusively addressed men and maleness. Finally, the fierce protection of white male privilege from minority encroachments rounds out a century of discourses of manliness and manhood, all of which have been designed to make white male masculinity equivalent to political personhood and public power.[1] A profound shift in our understandings of gender, politics, publicness, class, sexuality, and race can be engendered, I argue here, by refusing once and for all the marks of total abjection and dysfunction that make female masculinities seem uninhabitable.

Female masculinity, I have argued in a book by the same name, disrupts contemporary cultural studies accounts of masculinity within which masculinity always boils down to the social, cultural and political effects of male embodiment and male privilege. Such accounts can only read masculinity as the powerful and active alternative to female passivity and as the expression therefore of white male subjectivities. The term *female masculinity* stages several different kinds of interventions into contemporary gender theory and practice: first, it refuses the authentication of masculinity through maleness and maleness alone, and it names a deliberately counterfeit masculinity that undermines the currency of maleness; second, it offers an alternative mode of masculinity that clearly detaches misogyny from maleness and social power from masculinity; third, female masculinity may be an embodied assault upon compulsory heterosexuality, and it offers one powerful model of what inauthentic masculinity can look like, how it produces and deploys desire, and what new social, sexual and political relations it can foster. Finally, I hope that female masculinity can be provocative enough to force us to look anew upon male femininities and interrogate the new politics of manliness that has swept through gay male communities in the last decade.

THE GOOD: *AS GOOD AS IT GETS* AND HETEROSEXUAL CONVERSION NARRATIVES

Nineteen ninety-seven and 1998 saw the release of a series of films structured around triangles made up of two men and a woman. But unlike the triangles described and analyzed so well by Eve Sedgwick in *Between Men* as homosocial competitive relays of desire between seemingly heterosexual males, the desiring relations in these neo-homosocial triangles place an overtly gay man or a lesbian in the position of rival for the woman's affections. In either case, the gay man or the lesbian becomes a masculine competitor with the potential to unseat the white male as the object of the heterosexual woman's affection. These new triangles show some potential for reimagining dominant masculinity through alternative masculinities; unfortunately, they mostly sidestep this radical option in favor of a decidedly conservative narrative that props up heteromasculinity as "good" masculinity and casts both the gay man and the lesbian as "bad" substitutes. In this narrative structure, the straight homophobic man learns from the queer bonds between the others how to attain a fully human and socially viable model of manhood, and he achieves his "humanity" at the expense of theirs.

Films in the 1990s that deploy this neohomosocial narrative structure include *As Good As It Gets* (1997, dir. James L. Brooks), featuring a homophobic straight man, a gay man, and a straight woman, *Chasing Amy* (1997, dir. Kevin Smith), featuring a straight man, a bisexual woman, and a homophobic straight male friend, *The Opposite of Sex* (1998, dir. Don Roos), with a straight woman, a gay man, and a bisexual man, and, finally, *The Object of My Affections* (1998, dir. Nicholas Hytner), which uses the same formula as *As Good As It Gets* of a homophobic straight man, a gay man, and a straight woman. In nearly all these films, a heterosexual conversion narrative is set in motion by the desire of a heterosexual person for a seemingly unattainable gay person, and in some of them the conversion comes to fruition: *Chasing Amy, The Opposite of Sex*. This fairly repulsive genre of films has had enormous success, and *As Good As It Gets* even won Oscars in 1996 for its particularly cynical variation on the theme. The problems inherent to the genre however speak precisely to the problems produced by encounters between masculinity studies and feminist theory. In both the heterosexual conversion films and in masculinity studies, in both popular culture and academic discourse, maleness remains a protected provenance for the cultivation of privileged forms of masculinity, while feminism becomes in both arenas a diluted discourse about women's desires for domestic security, love, and family. By analyzing the structural contradictions of the new and popular genre of heterosexual conversion films, I believe we can attend to some of the problems that emerge from unsuccessful encounters between feminism and masculinity studies. Throughout, I will be offering a historically located model of female masculinity as one alternative site for feminist reformulations of masculinity.

Let us call the genre of films released between 1996–1997 and featuring neohomosocial triangles "heterosexual conversion fantasies."[2] Within the genre, stock characters act out their parts in a complex drama involving gender identity, class position, race, and sexuality. The straight woman in the heterosexual conversion fantasy is at least nominally a feminist; she is also a woman who (to use pop therapy lingo) loves too much, a Venetian who (to continue in this vernacular) inevitably ends up with a Martian (*Men Are from Mars, Women Are from Venus*) and wonders whether she can find someone to love who at least seems to inhabit her own planet (Gray, *Men*). Enter the gay man. The gay man in the heterosexual conversion fantasy plays the sensitive but masculine guy; he is a gay man who can pass for straight, and therefore becomes attractive to the leading lady, but he is also a male who does not demand sex from the woman. The gay man, unlike his heterosexual counterpart and rival, seems fully domesticated (except for the occasional episode of anonymous sex) and, again unlike the heterosexual man, he loves to cuddle, dance, eat out, cook, shop. In short, the narrative presents the masculine gay male as an ideal mate for the heterosexual woman in every aspect except sexual compatibility, and this is represented as a nonissue by casting women as domestic and asexual. The gay man ultimately offers perfect companionship for the heterosexual woman by being willing to do everything the "Martian" will not do with the woman. Enter the Martian. The alpha male within this triangle desires the woman but despises everything that goes with being with a woman—family responsibilities, financial obligations, domesticity, shopping, emotional exchange, and so on. But, when he finds himself in danger of being supplanted by the gay man, the heteromale feels justified in articulating his rage in protracted bouts of loud homophobic reaction followed by loud sexist outbursts.[3] By the narrative's end, the gay man rejects the woman and she either accepts the boorish straight man back into her life, having reformed him slightly, or she moves on from both the straight man and the gay substitute to a more realistic object of affection, one who, unlike the gay man, may want to have sex with her every now and then, and, unlike the bullying straight man, treats her with some respect. The new object of the heroine's affection is often coded as a minority masculinity and as neutralized in some way: in *Object of My Affection*, for example, Jennifer Aniston ends up with a sensitive black man; in *The Opposite of Sex*, Lisa Kudrow eventually marries a working-class shy guy. Curiously, in both films these alternative lovers are policemen—the connection between minority masculinities and the law, of course, leaves the space of outlaw or rogue male available for the insensitive, unloving, and utterly attractive (according to the film's logic) white heteromale. In almost every case, the films find alternative masculinities to be compromise choices, and this confirms once again the originary and authentic nature of white male heteromasculinity. The straight belligerent guy may not always get the woman he seems to desire, but he usually takes solace in a younger version of her for the time being. With everyone coupled up, at least temporarily, the gay man is no longer necessary and so he is also paired off.

So how is any of this relevant to the topic of feminism and masculinity? In all these films, the heterosexual conversion fantasy rests upon two crucial factors: first, heterosexual white male masculinity appears as naturally attractive and desirable despite any socially repulsive behaviors that may accompany it. In fact, the presence of a gay masculine rival allows the heteromale to voice his most homophobic and misogynist sentiments without repercussions of any kind. And, second, the heterosexual male is never really challenged by the alternative male masculinities with which he competes, and the choice of an alternative masculinity by the heroine is always cast as a compromise rather than a romantic resolution. These two factors, the naturalization of a particular form of heternormativity and the elimination of the threat of alternatives, combine with a weak feminist discourse in the narratives to produce profoundly conservative models of both masculinity and feminism. These films cast themselves as feminist by trying to depict the heroine as an agent in the drama of finding a mate and by representing her struggle to mate as a process of domesticating male sexuality. Audiences are supposed to recognize the heroine as feminist only in relation to her desire for self-determination, but the films are careful not to extend her feminist critique of male sexuality beyond what is necessary to her desire to reproduce and have a family.

This narrative trajectory varies only slightly when a lesbian rather than a gay man challenges the straight hero. In *Chasing Amy*, an avowedly bisexual woman, whom we would never recognize as queer outside the film's narrative frame, receives the attention of a very obnoxious straight male and, at first, she articulates all the right sentiments about his arrogance and her sexual preferences, but she then succumbs quickly and completely to his embrace. Our heroine is rarely seen interacting with lesbians, but she immediately invites her suitor to meet her at her local lesbian bar and then swaps oral sex stories with him and his buddy afterward. This woman never challenges the heterosexual suitor at the level of either sexuality or gender because she appears to have been straight all along. He feels good about having converted her, she feels good about being true to herself rather than following blindly the rules of a supposedly dominant and overbearing lesbian community, and her new boyfriend's roommate now gets to play the role of obnoxious and homophobic straight guy. The suitor's roommate, indeed, plays the very traditional triangulated role of the misogynist who masks his desire for his pal by mouthing the most woman-hating sentiments in relation to his bisexual girlfriend. However, this same character also articulates the dangerous truth that lies at the heart of the film: namely, that the heroine's bisexuality is merely a sexual ruse that amplifies her heterosexual attractiveness, and that real lesbianism has much more to do with masculinity. While one would not want to confirm the idea that authentic lesbianism requires masculine identification, lesbian masculinity in *Chasing Amy*, nonetheless, would have completely intervened in the heteromasculine fantasy of two feminine women that the film elaborated ad nauseum. *Chasing Amy* in fact deliberately refused even to imagine, outside of the roommate's homophobic imaginary, what lesbian masculinity would look like. In the case of most heterosexual conversion fantasies, the insertion of a viable female masculinity at any point in any of the narratives would be or could be cataclysmic. For example, how might the narrative play out in *As Good As It Gets* and *Opposite of Sex* or *Object of My Affection* if the gay rival for the heterosexual woman's affection was not a gay man but a gay masculine woman: in this scenario, the straight male rival would be forced to acknowledge an alternative version of masculinity that threatened him, if only because the sexual relationship between the heterosexual woman and the masculine woman would be far more possible.

I have only mentioned the most recent heterosexual conversion fantasies here, but there are numerous other queer and mainstream films that work around and within this triangle. When a serious model of female masculinity does emerge—as in *French Twist* (1995, dir. Josiane Balasko), for example—the threat deployed by the butch will inevitably be reduced to another form of femininity or else violently eradicated (she will be impregnated or killed or sexually humilated). But despite their unrelentingly conservative sexual agendas, heterosexual conversion narratives do indicate a prevailing crisis in heterosexuality that affects both men and women: in the conversion films, the straight man may exhibit all the symptoms of crisis and social/sexual impotence, but the straight woman is the one left at the end of the day with only dwindling opportunities for sexual and emotional satisfaction.

The title of one of these films suggests that heterosexual crisis emerges from a slippage between sexual aim and sexual object: by naming both a gay man and a straight man "the object of my affection," this film of the same title implies a psychoanalytic model of desire within which the woman's sexual aim (heterosexual sex) becomes trained upon an inappropriate sexual object (homosexual male). Freud discusses "deviations in respect of the sexual object" only in terms of same-sex objects of desire, but he does not mention the selection of an inappropriate opposite sex object—an object, in other words, constitutionally unwilling to return the woman's affection. The woman's perverse selection of an inappropriate sexual object can be best described as masochistic in the sense that, in Freud's words, "It appears to be that in which satisfaction is conditional upon suffering physical or mental pain at the hands of the sexual object" (*Three*, 24).

More often than not in the heterosexual conversion fantasy, the heroine chooses only between hetero- and homomasculinities, a gay man and a straight man, with lesbianism left completely out of the picture. In these rivalries, the superiority of the straight male is predicated always upon his natural assumption of masculinity and in contrast to the strained quality of the gay man's masculinity. Male narcissism also plays a huge role in these dramas, since the male lead never doubts that he is attractive nor that he is entitled to social power, social dominance, and all available sexual objects. In *As Good As It Gets,* the heteromale assumes that both the woman and the gay man desire him, and the film confirms his social reality but also exceeds his overtly narcissistic hopes by showing that even the gay man's dog is naturally (instinctually) drawn to the straight man over the gay man.

These heterosexual conversion films depend heavily upon a gay male character who presents as both masculine and respectable in order to offer some kind of challenge to the male heterosexual lover. The resolute depiction of gay maleness as properly masculine may lead us to ask what has happened to even the stereotyped versions of male femininity in contemporary queer discourse and popular representation. As masculinity is ever more naturalized in heterosexual, homosexual and transsexual male bodies, femininity becomes ever more degraded as a subject position and female masculinity becomes simply unimaginable. Good masculinity throughout these films is located in heterosexual male bodies and gay masculinity serves as a backup but not a substitute for the good and real masculinity of the hero. In my next section, I want to look at how "bad" masculinities—lesbian, female, racialized—might be far more suited to the task of representing phallicized masculinity.

THE BAD: MASCULINITY STUDIES

Any number of feminist theorists have remarked that the 1990s has witnessed a crisis of masculinity (Faludi, *Stiffed;* Bordo, *Male;* Solomon-Godeau, *Male*). In the various accounts produced by white feminists, this crisis revolves around inconsistencies in the function of fatherhood, competition in the workplace, new standards of sexual conduct as a result of sexual harassment discourse, new ideals for the male body, and the internalization of feminist ideologies by a new generation despite public backlashes against feminism. Crises in masculinity have also been analyzed by feminists of color in relation to the development of movements like the Million Man March, where a strengthened black masculinity comes at a high price for black women and accompanies conservative ideologies of family and culture. But the response to this widely acknowledged crisis from feminists has failed to deploy some of the most trenchant observations produced by queer theory about the liabilities of conventional masculinities within heteronormativity. The responses also assiduously refuse to acknowledge even the existence of fully realized nonmale masculinities, which come in the form of lesbian fatherhood, butch identities, drag king performances, female sports icons, and so on.[4]

Similarly, masculinity studies, I would venture to assert, has made little progress in generating either explanations for a perceived crisis in masculinity or imagining new social arrangements of gender, race, class, and sexuality that can compensate for and replace the binary gender systems that support and produce male dominance and heteronormativity. Almost without exception, the topic of masculinity and feminism has been reinterpreted as men and feminism. The work on men and feminism is wide-ranging, indeed, and makes many important contributions to gender studies. However the seamless translation of masculinity into men should give us pause. I propose that work on masculinity and feminism may want to begin (but not end) in the future with serious considerations of female masculinity in order not to reiterate the inevitable coupling of men and masculinity that I believe constitutes a serious obstacle to new and creative thought on gender and its relationship to social change.

This is not to say that there have been no developments of note on men and masculinity. Indeed, the most interesting work in recent years on male masculinity may not have taken female masculinity into consideration, but it has attempted to locate masculinity historically in relation to class and racial formations. While the work most typical of masculinity studies has depicted feminist work on masculinity as male bashing and has tended to call for "sympathy for the devil," in the words of one masculinity studies proponent,[5] other essays have tried to move away from individualistic accounts of the burden of white maleness in order to examine the pressures, the conventions, and the structural conditions they have organized white masculinities in the last few decades. Eric Lott's work on Elvis impersonation, for example, uses Elvis impersonation performances to talk about "how white working-class men currently live their whiteness" ("All the King's," 192–227). Lott sees these acts of impersonation as both the repository of a particular kind of cultural envy of black culture and black masculinities and as the imaginative response to "post white male politics," and to post-Fordist-era changes in the meaning of work. As he makes clear, when "work" for working-class men no longer simply signifies in terms of factories and manual labor then the terms *working class* and *masculinity* shift perceptibly in meaning. Lott's essay would have been richer for even a cursory examination of female masculinities, female Elvis impersonations, and female class identities and labor histories, but the attempt to map the effect of the emergence of "office styles of manhood" (196) upon male class identities provides a richly complex account of the interlocking structures that connect class to gender.

One way of shifting the discourse on masculinity might be to ask questions about the powerful forces that bind masculinity to realness. While normative masculinity depicts itself quite simply as real masculinity, it simultaneously exhibits some anxiety about the status of its own realness: male masculinity as an identity seems to demand authentication: Am I real? Is my masculinity real? The fact that male masculinities of all kinds seem to require recognition of some kind also has the counterintuitive effect of marking their instability and their distance from the real. This need for verification in the realm of male masculinity is so widespread and endemic to the identity that it is even readable within some female-to-male transsexual (FTM) narratives; indeed, transsexual theorist Henry Rubin, in his contribution to *Men Doing Feminism,* insists: "In general, I want to be unambiguously recognized as an authentic man even though I was not born with a male body. . . . I want to live manhood with the same authenticity as a man born with a male body" ("Reading," 316). But what constitutes the referent of Rubin's phrase "the same authenticity" in this desideratum? Do male bodies living male lives add up to authentic masculinity? Do heterosexual white men experience their masculinity as authentic most of the time or any of the time? In the age of viagra and penile enlargments, we might argue, male sexuality and male masculinity in general tends to be a mediated affair in all kinds of situations, and the apparent fragility of erectile function might stand as a symbol for other kinds of masculine vulnerabilities that move far beyond the psychoanalytic formulation of castration anxiety.

Perhaps not surprisingly, psychoanalysis has not been a very popular model for rethinking masculinity in masculinity studies. Paul Smith's essay, "Vas," stands out as one successful attempt to use feminist psychoanalytic formulations of desire to try to produce new models of masculine desire and embodiment that can respond to the shifting social landscape against which those desires play themselves out. In "Vas," Smith writes: "Male sexuality is both difficult and deadly easy" (1028), and he tries to return to what he thinks psychoanalysis has repressed, namely, the topic of masculinity. Since psychoanalysis is a model of human sexuality that takes the male subject as normative and understands the female body as the terrain for neurotic symptoms, he argues, then male failure will always be received as the presence of femininity. In this sense, the female body becomes a theater for the tragedy of embodiment, while the male body functions as a site of health and perfection. The male body is feminized when sick and the female body is masculinized when healthy, invigorated, and active. While Smith is adept at showing the liabilities and advantages that accrue to males within this metaphoric schema, his essay leaves aside the question of whether the masculinization of the female body can ever be recuperated for a new sexual politics of gender.

One immensely useful result of Smith's essay lies in his attempt to dislodge the phallus from its place as the primary signifier of masculinity. The phallus, he suggests, serves only as a metaphor for masculine power; what then can serve as a metaphor for masculine vulnerability? The term *vas* for Smith manages to avoid the singularity of the phallus and it includes the other stuff of masculinity, the other genital signifiers of maleness, all of which add up to an apparatus rather than an organ. He defines *vas* as: first, male genitalia in general, the testicles (site of vulnerability) as well as the penis (site of power); second, *vas* marks maleness as gear, stuff, equipment and not as the expression of an essential masculinity; finally, he discusses *vas* in terms of male orgasm, as a mode of spending or loss. Useful reformulations, like Smith's, of psychoanalytic readings of the male body, recognize that psychoanalysis is not a transhistorical model of human variability. Indeed, in order to continue to have meaning over time, the set of symbolic models created by

Freud to refer to the internalization of dominant systems of meaning must be updated in order to remain relevant to the social and political systems they describe. As gender relations shift and change over the course of the twentieth and twenty-first centuries, so too must the explanatory models we use to examine them. Accordingly, masculinity at the beginning of the twenty-first century can be recognized (in much the same ways as femininity was by Freud at the twentieth century's beginning) as a dynamic between embodiment, identification, social privilege, racial and class formation, and desire, rather than the result of having a particular body. And female masculinity, as Judith Butler's work has amply shown, provides a far better and more representative model for the workings of masculinity in a postmodern society.

In a pragmatic reading of Freud, we could say that he talks about phallic power as the representation of the power that seems to be available to men in social and political terms in a male-dominated culture.[6] Because we have so thoroughly naturalized and accepted the inevitability of male power, we might say, the coincidence of having a penis, performing heterosexual maleness, and accessing political power makes it unclear as to what comes first—the penis or the social power. Obviously, for Freud, the social power structure enables a reading of the penis as generative of social power; so, if the penis does not on its own generate social power, other body parts can also be phallic and other bodies can access the social power that seems to have been reserved for white males. This power can be accessed by female-bodied people not only by making the feminine livable and powerful but also by making maleness nonessential to masculinity. In *Bodies That Matter*, Judith Butler rereads Freud in order to highlight a slippage in his text between the penis and phallic power. Freud, Butler argues, cannot really sustain the possibility of the nonmale phallic body, and so he lapses into essentialism. Butler, however, stresses that in modern and postmodern society, where power works through bodies and desires rather than through repression, we can talk of the "transferability of the phallus," and even of the "lesbian phallus," by way of breaking down the seemingly insuperable bond between white male bodies and white male power (57–67).

In "The Lesbian Phallus," Butler returns to Lacan to reveal the structures of "normative heterosexuality" that undergird his descriptions of sex and sexual difference: Lacan, according to Butler, recognizes the subject as one founded upon lack, but, at the same time, he assumes that, in some sense, heterosexuality works: in other words, Lacan describes the way that threat (of castration) constitutes sex, but he assumes that the threatening and abject figures of the feminine male and the masculine female who represent the consequences of unsuccessful identifications will be sufficiently terrifying to the gendered subject to ensure normative gender identification. Butler asks of Lacan: "But what happens if the law that deploys the spectral figure of abject homosexuality as a threat becomes itself an inadvertent site of eroticization?" (97). In other words, the figures deployed by the unconscious to guarantee heteronormative gender and sexuality could themselves become cathected; Butler takes this one step further, however, and shows that even in terms of the mechanisms of identification that Lacan himself has pinpointed, maleness cannot be located as a privileged place for the development of masculinity. The body in Lacan's work, Butler emphasizes, is always a phantasmatic body; it always entails (as the mirror stage confirms) a misrecognition of self as coherent (Lacan, "Mirror"). Butler comments: "Lacan establishes the morphology of the body as a psychically invested projection, an idealization or "fiction" of the body as a totality and locus of control" ("Lesbian," 73). If all bodies are phantasmatic, then what makes the "lesbian phallus" impossible and the male phallus primary? Nothing, except Lacan's unconscious investment in the notion of a superior male body that produces male power; moreover, as Butler shows, neither Lacan nor Freud can really conceive of a powerful female masculinity.

The reading of female masculinity in "The Lesbian Phallus" is actually elusive, difficult, and hardly explicit, but it can be reduced more simply to three main points: first, the "lesbian phallus" signifies the possibility of a female body both being and having phallic power; this possibility is both a consequence of Lacan's theoretical framework and denied by him as a credible outcome of socialization. The lesbian phallus, moreover, intervenes in the relation between body parts and the body as a whole, which Lacan tends to essentialize. In other words, if, in the mirror stage, the image of the whole body is a fantasy within which the coherent body stands in for the coherent self, then the symbolic version of this misrecognition of coherence occurs when the phallic body stands in for social order. Butler's second main argument about the viability and suppression of female masculinity concerns forms of male narcisissm that allow men to misrecognize their penises as proof of their superiority and guarantor of their privileged relations to power, language, sexuality, desire. To the extent that they are unable to access the power they feel has been reserved for them, men tend to project their own misrecognition of the relationship between penises and male power onto the world around them.[7] Finally, for Butler, if the phallus symbolizes the penis, then it cannot *be* the penis. The phallus must therefore NOT be the penis and is bound to the penis by "determinate negation" (84).

Butler's work has been immensely useful to many different projects on gender and sexuality, but only rarely is it discussed directly in relation to "female masculinity." As my reading of "The Lesbian Phallus" hopefully shows, however, Butler's ability to finally, after years of debate among feminist psychoanalytic theorists, disassociate the phallus from the penis owes everything to a submerged but readable investment in the viability of nonmale masculinity. Because her example of gender performativity in *Gender Trouble* drew from the mostly gay male cultures of drag and female impersonation, theorists have perhaps tended to overlook the crucial focus of her intervention into psychoanalytic models of the gendered self—the butch body. The Butlerian phallus is above all accessed through a phallic dyke body, the butch body that has been repudiated by both psychoanalysis and feminism ("Lesbian," 86).

If we return for a moment to the heterosexual conversion narratives from the last section, we can see how the threat of the lesbian phallus, male narcissism, and the misrecognition of the part for the whole completely informs the models of masculinity and femininity that the films produce and affirm. Women, in these narratives, simply cannot be masculine; or, if they seem to present some form of credible masculinity, as occurs in *French Twist,* for example, it is still tempered by the notion that the butch resembles more closely the female object of her affection than the male object of her competitive instincts. In *French Twist,* the butch rival's temporary success with the heroine is explained by her willingness to play the male part in a domestic arrangement (fix a clogged drain, take out the garbage) in the temporary absence of a real man. Her threat to the heterosexuality of the heroine is tempered by, first, showing the heroine to be still fixated on male masculinity and settling for a supposedly counterfeit masculinity when the real thing is unavailable. But, second, the film continuously plays upon the butch rival's female and therefore "inadequate" body, showing her naked repeatedly and never allowing her body to become sexually phallic (through the use of a dildo, for example). Furthermore, the fact that the butch rival is able to pleasure the heroine at all becomes the ground for outrageous degrees of punishment that her character is forced to undergo.

The fact that male masculinity seems to stand, as I commented earlier, in constant need of verification confirms Butler's premise that all bodies are phantasmatic but that the male body has engaged in the most fabulous and extensive misrecognition of the realness of embodiment. In the next and last section of this essay, I want to consider the ways in which female masculinity has been cast historically as a completely abject, aesthetically displeasing, and uninhabitable position. In a culture that positively celebrates white masculinities of many different kinds, it is not obvious how masculinity can be reserved for white men over and against the threats levied by powerful and affirmative forms of female masculinity. The discourse of ugliness, I will argue, locates masculinity in females as abhorrent, repulsive, and unsustainable.

THE UGLY: HAIRY AND SCARY MASCULINE WOMEN

One indicator of changes in prevailing social attitudes to female masculinity has been the acceptance or rejection of women's sports. In 1999 women's sports took a huge step toward becoming viable entertainment in America. The women's U.S. World Cup soccer team and Women's National Basketball Association (WNBA) both signify the presence of sizable paying audiences willing to watch, play, and appreciate women's sports. Some have expressed amazement that it has taken this long to develop public acceptance for women's athleticism, but, then again, even in the masculinist space of the newspapers' sports pages, journalists have confirmed that a joint fear of lesbianism and masculinity in women has animated continued opposition to a serious appreciation of women's sports. During the Women's World Cup soccer finals, the *New York Times* journalist Robert Lipsyte, for example, wrote an editorial about the U.S. women's soccer team and the history of female sports. He commented: "For the World Cup team to crack into the male-dominated merchandising mart as a group and as individuals, they must dispel the aura of homosexuality that was hung on women's athleticism as a way of stifling their emerging physical and political power" ("Sports," 13).

Lesbianism has long been associated with female masculinity and female masculinity in turn has been figured as undesirable by linking it in essential and unquestionable ways to female ugliness. The dilemma of the masculine and therefore ugly woman functions as the specter that haunts feminine identification in order to ensure that few women cathect onto female masculinity through either identification or desire. One obvious signifier of the equation between ugliness and female masculinity can be traced through the association of female hirsute bodies with essential ugliness. Literature and history are full of examples of women with beards or women with excessive body hair. Many of these women have been dubbed "witch" or "freak" and displayed in circuses and fairs; some have married, some have had children, some were expelled from their communities, and others were adopted as divine figures.[8]

An early version of the heterosexual conversion narrative that revolves around a rivalry between a masculine/ugly woman and a male suitor for the heroine's attention can be found in a Wilkie Collins novel, *The Woman in White*. The discussions of female masculinity as a primary signifier of unattractiveness in this text also hint at the long history of social prejudices against even slight masculinity in women, prejudice, moreover, that lives on today in discussions of athletic and strong women. Collins's 1860 novel features a curious character, Marian Halcombe, whom Collins represents as both a sexual threat to the novel's heroine and a sexual rival to the novel's hero. Unlike contemporary heterosexual conversion fantasies, Collins's novel actually runs the risk of representing the figure that he wants to disdain and whom the reader will want the heroine to reject. Halcombe, like other masculine women in nineteenth-century literature, symbolizes not only the emergence of a model of active female sexuality but also a predatory form of female desire. In her first meeting with him, Marian is described by the hero Walter as follows. Walter has entered a room, and he sees a beautiful woman with her back to him. Observing her from behind, Walter observes her "easy elegance," her "comely shape," her "pliant firmness." He is filled with burning curiosity to see the beautiful woman face to face: "She left the window—and I said to myself, the lady is dark. She moved forward a few inches—and I said to myself, the lady is young. She approached nearer—and I said to myself (with a sense of surprise which words fail me to express). The lady is ugly!" Walter goes on to explain his definition of the ugly as it applies to Marian:

> Never was the old conventional maxim, that Nature cannot err, more flatly contradicted—never was the fair promise of a lovely figure more strangely and startlingly belied by the face and head that crowned it. The lady's complexion was almost swarthy and the dark down on her upper lip was almost a moustache. She had a large, firm, masculine mouth and jaw; prominent, piercing, resolute brown eyes; and thick, coal-black hair, growing unusually low down on her forehead. (25)

Significantly, Marian has a perfect figure and a lovely form; it is her face, with its dark skin, firm mouth, and shadow of a moustache, that gives her away and allows for Walter's singular exclamation, "The lady is ugly!" This remarkably explicit depiction of female ugliness also makes clear the ways in which masculinity and racial otherness tend to be linked within aesthetic displeasure. Marian is hairy and dark— "swarthy" in fact—and her ugliness is as much a function of not being "fair' (with its own double meaning) as it is of not being feminine. Quite obviously, then, in this sensational tale of sexual secrets, corrupt aristocracy, evil foreigners, and social climbers, the love and natural union between the hero and his "woman in white"—his fair heroine— is secured at the expense of the other characters, who all fall under the headings of either foreign, working class, oddly gendered, or sexually corrupt. Whereas the heroine's uncle is too effeminate to protect her, Laura's friend and companion Marian is too masculine to be safe with her. Laura and Walter's romance turns upon the ability of the novel to render the foreign Count Fosco, the effeminate Uncle Fairley, the butch Marian ugly and sexually deviant. Against this backdrop of freaks, Laura and Walter achieve beauty, harmony, and romantic union.

In an essay on the sensation novel, D. A. Miller has addressed the reading and writing effects of gender confusion in *The Woman in White*.

Miller argues that the novel "produces the configuration of incarcerated femininity" and simultaneously "cathects the congruent configuration of phobic male homoeroticism" ("Cage," 210). By employing the figure of "the woman in the man" or "the man in the woman," Miller shows that these twin fantasies of one gender locked up inside of the other serve the disciplinary purpose of defeminizing the man and refeminizing the female. While Miller is primarily concerned with the homoerotic tension between men in the text, and with the homosexual panic of the "nervous" or sensationalized man, *The Woman in White,* through the character of Marian, also predicates horror upon the masculinization of women rather than upon the feminization of men. The masculine woman in *The Woman in White,* Marian Halcombe, remains for Miller "a man in drag" (205). But Marian represents much more than a man in drag or the opposite of the contaminating femininity embodied in the novel's twinned heroines, Laura and Anne. Indeed, it is significant that Miller actually overlooks the configuration of "incarcerated masculinity" in this text, preferring to concentrate exclusively upon gay male formulations of desire and gender. Marian, quite obviously, represents female inversion, and at one point she even serves as a mentor for Walter, offering him instruction in masculinity and showing him how to master his passions successfully. But ultimately the novel punishes her for her hairy and scary demeanor, and she is abducted by the evil Count Fosco and reduced to a shell of her former self.

In much of the literature on masculine women between the 1860s and the 1910s there was a concerted effort to try to identify the perverse nature of female masculinity and simultaneously diffuse its potential power. Havelock Ellis, for example, rejected the image of the rapacious tribade with the three-inch clitoris and instead formulated female inversion in terms of ugly masculine women who pair up with plain but feminine women ("Sexual"). Similarly, in Wilkie Collins's sensation novel, Marian Halcombe menaces the hero with her own powerful virility but is then completely subjugated by her encounter with Count Fosco, which reduces her to a kind of wallflower spinster. With their beards and supposedly giant clitorises, their muscles and their swaggering ways, masculine women within this literature produced a hairy and scary threat that had to be transformed into the socially useless category of the ugly woman. Today, lesbian stereotypes confirm the persistence of this union of the ugly with the nonheterosexual in a kind of "inverse discourse," to misquote Foucault: in other words, heterosexual men find consolation in the noninterest shown toward them by lesbians in essentializing the category as undesirable.[9] For this reason, there are two types of lesbians who remain incredibly threatening to heterosexual men—the attractive lesbian who rejects them and the butch lesbian who rivals their masculinities.

Through an analysis of heterosexual conversion narratives from the nineteenth century to the present, and by offering a critique of masculinity studies and feminist studies based upon their indifference to viable models of female masculinity, I am proposing here that whether or not men can "do" feminism and whether or not men can express their feelings or be good fathers may not be the most important questions facing us today. Rather, why not ask whether men can "do" masculinity, whether anyone can do it better? Why not detail the forms of masculinity that emerge from the project of disentangling maleness, manhood, and masculinity. A story appeared recently in a magazine called *Our Sexual Health* telling of a gay man's experience with gay bashing in his early twenties. Richard Morrison writes of his encounter with some boys who threw bottles at him from a moving car as he walked down the street in New York City one evening: "The three kids across the street were talking loudly to one another until one of them started to call out, 'Hey Butch! Hey, Dyke!' " Morrison turned around, thinking they were actually after someone else, a butch woman in the street, perhaps. But there was no one else in sight, and Morrison realized that with his long hair and his slim figure he had been mistaken for a butch lesbian. This violent misrecognition alerted him to the fact that he actually did have an inarticulate relation to lesbian masculinity and that it was lesbian masculinity that actually informed his own self-presentation ("Masque"). This story is probably not unique; there must be many men who learn their masculinities from visible female masculinities but who would never acknowledge such an exchange precisely because it would endanger their carefully guarded sense of authenticity. It would also interfere in the smooth functioning of a legacy within which men pass on even imperfect forms of masculine self-understandings to other men. The possibility of a masculinity routed through a butch lesbian body short-circuits this natural history of masculine transmission and recognizes the quotidian, surprising, but not wholly unexpected ways in which female masculinity can form the basis for rather than the repudiation of active identifications.

At the end of *As Good,* Jack Nicholson gets the girl, the girl's son gets better, the girl gets laid, the black guy gets lost, the gay man gets his dog back, and that's as good as it gets. It can get much better, I would contend, but only when we find productive ways as feminists to theorize minority forms of masculinity.

NOTES

1. For a detailed analysis of this history see Bederman. And for specific consideration of the effects of this history of manliness on female homosexualities see Duggan, *Sapphic.*

2. Heterosexual conversion fantasies were not limited to the realm of popular culture in 1996–1998. In 1997, a right-wing Christian group took out an ad in the *New York Times* claiming to have converted willing homosexuals into reformed heterosexuals. These conversion narratives are fascinating, since the right wing has always accused gays and lesbians of trying to convert youth from straight to queer.

3. Jack Nicholson as Melvin in *As Good As It Gets* provides the most paradigmatic example of this role. Melvin is an obsessive compulsive and a misanthrope. The spectator is asked to believe that Melvin has no particular objects for his hostility; he is just a weird and reclusive guy who happens to vent his anger upon women and gay men. The film depicts this behavior as rudeness or male primitivism rather than as a politically motivated form of hate speech. One measure of the appeal of this kind of role lies in the fact that Nicholson was awarded an Oscar for playing America's most endearing racist, homophobic, sexist white guy.

4. The emergence in the 1990s of public debates over female sports has created a complicated discourse about female muscularity and the threat of sports activity to conventional femininities. The creation of a Women's National Basketball League in 1996, an unprecedented public interest in the Women's World

Cup Soccer series in 1999, and the appearance in women's tennis of well-built, strong female athletes, however, suggests that U.S. spectators might be willing in the near future to support women's sports even where the petite femme is replaced by the built butch.

5. See Pfeil, "Sympathy."

Pfeil argues that we have generalized too much in our depictions of white males and, as with any other group, the appellation *white guy* masks a wide array of differences, none more obvious than in the opposition between *men's movement* and *militias*. These kinds of responses to the crisis of white masculinity, he argues, should not be folded into one singular racist and fascist entity but rather carefully analyzed as different and differently problematic/effective responses. He also mounts a defense of the men's movement, saying that it is too easy to dismiss it as racist and misogynist; at least, he claims, the men's movement is an attempt to make things better coming from white guys.

Pfeil's discussion of white masculinities assumes huge distinctions between the kinds of defenses of white masculinity deployed by white supremacist militias and the kinds motivating men's movements, but he fails to examine what George Lipsitz has so trenchantly named "the possessive investment in whiteness" that animates both these groups (*Possessive*).

6. By "pragmatic" I mean to signal here a reading of psychoanalysis that recognizes its ability to comment upon social and political realities. Many psychoanalytic critics are drawn into an insular world of psychoanalytic terms and mechanism, and they forget completely about the relationship between the social and the psychic. I want to use psychoanalysis to talk about how people internalize social structures that are neither inevitable nor necessarily permanent. One critic who has mobilized psychoanalytic methods for the purpose of social inquiry is Avery Gordon. Method, according to Gordon, cannot be an "abstract" and "bloodless" professional question; method is where the investments of the discipline are readable; for sociology, method is the imagined route to pure knowledge, distilled from reports of human experience; for psychoanalysis, method is the mode of legitimizing a morbid interest in pathology; for Gordon, sociology needs to recognize the spirits that haunt it, and psychoanalysis needs to recognize the constraints of the social. Perhaps the best example of a pragmatic use of psychoanalysis occurs in Gayle Rubin, "The Traffic in Women." Rubin writes:

Psychoanalysis contains a unique set of concepts for understanding men, women and sexuality. It is a theory of sexuality in human society. Most importantly, psychoanalysis provides a description of the mechanisms by which the sexes are divided and deformed, of how bisexual, androgynous infants are transformed into boys and girls. Psychoanalysis is a feminist theory manque. (185)

7. A good example of this form of projection—violent projection—would be the recent phenomenon of the outraged white male supremacist who has misrecognized both his whiteness and his maleness, his skin and his penis, as signifiers of social power. When he finds his way to social power blocked (seemingly by blacks, Asians, and gays), then he begins shooting to correct the rift in the social order. On July 4, 1999, one young white man in Illinois went on a shooting rampage that left one black man dead and others, Asians and gays, wounded.

8. For more on the essential freakishness of the hairy female body see Thomson's informative work in *Extraordinary Bodies* and *Freakery*.

9. I refer here to Michel Foucault's formulation of a "reverse discourse" within which marginalized individuals (like homosexuals) begin to adopt and transform the terms that have been used to classify and control them (*History*, 101–2).

WORKS CITED

Bederman, Gail. *Manliness and Civilization*. Chicago: University of Chicago Press, 1995.

Bordo, Susan. *The Male Body: A New Look at Men in Public and Private*. New York: Farrar, Straus and Giroux, 1999.

Butler, Judith. "The Lesbian Phallus." In *Bodies That Matter: On the Discursive Limits of "Sex."* New York: Routledge, 1993.

Collins, Wilkie. *The Woman in White* [1860]. Oxford: Oxford University Press, 1973.

Duggan, Lisa. *Sapphic Slashers: Sex, Violence and American Modernity*. Durham: Duke University Press, 2000.

Ellis, Havelock. "Sexual Inversion in Women." In *Studies in the Psychology of Sex*. New York: Random House, 1900.

Faludi, Susan. *Stiffed: The Betrayal of The American Man.* New York: William Morrow, 1999.

Foucault, Michel. *The History of Sexuality.* Vol. 1: *An Introduction.* Trans. Robert Hurley. New York: Vintage, 1980.

Freud, Sigmund. *Three Essays on the Theory of Sexuality.* Ed. and trans. James Strachey. Intro. Steven Marcus. New York: Basic, 1975.

Gray, John. *Men Are from Mars, Women Are from Venus: A Practical Guide for Improving Communication and Getting What You Want in Your Relationships.* New York: Harper Collins, 1992.

Lacan, Jacques. "The Mirror Stage as Formative of the Function of the I." In *Ecrits: A Selection.* Trans. Alan Sheridan. New York: Norton, 1977 [1949].

Lipsitz, George. *The Possessive Investment in Whiteness: How White People Profit from Identity Politics.* Philadelphia: Temple University Press, 1998.

Lipsyte, Robert. "Sports and Sex Are Always Together." *New York Times,* "Sports Sunday," July 11, 1999, C13.

Lott, Eric. "All the King's Men: Elvis Impersonators and White Working Class Masculinity." In Barry Stephanoupolos, ed., *Race and the Subject of Masculinities,* pp. 192–230. Durham: Duke University Press, 1997.

Miller, D. A. "Cage Aux Folles: Sensation and Gender in Wilkie Collins' *The Woman in White.* In Elaine Showalter, ed., *Speaking of Gender,* p. 210. New York and London: Routledge, 1989.

Morrison, Richard. "Masque." *Our Sexual Health* 2.2 (Winter/Spring 1999): 3.

Pfeil, Fred. "Sympathy for the Devils: Notes On Some White Guys in the Ridiculous Class War." In *Whiteness: A Critical Reader,* pp. 21–34. New York: New York University Press, 1997.

Rubin, Gayle. "The Traffic in Women: Notes on the 'Political Economy' of Sex." In Rayna Reiter, ed., *Toward an Anthropology of Women,* pp. 157–210. New York: Monthly Review, 1975.

Rubin, Henry. "Reading Like a (Transsexual) Man." In Tom Digby, ed., *Men Doing Feminism,* p. 316. New York: Routledge, 1998.

Sedgwick, Eve Kosofsky. *Between Men: English Literature and Male Homosocial Desire.* New York: Columbia University Press, 1985.

Smith, Paul. "Vas." In Robyn Warhol and Diane Price Herndl, eds., *Feminisms: An Anthology of Literary Theory and Criticism,* pp. 1011–1029. New Brunswick, N.J.: Rutgers University Press, 1991.

Solomon-Godeau, Abigail. *Male Trouble: A Crisis in Representation.* London and New York: Thames and Hudson, 1997.

Thomson, Rosemarie Garland. *Extraordinary Bodies: Figuring Physical Disability in American Culture and Literature.* New York: Columbia University Press, 1997.

Thomson, Rosemarie Garland, ed. *Freakery: Cultural Spectacles of the Extraordinary Body.* New York: New York University Press, 1996.

CONTRIBUTORS

MICHAEL AWKWARD, professor of English and director of the Center for the Study of Black Literature and Culture at the University of Pennsylvania. He is author of *Inspiriting Influences: Tradition, Revision, and Afro-American Women's Novels* (Columbia, 1989), *Negotiating Difference: Race, Gender, and the Politics of Positionality* (Chicago, 1995), whose much anthologized essay, "A Black Man's Place in Black Feminist Criticism," argues for the possibilities of a black male feminism, and *Scenes of Instruction* (Duke, 2000), an autobiographical investigation of the sources of his interests in feminism. Also the editor of *New Essays on Their Eyes Were Watching God* (Cambridge, 1990), he is currently completing a study of cultural representations of black American identities following Martin Luther King Jr.'s assassination.

ISAAC D. BALBUS, professor of political science at the University of Illinois at Chicago, is author of *Emotional Rescue: The Theory and Practice of a Feminist Father* (Routledge, 1998), from which his essay in this book is adapted. His other publications include *Marxism and Domination: A Neo-Hegelian, Feminist, Psychoanalytic Theory of Sexual, Political, and Technological Liberation* (Princeton, 1982), *The Dialectics of Legal Repression: Black Rebels Before the American Criminal Courts* (Russell Sage, 1973), and numerous articles on feminist, psychoanalytic and critical theories, and law and politics. He was a cowinner of the C. Wright Mills Prize of the Society for the Study of Social Problems for *The Dialectics of Legal Repression*.

HARRY BROD is associate professor of philosophy and humanities at the University of Northern Iowa. He has previously taught at the University of Delaware, the women's studies program of the University of Pennsylvania, the gender studies program of the University of Southern California, and the intellectual heritage program at Temple University. He is a pioneer in the delineation of the field of men's studies and editor of important anthologies in the field, *The Making of Masculinities: The New Men's Studies* (Allen and Unwin, 1987), *A Mensch Among Men: Explorations in Jewish Masculinity,* and, with Michael Kaufman, *Theorizing Masculinities* (Sage, 1994). He has also written *Hegel's Philosophy of Politics* (Westview, 1992). He is a founding editor of the *Men's Studies Review* and subsequently on the advisory board of its successor journal, *Men and Masculinities* as well as guest editor of many journals. His essays on pornography and male sexuality, Jewish masculinity, men's studies, and pedagogy have been widely reprinted.

KING-KOK CHEUNG is professor of English and Asian American studies at the University of California, Los Angeles. She had been associate director of the Asian American Studies Center at UCLA and held visiting professorships at the University of Kansas and Harvard. She was a fellow at the Center for Advanced Study in the Behavioral Sciences at Stanford, a Fulbright lecturer at the University of Hong Kong, and held an ACLS fellowship. She has lectured extensively in the United States, Taiwan, Japan, Korea, and Thailand. She is the author of *Articulate Silences: Hisaye Yamamoto, Maxine Hong Kingston, Joy Kogawa* (Cornell, 1993) and editor of four volumes: *Words Matter: Conversations with Asian American Writers* (University of Hawai'i, 2000), *An Interethnic Companion to Asian American Literature* (Cambridge University, 1997), *Seventeen Syllables* (Rutgers, 1994), and *Asian American Literature: An Annotated Bibliography,* with Stan Yogi (Modern Language Assocation, 1988). Her essays on Asian American writers have appeared in numerous anthologies and journals.

NANCY J. CHODOROW is professor of sociology and clinical professor of psychology at the University of California at Berkeley, a faculty member at the San Francisco Psychoanalytic Institute, and a psychoanalyst in private practice. A foundational figure of feminist "mothering theory" and feminist uses of psychoanalysis, especially object relations theories, and of cultural feminism, she is the author of the pioneering book *The Reproduction of Mothering* (California, 1978; 2d ed. 1999), which was named one of the "Ten Most Influential Books of the Past Twenty-Five Years" by *Contemporary Sociology* in 1996. Her more recent scholarship includes *Feminism and Psychoanalytic Theory* (Yale, 1989), *Femininities, Masculinities, Sexualities* (Kentucky,

1994), and *The Power of Feelings: Personal Meaning in Psychoanalysis, Gender, and Culture* (Yale, 1999), which recently won the Boyer Prize from the Society for Psychological Anthropology. In addition to other grants, she has been awarded Guggenheim, National Endowment for the Humanities, and American Council of Learned Society Fellowships and has been a fellow at the Center for Advanced Study in the Behavioral Sciences. She is a member of the Committee on Research and Special Training of the American Psychoanalytic Association and is a founding member of the editorial board for *Studies in Gender and Sexuality*. Her essay in this volume reprints "The Enemy Outside: Thoughts on the Psychodynamics of Extreme Violence with Special Attention to Men and Masculinity," *JPCS: Journal for the Psychoanalysis of Culture and Society* 3.1 (Spring 1998): 25–38.

R. W. CONNELL is professor of education at the University of Sydney and was formerly professor of sociology at the University of California, Santa Cruz, and at Macquarie University. He is author or coauthor of eighteen books, including *The Child's Construction of Politics* (Melbourne, 1971), *Making the Difference* (Allen and Unwin, 1982), *Gender and Power: Society, the Person, and Sexual Politics* (Stanford, 1987), *Schools and Social Justice* (Temple, 1992), *Rethinking Sex: Social Theory and Sexuality Research* (Temple, 1993), *Masculinities* (California, 1995), *The Men and the Boys* (California, 2000), *Male Roles, Masculinities, and Violence: A Culture of Peace Perspective* (Unesco, 2000), and *Gender* (Polity, 2002). He is past president of the Sociological Association of Australia and New Zealand and a contributor to journals in sociology, education, political science, and gender studies. One of the most prominent figures in the academic study of masculinity, he is perhaps best known for the concept of "hegemonic masculinity." His chapter in this book reprints his contribution to Barbara Laslett and Barrie Thorne, eds., *Feminist Sociology: Life Histories of a Movement* (Rutgers, 1997).

JUDITH KEGAN GARDINER is professor of English and of gender and women's studies at the University of Illinois at Chicago, an editor of the interdisciplinary journal *Feminist Studies*, the author of *Rhys, Stead, Lessing, and the Politics of Empathy* (Indiana, 1989), and editor of *Provoking Agents: Gender and Agency in Theory and Practice* (Illinois, 1995). She has held a National Endowment for the Humanities Fellowship and a Rockefeller Foundation resident fellowship. She is currently working on a book about masculinity in feminist theory. Her essays on feminist and psychoanalytic theory, masculinity, and women writers appear in numerous books and journals.

JUDITH HALBERSTAM, professor of literature at the University of California at San Diego, is author of *Female Masculinity* (Duke, 1998) and *Skin Shows: Gothic Horror and the Technology of Monsters* (Duke, 1995) and coeditor of *Posthuman Bodies,* with Ira Livingston (Indiana, 1995), and of *The Drag King Book,* with Del La Grace Volcano (Serpent's Tale, 1999). Her interests include postmodern cultural studies, especially in relation to issues of gender and sexuality.

JUDITH NEWTON, director of women's studies and professor of English, University of California at Davis, coedited the first major anthology of materialist feminist literary criticism, *Feminist Criticism and Social Change: Sex, Class, and Race in Literature and Culture* (Methuen, 1985), as well as *Sex and Class in Women's History* (Routledge and Kegan Paul, 1983). She is also the author of *Women, Power, and Subversion: Social Strategies in British Fiction, 1778–1860* (Georgia, 1981). Her most recent book is *Starting Over, Feminism and the Politics of Cultural Critique* (Michigan, 1994). She has researched and published essays about the responses of 1960s male activists to feminism, and her review essay on masculinity studies appeared in *Feminist Studies* in 1998. Her current research and forthcoming publications address masculinity, race, and nation in the Christian men's movement.

FRED PFEIL is professor of English and American studies at Trinity College, having previously taught at Oregon State University. He is author of *White Guys: Studies in Postmodern Domination and Difference* (Verso, 1995) and *Another Tale to Tell: Politics and Narrative in Postmodern Culture* (Verso, 1990) as well as award-winning novels, short stories, and a libretto for chamber opera, including *What They Tell You to Forget* (Pushcart/Norton, 1996) and *Shine On and Other Stories* (Lynx House, 1987), *Heart of a Dog* (libretto comissioned by Boston Musica Viva, 1992), and *Goodman 202* (Indiana, 1986). He has coedited two volumes of *The Year Left: An American Socialist Yearbook* and written on issues of race, class, and gender in journals and anthologies. He held a resident fellowship at the Oregon State University Center for the Humanities and a Rockefeller Foundation Fellowship at the Wesleyan University Center for the Humanities. Since 1994 he has been coordinator and lead trainer for Alternatives to Violence workshops for the Connecticut Correctional Facility.

SALLY ROBINSON is associate professor of English at Texas A&M University, having previously taught in the departments of English and women's studies at the University of Michigan. She is the author of *Marked Men: White Masculinity in Crisis* (Columbia, 2000) and of *Engendering the Subject: Gender and Self-*

Representation in Contemporary Women's Fiction (SUNY, 1991). Her articles on masculinity in literature and contemporary culture have appeared in *Modern Fiction Studies, Genders, Cultural Critique, SubStance,* and other journals and anthologies.

MARLON B. ROSS is professor of English at the University of Virginia. He is completing a book entitled *The Color of Manhood: Racial Identity and Sexual Diversity in African American Men's Writing* and is the author of *Contours of Masculine Desire: Romanticism and the Rise of Women's Poetry* (Oxford, 1989) as well as many essays and articles on gender and sexuality theory and on British and U.S. literature and culture.

CALVIN THOMAS is associate professor of English at Georgia State University and has taught at Syracuse University and the University of Northern Iowa. He is the author of *Male Matters: Masculinity, Anxiety, and the Male Body on the Line* (Illinois, 1996) and primary editor of *Straight with a Twist: Queer Theory and the Subject of Heterosexuality* (Illinois, 2000). His essays in *Men and Masculinities, Novel, Literature and Psychology,* and other journals and collections concern eighteenth-century and contemporary writers, culture, and psychoanalytic and gender studies. He has also published fiction and poetry and is the English-language book review editor of the *South Atlantic Review.*

ROBYN WIEGMAN is Margaret Taylor Smith Director of women's studies at Duke University. She serves as codirector of the Dartmouth Institute on American Studies and is the North American editor for the journal *Feminist Theory.* She wrote *American Anatomies: Theorizing Race and Gender* (Duke, 1995) and is currently working on a book entitled "Object Lessons: Feminism and the Knowledge Politics of Identity." Her six edited collections include *Who Can Speak? Authority and Critical Identity* (Illinois, 1995), with Judith Roof, *The Futures of American Studies* (Duke, forthcoming), with Donald Pease, and the textbook, *Literature and Gender: Thinking Critically Through Fiction, Poetry, and Drama* (Longman, 1999), with Elena Glasberg. Her essays on film, masculinities, whiteness studies, and American literature appear in journals and anthologies.

INDEX